Asia and Global Production Networks

Asia and Global Production Networks

Implications for Trade, Incomes and Economic Vulnerability

Edited by

Benno Ferrarini

Senior Economist, Economics and Research Department, Asian Development Bank, Philippines

David Hummels

Professor of Economics, Department of Economics, Purdue University and Research Associate, National Bureau of Economic Research, USA

CO-PUBLICATION OF THE ASIAN DEVELOPMENT BANK AND EDWARD ELGAR PUBLISHING

Edward Elgar
Cheltenham, UK • Northampton, MA, USA

Published by
Edward Elgar Publishing Limited
The Lypiatts
15 Lansdown Road
Cheltenham
Glos GL50 2JA
UK

Edward Elgar Publishing, Inc.
William Pratt House
9 Dewey Court
Northampton
Massachusetts 01060
USA

Asian Development Bank
6 ADB Avenue, Mandaluyong City
1550 Metro Manila, Philippines
Tel +63 2 632 4444
Fax +63 2 636 2444
www.adb.org

A catalogue record for this book
is available from the British Library

Library of Congress Control Number: 2014938802

This book is available electronically in the ElgarOnline.com
Economics Subject Collection

ISBN 978 1 78347 208 6 (cased)
ISBN 978 1 78347 209 3 (eBook)

Typeset by Servis Filmsetting Ltd, Stockport, Cheshire
Printed and bound in Great Britain by T.J. International Ltd, Padstow

Contents

Contributors

Richard Baldwin is Professor of International Economics at the Graduate Institute, Geneva, Switzerland; a visiting Research Professor at the University of Oxford, UK; Director of the Center for Economic Policy Research (CEPR), UK; and Editor-in-Chief of *Vox*.

Menzie Chinn is Professor of Public Affairs and Economics at the Robert M. La Follette School of Public Affairs, University of Wisconsin, USA.

Hubert Escaith is the Chief Statistician of the World Trade Organization, Switzerland and Research Associate at the Centre de Recherche en Développement Économique et Finance Internationale, GREQAM/ DEFI Aix-Marseille University, France.

Benno Ferrarini is Senior Economist in the Economics and Research Department of the Asian Development Bank, Philippines.

Rikard Forslid is Professor, Department of Economics, Stockholm University, Sweden.

Thomas Hertel is Distinguished Professor of Agricultural Economics at Purdue University, USA and founder and Executive Director of the Global Trade Analysis Project (GTAP).

David Hummels is Professor of Economics, Department of Economics, Purdue University and a Research Associate of National Bureau of Economic Research, USA.

Andrei Levchenko is Associate Professor, Department of Economics, University of Michigan, USA; Faculty Research Fellow, National Bureau of Economic Research, USA; and Research Fellow, Centre for Economic Policy Research, UK.

Alyson C. Ma is Associate Professor of Economics, University of San Diego, USA.

Laura Puzzello is Senior Lecturer in the Department of Economics at Monash University, Australia.

Deborah Swenson is Professor of Economics, University of California – Davis, USA and a Research Associate of National Bureau of Economic Research.

Paul Raschky is Senior Lecturer in the Department of Economics at Monash University, Australia.

Ari Van Assche is Associate Professor of International Business at HEC Montréal and Research Fellow at CIRANO, Canada.

Terrie L. Walmsley is an Honorary Associate Professor in the Department of Economics at the University of Melbourne, Australia and Chief Economist at ImpactECON LLC, USA.

Jing Zhang is Senior Economist at the Federal Reserve Bank of Chicago, USA.

Foreword

The past few years have witnessed the emergence of a large and growing body of research on global value chains (GVCs), that is the creation of final goods and services through interlinked stages of production scattered across international borders. Although GVCs are hardly a new phenomenon, the attention devoted to the topic largely is. After years of neglect, policy makers, practitioners and scholars in the field of international economics have come to agree that global value chains should figure more prominently in policies, advice and research.

To be fair, there has been earlier work in the business and economics literature, focused primarily on measurement of the extent, geographic orientation, and growth in GVCs. But such work was sporadic, and only during the past three years or so has GVCs as a topic been receiving the full attention of the international policy community. Efforts have been directed mainly to gathering necessary statistics and correctly measuring the value-added trade associated with production fragmentation, as opposed to gross trade statistics, which mask the true origin of the value added embodied in goods and services traded internationally. Notably, the World Trade Organization (WTO) Secretariat launched its 'Made in the World' initiative in 2010, and has collaborated since with the Organisation for Co-operation and Economic Development (OECD) and other agencies to establish a statistical platform (OECD-WTO TIVA) that quantifies GVCs and to increase the measurement capacity of the national and international statistics agencies. Other notable efforts include the United Nations Conference on Trade and Development UNCTAD-Eora GVC database, as well as the World Input–Output Database (WIOD), which was established by a consortium of universities, think tanks and international bodies with funding by the European Commission and launched in 2012.

Proper measurement is an important first step in understanding the extent of GVCs, and a wealth of path breaking statistics and insights have accrued from recent efforts in that direction. But what remains is a far harder task: to understand how GVCs change the nature of global economic interdependence, and how that in turn changes our understanding of policies appropriate in this new environment. This volume attempts to take on some of this task, with particular focus on two broad themes.

The first explores the impact of greater integration and interdependence on economies' exposure to adverse shocks elsewhere in the world, such as natural disasters, political disputes, or recessions. Various chapters investigate to what extent do global value chains serve to transmit and even magnify shocks across national borders and, when a national economy absorbs the blow from an international shock, how firms respond. The second theme looks at the evolution of global value chains at the firm level and how this will affect competitiveness in Asia. Various chapters explore theory and data at the firm level to understand the evolution of GVCs within and across countries.

In this volume, authors bring to bear a wide variety of methodological tools and data, and perspectives ranging from the firm-level micro economy to the global macro economy to help understand how GVCs are reshaping interdependence in Asia. With its emphasis on analysis, rather than policy, this volume aims at providing scholars and stakeholders with an analytical toolbox useful to conceptualizing and assessing the relevant phenomena. Future work will have to complement these analytical aspects with in-depth discussions about the policy and regulatory implications stemming from the latest progress in this line of research, which largely represents a joint effort and work in progress by a large community of international and national policy makers, academia, and think-tanks.

I would like to thank Benno Ferrarini and David Hummels for their outstanding leadership, coordination and management of the research underlying this volume, and Cindy Castillejos-Petalcorin for invaluable administrative support and editorial assistance. The volume benefitted from excellent inputs from Richard Niebuhr as copy editor, and from helpful advice by Anna Sherwood of the ADB Department for External Relations on contractual matters concerning its publication. Joseph Zveglich Jr provided strategic support and guidance throughout the study. My special acknowledgement goes to the many scholars who contributed their invaluable expertise to this study.

Changyong Rhee
Chief Economist, Asian Development Bank

Abbreviations and acronyms

ADB	Asian Development Bank
AIO	Asian input–output
APL	average propagation length
ASEAN	Association of Southeast Asian Nations
B2B	business-to-business
BACI	Base pour l'analyse du commerce internationale
BEC	Broad Economic Classification
CAD	computer-aided design
CDE	constant difference of elasticity
CEPII	Centre d'Etudes Prospectives et d'Informations Internationales
CES	constant elasticity of substitution
CGE	computable general equilibrium
CIF	cost, insurance and freight
CNY	Chinese yuan
CO_2	carbon dioxide
COMTRADE	Commodity Trade Statistics Database
CPC	Central Product Classification
CPI	consumer price index
CRED	Centre for Research on Epidemiology of Disasters
CT	coordination technologies
DC	developing countries
DGP	data-generating process
EA	East Asia
EBOPS	Extended Balance of Payments Services Classification
ECLAC	Economic Committee for Latin America and the Caribbean
ELE	electrical equipment
EM-DAT	Emergency Events Database
Eora	Eora multi-region input–output database
EU	European Union
EUROSTAT	European Commission statistics
EXIOBASE	global, detailed multi-regional environmentally extended supply and use/input–output database

FAO	Food and Agriculture Organization
FDI	foreign direct investment
FOB	free on board
G5	Group of five (France, Germany, Japan, the United Kingdom, the United States)
G7	Group of Seven (Canada, France, Germany, Italy, Japan, the United Kingdom, the United States)
G-20	Group of Twenty (Argentina, Australia, Brazil, Canada, the People's Republic of China, France, Germany, India, Indonesia, Italy, Japan, the Republic of Korea, Mexico, the Russian Federation, Saudi Arabia, South Africa, Turkey, the United Kingdom, the United States, and the European Union)
GAD	Global Antidumping Database
GATT	General Agreement on Tariffs and Trade
GDP	gross domestic product
GTAP	Global Trade Analysis Project
GTAP-ICIO	Global Trade Analysis Project-Inter-Country Input–Output
GVCs	global value chains
HHI	Herfindahl–Hirschman Index
HP	Hodrick–Prescott
HQ	headquarters
HS	Harmonized System
ICIO	inter-country input–output
ICT	information and communication technology
IDE-JETRO	Institute of Developing Economies-Japan External Trade Organization
IIO	international input–output
IIT	intra-industry trade
ILO	International Labour Organization
IMF	International Monetary Fund
IO	input–output
IOT	input–output table
IRF	impulse response functions
ISIC	International Standard Industrial Classification of All Economic Activities
MNEs	multinational enterprises
MRIO	multi-region, input–output
NBER	National Bureau of Economic Research
NICs	newly industrialized countries
NSO	national statistical office

OECD	Organisation for Economic Co-operation and Development
OLS	ordinary least squares
PPP	purchasing power parity
PRC	People's Republic of China
RCA	relative comparative advantage
RER	real exchange rate
SC	supply chain
SCT	supply chain trade
SCV	supply chain vulnerability
SDR	Special Drawing Rights
SITC	Standard International Trade Classification
SNA	system of national accounts
SOE	state owned enterprise
SUT	supply and use table
TEC	trade by enterprise characteristics
TFP	total factor productivity
TiVA	OECD-WTO trade in value added database
TOSP	tasks, occupations, stages, products
ToT	terms of trade
UK	United Kingdom
UN	United Nations
UNCTAD	UN Conference on Trade and Development
UNIDO	United Nations Industrial Development Organization
US	United States
VA	value added
VAR	vector autoregressions
WDI	World Development Indicators
WIOD	World Input–Output Database
WTO	World Trade Organization
WTW	World Trade Web

ADB recognizes China by the name People's Republic of China.

1. Asia and global production networks: implications for trade, incomes and economic vulnerability

Benno Ferrarini and David Hummels

1. INTRODUCTION

Global value chains (GVCs) involve the production of goods and services through interlinked stages of production scattered across international borders. The international exchange of intermediate inputs, as opposed to final consumer goods, is a phenomenon as old as trade itself. What is new in the global economy is rapid growth in the extent and the complexity of global value chains. Nowhere in the world is production fragmented quite as much, or GVCs quite as complex or as fast growing, as in Asia.

As a consequence, there has been a widespread recognition by policy makers, practitioners and scholars in the field of international economics that global value chains should figure more prominently in their policies, advice and research. Early academic work focused primarily on measurement of the extent, geographic orientation, and growth in GVCs (Arndt and Kierzkowski 2001; Hummels, Ishii and Yi 2001; Grossman and Rossi-Hansberg 2008; Kimura 2006; Johnson and Noguera 2012). Among international bodies, the World Trade Organization (WTO) Secretariat launched its "Made in the World" initiative in 2010, and has collaborated since with the Organisation for Co-operation and Economic Development (OECD) to establish a statistical platform (OECD-WTO TiVA) to quantify GVCs and to increase measurement capacity. Reports have thus proliferated by international bodies, including the World Bank (Cattaneo et al. 2010), IDE/JETRO and WTO (2011), OECD (2013), and UNCTAD (2013), and various think tanks and other bodies, such as the World Economic Forum (2012) and the Fung Global Institute (Park et al. 2013; Elms and Low 2013).

New measures have opened up insights into the extent and complexity of global production networks. For example, Figure 1.1 shows a network graph based on the OECD-WTO TIVA indicator of value added embodied in 2009 gross exports by source country.[1] Three hubs – the United States

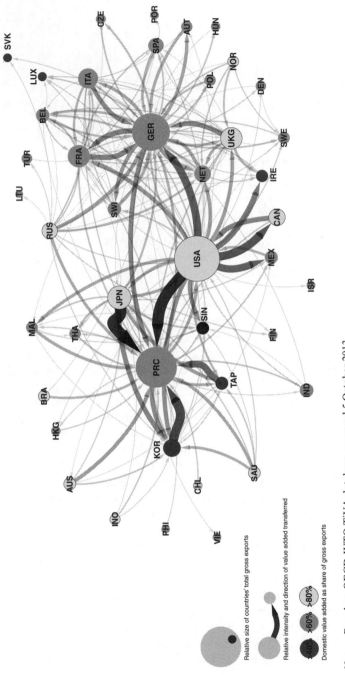

Note: Based on OECD-WTO TiVA database, accessed 5 October 2013.

Source: Authors' calculations.

Figure 1.1 Global value chains in 2009

(US), Germany and the People's Republic of China (PRC) – are seen at the center of a tightly knit web of value added transfers mainly among regional economies engaged in split production processes. The US is positioned at the center of the global supply chains both as the largest gross exporter of goods and services and as the main exporter of US value added embodied in other countries' exports. Germany and the PRC follow in the ranks in terms of gross (direct) and value added (indirect) exports. Compared to the US, these economies are positioned further downstream the value chains, involving a substantial share of value added inflows and outflows.[2] In the European regional network, horizontal integration prevails, with value added flowing in both directions among country pairs. Asian production networks are more hierarchical. At the top, countries such as Japan – and the US from outside the region – inject value added through the provision of key components and services to the PRC, the hub downstream, as well as through Malaysia, Thailand and to a lesser extent the other Association of Southeast Asian Nations economies as well as India. Other key players, right at the center of the regional networks, are the Republic of Korea, Taipei,China, as well as Singapore, each economy exporting high shares of foreign value added in reflection of their strong GVC involvement.

Baldwin and Forslid (Chapter 10) in this volume provide a deeper insight into the genesis and development of the Asian production networks, drawing on the latest data and insights that have become available during the past two years, while Escaith (Chapter 9) delves into methodological issues concerning measuring and mapping of trade associated with GVCs' activities.

Proper measurement is an appropriate first step in understanding the extent of GVCs, but it is only a beginning. What remains is a far harder task: to understand how GVCs change the nature of global economic interdependence, and how that in turn changes our understanding of policies appropriate in this new environment. The chapters in this volume are focused on this harder task. The authors bring to bear a wide variety of methodological tools and data, and perspectives ranging from the firm-level micro economy to the global macro economy to help understand how GVCs are reshaping interdependence in Asia.

2. ANALYTICAL TOOLS TO ASSESS THE IMPLICATIONS OF GVCS FOR TRADE, INCOMES AND ECONOMIC VULNERABILITY

We have two broad themes. We start with a topic of great concern to scholars and policy makers. Greater integration and interdependence can lead to efficiency gains, but it can also expose national economies to adverse shocks (natural disasters, political disputes, recessions) elsewhere in the world. This suggests several important but underexplored questions. One, to what extent do global value chains serve to transmit and even magnify shocks across national borders? Two, when a national economy absorbs the blow from an international shock, what are the most important response margins? That is, do firms respond to the failure of a key supplier or a drop off in foreign demand by shifting to new partners? If not, do these trade shocks result in large changes in output and employment, or are they absorbed through changes in factor and product prices? Of course, shocks need not be abrupt to have important effects at the macroeconomic level. Rebalancing current account surpluses may take years or decades, and the ways in which rebalancing is absorbed will depend critically on how nations are linked through GVCs in both consumption and production.

Our second theme is focused on the evolution of global value chains at the firm level and how this will affect competitiveness in Asia. Global value chains allow firms to specialize in stages of production in which they excel, leaving remaining stages to other firms or other nations. Conceptually this is a straightforward proposition – applying the principle of comparative advantage to exchanging stages of production rather than final goods. What remains unclear are the sources of advantage at the firm level. Perhaps firm advantages are based on technological sophistication, the realization of scale economies, arbitrage of policy differentials, or simply, factor input costs. Also unclear is how firm advantages trade off against the greater coordination costs of realizing these advantages in a far-flung "global factory". Various chapters explore theory and data at the firm level to understand the evolution of GVCs within and across countries.

2.1 Disaster Impact Assessments with the GTAP Supply Chain Model

Walmsley, Hertel and Hummels (Chapter 2 in this volume) and Hertel, Hummels and Walmsley (Chapter 3 in this volume) provide a set of tools for analyzing global value chains in a full general equilibrium context. Their approach can be thought of as a bridge between two important literatures related to GVCs: multi-region input–output (MRIO) analysis and computable general equilibrium (CGE) analysis. In a MRIO analysis researchers link national input–output tables with trade data to construct an international, multi-region IO table. Rather than examine total input usage for each industry, as is the case in national tables, a MRIO provides information on the source of these inputs. With this disaggregation a researcher can calculate the share of foreign versus domestic value added in output and exports for a particular industry, or further break foreign value added into specific source countries. That is, a MRIO distinguishes the value of Korean and Chinese steel used in the Japanese automobile industry, enabling researchers to examine how the Republic of Korea and the PRC are differentially affected by a shock to Japan. Such tables provide the basis of most trade in value added statistics and macro level assessments of global value chains. Additional details on the strengths and weaknesses of this approach can be found both in Walmsley et al. (Chapter 2) and in Escaith (Chapter 9).

The challenge for a MRIO comes when a researcher wants to go beyond a static look at the data and consider changes to the world economy. That is, a MRIO describes a particular pattern of input–output use that prevailed at a point in time, but is not well suited to analyzing what will happen to that pattern should there be a significant shock to an economy. To answer such questions requires a full computable general equilibrium model that can track behavioral responses in production, consumption, and trade.

Walmsley et al. (Chapter 2) provide a detailed discussion of how to embed MRIO-like data on global value chains into GTAP, a widely used CGE tool for world trade analysis. The resulting model is called GTAP-SC ("Supply Chain"). This methodological piece includes a discussion of the challenges and choices involved in reconciling disparate data sources on GVCs. The chapter then provides a series of exercises meant to illustrate how MRIO and CGE approaches differ when analyzing changes to global value chains. The authors show that standard MRIO analysis is actually an extremely restrictive version of a CGE analysis in which one assumes that output can instantaneously and costlessly adjust to any shock to the system. The GTAP-SC model allows for much more general responses, including evaluating how shocks lead to price changes, which in turn induce substitution in production and consumption, both within and across countries. The results here are illuminating in themselves, but readers may find them even more useful as a kind of guidebook to pursuing their own analysis of GVCs.

Hertel et al. (Chapter 3) employ the GTAP-SC model to evaluate two major disasters that reduce output and productivity: the first in the electronics sector in Taipei,China and the second at the Port of Singapore. The model traces through effects on goods and factor markets, focusing on the distribution of effects as a function of GVC linkages to these sectors. A clear distinction arises between sectors and countries that are vertically linked to the disrupted area versus sectors and countries that are substitutes. Vertically linked sectors suffer while substitutes enjoy tremendous growth as they at least temporarily replace the disrupted production.

A novel part of the analysis is the ability to evaluate changes that occur at different time horizons. For example, at very short time horizons, output quantities may be slow to respond to shocks, so all adjustment must occur through prices. At medium horizons, some factors of production (unskilled labor) may be mobile across firms, while others (capital to build factories) are not, which allows for adjustment to occur through a mix of price and quantity changes. Similarly, by varying substitution parameters in the model, the authors can experiment with inputs as vitally necessary (very difficult to replace), or commodities (easy to replace) to gauge the resulting impact.

2.2   Natural Disasters Impact Assessment through Regression Analysis

We can think of Hertel et al. (Chapter 3) as a stylized simulation of what might happen in some future disastrous event, tracing through the effects on output, trade, employment, wages, and prices. Puzzello and Raschky (Chapter 4) also examine natural disasters, but they focus on disasters that have actually occurred and econometrically examine the linkage between these disasters and trade flows. They draw on a comprehensive database of natural disasters (drought, earthquakes, floods, wind storms) that provides data on the number of persons affected, numbers killed, and estimated dollar damage for all countries worldwide during the period 1995–2010. Using this data, they construct measures of the vulnerability of global value chains to natural disasters. For each country and industry, these measures capture the proportion of inputs provided by suppliers struck by at least one large natural disaster in a given year.

Next, they estimate a regression model that explains a country's exports at the industry level as a function of, among other factors, the vulnerability to natural disasters of that country-industry's supply chain. The causal channel here is straightforward. If an industry relies heavily on inputs whose supply is disrupted by a disaster, it should raise costs or lower production for that industry, and this will show up in reduced international competitiveness and exports. This is not inevitable, of course. It may be that, while firms purchase inputs from abroad they are not truly dependent on them. Rather, they may find it relatively easy to switch away from a disaster-struck supplier to an alternative vendor, with costs, competitiveness and exports unimpeded.

These authors reveal a set of interesting facts. They find that manufacturing products are highly exposed to large natural disasters abroad, which is consistent with the high incidence of input trade in the manufacturing sector. Asia and North America are the regions most vulnerable to large natural disasters both at home and abroad, both because they are more disaster prone and because production there is more globalized. The regression estimates show that higher supply chain vulnerability to large natural disasters significantly reduces exports, and that the effects are larger when large disasters happen at home. More complex industries are little affected by disasters at home, but are affected by disasters abroad. This is consistent with the idea that firms find it relatively easy to substitute away from affected inputs when they are domestically sourced inputs, but find it difficult to do the same for imported inputs.

2.3 Impact Assessment of Current Account Rebalancing in Asia

While natural disasters are an excellent laboratory for examining abrupt changes to GVCs and the world economy, not all shocks are abrupt or unanticipated. Even slow moving changes can have profound effects if they fundamentally reorder patterns of production and consumption. Levchenko and Zhang (Chapter 7) examine one such shock, current account rebalancing in Asia. A country running a trade surplus is spending less than the value of its output. Rebalancing – an elimination of the trade surplus – then by construction increases the country's total spending. Classical theory predicts that an elimination of a trade surplus in a country: (i) increases both relative and real incomes; (ii) appreciates the real exchange rate; (iii) increases the employment share in the non-traded sector; and (iv) reduces exports. All of these effects are reversed in the trade deficit countries as the trade imbalance is eliminated.

While useful starting points, classic theory on rebalancing is based on stylized small-country or two-country models that are too simplistic to reliably gauge the magnitudes involved. The real world features many heterogeneous countries with highly asymmetric trade relationships between them. While this distinction is non-existent in two-country models, in the real world the elimination of the PRC's trade surplus will likely have a very different global impact than the elimination of Japan's trade surplus, as those two countries occupy different positions in the world trading system. Since there are differences in the nature and orientation of global value chains feeding inputs into traded and nontraded sectors, rebalancing will have differential effects on these suppliers.

Levchenko and Zhang base their analysis on a quantitative Ricardian–Heckscher–Ohlin framework that features 75 countries (including 14 from developing Asia), 19 tradeable and 1 non-tradeable sector, multiple factors of production, as well as the full set of cross-sectoral input–output linkages forming a global supply chain. They begin with a baseline equilibrium that matches the observed levels of trade imbalances in each country in 2011, and then compare outcomes to a counterfactual scenario in which each country is constrained to have balanced trade.

In their sample of 14 developing Asia countries, seven have trade surpluses and seven trade deficits in 2011. Rebalancing leads to the following effects. The surplus countries experience a large increase in wages relative to the US, 17.5 percent on average. There is a modest (at the median, 4 percent) increase in the share of labor employed in the non-traded sector as these countries stop transferring income abroad and instead use it to purchase domestically produced goods and services. The trade-weighted real exchange rate (RER) for the surplus countries in developing Asia appreciates slightly, 1.47 percent on average. While one might expect larger adjustments given the magnitude of the rebalancing involved, it is important to keep in mind patterns of trade. Much of these countries' trade is with each other, and thus even as they are all appreciating relative to the US, their trade-weighted appreciation is much smaller. The Republic of Korea and Taipei,China even experience modest RER depreciations.

The impact of external rebalancing on welfare is much smaller than on either relative wages or RERs. At the median, these countries experience a rise in welfare of 0.4 percent, two orders of magnitude less than the average increase in the relative wage. This is sensible: as these countries' relative wages rise dramatically, so do domestic prices. The net impact is positive (with the sole exception of the Republic of Korea), but much smaller than the gross changes in either wages or price levels. For countries running deficits, the adjustments are the opposite of the surplus countries, and of similar magnitudes, though welfare losses are much more substantial. Finally, the authors track the changes due to rebalancing through global value chains. A country's welfare changes due to global rebalancing are strongly positively correlated with whether it exports mostly to the deficit or to surplus countries. Thus, multilateral trade relationships are crucial for fully understanding the importance of rebalancing.

2.4   Monetary, Exchange Rate Policy and Business Cycle Analysis in Light of GVCs

Continuing with a macroeconomic focus, Chinn (Chapter 8) offers a broad look at how GVCs change the measurement and estimation of key macroeconomic variables and relationships. In a world where all trade is in final goods and all goods are traded, the real exchange rate is easily defined and measured as the nominal exchange rate net of the price level for final goods at home and abroad. In the presence of global value chains, real exchange rates are conceptually difficult. Chinn reviews two approaches in the literature, which turn on whether consumers have preferences over value-added (i.e. consumers care about each stage in production and so real exchange rates must reflect where each stage took place), or only over the final good, in which case global value chains only matter to the extent that multi-stage production reduces the price of that good. This literature shows that accounting for GVCs gives a picture of the RER that differs significantly from conventional measures. For example, using a GVC adjusted RER, the PRC's effective exchange rate appreciated 11.4 percentage points more than was implied using conventional measures. These adjusted measures also significantly change our measurement and interpretation of how the RER affects trade quantities (i.e. the elasticity of trade with respect to movements in the RER) and prices (the degree of pass-through).

Chinn next turns to business cycles. A number of researchers have claimed that deeper integration via global value chains causes a greater degree of business cycle synchronization. Chinn provides static and dynamic exercises to examine whether there have been changes in the extent of synchronization in Asia over time. First, he calculates the correlation of quarterly GDP growth for Asian country pairs over the 1990–1996 and 1999–2012 periods, using a variety of techniques (HP filters, quadratic and log detrending) to isolate business cycle components. Correlation coefficients among Asian country pairs rise significantly, especially those pairs involving the PRC. As an accompanying exercise focused on dynamics, Chinn estimates a non-structural VAR to evaluate the impulse response of each country to output gaps in other countries.

Finally, Chinn analyzes whether global value chains alter the conduct of monetary and exchange rate policy. The starting point is the idea that policymakers will value a stable exchange rate when there is more production sharing, and therefore more commercial transactions whose value will be made uncertain by a fluctuating exchange rate. Further, if countries desire to stabilize, do they stabilize against the US dollar or, owing to the centrality of the PRC in Asian value chains, do they stabilize against the Chinese yuan (CNY)? Previous work using daily currency movements has shown that central banks now place more weight on the CNY than they did prior to 2005. Chinn extends this work to longer horizons, monthly and quarterly movements, and confirms the primary finding that the CNY has risen in importance as a nominal anchor for the region's currencies.

2.5 The Progression of People's Republic of China's Trade through GVC Participation

We turn next to two chapters that are focused on the microeconomics of global value chains at the firm level. Previous chapters in the volume have employed input–output tables to measure GVCs. This is a standard approach, which is useful for comparability across countries and over time, but it fails to capture significant heterogeneity across firms within industries. An alternative approach is to rely on firm-level data that provides a highly detailed picture of which firms are deeply integrated into GVCs, relying on foreign suppliers and selling to foreign customers, and which are not. Chapters by Swenson (Chapter 6) and Ma and Van Assche (Chapter 5), make use of Chinese customs data that provides a rich picture of these transactions, including product and origin country information for inputs and product and destination detail for exports. These data are further broken out by "processing firms", which import inputs free of charge and sell their products outside the PRC, and "ordinary firms", which do not enjoy duty free imports, but can sell output domestically and abroad.

One of the central questions of development relates to the progression of countries through a rising level of production sophistication. At the crudest level this can be characterized as a switch from agriculture to "light" manufacturing to more complex manufacturing, and the literature has provided a variety of ways to characterize technological sophistication. The rise of global value chains upends these traditional distinctions. While a laptop computer may be a highly complex piece of machinery, embodying advanced parts and technology, not all stages of its production are complex or sophisticated. Some assembly stages may be labor intensive, produced capably by workers with few skills or training. This raises the question of whether the apparent rise in the sophistication of Chinese exports (for example, a switch from textiles and apparel to electronics) simply captures Chinese participation in the simplest stages of production.

Swenson (Chapter 6) uses the rich detail in Chinese customs data to characterize changes in the production stage position of PRC firms. Key to her analysis are measures of "upstreamness" and "stages" in production developed by Fally (2012 a, 2012b). Suppose we have a production process involving 10 sequential steps. A firm that produces the seventh step has six previous "stages", and is "upstream" from three subsequent steps. By using very detailed IO tables to measure how far a production stage is from final consumption, then matching this data to traded products, Fally is able to characterize the "upstream" and "stage" measure of a given product. Taking these measures, Swenson can then characterize where Chinese firms sit in sequencing based on the inputs they purchase and the outputs they produce. Over time, a firm can change its position in two ways. For a given production process it can move closer to the point of final consumption (increasing stages and decreasing upstreamness), or further away. Or it can switch to a more complex production process involving more steps (conceivably increasing both stages and upstreamness).

In the aggregate, Swenson finds that Chinese firms have increased both the stages and upstreamness, consistent with the view that they are switching to production processes that involve increasingly long production chains. Swenson next provides an alternative measure of complexity, the number of distinct inputs used in production. Based only on a count of distinct HS6 product lines imported, there is a decline in the number of inputs. This could reveal falling complexity, or it could reveal a move along the production chain further from final consumption. For example, production of a microchip could involve relatively few parts, while assembly of a laptop computer could involve many parts.

The initial work focuses on aggregate behavior of the Chinese economy so Swenson next exploits firm-level data. She relates growth in imports and exports to the position of these products in the value chain as measured by Fally's stages/upstreamness variables, while using fixed effects to control for unobservables. There are striking differences between imports and exports. Import growth is greater for products that exhibit higher stages and upstreamness (products with longer chains), while export growth is smaller for these products. Swenson also explores an alternative way to see a similar relationship. She focuses on the probability of exit, that is, identifying products that were imported (or exported) at some point by a Chinese firm, but then cease to be, as a function of their position in the value chain. Here the results are mixed and depend highly on goods type. All in all, this chapter represents a wholly novel way to evaluate the changing advantages of firms within multi-stage production processes.

2.6　Trade Policy Shocks and Production Relocation by Processing Firms in the People's Republic of China

Ma and Van Assche (Chapter 5) also employ the PRC customs data, but in pursuit of a very different objective. They are interested in how global value chains allow firms to circumvent trade policy barriers. The authors begin with a model of heterogeneous firms similar to Melitz (2003), but introduce two vertical stages of production: headquarters services produced at home, and manufacturing, which is footloose. The mobility of manufacturing makes it profitable for some firms to circumvent tariffs and produce abroad. A key insight is that global value chains increase the elasticity of bilateral exports with respect to tariffs. The reason is that a tariff hike has two effects. First it raises prices and lowers export sales for firms who continue to produce at home. Second, it induces a subset of firms to stop exporting and relocate production to avoid the tariff. Note that while global value chains amplify the effect of the tariff on manufacturing at home, it dampens the effect on headquarters activities, which continue to operate and provide services to manufacturing plants abroad. This result is complementary to recent studies that find offshored assembly activities are more vulnerable to business cycle shocks than corresponding domestic activities.

Next, Ma and Van Assche investigate the prediction that vertically specialized trade is more sensitive to a country-specific tariff hike than exports that are part of local value chains. They draw on both firm-level (2000–2006) and provincial level (1997–2009) data from the PRC's customs statistics, distinguishing Chinese firms based on customs regimes (processing and ordinary trade). The processing trade regime is used primarily by exporting firms in the PRC that are part of a global value chain, while the ordinary trade regime is used by exporting firms that have more extensive domestic value chains. Apart from legal treatment, this distinction is clear in the data: processing exports embody less than half as much domestic value added than ordinary exports, and foreign-owned firms play a much more dominant role in the processing trade regime than in the ordinary trade regime. To measure country-specific trade policy shocks, they use antidumping cases against the PRC at the HS6 digit level as identified in the World Bank's Global Antidumping Database (GAD). Ma and Van Assche find strong evidence that processing exports are more sensitive to the imposition of antidumping measures than ordinary exports, and consistent with the theoretical model, this is mostly due to the extensive margin effect.

2.7   Measuring Global Value Chains

We conclude with two chapters that address broad conceptual issues highlighting the rise and future development of global value chains in Asia.

Escaith (Chapter 9) returns to the issue of measurement of global value chains, setting in context the varied efforts by researchers and policy institutes around the world. He strongly advocates for a process of theory before measurement, or put another way, for researchers to understand what questions they are trying to answer, and what measurement and data organization tools are appropriate in that context. He reviews work on input–output table based approaches, such as those used in the chapters by Walmsley et al., Puzzello and Raschky, and to some extent in those by Chinn and by Levchenko and Zhang. While these authors draw on extensive work elsewhere and employ it in varied applications, readers may find their explanations somewhat terse. Escaith's chapter provides a more detailed exegesis, including the economic assumptions implicit in these calculations. As an example, Chinn describes two methods for calculation of the real exchange rate in the presence of GVCs, and these approaches turn on whether consumers have preferences over value added or preferences over final goods. This is conceptually very close to the problem described by Escaith in terms of using network theory to understand GVCs. Can we think of consumers valuing electronic components from Thailand independently of the way they are integrated into the network of computer production throughout Asia?

When a methodology becomes dominant, as the MRIO approach has in measuring GVCs, it can become easy to forget its limitations. Escaith reminds us of these problems, and then highlights the different sorts of conceptual questions and problems that can be answered with reference to firm-level data. This points clearly to the strengths of the data approaches employed by Swenson and by Ma and Van Assche.

As we noted at the outset of this chapter, the study of global value chains has progressed beyond infancy but is at best an adolescent literature. There remain a host of interesting questions about GVCs that are little understood. Indeed, Escaith's simple enumeration of "what should be counted" with respect to GVCs illustrates the fairly limited dimensions of "what has been counted" in the literature extant. Ultimately Escaith's chapter provides a useful overview of the work to date, and a rich outline of work to do for the ambitious researcher or concerned policy maker.

2.8 The Development and Future of Production Networks in Asia

In a similar vein, Baldwin and Forslid's Chapter 10 provides a useful overview of how global value chains arose in Asia, and where they are going. They begin with the history, describing globalization as two unbundlings driven first by lower trade costs (tariffs, transportation costs), and second by improvements in information and communication technology (ICT). The first unbundling allowed production and consumption to be separated by great distances, but production stages remained bundled locally, in factories and industrial districts. The ICT revolution unbundled the factories themselves. They illustrate these facts with a series of data displays meant to illustrate the sharp changes in trade volumes and patterns of trade in value added corresponding to the period of the ICT revolution. These displays also provide a useful set of indicators going forward to track the extent and growth of GVCs.

The second part of the chapter provides some simple conceptual theory to help the reader understand driving forces between the second unbundling. The first organizes production into a TOSP (tasks, occupations, stages, and products) hierarchy, where tasks, or the most granular activities, are bundled in groups to workers of particular occupations, who are themselves bundled into stages, with these stages ultimately bundled into products. For a product like a laptop computer, we could separate design, parts production, assembly, and marketing into four distinct stages. The design stage could involve occupations like electrical engineers or software coders, each of whom has a large set of discrete tasks that must be completed to design a microchip or the computer's hardware BIOS.

With this setup in hand, the challenge is to think in terms of the optimal aggregation of occupations and stages, that is, how many tasks should be completed by each occupation, and how occupations should be bundled into a given stage. The ICT revolution lowers the cost of communicating between disparate stages (making it lower cost to disaggregate occupations), but it also lowers the marginal benefit of specialization as automation enables individual workers to master more tasks without the loss of efficiency. This simple framework helps us to think through the extent of unbundling, trading off efficiency and coordination costs. A key point here is that relationships are not monotonic; in other words, the model reveals tipping points at which offshoring can increase rapidly or even decrease as costs fall. Further, these costs interact with traditional sources of comparative advantage that may itself evolve. In short, it is not at all obvious whether global value chains in Asia will continue to grow in size and complexity, or whether we have hit a high water mark in their importance.

NOTES

1. Figure 1.1 was drawn with the help of Cytoscape, an open-source platform for complex network analysis and visualization (www.cytoscape.org). The network graph extends across all country pairs, involving more than 3000 connections. To avoid clutter, only the top 5 percent are shown on this map. Also omitted from the map are value added transfers to and from the rest of the world aggregate, as well as self-looping arches in relation to countries' domestic value added. Shown are the top 5 percent of value added flows among country pairs in 2009, connected by arches whose width is proportional to source countries' value added embodied in recipient countries' exports. Individual economies are shown as nodes whose size relates to the gross value of goods and services exports. Darker shades denote economies with lower shares of domestic value added in gross exports, compared to more brightly shaded nodes. The method is described further in Ferrarini (2013).
2. In fact, exports by the US (89 percent) contain a considerably higher share of domestic value added compared with that of Germany (73 percent) and the PRC (68 percent).

REFERENCES

Arndt, S.W. and H. Kierzkowski (2001), *Fragmentation: New Production Patterns in the World Economy*, Oxford University Press.

Cattaneo, O., G. Gereffi, and C. Staritz (eds) (2010), *Global Value Chains in a Postcrisis World – A Development Perspective*, The World Bank, Washington, DC.

Elms, D.K. and P. Low (eds) (2013), *Global Value Chains in a Changing World*, Fung Global Institute, Nanyang Technological University, and World Trade Organization.

Fally, T. (2012a), 'Production staging: measurement and facts', University of Colorado, Boulder, Manuscript.

Fally, T. (2012b), 'Data on the fragmentation of production in the U.S.', University of Colorado, Boulder, Manuscript.

Ferrarini, B. (2013), 'Vertical trade maps', *Asian Economic Journal*, 105–123.

Grossman, G.M. and R.-H. Esteban (2008), 'Trading tasks: a simple theory of offshoring', *American Economic Review*, **98**, 1978–1997.

Hummels, D., J. Ishii, and K.-M. Yi (2001), 'The nature and growth of vertical specialization in world trade', *Journal of International Economics*, **54**, 75–96.

IDE/JETRO (Institute of Developing Economies/Japan External Trade Organization and World Trade Organization) (2011), *Trade Patterns and Global Value Chains in East Asia: From Trade in Goods to Trade in Tasks*, Geneva: World Trade Organization.

Johnson, R.C. and G. Noguera (2012), 'Accounting for intermediates: production sharing and trade in value added', *Journal of International Economics*, **86**, 224–236.

Kimura, F. (2006), 'International production and distribution networks in East Asia: eighteen facts, mechanics, and policy implications', *Asian Economic Policy Review*, **1**, 326–344.

Melitz, M.J. (2003), 'The impact of trade on intra-industry reallocations and aggregate industry productivity', *Econometrica*, **71**, 1695–1725.

OECD (2013), *Interconnected Economies – Benefitting from Global Value Chains*, OECD Publishing.

Park, A., G. Nayyar, and P. Low (eds) (2013), *Supply Chain Perspectives and Issues – A Literature Review*, Fung Global Institute and World Trade Organization.

UNCTAD (2013), *World Investment Report 2013 – Global Value Chains: Investment and Trade for Development*, Geneva: United Nations.

World Economic Forum (2012), *The Shifting Geography of Global Value Chains: Implications for Developing Countries and Trade Policy*, Cologny/Geneva, Switzerland.

2. Developing a GTAP-based multi-region, input–output framework for supply chain analysis

Terrie L. Walmsley, Thomas Hertel and David Hummels*

1. INTRODUCTION

With the global economy increasingly inter-connected through international trade in intermediate inputs as well as consumer goods, the demand for analytical tools that trace out the implications of these linkages has grown significantly. Examples include studies of international supply chains and trade in value added (Koopman et al., forthcoming; and Johnson and Noguera, 2012), virtual water trade (Konar et al., 2013), life cycle assessment of environmental impacts (Hendrickson et al., 1998), and greenhouse gas (GHG) emissions associated with global trade flows (Peters et al., 2011). All of these studies require a global database that traces out these trade flows between sectors and between producers and consumers of final goods and services, that is, a multi-region, input–output (MRIO) database. In response to these demands, several projects have been formed with the goal of producing new MRIO databases, including EXIOBASE (Tukker et al., 2009), WIOD (Timmer, 2012), OECD-TiVA (OECD, 2012) and Eora (Lenzen et al., 2013 and Lenzen et al., 2012).

An alternative source of global economic data suitable for MRIO- type analysis is the Global Trade Analysis Project (GTAP) database (Narayanan et al., 2012), first released in 1993, which has been updated and encompasses eight releases covering the period 1990 to 2007; a 2011 update is being prepared. The GTAP database is most commonly used as the foundation for global computable general equilibrium (CGE) models. At its core, it is very similar to a MRIO database in that there is an input–output structure for each country that is linked via trade flows to partner countries. However, while it contains far more policy detail than a MRIO, the existing GTAP data contains less import-sourcing detail than is found in a typical MRIO database. Rather than tracing bilateral trade flows to individual agents (intermediate and final), the existing GTAP database aggregates these flows at the border. In this chapter we adopt procedures found in the MRIO literature to disaggregate these flows, thereby creating a complete MRIO from the GTAP database. The benefit of adapting the GTAP database is that it offers broad geographical coverage, and has long term support from a community of researchers and policy makers who employ and update the data on an ongoing basis.

A MRIO database is most useful if it is integrated with tools that can be used to understand the evolution of supply chains in response to changes in technology, final demands, policy and other shocks. That is, global supply chains represent a complex set of general equilibrium interdependencies between countries that reflect a combination of preferences, technology, endowments, and policy. Shocks to income or changes in trade policy, for example, may result in subtle ripple effects throughout supply chains that are difficult to understand by considering only retrospective patterns of output and trade, or by fixing relative prices in prospective analyses. By relaxing these restrictive assumptions, CGE analysis of global supply chains can be considerably more flexible and powerful.

In its simplest form, MRIO-based supply chain analysis investigates the strength of forward and backward linkages from a critical sector or region to the rest of the global economy. If the Japanese automobile sector expands by 10 percent, we can use MRIO tools to calculate the quantity of Korean steel and Thai electronics embodied in a Japanese car, and assume these sectors expand accordingly. This type of fixed-price, IO-multiplier analysis relies on some very strong assumptions. In particular, it requires that there is an infinitely elastic supply of factors available to the economy. In contrast, CGE analysis would typically take supplies of factors as fixed and allow prices to adjust and factors to be reallocated across sectors in order to achieve a new, general equilibrium. That is, an expansion of the Korean steel sector incurs an opportunity cost in terms of output foregone elsewhere in the Korean economy and the adjustment mechanism is through changes in factor and commodity prices that cascade throughout the economy.

We can then think of MRIO supply chain analysis as a special case of CGE analysis in which there is a perfectly elastic supply of primary factors that can expand or contract at constant wage and rental rates. By imposing these factor supply conditions as special restrictions on the CGE model, we can alternately explore the implications of a given shock in the presence of MRIO assumptions or in a more general environment in which these assumptions are relaxed.

Having built a GTAP-based MRIO, this chapter illustrates its usefulness through two applications, which have been selected in order to highlight key features of MRIO analysis and extensions thereof. First, we examine the global labor market implications of economic growth. We start with a fixed-price IO multiplier model then sequentially relax the model's closure assumptions to demonstrate the flexibility of the full CGE. This application also capitalizes on recent work to disaggregate labor endowments in GTAP into five occupational categories to understand how economic growth will affect direct and indirect labor market demands in major Asian markets. We find that the linkages within Asia and between Asia and the rest of the world make it a true engine for growth in the world economy. However, sourcing splits are ultimately endogenous – suggesting that more formal economic modeling is required to understand how these are likely to evolve.

Our second application highlights both the importance of disaggregating import sources in a MRIO database, and of analyzing them in a CGE policy setting. Specifically, a key aspect of developing a full MRIO is attributing import sources for both intermediate and final demands to individual source countries. For example, it might be that both Thailand and Japan export large volumes of electronics, but Thailand exports electronics inputs while Japan exports electronics final goods. To illustrate this distinction we analyze the effect of eliminating tariffs on imported intermediates, while leaving tariffs on final goods unchanged. We find that the additional detail on sourcing can significantly improve our ability to examine the impact of trade liberalization policies aimed specifically at firms. Indeed we find that different sourcing shares can affect the size of the tariff shock and the extent to which other countries gain from increased exports.

2.   BACKGROUND TO MRIO DATABASES

With the increased interest in life cycle and supply chain analyses at the global or multi-regional level there has been a significant escalation in the development of databases linking country input–output tables (IOT).[1] Since the motivation behind the development of these datasets is the examination of supply chains, these databases require information on the value of imports of commodity i by agent (firms, government, households etc), from source s, by region r. At this time, however, there is no global source for this kind of detailed information and data on individual countries (databases built by IDE-JETRO using industry surveys being the exception). Most of the global datasets must therefore rely on the proportionality assumption or the use of the UN Broad Economic Classification (or BEC concordance) with HS6 COMTRADE data to split imports sources by agent.

Table 2.1   Creating a multi-region input–output database

Sources	Intermediate	Final			Constraints
	Sectors 1…j	Investment	Private Consumption	Government Consumption	
Import sources 1…s	$VIFMS_{i,j,s,r}$	$VIFMS_{i,s,r}$	$VIPMS_{i,s,r}$	$VIGMS_{i,s,r}$	$VIMS_{i,s,r}$ (COMTRADE)
Domestic r (IO Data)	$VDFM_{i,r}$	$VDEM_{i,r}$	$VDPM_{i,r}$	$VDGM_{i,r}$	$VDM_{i,r}$ (IO data)
Constraints (IO Data)	$VFM_{i,j,r}$	$VEM_{i,r}$	$VPM_{i,r}$	$VGM_{i,r}$	

Note: COMTRADE = United Nations Commodity Trade Statistics Database; IO = input–output.

Source: Authors' calculations.

Table 2.1 can be used to better explain the challenge faced by those undertaking global MRIO analyses. (The table follows GTAP notational conventions, since they are widely used and well defined.) In an ideal world data would be available on the commodity (i), source (s), destination (r), and agent ($VIFMS_{i,j,s,r}$: intermediate firms (1 … j), $VIPMS_{i,s,r}$: household private consumption, $VIGMS_{i,s,r}$: Government consumption (G) and $VIEMS_{i,s,r}$: Investment).[2]

Country IO tables or supply and use tables provide the total purchases of intermediate inputs by firm j($VFM_{i,j,r}$) and the total purchases of final goods by households, government and for investment ($VPM_{i,r},VGM_{i,r}$ and $VEM_{i,r}$), as well as the value of domestic sales ($VDM_{i,r}$) and the value of imports ($VIM_{i,r}$). Note that the latter are typically not broken out by source. In some tables there may also be reasonable detail on the split of intermediate and final purchases into domestically produced ($VDFM_{i,j,r},VDPM_{i,r},VDGM_{i,r}$ and $VDEM_{i,r}$) and imported items ($VIFM_{i,j,r},VIPM_{i,s,r},VIGM_{i,s,r}$ and $VIEM_{i,s,r}$), but again, none of these imports are disaggregated by source country. Rather, imports are simply aggregated into a single category.

From the United Nations' COMTRADE database we can obtain imports ($VIMS_{i,s,r}$) of commodity (i) by source (s) and destination (r), but these are not disaggregated by use within the importing country and, once aggregated, they do not match the data reported in the IO tables. Two approaches have therefore been used to estimate $VIFMS_{i,j,s,r}$ and $VIPMS_{i,s,r},VIGMS_{i,s,r}$ and $VIEMS_{i,s,r}$, thereby constructing an MRIO database.

2.1 The Proportionality Method

This is the simplest method, and has therefore been frequently used in the MRIO literature. It assumes that all uses of a good are sourced in the same way. That is, if 10 percent of all Chinese imports of electronics come from Thailand, we assume that the same 10 percent share applies whether they are used as intermediate inputs, investment, by the government sector or household final demand, so that:

$$\frac{VIFMS_{i,j,s,r}}{\sum_s VIFMS_{i,j,s,r}} = \frac{VIPMS_{i,s,r}}{\sum_s VIPMS_{i,s,r}} = \frac{VIGMS_{i,s,r}}{\sum_s VIGMS_{i,s,r}}$$

$$= \frac{VIEMS_{i,s,r}}{\sum_s VIEMS_{i,s,r}} = \frac{VIMS_{i,s,r}}{\sum_s VIMS_{i,s,r}}$$

2.2 The BEC Concordance Method

This method uses the detailed BEC concordances to split commodities at the HS6 level into intermediate goods, final goods or mixed. Within electronics, for example, a microchip would likely be classified as an intermediate input, while a laptop could be a final good. Using the COMTRADE HS6 data with source countries disaggregated, in conjunction with these BEC-derived splits into final, intermediate and mixed, then allows us to determine the sourcing shares of both intermediate and final goods independently. If in the trade data Thailand exports microchips and the People's Republic of China (PRC) exports laptops, we will obtain different sourcing shares for the aggregated category of electronics, even though we have no independent information on sourcing shares at the HS6 level.

These BEC-influenced sourcing shares for aggregated commodities are then applied and the data are rebalanced to ensure the adding up constraints given in Table 2.1. Given the limited information about sourcing in the BEC concordance, this method only provides sourcing shares for total intermediates (i.e., $VINMS_{i,s,r} = \Sigma_j VIFMS_{i,j,s,r}$) and total final goods ($VILMS_{i,s,r} = VIPMS_{i,s,r} + VIGMS_{i,s,r} + VIEMS_{i,s,r}$).[3] It does not distinguish between the sources of, for example, imported steel used in the motor vehicle industry as opposed to the coal industry for a given destination country. Nor does it distinguish between the sources of imported leather for private consumption as opposed to investment or government uses. To further split these data across intermediate or final uses the proportionality assumption must be used. Hence:

$$\frac{VIFMS_{i,j,s,r}}{\sum_s VIFMS_{i,j,s,r}} = \frac{VINMS_{i,s,r}}{\sum_s VINMS_{i,s,r}}$$

and

$$\frac{VIPMS_{i,s,r}}{\sum_s VIPMS_{i,s,r}} = \frac{VIGMS_{i,s,r}}{\sum_s VIGMS_{i,s,r}} = \frac{VIEMS_{i,s,r}}{\sum_s VIEMS_{i,s,r}} = \frac{VLMS_{i,s,r}}{\sum_s VLMS_{i,s,r}}$$

But

$$\frac{VINMS_{i,s,r}}{\sum_s VINMS_{i,s,r}} \neq \frac{VLMS_{i,s,r}}{\sum_s VLMS_{i,s,r}}$$

A number of efforts are currently being undertaken to develop regional and/or global MRIO datasets. Some of these tables do not yet include the additional MRIO detail on sourcing by agent, while others have developed MRIO variants using the proportionality method – for example, EXIOBASE (Tukker et al., 2009) and various GTAP-based MRIOs (Andrew and Peters, 2013 and Johnson and Noguera, 2012). The World Input–Output Database (WIOD) (Timmer, 2012), the TiVA database (OECD, 2012) and the GTAP-Inter-Country Input–Output (GTAP-ICIO) (Koopman et al., 2010) are examples of global databases where the BEC concordance has been used to improve the sourcing splits. Table 2.2 lists some of these projects and the differences in their approaches to the inclusion of the supply chain detail.[4]

Since IO tables are not produced on an annual basis, all of the datasets discussed above will have had to rely on external data to update the MRIO to a consistent 'base year' and/or 'fill in' missing information in the IO tables to ensure consistency in the data across countries. Another feature of many of these datasets is the availability of time series. The underlying idea/assumption behind the updating of these IO tables to a new base year or the creation of time series data is that it is the IO shares that matter and that these shares do not change significantly between releases of new IO tables by statistical agencies. In some cases the producers of these datasets have chosen to release only those years for which they have IO tables (e.g., the OECD-WTO TiVA and JETRO databases), while in other cases constrained optimization techniques have been used to fill in missing years using the structure given in the IO table for another year as the starting point and updating it with additional macroeconomic and/or production data (e.g., WIOD and Eora). In the case of GTAP and EXIOBASE the data are released for one year (or two in the case of the recent GTAP v.8

Table 2.2   Summary of datasets

Database	Reference	Primary approach used to include supply chain detail	Balancing
IDE-JETRO Asian International Input–Output Tables	Meng et al. (2013)	Country foreign trade data and imported input surveys	Manual identification of errors/reasons for differences, followed by manual adjustment
OECD-WTO TiVA database	OECD (2012)	OECD tables and BEC concordances approach with HS6 trade data	OECD IO Tables were adjusted to ensure balanced bilateral trade
GTAP Database GTAP-MRIO	Narayanan et al. (2012) Andrew and Peters (2013) and Johnson and Noguera (2012)	Does not include MRIO detail Proportional	Trade data given priority Re-balancing not required
GTAP-ICIO	Koopman et al. (2010)	BEC concordance plus additional detail on special processing zones in People's Republic of China, and Mexico.	Trade data given priority
WIOD	Timmer (2012)	BEC concordances approach with HS6 trade data	IO/SUT data given priority. No balancing undertaken
EXIOBASE	Tukker et al. (2009)	Proportional	IOT given priority but RAS used to rebalance and ensure non-negative trade

Table 2.2   (continued)

Database	Reference	Primary approach used to include supply chain detail	Balancing
EORA	Lenzen, Moran et al. (2013) and Lenzen, Kanemoto et al. (2012)	IO tables where available and BEC concordances approach with HS6 trade data	Re-balanced: preferences are based on estimated standard deviations. In current version national IO tables (e.g., IDE/ JETRO) have highest priority, COMTRADE the lowest

Notes:
BEC = Broad Economic Classification; EXIOBASE = global, detailed Multi-regional Environmentally Extended Supply and Use/Input Output; GTAP = Global Trade Analysis Project; IDE-JETRO = Institute of Development Economics-Japan External Trade Organization; IO = input–output; MRIO = multi-region, input–output; OECD = Organisation for Economic Co-operation and Development; SUT = supply and use table; TiVA = trade in value added; WIOD = World Input–Output Database; WTO = World Trade Organization.
Primary approach is the primary source of the additional MRIO sourcing detail. Where the primary source is unavailable other methods, such as proportionality, are likely to have been used.

Source: Sources of information listed in column 2.

database),[5] however, not all IO tables derive from the base year and hence they use similar optimization techniques to update the data to the relevant year.

3.   BUILDING A GTAP-BASED MRIO

In this section we describe in detail the process of converting the GTAP database to a global MRIO by disaggregating imports of commodity i from source s by region r into distinct uses (intermediate versus final). By going through this process in some detail, we gain better insight into the alternative approaches currently employed in this literature.

3.1 How to Build a GTAP-MRIO

The following sections provide an overview of the assumptions made and procedures used in constructing our extended GTAP database.

Application of the BEC concordance

As described above, we use a concordance from the UN Broad Economic Classification (BEC), applied at the HS6 level, to allocate commodities to intermediate, final or mixed demand. The commodities are then aggregated from HS6 to the GTAP level using COMTRADE weights to provide the allocation of bilateral GTAP imports ($VIMS_{i,s,r}$) across final ($VILMS_{i,s,r}$) and intermediate ($VINMS_{i,s,r}$) uses by source (Table 2.3).[6] To allocate across intermediate sectors and final demand types (private and government consumption, and investment) the proportionality assumption is then used, as is customary in all those datasets using the BEC concordance (WIOD and GTAP-ICIO). Like Koopman et al. (2010) we also find significant variation between the sources of intermediate and final use.

International trade data are available for 45 GTAP commodities, 159 importing regions and 231 exporting regions. Missing commodities include water, construction, trade, other transport, water transport, air transport,

Table 2.3   Creating a GTAP-MRIO

Sources	Intermediate	Final	Constraints (GTAP data)
Imports 1...s	$VINMS_{i,s,r}$	$VILMS_{i,s,r}$	
	$(=\Sigma_j VIFM_{i,j,r})$	$(=VIEM_{i,r}+VIPM_{i,r}+VIGM_{i,r})$	$VIMS_{i,s,r}$
Domestic r	$VDNM_{i,r}$	$VDLM_{i,r}$	
	$(=\Sigma_j VDFM_{i,j,r})$	$(VDEM_{i,r}+VDPM_{i,r}+VDGM_{i,r})$	$VDM_{i,r}$
Constraints (GTAP data)	$VNM_{i,r}=\Sigma_j VFM_{i,j,r}$	$VLM_{i,r}=VEM_{i,r}$ $VPM_{i,r}+VGM_{i,r}$	

Notes:
GTAP = Global Trade Analysis Project; MRIO = multi-region, input–output.
For 'Final', we are using E for investment: $VEM_{i,j,r}=\Sigma_{j \in cgds}, VFM_{i,j,r}$ in GTAP notation.

Source: Authors' calculations.

communication services, other financial services, insurance, other business services, recreational services, government services and dwellings. Since the UN COMTRADE database does not cover services it is not surprising that these data are unavailable. In these cases the proportionality assumption is used to allocate bilateral GTAP imports ($VIMS_{i,s,r}$) across final ($VILMS_{i,s,r}$) and intermediate ($VINMS_{i,s,r}$) uses by source.

The 159 importers cover a substantial proportion of trade between the 244 countries underlying the GTAP database. However, there are five primary[7] countries in GTAP that have no import data shares from the application of BEC: Taipei,China, Egypt, Iran, Lao People's Democratic Republic (Lao PDR) and Nepal. Taipei,China is also not recorded as an exporter, although Egypt, Iran, Lao PDR and Nepal are included in the 231 exporters. In these cases the proportionality rule is applied.

Rebalancing

The aim of this data construction exercise is to create a globally consistent, bilaterally-sourced GTAP-MRIO database while minimizing changes to the underlying economic flows recorded in the original GTAP database. Table 2.3 illustrates the balancing problem. We need to find values for intermediate ($VINMS_{i,s,r}$) and final ($VILMS_{i,s,r}$) demand by source that add up to total imports by source ($VIMS_{i,s,r}$), and that, when combined with domestic sales, add up to the total value of intermediate ($VNM_{i,r}$) and final ($VLM_{i,r}$) demand.

Given the high priority which the GTAP database construction procedures afford the trade data, the decision was first made to benchmark to the underlying GTAP trade data ($VIMS_{i,s,r}$), thereby keeping the trade data intact. The shares obtained from the BEC concordance are applied to bilateral trade in GTAP ($VIMS_{i,s,r}$) to provide estimates of intermediate (N) imports, $VINMS_{i,s,r}$, and final imports (L), $VILMS_{i,s,r}$. This is consistent with what was done by Koopman et al. (2010), although it is not consistent with what has been done in the WIOD database, where the IO data are given the highest priority.[8]

The first issue that results from this decision is that any changes in $VINMS_{i,s,r}$ and $VILMS_{i,s,r}$ resulting from application of the BEC shares will likely cause a deviation from the original total in the standard GTAP database (for instance, in the case of intermediates $\Sigma_s VINMS_{i,s,r} \neq \Sigma_j VIFM_{i,j,r}$).

Since this split between domestic and imported goods, is generally thought to be the weakest part of the IO table construction, it would seem to make sense to allow these splits to adjust to reflect the new information contained in the BEC shares. Under this assumption, these changes will need to be offset by corresponding changes in domestic intermediate ($VDNM_{i,r}$) and domestic final ($VDLM_{i,r}$) to retain a balanced IO table and retain total intermediate and final demand (i.e., the final row of Table 2.3). Moreover, if those changes were to cause either of these domestic values ($VDNM_{i,r}$ or $VDLM_{i,r}$) to fall below zero, then the sourcing implied by BEC would have to adjust to restore balance. Under this approach, the only constraints applied in the rebalancing procedure are those represented by the shaded areas in Table 2.3.

The alternative is to assume that the domestic-import splits in the IO table do indeed contain meritorious information, therefore suggesting that the sourcing shares should adjust to retain the domestic/imports split reported in the IO tables. Under this option the italicized and bolded items in brackets in Table 2.3 are imposed as constraints on the new database, along with the GTAP trade data ($VIMS_{i,s,r}$).[9]

Since each approach yields a different MRIO, which in turn may result in different conclusions from a given study, we construct and compare outcomes from three alternative datasets in the subsequent analyses:

1. GTAP prop:[10] GTAP sourcing shares (i.e., the proportionality assumption is applied as in EXIOBASE; Peters et al., 2011; and Johnson and Noguera, 2012).
2. GTAP-BEC: BEC sourcing shares are applied to intermediate and final imports; however the splits between intermediate and final imports, and hence domestic goods obtained from the GTAP database, are also applied as constraints on the rebalancing. This is akin to the alternative listed above wherein the italicized items in Table 2.3 are imposed as constraints on the new database.
3. BEC: the IO data are rebalanced, thereby allowing BEC to alter the intermediate/final import shares in the IOT, as well as the sourcing shares. The balancing constraints are therefore those shaded in Table 2.3.

For the sake of illustration, Table 2.4 reports the shares of imports of Japanese wearing apparel to help illustrate what has been held constant under the three alternative dataset options. There is a considerable difference between the proportionality assumption (option 1) and using the BEC concordance (options 2 and 3) in this simple example: Japan imports much more 'intermediate' wearing apparel from the EU and more 'final' wearing apparel from the PRC and Viet Nam under the BEC concordance than is suggested by the proportionality assumption. Since it is these differences in bilateral flows that underlie supply chain analysis, there appears to be an important role for the BEC concordance in this case. The difference between GTAP-BEC and BEC is less obvious. Since Japan imports significantly more wearing apparel overall from the PRC than it

Table 2.4   Japanese imports of wearing apparel (%)

		Share in total imports	Share in total demand	Share of imports from		
				PRC	EU	Viet Nam
Intermediate	GTAP	3.6	4.3	77.8	9.8	4.2
imports	GTAP-BEC	3.6	4.3	55.4	31.6	0.5
	BEC	2.8	3.4	53.8	32.1	0.5
Final imports	GTAP	96.4	44.7	77.8	9.8	4.2
	GTAP-BEC	96.4	44.7	78.6	9.0	4.3
	BEC	97.2	45.0	78.5	9.2	4.3

Notes:
BEC = Broad Economic Classification; EU = European Union; GTAP = Global Trade
Analysis Project; PRC = People's Republic of China.
Share in total imports = Sum to 100.
Share in total demand = Share of imported intermediate in total intermediated and share of
imported final goods in total final goods. Domestic share = 1 – import share.
Share of imports from People's Republic of China/European Union/Viet Nam = Sum to
100% across all sources.

Source: Authors' calculations.

does from the EU, the share of intermediate goods in total imports goes
down from 3.6 percent to 2.8 percent because Japan purchases mostly final
wearing apparel from the PRC. Hence the share of imported intermediates
in the production of wearing apparel goes down and the share of domestic
increases (and vice versa for final wearing apparel). To keep those import
shares the same (GTAP-BEC), the sourcing shares must adjust back
toward the proportionality shares – in this case the required adjustment in
sourcing shares is relatively small.

Preferences for either the second or the third option will depend on
the extent to which one 'believes' that the import shares in the IO tables
(GTAP-BEC) are more realistic than those implied by the BEC shares
(BEC). Which approach is best ultimately depends on the quality of the
IO data relative to the BEC data. Since the split between imports and
domestically produced goods is the weakest part of many IO tables, focusing on total intermediate and final demand as the balancing constraint
(BEC) is a reasonably sound choice. However if a national statistical
office (NSO) has made a serious attempt to estimate these, then it is difficult to believe that the BEC concordance – one that arbitrarily allocates
goods into mixed, final or intermediate goods at the HS6 level – would
produce better import shares by intermediate and final agents than the
NSO. In future work we would hope to utilize the information we collect

from contributors to ascertain how reliable this aspect of each GTAP IO table might be. Indeed, the best strategy may well be to employ a mixed approach in which the choice between BEC and GTAP-BEC depends on the country in question.

Koopman et al. (2010) bring another level of sophistication to the construction of a MRIO database by taking into account the trade reporter reliability indexes prepared in constructing the underlying GTAP trade data as discussed in Gehlhar et al. (2008). This suggests that there may be a preference for data reported by the exporter in some cases, thereby overruling the importer-based data. It is hoped that once the MRIO construction process is rolled into the GTAP database construction process, the underlying BEC shares would come from the same source as the trade data, namely the work of Mark Gehlhar, and hence the reliability of reporters will have been taken into account. This would increase the quality of the implied BEC shares and our belief in them.

One can also alter the objective function used in the constrained optimization, rebalancing exercise. For example, Koopman et al. (2010) use a quadratic optimization process, while we use an entropy-based objective function. The Koopman et al. (2010) approach targets total intermediate and final demands in the GTAP IO table shares, and therefore their data are more akin to option 3: BEC, although there are additional differences in their procedures that would cause other differences in their database.

Figure 2.1 offers a summary of the resulting demand for Asia's exports under the BEC database produced for this chapter. It clearly illustrates that intra-regional trade within Asia is dominated by intermediate goods: approximately 75 percent of Asian exports to inside Asia are intermediate, while less than 50 percent of Asian exports to outside Asia are intermediate. This is consistent with the characterization of 'Factory Asia' by Baldwin and Forslid elsewhere in this volume. (Comparable figures for the GTAP-BEC and GTAP proportional methods can be found in Appendix 2A.2: at this aggregated level the differences between the datasets are not significant.)

Other adjustments

Having determined the aggregated intermediate and final import source splits, these are then applied within the broad categories of intermediate and final demands, using the proportionality rule (i.e. across sectors in the case of intermediates, and across private and government consumption and investment for final demands). Adjustments are also made to separate any taxes, import duties and transportation margins by agent, assuming the same rate regardless of the agent purchasing the import.

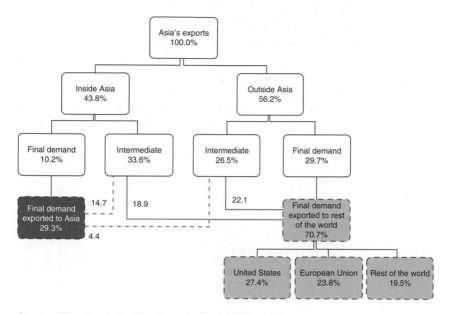

Source: Based on Asian Development Bank (2010), p. 33.

Figure 2.1   Final demand for Asia's exports: broad economic classification database

An aside on labor splits

Since the impact of supply chains on value added and employment is an important consideration for this chapter, we also incorporate recent work that splits labor into five categories within the GTAP-MRIO. These five categories are based on International Labour Office (ILO) data and include labor cost shares by sector for:

- Professionals
- Technicians and associate professionals
- Clerks
- Service workers, shop and sales workers
- Agricultural, machine operators, assemblers and unskilled workers

Details on how the ILO data were processed and incorporated into the GTAP database can be obtained from Weingarden and Tsigas (2010) and Walmsley and Carrico (2013).

Table 2.5   Commodity and regional aggregation

Regions	Commodities
Japan	Cereals
Korea, Republic of	Other crops
China, People's Republic of	Livestock and raw milk
Taipei,China	Forestry and fishing
Other East Asia	Resources
Singapore	Meat and dairy
Philippines	Processed rice
Thailand	Other food
Indonesia	Textiles
Malaysia	Wearing apparel
Viet Nam	Lumber and paper
Other Southeast Asia	Resource products
India	Chemicals, rubbers and plastics
Bangladesh	Metals
Pakistan	Metal products
Other South Asia	Motor vehicles
Central Asia	Electronic goods and other equipment
Pacific Islands	Other manufactures
Australia and New Zealand	Non-tradable services
European Union	Services
North America	
Other developing countries	

Source: Authors' calculations.

3.2   Comparing the Alternative GTAP-MRIO Data Sets

For purposes of this chapter the final GTAP-MRIO database is then aggregated into 20 commodities and 22 regions (Table 2.5). The choice of aggregation reflects the fact that we are interested in examining the impact of Asia-Pacific growth on the developing member countries of the Asian Development Bank.

In comparing the three alternative datasets, there are two shares that are of special interest. First, we look at the share of intermediate (or final) imports to total imports under option 3 compared to the same GTAP share.[11]

$$\frac{\sum_r VINMS_{i,r,s}}{\sum_r VINMS_{i,r,s} + \sum_r VILMS_{i,r,s}} \text{ vs } \frac{\sum_j VIFM_{i,j,s}}{\sum_j VIFM_{i,j,s} + VIPM_{i,s} + VIGM_{i,s} + VIEM_{i,s}}$$

The comparison shows that in all but two cases the main differences between he original GTAP shares and the BEC shares (option 3) are in the agricultural commodities. This could be due to a number of factors.

First, certain countries (e.g., Australia) require that agricultural goods, such as sugar or processed rice, be sold first to a domestic firm which then checks and packages the product before selling it to final consumers. The BEC concordance misses these types of country specific issues, while the IO table is likely to capture these idiosyncrasies.

Second, many IOT/SUTs do not include individual agriculture commodities, reporting instead flows only for a single agricultural industry. This single industry is then disaggregated/processed in-house at the GTAP center using econometric estimates based on FAO data which means that there is no country-specific inter-industry information brought to bear at the sub-sector level.

In those countries that do break out agriculture in the IO tables we often find that the distinction between raw and processed agricultural products (such as rice and grains) is more complicated than the BEC concordance would suggest. In some cases basic processing may take place on the farm and/or unprocessed or semi-processed grains may be sold directly to households, particularly in developing countries.

The countries appearing more than twice in the top 100 are listed in the right hand column of Table 2.6. While 17 commodities continuously appear in the top 100, many more countries (57) appeared in the top 100 differences, suggesting this is more of an issue with agriculture than with specific countries. Not surprisingly, developing countries were more likely than developed countries to be in the top 100. Of the Asian countries, Mongolia, India, Sri Lanka, Kazakhstan and the Kyrgyz Republic appear twice in this list. The top 25 commodity-country pairs, in terms of largest differences between GTAP and BEC, for the aggregation presented in this chapter, are listed in Appendix Table 2A.1.

The second key point of comparison in the databases is the sourcing shares and the differences between sourcing of intermediate and final as opposed to using the proportional assumption

$$\frac{VINMS_{i,r,s}}{\sum_r VINMS_{i,r,s}} \text{ vs } \frac{VIMS_{i,r,s}}{\sum_r VIMS_{i,r,s}} \text{ or } \frac{VILMS_{i,r,s}}{\sum_r VILMS_{i,r,s}} \text{ vs } \frac{VIMS_{i,r,s}}{\sum_r VIMS_{i,r,s}}$$

In Appendix Table 2A.2, the top differences between these shares in the aggregated data are listed. As in the case above, the differences are most pronounced in agriculture, with processed rice featuring most prominently.

Table 2.6   Largest changes in the share of intermediate imports to total imports in disaggregated GTAP 8 Database

Commodities appearing in top 100	Number of times commodity appears in top 100	Countries appearing more than twice in top 100	Number of times country appears in top 100
Grains	21	Morocco	6
Processed rice	19	Ethiopia	6
Other animal products	10	Bolivia	4
		Turkey	4
Cattle	9	Kenya	4
Vegetables and fruit	9	Honduras	3
Oil seeds	6	Ivory Coast	3
Paddy rice	5	Ghana	3
Fish	4	Malawi	3
Forestry	4		
Sugar	3		
Plant fibers	2		
Vegetable oils	2		
Wheat	2		
Electricity	1		
Other meat	1		
Wool	1		
Wearing apparel	1		
Sum	100		

Source: Authors' calculations.

Other goods include wearing apparel and non-tradable services, which is related to electricity imports by Thailand from neighboring countries.

4.   GTAP-SC ANALYSIS

In order to accommodate this MRIO database, we have also constructed a new version of the GTAP model, complete with sourcing splits, and designed to be used in analyzing supply chains. We call this new model GTAP-SC and illustrate its use through several applications in this section.

In the first section, we use a special closure and parameters file to turn the GTAP-SC model into a fixed-price IO multiplier model. We then use this model to examine the impact of a 10 percent increase in net national income in each country under a succession of three alternative datasets (options 1–3 discussed above). The assumptions underlying the fixed-price, IO multiplier model are then progressively relaxed. Overall, the results show insignificant differences resulting from the incorporation of the sourcing splits and the different balancing assumptions used – particularly when contrasted with the very large changes which result from relaxing the economic assumptions behind the fixed-price multiplier model.

To illustrate how the additional sourcing information can alter results, we then use GTAP-SC as a policy-oriented CGE model to examine the impact of removing tariffs on all intermediate imports. We compare the results from the GTAP-SC model under the three alternative datasets with those obtained from the GTAP model using the standard GTAP database. Here, the differences are more significant, suggesting that the approach to construction of MRIO databases is indeed an important topic for further investigation.

4.1 The GTAP-SC Model

In the standard GTAP model for every region, each agent (firms, government, and private households) chooses quantities of domestic and imported intermediate inputs (Figure 2.2, left hand side). The three demands for imports are then aggregated, as indicated below the dashed line in the left hand side of Figure 2.2 to obtain total demand for imports. Finally, sourcing decisions for those imports are made at this aggregated level. This was done because of the lack of data on sourcing by agents and to keep the model tractable computationally as the number of regions in the database proliferated.

In GTAP-SC (Figure 2.2, right hand side) for each region, individual agents choose quantities of domestic and imported intermediates, as well as determining where to source those imported intermediates ($QIFS_{i,j,s,r}$, where Q is used for quantity). This acknowledges the fact that firms may source the same goods from different sources than private households or government, as shown above. Agents therefore make their decision on the price paid by them for the imported good, including any taxes and tariffs. The Armington assumption is still in place, it is just now at the agent level. Similar structures exist for private and government consumption.

Importantly, this treatment in GTAP-SC allows import prices to differ by agent, as would be the case if there are differential import taxes or duties applied to intermediate vs. final goods. Such differences are pervasive at the GTAP commodity level, once the BEC concordance is used to aggregate commodities from the HS6 level, since tariffs vary considerably across HS6 commodities within a given GTAP sector. Another instance in which such differences in tariffs will arise is in those countries where duty drawbacks

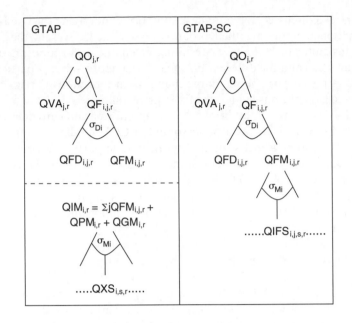

Note: GTAP = Global Trade Analysis Project; SC = supply chains.

Source: Authors' illustration.

Figure 2.2   Firm structure in GTAP and GTAP-SC

are offered on imports used to produce goods produced in export processing zones. Without the additional detail on imports by agent, such differences in tariffs will not show up in the database. (Of course, a full treatment
of duty-drawbacks requires the disaggregation of sectors into those within
export-processing zones and those producing for the domestic market. For
a GTAP-based application of this approach, see Ianchovichina, 2003).
where:

$QO_{j,r}$: quantity of output of industry j in region r.
$QVA_{j,r}$: quantity of value added purchased by industry j in region r
$QF_{i,j,r}$: quantity of intermediate good i purchased by industry j in
region r
$QFD_{i,j,r}$: quantity of domestic intermediate good i purchased by industry j in region r
$QIM_{i,r}$: quantity of imported goods i purchased by ALL agents in
region r
$QFM_{i,j,r}$: quantity of imported intermediate good i purchased by
industry j in region r

$QPM_{i,r}$: quantity of imported good i purchased by private households in region r

$QGM_{i,r}$: quantity of imported good i purchased by government in region r

$QXS_{i,s,r}$: quantity of total imports of good i from region s in region r

$QIFS_{i,j,s,r}$: quantity of imported intermediate good i from region s in region r

σ_{Di} or $ESUBD_i$ (in GTAP): constant elasticity of substitution (CES) between domestic and imported good i (same for all agents)

σ_{Mi} or $ESUBM_i$ (in GTAP): CES elasticity of substitution between imports by source s (same for all agents)

We impose a balancing constraint that the quantity of imports demanded[12] from each source by each agent must equal the quantity exported.

$$QXS_{i,s,r} = \sum_j QIFS_{i,j,s,r} + QIPS_{i,s,r} + QIGS_{i,s,r}$$

where:

$QIPS_{i,s,r}$: quantity of imported good i for private consumption from region s in region r

$QIGS_{i,s,r}$: quantity of imported good i for government consumption from region s in region r

Note: $QIFS_{i,cgds,s,r}$: quantity of imported good i for investment from region s in region r

Finally, the model allows for the possibility that technological change, taxes and import duties may be applied at different rates depending on the agent purchasing the commodity, and hence these can be shocked independently in GTAP-SC. On the other hand, international transportation margins are not differentiated by agent.

4.2 GTAP-SC as a Fixed Multiplier Model

Supply chain analysis in its simplest form involves investigation of the forward and backward linkages from a critical sector/region of the global economy. This type of 'multiplier analysis' is a special case of CGE analysis in which the aggregate supply of primary factors is perfectly elastic and can therefore respond endogenously to a 'shock' in the economy. In CGE analysis, the supply of factors is often (but not always) fixed, and any increase in demand leads to a change in prices and reallocation of factors across sectors. The closure of a CGE model must therefore be adjusted to convert the model into a fixed-price IO multiplier model as follows:

1. By fixing real factor prices in all regions and endogenizing their aggregate supplies. As aggregate income rises, demand rises and firms can simply produce whatever is demanded without an increase in costs. They are able to do this because their access to factors is limitless. Output is therefore fully demand-driven.
2. The GTAP model has a non-homothetic demand system (constant difference of elasticity or CDE) for private consumption that causes budget shares to change as incomes rise. In order to neutralize these changes in the budget shares, the non-homotheticity in the CDE function must be 'turned off' by appropriately changing the parameter file.[13]
3. Finally, in order to shock a variable, in this case regional income, this variable must be fixed. However, in a CGE framework, regional income is endogenously determined by changes in factor earnings and net tax receipts. And since we have already artificially endogenized endowments, it makes sense to fix regional incomes. Of course, fixing a region's income destroys the link between expenditure and income and eliminates the general equilibrium characteristics of the model and therefore further adjustments must be made. In particular, since Walras's Law no longer applies, we must impose equilibrium in the (normally omitted) market for global savings and investment. In adding another equation, we must also add another variable – in this case the global index of primary factor prices, which is normally the (fixed) numeraire. Since all prices are fixed in this closure anyway, the issue of a numeraire does not come up.

Exploring the impacts of a 10 percent increase in income
In Table 2.7 we use the fixed price multiplier model to analyze how a 10 percent rise in income within one country results in changes in real GDP within that country and throughout all other economies. Each column refers to a separate experiment, with the matrix of results showing the impact on every country of an increase in its own income (along the diagonal), and of an increase in the income of every other country (off diagonal elements in the table). There are several items worthy of discussion.

First, countries tend to gain most from their own growth, rather than that of others. However, countries that are more globally integrated (e.g. Singapore, Malaysia, Thailand and Viet Nam) see a larger share of the 10 percent income shock absorbed by their trading partners. All of these countries have high import and export shares relative to GDP (Figure 2.3

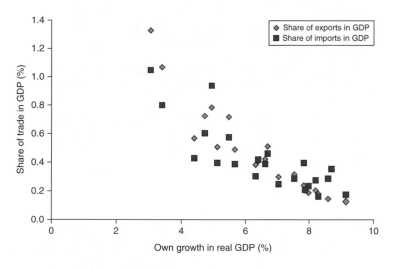

Note: GDP = gross domestic product.

Source: Authors' illustration.

Figure 2.3   *Scatterplot of import and export to GDP shares against own growth in real GDP*

and Table 2.8), leading to 'leakage' of the income shock into the rest of the world and vice versa. The higher the import to GDP share the greater the leakage.

Moreover, larger countries/regions (Japan, the PRC, the EU, North America and DCs) tend to induce higher growth elsewhere simply because even a small outward leakage in percentage change terms for them is a large inward leakage for the smaller economies. Of course this is only part of the story – while the EU and North America are of similar economic size, the gains from EU growth are much larger due to the region being more integrated into the world economy. Similarly the gains from the DCs are closer to those of North America despite being half their size, simply because they are more integrated with the rest of the world (Table 2.8).

Table 2.8 also shows the contribution of own and others' growth in the total percentage change in real imports and exports. Not surprisingly the changes in imports from own and others' growth tends to follow the same pattern as the change in real GDP. Exports on the other hand are not greatly affected by own growth, although they do rise considerably as a result of others' growth. This follows from the fact that own growth increases imports, which in turn raises exports of the trade partners (others). The exceptions are the EU, North America and DCs

Table 2.7 Impact of a 10 percent increase (shock) in income on real GDP in own and other economies

Impacted region	Region in which income is shocked											
	Japan	Korea, Rep. of	PRC	Taipei, China	OEA	Singapore	Philippines	Thailand	Indonesia	Malaysia	Viet Nam	OSE
Japan	8.27	0.09	0.41	0.06	0.00	0.03	0.01	0.03	0.03	0.03	0.01	0.00
Korea, Rep. of	0.28	6.60	0.69	0.06	0.00	0.03	0.02	0.03	0.05	0.04	0.02	0.01
PRC	0.37	0.15	6.30	0.06	0.01	0.04	0.02	0.04	0.05	0.04	0.02	0.01
Taipei,China	0.36	0.14	1.06	5.48	0.01	0.03	0.03	0.05	0.05	0.05	0.04	0.01
Other East Asia	0.23	0.13	0.72	0.03	4.41	0.04	0.01	0.05	0.04	0.04	0.01	0.00
Singapore	0.51	0.24	0.93	0.08	0.01	3.07	0.05	0.11	0.27	0.16	0.05	0.02
Philippines	0.39	0.11	0.70	0.05	0.00	0.03	6.68	0.04	0.05	0.05	0.02	0.00
Thailand	0.52	0.13	0.68	0.07	0.01	0.05	0.05	4.72	0.13	0.10	0.06	0.08
Indonesia	0.53	0.17	0.38	0.08	0.00	0.04	0.03	0.05	7.00	0.07	0.02	0.01
Malaysia	0.64	0.21	0.86	0.13	0.01	0.12	0.06	0.12	0.16	3.40	0.05	0.03
Viet Nam	0.56	0.14	0.48	0.08	0.00	0.05	0.08	0.06	0.15	0.09	4.92	0.04
Other Southeast Asia	0.71	0.21	0.31	0.03	0.00	0.03	0.01	0.42	0.25	0.04	0.05	5.67
India	0.08	0.04	0.25	0.02	0.00	0.02	0.01	0.02	0.02	0.02	0.01	0.00
Bangladesh	0.04	0.02	0.12	0.02	0.00	0.01	0.00	0.01	0.01	0.01	0.00	0.00
Pakistan	0.04	0.03	0.14	0.02	0.00	0.01	0.00	0.01	0.01	0.01	0.00	0.00
Other South Asia	0.08	0.03	0.15	0.02	0.00	0.02	0.00	0.02	0.02	0.01	0.00	0.00
Central Asia	0.14	0.07	0.43	0.03	0.00	0.03	0.01	0.02	0.03	0.02	0.00	0.00

Table: Region in which income is shocked

Impacted region	India	Bangladesh	Pakistan	Other South Asia	Central Asia	Pacific Islands	Australia New Zealand	European Union	North America	Other DCs
Pacific Islands	0.42	0.09	0.44	0.05	0.00	0.06	0.03	0.03	0.01	0.00
Australia and New Zealand	0.31	0.11	0.38	0.05	0.00	0.03	0.04	0.03	0.01	0.00
European Union	0.09	0.04	0.24	0.03	0.00	0.02	0.02	0.02	0.00	0.00
North America	0.07	0.04	0.16	0.02	0.00	0.01	0.01	0.01	0.00	0.00
Other DCs	0.21	0.09	0.31	0.04	0.01	0.03	0.03	0.02	0.01	0.00
Japan	0.02	0.00	0.00	0.00	0.01	0.00	0.05	0.36	0.25	0.33
Korea, Rep. of	0.06	0.00	0.00	0.00	0.03	0.00	0.06	0.77	0.56	0.68
PRC	0.08	0.01	0.01	0.00	0.03	0.00	0.09	1.05	0.94	0.69
Taipei,China	0.07	0.01	0.01	0.00	0.02	0.00	0.09	0.96	0.98	0.55
Other East Asia	0.10	0.00	0.01	0.00	0.02	0.00	0.11	2.14	0.95	0.95
Singapore	0.32	0.01	0.02	0.02	0.03	0.01	0.21	1.87	1.10	0.91
Philippines	0.04	0.00	0.00	0.00	0.01	0.01	0.06	0.74	0.66	0.35
Thailand	0.09	0.01	0.02	0.01	0.02	0.01	0.21	1.29	0.91	0.81

Table 2.7 (continued)

Impacted region	Region in which income is shocked									
	India	Bangladesh	Pakistan	Other South Asia	Central Asia	Pacific Islands	Australia New Zealand	European Union	North America	Other DCs
Indonesia	0.12	0.01	0.02	0.01	0.01	0.00	0.09	0.57	0.38	0.39
Malaysia	0.25	0.02	0.05	0.02	0.02	0.01	0.24	1.42	1.33	0.87
Viet Nam	0.05	0.00	0.01	0.00	0.01	0.01	0.39	1.27	1.08	0.53
Other Southeast Asia	0.28	0.02	0.01	0.00	0.01	0.00	0.21	0.72	0.69	0.31
India	7.96	0.02	0.01	0.03	0.01	0.00	0.03	0.63	0.31	0.50
Bangladesh	0.03	8.17	0.01	0.00	0.01	0.00	0.01	0.85	0.46	0.22
Pakistan	0.02	0.01	8.58	0.05	0.01	0.00	0.02	0.43	0.27	0.36
Other South Asia	0.20	0.01	0.02	7.82	0.01	0.00	0.03	0.78	0.37	0.38
Central Asia	0.05	0.01	0.01	0.01	5.10	0.00	0.03	1.96	0.47	1.57
Pacific Islands	0.09	0.00	0.00	0.00	0.02	6.39	0.40	1.00	0.43	0.46
Australia and New Zealand	0.09	0.00	0.00	0.00	0.01	0.02	7.87	0.45	0.17	0.34
European Union	0.04	0.00	0.00	0.00	0.02	0.00	0.03	8.69	0.20	0.53
North America	0.02	0.00	0.00	0.00	0.01	0.00	0.02	0.27	9.13	0.22
Other DCs	0.10	0.00	0.01	0.00	0.03	0.00	0.03	1.03	0.47	7.53

Note: DCs = developing countries; OEA = Other East Asia; OSE = Other Southeast Asia; PRC = People's Republic of China.

Source: Authors' calculations.

Table 2.8   *Impact of a 10 percent increase (shock) in income on real values of GDP, imports and exports from own and other economies*

	GDP US$ million	Share of exports in GDP (%)	Share of imports in GDP (%)	% change in real GDP		% change in imports		% change in exports	
				From own growth	From others' growth	From own growth	From others' growth	From own growth	From others' growth
Japan	4377945	18.1	16.2	8.29	1.71	7.53	2.47	0.31	9.69
Korea, Rep. of	1049236	42.3	38.9	6.61	3.39	5.37	4.63	0.14	9.86
PRC	3701129	38.3	30.3	6.31	3.69	5.71	4.29	0.79	9.21
Taipei,China	393763	71.7	57.5	5.48	4.52	3.85	6.15	0.06	9.94
Other East Asia	36902	56.8	42.9	4.40	5.60	4.87	5.13	0.01	9.99
Singapore	176760	132.8	104.1	3.06	6.94	2.25	7.75	0.05	9.95
Philippines	144071	51.1	46.2	6.69	3.31	4.89	5.11	0.03	9.97
Thailand	247110	72.4	60.3	4.73	5.27	4.38	5.62	0.04	9.96
Indonesia	432103	29.8	24.8	7.03	2.97	6.99	3.01	0.09	9.91
Malaysia	186642	106.8	79.5	3.41	6.59	3.27	6.73	0.06	9.94
Viet Nam	68435	78.4	93.2	4.94	5.06	4.73	5.27	0.07	9.93
Other Southeast Asia	41246	48.9	38.8	5.67	4.33	6.57	3.43	0.15	9.85
India	1232816	18.8	23.5	7.98	2.02	7.49	2.51	0.09	9.91
Bangladesh	68416	20.4	27.5	8.20	1.80	7.52	2.48	0.02	9.98

Table 2.8 (continued)

	GDP US$ million	Share of exports in GDP (%)	Share of imports in GDP (%)	% change in real GDP		% change in imports		% change in exports	
				From own growth	From others' growth	From own growth	From others' growth	From own growth	From others' growth
Pakistan	143 170	14.6	28.7	8.59	1.41	8.47	1.53	0.02	9.98
Other South Asia	54 651	23.9	39.6	7.83	2.17	7.78	2.22	0.10	9.90
Central Asia	199 769	50.6	39.6	5.12	4.88	6.44	3.56	0.37	9.63
Pacific Islands	31 830	40.8	41.9	6.39	3.61	6.83	3.17	0.11	9.89
Australia and New Zealand	995 228	20.4	20.9	7.87	2.13	8.13	1.87	0.52	9.48
European Union	17 638 780	35.3	35.3	8.69	1.31	8.53	1.47	5.75	4.25
North America	16 519 626	12.7	17.5	9.13	0.87	8.83	1.17	3.95	6.05
Other DCs	8 091 719	31.6	28.6	7.53	2.47	7.97	2.03	2.20	7.80

Notes:
GDP = gross domestic product; DCs = developing countries; PRC = People's Republic of China.
'From own growth' are the diagonal elements of the matrix in Table 2.6. It shows the gains to a country from its own growth. Others' growth is the sum of the off diagonal elements (across the row). It is the gains to a country from growth in all other countries, except itself.

Source: Authors' calculations and GTAP database.

that are aggregate regions that trade a lot with other countries in their regions – hence imports from the EU to the EU also appear as EU exports.

Greater global integration means that a country has more to gain from positive income shocks (and more to lose from negative shocks), and most Asian countries have trade to GDP shares significantly greater than 30 percent. This suggests that Asia as a whole will be more affected by international shocks. To investigate this, we calculate the average regional growth for 'Asia (developing and developed)' and the rest of world in response to the 10 percent increase in income in particular economies. We find that on average 'Asia (developing and developed)' gains more than the rest of the world from growth in income in any given country (Figure 2.4). Although not shown, breaking this down into growth in East vs Southeast vs South Asia the pattern remains, with Southeast Asia gaining the most and South Asia the least. In fact the lower integration of South Asia means that its gains are more in line with the non-Asian regions.

Finally we explore the impacts of these income shocks on employment of the five labor types (Table 2.9). In the fixed multiplier model, employment of all endowments rises, as there are no constraints on endowments. In general, the results are consistent with the overall impact on real GDP from own and others' growth, although there are some notable differences. First, when compared to the other occupational categories, agricultural/unskilled workers gain less from own growth and more from others' growth in all countries. This is due to the fact that these laborers primarily work in industries producing tradable commodities. In contrast, highly skilled professional or technical workers are employed more intensively in the non-tradable service sectors, which means they are more sensitive to shocks at home rather than shocks abroad.

Recall that we constructed three alternative MRIO datasets, each differing in its import sourcing splits. When we applied the same 10 percent increase in real income shock to each of the three MRIO datasets we found no differences (at the second decimal point) relative to the results in Tables 2.7–2.9. This suggests that the additional detail on supply chains had no impact on the results under this scenario.

Introducing economics into the multiplier model
In this section the assumptions underlying the fixed-price, input–output multiplier model are gradually dismantled, ultimately returning us to a full-fledged, CGE model. Three alternatives are considered:

1. Multiplier: Results from fixed multiplier model
2. Behavioral: In the fixed multiplier scenario final demand is assumed to be homothetic, while under this scenario, the standard GTAP

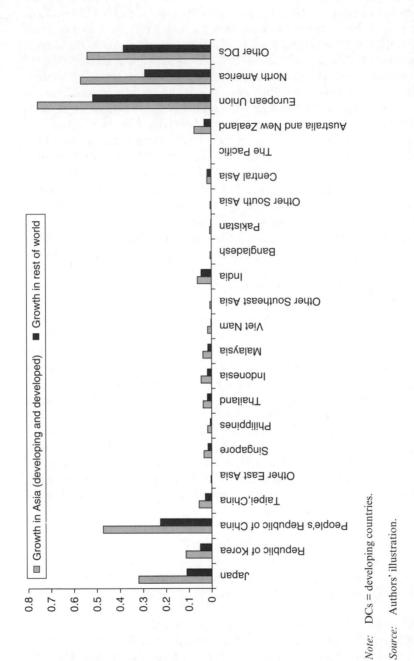

Figure 2.4   Impact of a 10 percent increase in income in each country's growth on real GDP of the Asia region and rest of the world (excludes own growth) (%)

44

Table 2.9 Impact on employment by labor type of 10 percent shock to regional income

	Professionals		Technicians and associate professionals		Clerks		Service workers, shop and sales workers		Agricultural, machine operators, assemblers and unskilled workers	
	Own growth	Others' growth	Own growth	Others' growth	Own growth	Others' growth	Own growth	Others' growth	Own growth	Others' growth
Japan	8.7	1.3	8.3	1.7	8.1	1.9	8.9	1.1	7.3	2.7
Korea, Rep. of	7.4	2.6	6.8	3.2	6.2	3.8	7.5	2.5	6.1	3.9
PRC	7.2	2.8	7.0	3.0	6.2	3.8	6.6	3.4	6.0	4.0
Taipei,China	6.7	3.3	5.8	4.2	5.2	4.8	6.3	3.7	3.8	6.2
Other East Asia	5.5	4.5	4.2	5.8	3.9	6.1	4.5	5.5	4.1	5.9
Singapore	2.7	7.3	3.9	6.1	3.0	7.0	3.6	6.4	2.2	7.8
Philippines	7.3	2.7	7.5	2.5	7.2	2.8	7.6	2.4	6.7	3.3
Thailand	6.2	3.8	4.8	5.2	5.8	4.2	7.2	2.9	4.1	5.9
Indonesia	8.5	1.5	7.6	2.4	7.4	2.6	8.3	1.7	6.7	3.3
Malaysia	3.6	6.4	3.7	6.3	4.2	5.8	4.1	5.9	2.9	7.1
Viet Nam	5.6	4.4	5.2	4.8	5.2	4.8	6.0	4.0	4.5	5.5
Other Southeast Asia	6.2	3.8	5.7	4.3	6.7	3.3	6.5	3.5	5.8	4.2
India	8.4	1.6	8.4	1.6	7.8	2.2	8.0	2.1	8.0	2.1
Bangladesh	7.6	2.4	8.5	1.5	8.4	1.6	8.3	1.7	7.5	2.5

Table 2.9 (continued)

	Professionals		Technicians and associate professionals		Clerks		Service workers, shop and sales workers		Agricultural, machine operators, assemblers and unskilled workers	
	Own growth	Others' growth	Own growth	Others' growth	Own growth	Others' growth	Own growth	Others' growth	Own growth	Others' growth
Pakistan	8.6	1.4	8.9	1.1	8.8	1.2	8.8	1.2	8.6	1.4
Other South Asia	8.2	1.8	8.1	1.9	7.8	2.2	8.0	2.0	7.8	2.2
Central Asia	6.2	3.8	6.3	3.7	5.7	4.3	6.3	3.7	5.6	4.4
Pacific Islands	6.8	3.2	6.6	3.4	6.5	3.5	7.1	2.9	5.3	4.7
Australia and New Zealand	8.2	1.8	8.1	1.9	8.1	1.9	8.4	1.6	7.3	2.7
European Union	8.8	1.2	8.7	1.3	8.6	1.4	9.0	1.0	8.3	1.8
North America	9.2	0.8	9.2	0.8	9.2	0.8	9.1	0.9	8.7	1.3
Other DCs	8.2	1.9	8.4	1.6	8.1	1.9	8.3	1.7	7.8	2.2

Note: DCs = developing countries; PRC = People's Republic of China.

Source: Authors' calculations.

non-homothetic CDE utility structure causes rising income to shift consumption shares toward the service sector and away from food.

3. Factors: In the multiplier scenario, factor prices are fixed and supplies are perfectly elastic. In this scenario, total factor employment is fixed for each country, and factor prices adjust to maintain this equilibrium. Because endowments cannot expand to increase output, factors will reallocate across sectors and any increase in aggregate labor demand will cause wages to rise.

The impacts on employment (Multiplier and Income) and on real factor prices (Factors) of the 10 percent shock in income are shown in Table 2.10. By introducing non-homothetic preferences, rising income causes consumers to shift away from agricultural products toward services. The impact of this on the budget shares are shown in Appendix Table 2A.3. They cause the employment of low skilled agricultural workers to fall relative to real GDP in both the own growth and others' growth cases. The worsening position of agricultural/low skilled workers relative to other workers becomes most apparent when factor employment is also fixed. In this last scenario the real wages of these agricultural/low skilled workers actually falls in some cases as a result of the shock to real income (Table 2.10).

Of course, the differences between analyzing supply chains using a fixed price IO multiplier and a full CGE approach will depend on the particular question and experiment at hand. The value of integrating a MRIO into GTAP is the ability to more fully understand which kinds of adjustments matter and the magnitudes of those adjustments. In this example we focus on the distribution of impacts from an income shock. Allowing non-homothetic preferences and price adjustments does little to change the country distribution of effects. That is, an income shock in Japan mostly stays at home while the same shock in Singapore is absorbed abroad. However, we do see significant effects on both the distribution of activity across broad sectors (agriculture as compared to services) and large effects on relative wages for different worker types.

In our example, the way in which income shocks are distributed across nations depends primarily on the degree of outward orientation and not on the subtle differences in import sourcing splits between intermediate inputs and final goods. We turn next to an experiment where these splits are more central to the story.

4.3   The Elimination of Tariffs on Intermediate Imports

In this section we utilize GTAP-SC to examine the impact of reducing all tariffs on intermediate imports across the entire world, as well as the

Table 2.10 Impact on employment or real factor prices of selected labor types of 10 percent shock to own regional income (i.e., own growth only)

	Technicians and associate professionals			Service workers, shop and sales workers			Agricultural, machine operators, assemblers and unskilled workers		
	Growth in employment		Change in real wages	Growth in employment		Change in real wages	Growth in employment		Change in real wages
	Multiplier	Behavioral	Factors	Multiplier	Behavioral	Factors	Multiplier	Behavioral	Factors
Japan	8.26	8.34	1.04	8.88	9.00	2.47	7.26	7.10	-1.77
Korea, Rep. of	6.84	7.00	1.57	7.48	7.66	2.89	6.11	5.66	-0.02
PRC	6.97	7.17	1.87	6.59	6.60	1.14	6.03	5.69	-0.32
Taipei;China	5.83	5.95	1.26	6.31	6.41	1.89	3.76	3.53	-2.00
Other East Asia	4.19	4.36	0.69	4.49	4.62	0.99	4.13	4.06	0.02
Singapore	3.91	3.95	1.74	3.59	3.63	1.59	2.17	2.15	0.03
Philippines	7.48	7.99	2.37	7.61	8.27	2.73	6.70	5.76	-0.56
Thailand	4.77	4.86	1.19	7.15	7.37	4.29	4.11	3.63	-0.24
Indonesia	7.56	8.06	2.10	8.34	8.94	3.54	6.73	6.27	-0.61
Malaysia	3.74	3.86	1.29	4.10	4.24	1.68	2.92	2.81	0.05
Viet Nam	5.21	5.78	3.04	5.96	6.59	3.88	4.51	4.50	1.29
Other Southeast Asia	5.69	6.87	1.66	6.48	7.55	2.58	5.81	5.87	0.24

India	8.38	9.00	1.93	7.95	8.54	1.08	7.95	7.16	−0.45
Bangladesh	8.50	9.28	2.31	8.30	9.04	1.83	7.52	7.26	−0.94
Pakistan	8.90	9.52	2.55	8.77	9.35	2.15	8.58	8.00	0.64
Other South Asia	8.13	9.13	3.30	8.02	9.00	3.05	7.83	6.90	0.77
Central Asia	6.27	6.68	3.06	6.28	6.58	2.98	5.63	5.15	0.84
Pacific Islands	6.62	6.84	2.05	7.13	7.43	2.94	5.34	5.37	−0.46
Australia and New Zealand	8.10	8.18	1.59	8.41	8.52	2.31	7.32	7.33	−0.33
European Union	8.69	8.74	0.75	9.02	9.12	1.71	8.25	8.08	−0.54
North America	9.19	9.25	1.22	9.06	9.12	0.91	8.67	8.65	−0.94
Other DCs	8.39	8.69	2.21	8.31	8.66	2.24	7.77	6.99	0.07

Note: DCs = developing countries; PRC = People's Republic of China.

Source: Authors' calculations.

impact of unilateral elimination of these tariffs on intermediates by each country. The policy experiment is designed to illustrate some of the benefits of using a supply chain model, rather than being a true reflection of how such a policy might be implemented. Tariffs on all commodities purchased by all firms, producing any commodity, are completely removed.

The fixed price multiplier model, outlined above, is not adequate for this purpose, since we need a model that will allow for the tariffs' impact on price. In the GTAP-SC model the price at which firms in region r import commodity i from region s ($pfms_{i,f,s,r}$) depends on the cif price ($pcif_{i,s,r}$) and the *ad valorem* tariff ($tfms_{i,j,s,r}$), which are now sector and source specific. This *ad valorem* tariff on intermediate imports can therefore be eliminated while leaving all tariffs on final goods unchanged. Moreover the countries from which intermediates and final goods are sourced differ and therefore we would expect the impact of this partial removal of tariffs to have differential impacts on the source countries.

Three alternative models/data sources are used to examine the impact of removing tariffs on intermediate goods:

1. BEC: Uses the BEC sourcing shares examined above with the GTAP-SC model.
2. GTAP-BEC: Using the GTAP-BEC sourcing shares examined above with the GTAP-SC model.
3. GTAP Proportional: Uses the GTAP based on proportional sourcing shares examined above with the GTAP-SC model.

In addition to the three experiments above, we are also interested in how these results compare to those obtained using the standard GTAP model. The results of two additional experiments are therefore noted:

4. GTAP: Using the standard GTAP model and database.
5. GTAP-SC: Using the BEC sourcing shares but removing tariffs on both intermediate and final goods.

Overview: impacts on real GDP
The impact of these five experiments on real GDP is shown in Table 2.11. Taking each panel in the table in turn:

First, as expected the liberalization of trade in intermediate goods (Columns I-III, Table 2.11) benefits most of the world's economies, particularly in Asia where intra-regional trade tends to be primarily in intermediate goods (Figure 2.1). With the exception of Japan and Viet Nam, the impact of the three alternative MRIO datasets is relatively insignificant. As we dig down deeper into the trade results however, further differences can be seen, and in this section we focus on the results for Viet Nam.

Table 2.11   *Percent changes in real GDP from the liberalization of tariffs on intermediate inputs*

	From world liberalization of intermediates			From world liberalization of final and intermediates		From own liberalization of intermediates		
	I BEC	II GTAP- BEC	III GTAP Prop	IV Standard GTAP	V GTAP-SC (BEC)	VI BEC	VII GTAP- BEC	VIII GTAP Prop
Japan	0.09	0.18	0.18	0.32	0.31	0.04	0.14	0.14
Korea, Republic of	0.42	0.48	0.45	0.81	0.95	0.50	0.56	0.51
PRC	2.06	2.06	2.08	2.53	2.55	2.01	2.00	2.01
Taipei,China	−0.01	−0.02	−0.02	0.06	0.06	0.05	0.05	0.05
Other East Asia	0.03	0.02	0.03	0.13	0.15	0.01	0.01	0.01
Singapore	0.03	0.02	0.03	0.04	0.04	0.03	0.02	0.03
Philippines	0.06	0.07	0.07	0.17	0.18	0.08	0.09	0.09
Thailand	0.69	0.68	0.67	1.44	1.50	0.72	0.70	0.71
Indonesia	0.07	0.06	0.06	0.14	0.15	0.06	0.06	0.06
Malaysia	0.43	0.45	0.46	0.58	0.83	0.47	0.48	0.48
Viet Nam	1.85	1.96	2.08	3.26	3.91	1.86	1.93	1.95
Other South-east Asia	0.12	0.12	0.13	0.30	0.33	0.13	0.13	0.13
India	0.69	0.60	0.61	1.22	1.19	0.68	0.60	0.59
Bangladesh	0.29	0.29	0.29	0.53	0.48	0.24	0.25	0.24
Pakistan	0.24	0.21	0.26	0.42	0.44	0.21	0.19	0.20
Other South Asia	0.26	0.27	0.24	0.49	0.54	0.20	0.20	0.18
Central Asia	0.04	0.04	0.04	0.10	0.09	0.05	0.06	0.05
Pacific Islands	1.98	1.94	1.92	2.25	2.39	1.89	1.86	1.88
Australia and New Zealand	0.01	0.01	0.01	0.12	0.12	0.02	0.02	0.02
European Union	0.01	0.02	0.03	0.08	0.09	0.01	0.01	0.02
North America	0.04	0.04	0.04	0.06	0.07	0.00	0.00	0.01
Other DCs	0.09	0.08	0.08	0.17	0.17	0.09	0.08	0.09

Note: BEC = Broad Economic Classification; DCs = developing countries; GTAP = Global Trade Analysis Project; PRC = People's Republic of China; Prop =proportionality.

Source: Authors' calculations.

Second, the differences between the three MRIO databases (Columns I-III) and the standard GTAP model and database (Column IV) are much more significant. The reason for this is simply that the standard GTAP model cannot examine the impact of more complex trade policies that liberalize tariffs on intermediate and final goods at different rates. Of course when we compare the standard GTAP model with the GTAP- SC model applying the same shocks (liberalization of both intermediate and final imports) the differences between the two models are less stark (Columns IV and V). However, there are some notable differences – in those countries that are highly integrated into the global supply chain for processing intermediates (Viet Nam, Thailand and Malaysia), the gains under the GTAP-SC model are larger than for the standard GTAP model. India on the other hand is not well integrated into the global supply chain, and hence the gains are lower under the GTAP-SC model than under the GTAP model. This is due to the fact that countries that import intermediates more intensely than final goods are more likely to see greater indirect benefits from trade liberalization, due to lower costs of production, which in turn flow on to further increase wages, capital rentals, incomes, final consumption, investment and so forth.

Third, the benefits from liberalizing trade in intermediates are less than if all trade was liberalized (see Columns IV and V, Table 2.11), however for many economies (most notably the PRC,[14] Malaysia, Singapore and North America) more than half of the benefits that could have been obtained from liberalization accrue from the liberalization of intermediate goods.

Columns VI–VIII illustrate the impact on the region of its own liberalization of intermediate tariffs. They reveal that most of these gains from liberalization of intermediates are due to each country's own liberalization (compare Columns I-III with VI-VIII in Table 2.11). In order to focus in on some of the differences, it is advantageous to consider just one or two countries. For this reason in the remainder of this section we focus on Viet Nam and India to see the impact on each economy of its own liberalizations and consider their sectoral effects.

Sectoral results
As expected, when the tariffs on intermediate goods fall, variable costs fall, prices drop, and firms substitute toward imported intermediate inputs (Tables 2.12 and 2.13) and away from domestic inputs. In the GTAP-SC model where there is a separation of tariffs on imported intermediates and final goods, final consumers will then substitute toward domestic goods as the price of these domestically produced goods falls (Tables 2.12 and 2.13), while the tariffs on their imports of final goods have not changed. This

effect is somewhat muted by the fact that households will also have more income as a result of higher returns to factors, and hence their demand for imports may also rise: this is the case in Viet Nam (Table 2.12), but it is less apparent in the case of India (Table 2.13).

Production in some sectors rises, while in others it falls as resources are shifted toward those that benefit most from the liberalization. The sectors that gain are those with high shares of imported intermediates, high initial tariffs and price-responsive demand for their products (as exports or consumer goods), since there is less demand for domestic intermediates (Tables 2.12 and 2.13). For instance, a comparison of the other food production and the wearing apparel sectors in Viet Nam reveals that while both rely on intermediate imports, there are more opportunities for the wearing apparel industry to switch to cheaper inputs of textiles and wearing apparel following the liberalization. The food industry, on the other hand, can purchase cheaper imported food, but other important primary inputs, such as livestock and raw milk, do not have high initial tariffs and do not benefit to the same degree as the apparel industry. Moreover, domestically produced food for intermediate use is an important element of the demand for food production in Viet Nam, and the switch to imports causes demand for food production to fall significantly. Textiles and wearing apparel on the other hand are generally produced for export, demand for which rises. As a result resources move toward textiles and away from food production. In general production becomes more import intensive and the share of value added in output also rises as the returns to factors rise (Tables 2.12 and 2.13).[15]

Differences in sourcing
While the differences in the macro results for the three different datasets are quite small, there are sectoral differences owing to the differential sourcing of the imports underlying the three different datasets. Tables 2.14 and 2.15 show two examples of how differences in shares lead to differences in the tariff shocks applied and hence differences in the results. Table 2.14 gives the example of the food industry in India. The average tariffs on cereals and food imported into India are 99 percent and 89 percent respectively in the BEC database (Table 2.13), and since cereals and food are important intermediate inputs into the food industry this translates to some large source specific shocks to the food industry in Table 2.14.[16] As expected the tariff shock drives the price of food down and final demand rises. Despite the fall in domestic prices output does not rise as intermediate demand for domestic food has fallen considerably. For those sources where Indian tariffs on intermediate inputs into the food industry fall,

Table 2.12 Percent changes in Viet Nam's output, value-added to output shares, intermediate and final demand resulting from the liberalization of tariffs on intermediate inputs by Viet Nam (BEC)

Sector/Commodity	Output by sector		Share of value added/Output by sector		Intermediate input demand by sector		Private household demand for commodity		Initial average tariff rate on intermediate commodity
	Initial value (US$ mn)		Initial	After simulation	Domestic	Imports	Domestic	Imports	
	All	%	%	%	%	%	%	%	%
Cereals	4027	−4.16	66	66	−4.3	5.4	−0.5	4.7	3.9
Other crops	5520	−4.48	72	73	−4.7	29.1	0.3	3.3	10.1
Livestock and raw milk	2558	1.31	48	49	−1.0	−2.9	2.0	4.9	0.9
Forestry and fishing	4939	−6.77	60	61	−11.0	−6.7	1.8	6.1	1.8
Resources	9664	−6.02	60	60	−9.6	9.6	2.4	5.8	2.4
Meat and dairy	849	−10.55	21	25	−38.3	17.8	1.6	3.0	18.2
Processed rice	4616	−3.05	10	12	−4.9	3.4	1.1	9.8	0.0
Other food	10383	−6.95	23	26	−15.4	17.5	−0.4	5.2	15.5
Textiles	5097	35.08	29	34	−7.1	86.6	23.3	−6.3	28.9
Wearing apparel	14259	78.85	27	31	47.9	110.8	19.5	−15.6	16.4
Lumber and paper	5215	−17.28	21	25	−20.7	12.8	−2.4	9.2	7.8
Resource products	5603	−17.68	28	32	−19.4	14.3	−6.0	5.5	12.7

Chemicals, rubbers and plastics	7058	−8.70	20	24	−7.4	13.4	−1.9	7.1	4.5
Metals	1373	−18.46	3	4	−1.1	0.7	−12.6	8.6	2.5
Metal products	928	−1.28	19	22	10.7	8.4	1.4	3.1	10.9
Motor vehicles	3904	2.14	25	29	1.9	11.9	5.9	1.9	17.6
Electronic goods and other equipment	7050	−9.94	18	21	−10.8	5.8	−2.1	3.2	4.7
Other manufactures	2503	−9.04	18	21	−13.1	78.7	2.3	3.5	21.7
Non-tradable services	18665	−4.90	72	76	−6.4	20.8	−0.5	25.4	0.8
Services	35087	4.61	44	50	10.1	15.0	−0.2	10.1	0.0

Notes:
BEC = Broad Economic Classification; mn = million.
The initial average tariff rate on intermediate commodity is the average tariff across all sectors applied on this commodity; it is not the average tariff on all intermediates purchased by this sector.

Source: Authors' calculations.

Table 2.13 *Percent changes in India's output, value-added to output shares, intermediate and final demand resulting from the liberalization of tariffs on intermediate inputs by India (BEC)*

Sector/Commodity	Output by sector		Share of value added/ Output by sector		Intermediate input demand by sector		Private household demand for commodity		Initial average tariff rate on intermediate commodity
	Initial value (US$ mn) All	%	Initial	After simulation	Domestic	Imports	Domestic	Imports	
		%	%	%	%	%	%	%	%
Cereals	43424	−9.56	48	47	−13.6	514.1	0.8	−12.5	99.6
Other crops	141160	0.07	71	72	−1.1	85.6	0.6	−3.8	27.6
Livestock and raw milk	71741	0.21	66	67	−1.0	23.1	0.6	−4.8	12.2
Forestry and fishing	21248	−0.74	83	83	−3.5	8.1	0.1	0.4	6.5
Resources	40645	−4.74	64	63	−25.1	11.6	2.1	−20.8	10.6
Meat and dairy	24271	0.74	16	16	−1.9	160.1	0.5	−5.3	28.5
Processed rice	33452	0.79	28	29	−0.4	146.8	0.4	−5.8	33.6
Other food	86674	−1.97	19	20	−32.4	80.5	1.1	−7.9	89.8
Textiles	57080	1.50	26	26	−4.1	60.2	0.7	−4.3	15.8
Wearing apparel	22743	4.68	28	29	−3.8	42.0	0.7	−4.4	12.3
Lumber and paper	23738	−4.90	30	31	−7.2	32.8	0.7	−2.2	13.5
Resource products	141450	3.47	13	14	−1.6	14.0	1.8	−11.9	13.9

Chemicals, rubbers and plastics	108 532	−0.66	20	22	−7.2	22.9	2.1	−10.0	13.8
Metals	77 819	−6.11	25	26	−11.3	27.1	4.0	−4.7	16.1
Metal products	45 385	0.97	28	29	−1.0	32.2	1.5	−9.7	14.9
Motor vehicles	51 110	2.17	24	25	0.7	5.2	1.2	−6.2	10.0
Electronic goods and other equipment	122 836	3.71	20	21	1.2	5.6	5.1	−7.6	10.3
Other manufactures	51 287	2.93	35	36	−0.7	23.4	0.9	−4.9	14.9
Non-tradable services	290 364	−0.83	75	76	−1.3	2.0	0.0	1.6	0.0
Services	876 717	0.89	58	59	1.4	1.4	0.1	0.4	0.0

Notes:
BEC = Broad Economic Classification; mn = million.
Initial average tariff rate on intermediate commodity is the average tariff across all sectors applied on this commodity; it is not the average tariff on all intermediates purchased by this sector.

Source: Authors' calculations and GTAP database.

Table 2.14   *India's intermediate imports used in the food industry and production and price response to tariff liberalization of intermediates*

	Value of intermediate imports by source (in millions of dollars)			%		
	BEC	GTAP-BEC	GTAP Prop	BEC	GTAP-BEC	GTAP Prop
Tariff shock						
Price (% change)				4.84	−3.59	−3.51
Output (% change)				1.97	−0.95	−0.81
Tariff rate						
Japan	120	103	94	13	12	12
Korea, Republic of	95	83	74	14	14	13
PRC	293	282	315	14	14	14
Taipei,China	30	30	44	12	13	13
Other East Asia	5	4	4	7	6	7
Singapore	163	154	155	9	8	8
Philippines	4	4	4	9	8	9
Thailand	65	37	49	44	20	27
Indonesia	2 546	1 048	778	97	93	92
Malaysia	98	58	127	31	16	50
Viet Nam	5	5	5	25	29	27
Other Southeast Asia	15	29	67	8	22	27
India	0	0	0	0	0	0
Bangladesh	5	6	6	8	13	9
Pakistan	30	25	29	76	54	64
Other South Asia	81	80	74	25	24	13
Central Asia	6	3	13	54	10	75
Pacific Islands	3	1	2	8	11	10
Australia and New Zealand	49	63	62	13	18	18
European Union	747	714	693	11	11	12
North America	484	496	578	20	21	22
Other DCs	1 446	1 143	1 195	42	40	41
Total/Average	6 289	4 368	4 368	46	34	33

Note: BEC = Broad Economic Classification; DCs = developing countries; GTAP = Global Trade Analysis Project; PRC = People's Republic of China; Prop = proportionality.

Source: Authors' calculations.

Table 2.15   Viet Nam's intermediate imports used in motor vehicle and transportation production and production and price response to tariff liberalization of intermediates

	Value of intermediate imports by source (in millions of US dollars)			%		
	BEC	GTAP-BEC	GTAP Prop	BEC	GTAP-BEC	GTAP Prop
Tariff shock						
Price (% change)				−1.19	−0.77	−2.13
Output (% change)				2.14	−0.74	0.44
Tariff rate						
Japan	205	182	231	10	9	14
Korea, Republic of	126	114	215	7	6	13
PRC	695	634	548	13	12	13
Taipei,China	28	25	132	12	12	8
Other East Asia	0	0	0	4	2	7
Singapore	30	27	32	7	7	11
Philippines	37	35	24	4	4	3
Thailand	195	193	124	5	5	5
Indonesia	87	86	48	9	9	7
Malaysia	100	99	82	2	2	2
Viet Nam	0	0	0	0	0	0
Other Southeast Asia	15	13	13	0	0	2
India	18	16	16	2	2	3
Bangladesh	0	0	0	13	13	13
Pakistan	0	0	0	10	11	11
Other South Asia	0	0	0	6	6	5
Central Asia	2	2	2	4	4	3
Pacific Islands	0	0	0	1	1	8
Australia and New Zealand	74	71	60	2	2	2
European Union	518	494	439	7	7	9
North America	42	39	116	4	3	28
Other DCs	195	193	143	15	15	12
Total	2367	2225	2225	9	9	11

Notes: BEC = Broad Economic Classification; DCs = developing countries; GTAP = Global Trade Analysis Project; PRC = People's Republic of China; Prop = proportionality.

Source: Authors' calculations.

demand increases (Japan, Indonesia and Thailand), while those where tariffs are small experience declines.

What is surprising, however, is the extent to which differences in tariffs among the three different databases in turn alter the results. In the first case (BEC), inputs used in food production are more intensively obtained from Indonesia, where tariffs are initially substantially higher than elsewhere. This higher share of Indonesian food in India's food production in the BEC database raises the average tariff faced by the food industry on its imported intermediates to 46 percent (as opposed to about 34 percent in the GTAP proportional and GTAP-BEC databases, see total row, Table 2.14). The reason for the lower tariff in the GTAP-BEC database is that, while the sourcing data from BEC indicates that the share of imported food for intermediate use from Indonesia should be higher than that specified in GTAP prop (40 percent as opposed to 18 percent), this raises the share of imported intermediates in total imported and domestic use. In order to adjust for this the GTAP-BEC database must lower the values to match the original GTAP total intermediate imports (see totals row in Table 2.14). In doing so the value of imports purchased from Indonesia must fall in order to maintain balance and the share also falls back toward the original GTAP share. However, the rebalancing causes the total intermediate imports to fall, which has the effect of reducing the shares of imports from Indonesia, thereby reducing the impact of the tariff shock on the price of food in India.

In the second example, we examine the impact of tariff shocks on the motor vehicle and transportation sector in Viet Nam. Unlike the previous example, in this case the BEC shares suggest that Viet Nam's motor vehicle and transportation industry purchase more of its intermediate inputs (metal and motor vehicle parts) from Southeast Asia, where tariffs are already low due to ASEAN trade preferences. As a result, the removal of these smaller tariffs on intermediate inputs has a much smaller effect (in absolute terms) on the price of motor vehicles than would have been the case if the proportionality assumption had been used (–1.19 percent as opposed to –2.13 percent).

Turning to GTAP-BEC, the increased use of imports from Southeast Asia raises intermediate imports relative to final imports under BEC, which means that the total value of intermediate imports must fall again to the GTAP level under GTAP-BEC. As a result of the rebalancing, the value of intermediate imports falls, but the share of Southeast Asian imports remains high.[17] The result is that tariffs are still lower than in GTAP (see totals row in Table 2.15) and intermediate imports are also lower. The result is that the impact of the tariff shock on the price of motor vehicles is even less pronounced (–0.77 percent as opposed to –1.19 percent).

Given these changes in prices resulting from the three alternative datasets, the large positive change in production of motor vehicles under the BEC database, as compared to the negative change in the GTAP-BEC, is somewhat unexpected. The reason for the increase in production under BEC is an increase in demand for domestic motor vehicles for investment purposes. Under BEC, motor vehicles are mainly imported for intermediate use, rather than final use (or investment). Hence the share of imported (domestic) motor vehicles in investment is lower (higher) in the BEC database. Moreover, trade liberalization generally results in an expansion in investment, due to the higher rates of return on capital in Viet Nam following trade reforms. Thus the slightly larger domestic share of motor vehicles in investment in the BEC database means that the rise in investment will result in an additional source of demand for domestic motor vehicles that, in turn, causes production to rise in the BEC case, as opposed to falling in the other case.

5. CONCLUSIONS

With firms increasingly reliant on international trade to source their intermediate inputs into production, the need to be able to undertake supply-chain analyses has risen. This is particularly true in Asia, where the inter-connectedness of trade and production has made the region a powerful engine for growth. Our aim in this chapter has been to develop and examine some of the tools that can be used to understand the evolution of supply chains in response to policy and other shocks.

In order to do this, however, we first needed to construct a global MRIO database suitable for supply chain analysis. We found that this could be done using the GTAP database as our foundation. The benefits of starting from the GTAP database are clear: the GTAP database offers a publicly available and continuously updated source of globally reconciled trade data covering 134 countries/regions and 57 sectors. As in other MRIO datasets, the GTAP database can be augmented with shares obtained from the trade data and application of the BEC concordance.

Like others (Koopman et al. 2010), we find that there are significant differences in the sourcing of intermediate versus final goods, obtained through the use of BEC concordances, and that these differences are important for the analysis of supply chains. We find, however, that there is still a great deal of work to be done on improving the quality of these data and reconciling it with the underlying trade and IO tables in GTAP. Most of the work done to date in this area has invoked extreme assumptions aimed at simplifying the task of creating a MRIO. Future efforts must factor in more information on the provenance of source data and how this should influence the relative priority given to conflicting information.

With our database in hand, the task of developing tools for analysis of supply chains was then considered. Using the GTAP model as our starting point, we implemented the additional detail on supply chains (GTAP-SC) and then used 'closure' swaps and parameter changes to turn the GTAP-SC model into a fixed price multiplier model. From this we were able to see very clearly the linkages between economies and how growth in aggregate demand in one region could affect other regions through trade. We found that the Asian region in particular, through its interconnectedness with the rest of the world, was a powerful driver behind the spread of growth. However, we also found that the addition of the sourcing information did not significantly affect this result. Moreover, the assumption that prices are fixed had a significant effect on the results and limited our ability to analyze trade policy.

For this reason we then chose to use the GTAP-SC in its original CGE form to show how CGE models can be used to analyze some of the key issues in supply chain analysis. We then used this model to examine the impact of removing all tariffs on imported intermediate goods, as the PRC and others have done for export-oriented firms in the special economic zones. We find that the additional detail on the sourcing of imports by agent can have considerable effects on the impact of trade liberalization, particularly in countries that are highly integrated in global supply chains, such as Viet Nam, Malaysia and Thailand. We also find that a large proportion of the gains from full trade liberalization can be achieved from the removal of these tariffs on intermediate goods. There is a general increase in intermediate imports as firms switch to foreign sources for their intermediate inputs and away from domestic sources, resulting in growth in the PRC and abroad. The source of these new imports depends on the current sourcing of intermediate inputs and the tariffs imposed. We find that the tariffs can differ significantly as a result of the additional information on the supply chains.

The scope for future analysis in this area is considerable. Currently, the differences in tariffs between intermediate and final goods reported here are due only to differences in weights applied in aggregating up from the GTAP level. There are other sources of differences that are not captured here. First, these differential weights should be applied when aggregating tariffs from the HS6 level up to the GTAP level. This is likely to have a considerable impact on the tariffs applied on intermediate versus final goods and hence for the results of this analysis. Moreover, countries may have differential policies with regards to the treatment of intermediate and final imports, such as the duty drawbacks schemes in the PRC and other countries. By factoring in these differences into a global MRIO database and supply chain model, future analysis can better capture the impacts of exogenous shocks as well as policy reforms on the global supply chain.

NOTES

*   This chapter has been commissioned as part of the Asian Development Bank study on Supply Chains in Asia, led by David Hummels and Benno Ferrarini. The authors would like to thank Angel Aguiar for discussions comparing the various new MRIO datasets.
1.   Supply and use tables may also be used where input–output tables are not available.
2.   GTAP notation is being used where possible. *VIFMS* is Value of Imported Intermediate/ Firm goods at Market prices from Source s. In general, note V is value, I is imports, D domestic output, M market prices, F firms, P private consumption, and G government consumption. Where a letter is missing it means that the variable is aggregated over that set or type: for example, if D or I is missing then the variable is aggregated over domestic output or imports; and if S is missing then the value is aggregated over all sources. Instead of using the GTAP notation for invEstment ($VIFM_{i,cgds,r}$), E is used ($VIEM_{i,r}$) to emphasize its place in final demand. Below N and L are also used to represent aggregate iNtermediate demand (i.e., the sum of 1 to j in intermediate demand F) and aggregate finaL demand (the sum of P – private consumption, G – government consumption and E – Investment).
3. N and L are also used to represent aggregate iNtermediate demand (i.e., the sum of all 1 . . . j in intermediate demand F) and aggregate finaL demand (the sum of P private consumption, G government consumption and E Investment). In Table 2.1 these are shown by the double bordering around final and intermediate imports.
4.   Appendix 2A.1 provides a summary of a number of initiatives in the area of Global MRIO datasets. A full summary of the approaches can be found in Murray and Lenzen (2013).
5.   The GTAP 8 database was released with two base years, 2004 and 2007. It is expected that GTAP will update all previous years and add (at least) one additional base year with each new release in future. The decision to expand to multiple base years reflects the fact that the GTAP data construction techniques and the data inputs have continuously improved and expanded with each version, making comparison of GTAP databases across versions difficult.
6.   Table 2.3 is similar to Table 2.1, except that Table 2.3 simplifies the problem in terms of aggregated intermediates and final demand.
7.   Primary countries in GTAP are those countries that have an IO table and are therefore separately identified in the GTAP database. Other countries may also be missing from the BEC, however they are contained in regional aggregates in the GTAP database and therefore their non-inclusion in BEC is less significant, since the sourcing shares can be obtained from other countries in that aggregated region.
8.   The decision of which data to prioritize depends on your beliefs about which data are most reliable. In the case of GTAP there are many more countries included than in other databases, and not all IO tables are of equal quality. Moreover, the ultimate aim of this database is for use with a CGE trade model that requires that the IO table be globally balanced. Country IOTs are not globally balanced and any attempt to keep all the trade information in country IOTs results in negative trade with the rest of the world (as in WIOD). Given the ultimate use of the GTAP database, negative trade is not an option and hence the data are benchmarked against the trade data.
9.   Note that the shaded items will also be maintained since the initial GTAP database is already balanced.

10. Where 'prop' stands for proportionality.
11. Note that there is no difference between the GTAP shares and the GTAP-BEC shares (option 2) since these shares are benchmarked in option 2.
12. Note that investment is a sector and therefore part $QIFS_{i,j,s,r}$
13. This is equivalent to using the 'altertax' closure in RunGTAP (Malcolm, 1998).
14. Note that we have not taken into account any pre-existing duty drawbacks. It was assumed that at the GTAP sectoral level all tariffs on intermediate and final goods were the same. Once the data are aggregated, however, these tariff rates on intermediate and final goods will differ due to differences in the import shares of intermediate and final demand goods.
15. Although this is very small, since the GTAP-SC assumes a Leontief structure at the top level.
16. Note that we assumed that tariffs in the GTAP database applied equally to intermediate and final goods. Hence all differences in tariffs across the three datasets are the result of aggregating tariffs using different weights from GTAP to the aggregation provided in Table 2.4. Further differences in tariffs are likely to be considerable if these alternate weights are applied to aggregate tariffs from the HS6 level to GTAP.
17. This is in stark contrast to the Indian food case where the share of Indonesian imports falls in order to restore balance in intermediate imports.

REFERENCES

Andrew, R., and G. Peters (2013), 'A multi-regional input–output table based on the Global Trade Analysis Project Database (GTAP-MRIO)', *Economic Systems Research*, **25**, 99–121.

Asian Development Bank (2010), *Institutions for Regional Integration – Toward an Asian Economic Community*, Manila: Asian Development Bank.

Gehlhar, M., Z. Wang, and S. Yao (2008), 'GTAP 7 Data Base documentation – Chapter 9.A: Reconciling merchandise trade data', in B. Narayanan and T.L. Walmsley (eds), *Global Trade, Assistance, and Production: The GTAP 7 Data Base*, Center for Global Trade Analysis, Purdue University.

GRAM (2012), *Ein globales Modell zur Berechnung der Ökologischen Rucksäcke des internationalen Handels*, Sustainable Europe Research Institute (SERI), Wien, Austria.

Hendrickson, C., A. Horvath, S. Joshi, and L. Lave (1998), 'Economic input–output models for environmental life-cycle assessment', *Environmental Science and Technology Policy Analysis*, **32**, 184A–191.

Ianchovichina, E. (2003), 'GTAP-DD: A model for analyzing trade reforms in the presence of duty drawbacks', GTAP Technical Papers 21, Center for Global Trade Analysis, West Lafayette, IN, USA.

Inomata, S., and B. Meng (2013), 'Transnational interregional input–output tables: an alternative approach to MRIO?', Chapter 4 in J. Murray and M. Lenzen (eds), *The Practitioners Guide to Multi-Regional Input–Output Analysis*, Champaign, IL: Common Ground.

Johnson, R.C., and G. Noguera (2012), 'Accounting for intermediates: production sharing and trade in value added', *Journal of International Economics*, **86**, 224–236.

Konar, M., Z. Hussein, N. Hanasaki, D.L. Mauzerall, and I. Rodriguez-Iturbe (2013), 'Virtual water trade flows and savings under climate change', *Hydrology and Earth System Sciences*, **10**, 67–101, doi:10.5194/hessd-10-67-2013.

Koopman, R., W. Powers, Z. Wang, and S. Wei (2010), 'Give credit where credit is due: tracing the value-added in global production chains', NBER Working Paper No. 16426, available at http://www.nber.org/papers/w16426.

Koopman, R., Z. Wang, and S. Wei (forthcoming), 'Tracing value-added and double counting in gross exports', *The American Economic Review*.

Lenzen, M., K. Kanemoto, D. Moran, and A. Geschke (2012), 'Mapping the structure of the world economy', *Environmental Science & Technology*, **46**, 8374–8381.

Lenzen, M., D. Moran, K. Kanemoto, and A. Geschke (2013), 'Building Eora: a global multi-region input–output database at high country and sectoral resolution', *Economic Systems Research*, **25**, 20–49.

Malcolm, G. (1998), 'Adjusting tax rates in the GTAP data base', GTAP Technical Paper No. 12, Center for Global Trade Analysis, West Lafayette, IN, USA.

McDougall, R. (1999), 'Entropy theory and RAS are friends', GTAP Working paper No. 6, Center for Global Trade Analysis, West Lafayette, IN, USA.

Meng, B., Y. Zhang, and S. Inomata (2013), 'Compilation and application of IDE-JETRO's international input–output tables', *Economic Systems Research*, **25**, 122–142.

Murray, J., and M. Lenzen (2013), *The Practitioners Guide to Multi-regional Input–Output Analysis*, Champaign, IL: Common Ground.

Narayanan, G.B., A. Aguiar, and R. McDougall (2012), *Global Trade, Assistance, and Production: The GTAP 8 Data Base*, Center for Global Trade Analysis, Purdue University.

OECD (Organisation for Economic Co-operation and Development) (2009), *OECD Input–Output Tables: 2002, 2006 and 2009 Editions*, Paris, France: OECD.

OECD (2012), *Measuring Trade in Value-Added; An OECD-WTO Joint Initiative*, Paris, France: OECD.

Peters, G., R. Andrew, and J. Lennox (2011), 'Constructing an environmentally extended multi-regional input–output table using the GTAP Data Base', *Economic Systems Research*, **23**, 131–152.

Reimer, J. (2010), 'The domestic content of imports and the foreign content of exports', *International Review of Economics and Finance*, **20**, 173–184.

Rutherford, T., J. Carbone, and C. Böhringer (2011), 'Using embodied carbon to control carbon leakage', paper presented at the 14th Annual Conference on Global Economic Analysis, Venice, Italy.

Timmer, M.P. (2012), 'The World Input–Output Database (WIOD): contents, sources and methods', WIOD Working Paper No. 10.

Tukker, A., E. Poliakov, R. Heijungs, T. Hawkins, F. Neuwahl, J. Rueda-Cantuche, S. Giljum, S. Moll, J. Oosterhaven, and M. Bouwmeester (2009), 'Towards a global multi-regional environmentally extended input–output database', *Ecological Economics*, **68**, 1929–1937.

Walmsley, T.L., and C. Carrico (2013), 'Disaggregating labor payments by skill level in GTAP', Unpublished manuscript, Center for Global Trade Analysis.

Weingarden, A., and M. Tsigas (2010), 'Labor statistics for the GTAP Database', paper presented at 13th Annual Conference on Global Economic Analysis, Malaysia, Penang.

APPENDIX 2A.1   OVERVIEW OF DATASETS[1]

IDE-JETRO Asian Input–Output Tables

The Institute of Developing Economies Japan External Trade Organization (IDE-JETRO) is the longest standing producer of international input–output tables, with more than 30 years of experience in producing input–output tables for the Asia-Pacific region (Inomata and Meng, 2013). Recently the IDE-JETRO released its latest version of the Asian International Input–Output tables covering 10 countries, 76 sectors and value-added (compensation of employees, operating surplus, capital depreciation, and net indirect taxes less subsidies). The base year for these tables is 2005. The MRIO information is obtained from each country's trade statistics (concordances are used if required) and this is supplemented by imported input surveys. The rebalancing involves manually identifying differences/errors in data sources, analyzing causes and then making adjustments to remove the cause and the error (Meng et al., 2013).

The OECD Input–Output Tables and TiVA Database

The OECD tables (OECD, 2009) include 37 independent, harmonized, industry by industry country IO tables covering 48 sectors, two of which are in food and agriculture, and two endowments (capital and labor). In 2006 the OECD released version 3 with a base year of 2000, and they are working on version 4. The OECD obtains input–output or supply and use tables from the various national statistical offices and then process the data to harmonize the structure and sectoral coverage in-house; no reconciliation with other external data sources or to ensure any cross-country balance constraints is undertaken.

These OECD tables have been used to produce trade in value added measures (TiVA: OECD, 2012) in a joint initiative by the OECD and WTO. The TiVA database includes indicators for 57 economies (including all OECD countries, Brazil, the PRC, India, Indonesia, Russian Federation and South Africa) and 18 industries. It also covers the years 1995, 2000, 2005, 2008 and 2009. The TiVA database reconciles bilateral trade and uses BEC concordances and the proportionality assumption to allocate trade when other data are not available. The IO table for the PRC has also been revised to include export processing zones, as was done in the GTAP-ICIO database below. Available indicators include: decomposition of gross exports by industry into their domestic and foreign content; the services content of gross exports by exporting industry (broken down by foreign and domestic origin); bilateral trade balances based on flows of value added embodied in domestic final demand; and intermediate imports embodied in exports.

The GTAP Database

The GTAP database (Narayanan et al., 2012) is the most longstanding of all the global datasets, with version 8.1 released in 2013. The current version has two base years (2004 and 2007) and covers 134 regions (including approximately 20 rest of world[2] aggregates). The underlying country data are based on contributed[3] input–output or supply and use tables. The GTAP database covers 57 industries/commodities, including 8 food and 12 agricultural products, and 5 endowments (land, capital, skilled and unskilled labor[4] and natural resources). Satellite datasets also include CO_2 emissions, energy volumes, international migration and 18 agro-ecological zones. Unlike the other global datasets, the GTAP database was established by economists and policy makers interested in trade policy analysis and hence special attention has been paid to the trade data and to reconciling the country data to the trade and macro (GDP, private and government consumption and investment). Trade is taken from the UN COMTRADE database and reconciled depending on the reliability of the reporter (importer versus exporter). Trade is therefore globally reconciled, although trade balances do not match national statistical office data. Estimates are also produced for international transportation margins and protection on imports and exports; as well as for energy commodities.

A number of research papers (Peters et al., 2011; Andrew and Peters, 2013; Johnson and Noguera, 2012; Rutherford et al., 2011; Reimer, 2010; Ianchovichina, 2003) have taken the GTAP Database and used the proportionality assumption to further split imports by agent by source, thereby producing a basic MRIO.

GTAP-ICIO Database

Koopman et al. (2010) utilized additional information from the trade data to construct a GTAP MRIO that more accurately depicts the differences between agents' sourcing of imports. They constructed a global ICIO table from the GTAP 8 database using detailed trade data from UN COMTRADE and processing export information from two additional IO tables – Mexico and the PRC. Emphasis is placed on minimizing deviation from the original GTAP data, and in particular in the sectoral bilateral trade data. They also utilized the reliability indexes used to reconcile the standard GTAP trade data to assist them in obtaining the sourcing shares by agent, and hence produce more reliable estimates. The resulting database covers 63 countries/regions and 41 sectors for the two base years, 2004 and 2007.

WIOD

The World Input–Output Database (Timmer, 2012), released in 2012, was funded under the European Commission 7th framework program. It is a time series database (1995–2009) covering 41 countries (including Rest of World), 35 industries and 59 commodities, two of which are in food and agriculture, and four endowments (capital and three labor). The underlying country data are based on publicly available input–output (IOT) or supply and use (SUT) tables, usually from national statistical offices.[5] Two versions are produced, an industry by industry variant and a commodity by industry version. Special attention was paid to keeping with UN SNA concepts, such as price definitions, the treatment of domestic margins and changes in stocks; and to limiting the number of changes made to the underlying country data from the national statistical offices. Sectoral output and macro aggregates (private and public consumption and investment) were reconciled over time to the national account statistics. Trade was taken from the country IO or SUT data and hence trade balances match the underlying country statistics. International trade data were then used to obtain bilateral imports by use and adjustments were made for international margins. Since trade is not globally reconciled and differences were included as a residual in exports to rest of the world, exports to the rest of the world could be negative. Detailed bilateral trade data are also used to obtain estimates of imports by intermediate and final demanders and hence it is a MRIO. The method used by WIOD is similar to that undertaken in this chapter for the GTAP-MRIO database.

EXIOBASE

The EXIOBASE Database, first released in 2010, was funded under the European Commission 6th framework program (Tukker et al., 2009). The base year is 2000 and covers 44 countries (including Rest of World), 129 industries/commodities, with extensive coverage of food and agriculture, and numerous endowments (capital, 3 types of labor, land, and 80 resources and water). The EXIOBASE database also includes around 30 emissions and 60 IEA energy carriers. The underlying country data are based on input–output (IOT) or supply and use (SUT) tables, usually from national statistical offices. Trade was taken from the country IOT or SUT, and hence trade balances match underlying country statistics. International trade data were then used to obtain bilateral imports by use, and adjustments were made for international margins. Unlike WIOD, RAS[6] was used to reconcile the trade and ensure no negative residuals. The proportionality assumption was used to produce a MRIO, as done by Peters et al., 2011 and others with the GTAP database (discussed above).

The Eora MRIO

The Eora MRIO database (Lenzen et al., 2013) is a time series database covering the period 1990–2011 and 187 countries. Each country has a unique set of sectors (between 25 and 400) depending on the underlying data from the original source. The database also includes around 35 environmental indicators and estimates of the level of uncertainty or standard deviations associated with each element of the global matrix. Behind the Eora database is an optimization program that ensures that conflicting data are reconciled and the global IO table is balanced.

APPENDIX 2A.2 SUMMARY OF FINAL DEMAND FOR ASIA'S EXPORTS[7]

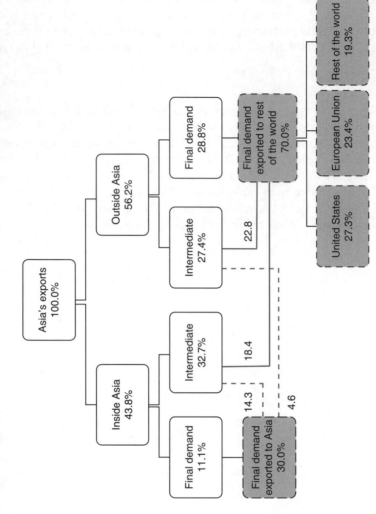

Source: Authors' calculations using GTAP-BEC database.

Figure 2A.1 Using final demand for Asia's exports: GTAP-BEC database

71

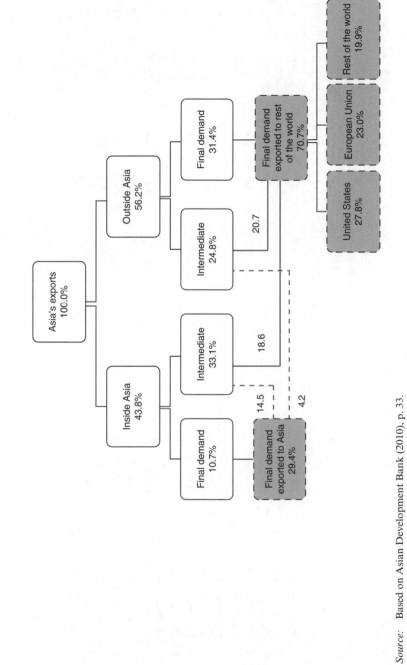

Source: Based on Asian Development Bank (2010), p. 33.

Figure 2A.2 Using final demand for Asia's exports: GTAP proportionality database

Table 2A.1 Top 25 differences in the share of imported intermediates in 20 commodities by 22 region aggregation

			Values			Shares %		
			1 Prop	2 GTAP-BEC	3 BEC	1 Prop	2 GTAP-BEC	3 BEC
1	Processed rice	Malaysia	209.7	209.7	1.3	62	62	0
2	Processed rice	Japan	1301.5	1301.5	24.0	67	67	1
3	Processed rice	Australia and New Zealand	112.2	112.2	28.3	98	98	25
4	Processed rice	Other East Asia	29.1	29.1	0.7	24	24	1
5	Livestock and raw milk	Pakistan	6.8	6.8	38.0	10	10	57
6	Processed rice	Korea, Republic of	23.2	23.2	5.2	65	65	14
7	Processed rice	Philippines	122.4	122.4	0.4	12	12	0
8	Livestock and raw milk	India	105.9	105.9	328.5	29	29	89
9	Processed rice	PRC	323.5	323.5	68.5	54	54	12
10	Livestock and raw milk	Viet Nam	38.2	38.2	131.0	21	21	70
11	Forestry and fishing	India	482.7	482.7	1240.2	38	38	98
12	Other food	India	2350.4	2350.4	6364.1	27	27	73
13	Forestry and fishing	Bangladesh	30.3	30.3	64.5	47	47	99
14	Processed rice	Thailand	2.4	2.4	0.8	47	47	16
15	Cereals	PRC	185.1	185.1	348.5	50	50	95
16	Livestock and raw milk	Malaysia	34.6	34.6	69.6	36	36	72

17	Cereals	Central Asia	415.5	415.5	723.3	51	51	89
18	Livestock and raw milk	Bangladesh	12.8	12.8	23.4	41	41	74
19	Processed rice	North America	309.8	309.8	139.3	46	46	20
20	Other crops	India	1 555.4	1 555.4	689.5	41	41	18
21	Processed rice	Indonesia	35.7	35.7	1.0	5	5	0
22	Processed rice	European Union	683.5	683.5	321.7	42	42	20
23	Processed rice	Bangladesh	10.0	10.0	0.1	3	3	0
24	Processed rice	Viet Nam	0.7	0.7	0.3	20	20	0
25	Wearing apparel	Philippines	266.6	266.6	161.7	56	56	34

Notes: BEC = Broad Economic Classification; GTAP = Global Trade Analysis Project; Prop = proportionality.

Source: Authors' calculations.

Table 2A.2   Top differences in sourcing share in 20 commodities by 22 region aggregation

Commodity	Source	Destination	Values			Shares %		
			1 Prop	2 GTAP-BEC	3 BEC	1 Prop	2 GTAP-BEC	3 BEC
Processed rice	Viet Nam	Indonesia	27	14	0	74.30	39.44	0.00
Processed rice	India	Bangladesh	10	5	0	97.97	47.69	0.10
Processed rice	Viet Nam	Philippines	93	61	0	76.19	50.05	0.01
Processed rice	Thailand	Viet Nam	0	0	0	45.55	5.47	0.00
Processed rice	Thailand	Malaysia	125	109	0	59.42	52.01	0.00
Processed rice	North America	Japan	675	517	0	51.85	39.75	0.02
Processed rice	PRC	Korea, Rep. of	11	7	0	47.94	31.83	0.03
Processed rice	Other Southeast Asia	Viet Nam	0	0	0	33.41	13.33	0.00
Processed rice	Other DCs	Indonesia	0	1	1	0.07	1.49	51.82
Processed rice	Other DCs	Philippines	0	0	0	0.02	0.14	41.06
Processed rice	Viet Nam	Malaysia	68	74	0	32.43	35.44	0.00
Processed rice	Other DCs	Bangladesh	0	0	0	0.01	0.23	33.77
Processed rice	Pakistan	Other South Asia	7	8	0	24.91	28.07	0.00
Processed rice	India	Thailand	0	0	0	18.91	2.74	0.00
Processed rice	Other DCs	Malaysia	0	1	1	0.18	0.28	44.10
Processed rice	Thailand	Indonesia	9	12	0	24.23	33.56	0.00
Processed rice	Pakistan	Thailand	0	0	0	20.85	16.56	0.00
Processed rice	Other DCs	Japan	8	13	13	0.64	0.96	52.10
Processed rice	Thailand	India	0	0	0	17.27	0.00	0.00
Processed rice	Thailand	Japan	220	265	0	16.93	20.37	0.00
Processed rice	Other DCs	Other East Asia	0	0	0	0.22	0.92	39.11

Sector	Origin	Destination						
Processed rice	Thailand	Philippines	28	51	0	22.62	41.31	0.01
Processed rice	Thailand	Other East Asia	21	9	0	72.93	30.46	7.31
Processed rice	Taipei,China	Bangladesh	0	0	0	0.00	0.11	16.31
Processed rice	Indonesia	Philippines	0	0	0	0.01	0.06	17.33
Wearing apparel	Philippines	Malaysia	30	0	0	8.49	0.00	0.00
Processed rice	PRC	Japan	217	262	0	16.64	20.11	0.01
Processed rice	Thailand	Pakistan	0	0	0	12.24	0.00	0.00
Processed rice	North America	Korea, Rep. of	5	5	0	20.82	20.41	0.07
Processed rice	Indonesia	Malaysia	0	0	0	0.08	0.12	18.87
Processed rice	Thailand	Pacific Islands	9	0	0	20.49	0.22	0.19
Processed rice	Other Southeast Asia	Indonesia	-0	0	0	0.02	0.40	13.91
Processed rice	Indonesia	Bangladesh	0	0	0	0.00	0.07	10.49
Processed rice	Taipei,China	Japan	3	5	5	0.26	0.38	20.72
Processed rice	Viet Nam	Bangladesh	0	0	0	0.00	0.07	9.91
Processed rice	Other Southeast Asia	Philippines	0	0	0	0.00	0.04	11.07
Processed rice	Philippines	Indonesia	0	0	0	0.02	0.37	13.03
Processed rice	Viet Nam	Japan	89	119	0	6.84	9.12	0.00
Processed rice	Australia and New Zealand	Pacific Islands	8	0	0	17.76	0.26	0.23
Processed rice	Other DCs	Viet Nam	0	0	0	3.82	19.03	36.41
Non-tradable services	Malaysia	Thailand	6	18	92	6.27	19.42	43.74
Processed rice	Thailand	Korea, Rep. of	1	2	0	5.42	7.91	0.00
Wearing apparel	PRC	Bangladesh	12	1	2	37.81	3.68	5.19
Processed rice	Other DCs	Korea, Rep. of	1	2	2	6.01	9.28	40.08
Other crops	Other Southeast Asia	India	180	57	0	11.60	3.67	0.04

Table 2A.2 (continued)

Commodity	Source	Destination	Values			Shares %		
			1 Prop	2 GTAP-BEC	3 BEC	1 Prop	2 GTAP-BEC	3 BEC
Processed rice	Australia and New Zealand	Thailand	0	0	0	11.10	2.50	0.04
Processed rice	Philippines	Malaysia	0	0	0	0.05	0.07	11.39
Processed rice	Pakistan	Viet Nam	0	0	0	5.46	5.65	0.00
Other manufactures	PRC	Pakistan	5	1	1	36.32	4.16	5.09
Cereals	Thailand	Viet Nam	1	1	61	0.19	0.30	13.69
Other crops	PRC	Singapore	97	8	6	21.53	1.78	1.35
Processed rice	Malaysia	Bangladesh	0	0	0	0.00	0.04	6.41
Processed rice	Philippines	Bangladesh	0	0	0	0.00	0.04	6.34
Metals	Taipei,China	Viet Nam	555	0	1	8.97	0.00	0.02
Forestry and fishing	Australia and New Zealand	Australia and New Zealand	29	13	4	32.65	14.70	5.07
Livestock and raw milk	Taipei,China	Viet Nam	4	0	0	9.96	0.00	0.06
Other food	Pacific Islands	Thailand	191	0	0	5.89	0.00	0.00
Processed rice	Other DCs	Thailand	0	0	0	10.68	18.62	44.79
Processed rice	Korea, Rep. of	Philippines	0	0	0	0.00	0.02	6.32
Other manufactures	PRC	North America	5 553	887	1808	41.54	6.63	9.75
Wearing apparel	PRC	North America	4 256	1 557	973	52.83	19.32	15.84
Processed rice	Taipei,China	Indonesia	0	0	0	0.01	0.19	6.75

Processed rice	European Union	Indonesia	0	0	0	0.01	0.19	6.70
Processed rice	Australia and New Zealand	Japan	81	109	0	6.23	8.39	0.01
Resource products	Taipei,China	Viet Nam	1351	42	121	18.97	0.59	1.67
Forestry and fishing	Viet Nam	Other Southeast Asia	3	2	0	47.15	43.79	13.53
Processed rice	Taipei,China	Philippines	0	0	0	0.00	0.02	5.37
Metal products	Taipei,China	Viet Nam	72	2	2	11.16	0.24	0.25
Processed rice	Indonesia	Other East Asia	0	0	0	0.04	0.18	7.87
Other manufactures	Other DCs	North America	1888	7083	8681	14.12	52.98	46.82

Note: BEC = Broad Economic Classification; DC= developing countries; GTAP = Global Trade Analysis Project; PRC = People's Republic of China; Prop = proportionality.

Source: Authors' calculations.

77

Table 2A.3   Percent changes in private households' budget shares of selected commodities resulting from non-homothetic preferences due to a 10 percent increase in every region's income

	Cereals	Other crops	Livestock and raw milk	Forestry and fishing	Meat and dairy	Processed rice	Wearing apparel	Motor vehicles	Electronic goods and other equipment	Non-tradable services	Services
Japan	-9.77	-9.57	-1.49	-0.84	-1.53	-9.75	-0.29	0.32	0.34	0.33	0.38
Korea, Rep. of	-9.49	-9.65	-1.94	-1.79	-2.09	-9.49	-0.35	0.68	0.69	0.68	0.79
PRC	-4.41	-4.58	-1.91	-2.33	-1.93	-4.55	-1.01	0.32	0.54	0.90	2.06
Taipei;China	-9.30	-9.28	-2.40	-2.80	-2.47	-9.28	-0.58	0.53	0.62	0.61	0.75
Other East Asia	-4.39	-4.30	-1.17	-1.25	-1.19	-4.26	-1.26	-0.43	-0.44	0.55	1.32
Singapore	-9.47	-9.53	-2.02	-2.21	-2.09	-9.65	-0.60	0.19	0.20	0.18	0.32
Philippines	-5.20	-5.11	-2.25	-2.49	-2.32	-5.20	-1.37	0.17	0.49	0.73	2.03
Thailand	-6.17	-5.98	-3.01	-3.35	-3.10	-6.13	-1.53	0.36	0.56	0.58	1.64
Indonesia	-4.90	-4.73	-1.93	-2.57	-2.09	-4.87	-1.04	0.40	0.91	1.21	2.20
Malaysia	-7.40	-6.86	-3.34	-3.70	-3.43	-7.15	-1.39	0.65	0.71	0.64	1.09
Viet Nam	-4.05	-3.30	-0.21	-0.71	-0.45	-4.06	-0.67	0.50	0.45	1.25	2.95
Other Southeast Asia	-3.17	-3.94	0.54	-0.02	0.73	-3.76	-0.49	-0.29	-0.37	1.33	2.47

India	−4.64	−4.59	−0.68	−0.45	−0.89	−4.53	−0.71	0.49	0.51	1.36	2.77
Bangladesh	−3.89	−3.77	1.07	0.51	0.92	−3.86	−0.22	1.07	−0.03	1.79	2.94
Pakistan	−3.89	−4.03	−0.84	−1.14	−0.94	−3.93	−0.51	0.82	0.88	1.43	2.12
Other South Asia	−4.00	−4.36	1.06	−0.89	−0.51	−4.42	−0.41	0.71	0.35	1.79	2.54
Central Asia	−6.13	−4.87	−1.83	−0.25	−2.26	−6.33	−0.26	1.95	1.44	1.79	2.35
Pacific Islands	−6.23	−6.15	−3.39	−1.68	−3.45	−6.27	−1.82	−0.13	0.25	0.35	1.31
Australia and New Zealand	−9.68	−9.68	−1.40	−1.37	−1.48	−9.78	−0.35	0.19	0.21	0.20	0.28
European Union	−9.59	−9.58	−1.76	−1.02	−1.63	−9.71	−0.35	0.20	0.23	0.21	0.41
North America	−9.10	−9.62	−1.66	−0.34	−1.31	−9.76	−0.30	0.10	0.13	0.12	0.22
Other DCs	−5.49	−5.53	−2.30	−1.25	−2.81	−6.22	−0.76	0.81	0.96	1.00	1.61

Note: DC= developing countries; PRC = People's Republic of China.

Source: Authors' calculations.

Notes

1. Another dataset not discussed here is GRAM (2012). The Global Resource Accounting Model (GRAM) is a multi-regional input–output (MRIO) model, covering 53 countries and 48 sectors and the years 1995 and 2005. It is based on an OECD IOT and trade data.
2. The reason for 20 'rest of' regions is to facilitate the analysis of regional free trade agreements, the main reason for the development of the GTAP database in the early 1990s.
3. The GTAP project relies on individuals from the network contributing their country data. These country data may be based on data from the national statistical office or on other data sources if national statistical office data do not exist. Contributions are then checked and reviewed in-house.
4. In the database used in this chapter labor includes five categories, raising the number of endowments to eight. This new feature is expected to be included in version 9 of the GTAP database.
5. Not all of the countries in the WIOD database are based on official country data, a limited number were engineered.
6. RAS is an iterative scaling method commonly used for balancing matrices (McDougall, 1999).
7. Figures are based on Asian Development Outlook, 2010, p. 33. Asia includes all 18 Asian countries, country groups and Pacific Islands listed in Table 2.5.

3. The vulnerability of the Asian supply chain to localized disasters*

Thomas Hertel, David Hummels and Terrie L. Walmsley

1. INTRODUCTION

There are good reasons to believe that globalization of supply chains leads to significant productivity gains for national economies. But heightened interdependence comes with a down side: shocks to one economy may create ripples, or in some cases, tidal waves which come crashing down on the economies of its trade partners.

Economic shocks to global supply chains can take many forms. At the micro scale, key input suppliers may fail to meet quality and scheduling targets or simply go out of business. Shocks of this sort can be extraordinarily harmful to agents with close vertical links to the failing firm, but may have few discernible effects on the economy as a whole. In contrast, macro scale shocks such as deep recessions, wars and terrorist attacks, and large natural disasters may create widespread damage. Regrettably, there is good reason to believe that the severity of these macro scale shocks is on the rise. The Great Recession and subsequent trade collapse of 2008–2009 represents the largest downturn in international transactions on record. Climate change is expected to increase the frequency and intensity of natural disasters. And high profile terrorist attacks against vital infrastructure, waged in person or online, may significantly impede movements of goods, services and people.

In this chapter, we use the GTAP-SC (Supply Chain) CGE model to explore the consequences of two major disruptions to Asian trade and global production networks: a natural disaster that significantly damages Taipei,China's electronics equipment sector, and a severe disruption of Singapore's port and entrepot operations. By examining these two, very different, types of supply chain disruptions, we seek to learn more about the way in which disasters that are specific to a given industry or entrepot spread around the world.

The existing literature, detailed below, has focused on several dimensions of response to natural disasters. We extend previous work in a number of ways. First, we introduce a globally consistent multi-region input–output (MRIO) framework (see Chapter 2 by Walmsley, Hertel and Hummels for details) that provides an exhaustive framework for global supply chain analysis. Notably, we can measure the effect of a well-defined shock to final demand, outputs, and trade. Second, and in contrast to input–output multiplier approaches, we model temporary scarcities and market-mediated economic adjustments to the disaster. That is, rather than assuming that all foreign market outputs adjust costlessly to absorb the shock, we consider how market prices of goods and factors will adjust to supply chain disruptions. Third, we address a common criticism of computable general equilibrium (CGE) analysis, namely that it focuses excessively on the post-shock, long run equilibrium. In the same spirit as the analysis of regional impact of municipal water supply disruptions by Rose and Liao (2005), we develop model variants that replicate short run versus long run adjustments within the context of a global supply chain. These include: allowing labor to be imperfectly mobile across sectors, allowing for short run changes in aggregate employment levels, and allowing for different degrees of substitutability across input sources in response to price changes.

The existing literature has examined how natural disasters affect trade, firm-level outcomes, and economy-wide growth. The focus on disasters and global supply chains is especially relevant because important theories of offshoring have at their core the possibility of supply disruptions. In these models (for example, Antras and Helpman, 2004), firms face a choice between producing inputs internally and offshoring those inputs. Internal production comes at higher cost but with no chance of supply disruption, while external production is lower cost but subject to the chance that foreign suppliers will not deliver the input. In these models the disruption is often cast in terms of agency problems, often a deliberate defection by the foreign supplier. But these models can also be understood in terms of a disruption caused by a natural disaster or political unrest.

The empirical literature on disasters, output and trade employs two disparate approaches. The first focuses on a particular outcome and relates changes in that outcome to the event of natural disasters. For example, Noy and Nualsri (2007) employ country-level, panel data to look at the impact of disasters on economic growth in a dynamic context.[1] Leiter et al. (2009) delve into firm-level data in order to analyze the impact of flooding in Europe on firm-level productivity, employment, capital accumulation and growth. Several papers use panel data on natural disasters and trade, and estimate the decline in bilateral trade for countries afflicted by natural disasters of varying severity. In Chapter 4 of this volume, Puzzello and Raschky show that natural disasters have greater effects on trade volumes when two countries have tightly linked supply chains.

These analyses excel at showing, retrospectively, the effects of observed shocks on particular outcome variables. A limitation of these exercises is that one cannot trace through broader impacts, nor can one definitively identify the channels (income effects, supply disruption, and price changes that induce substitution in sourcing, etc.) through which a shock affects trade or output. To capture these 'higher order' effects, one needs a model-based analysis (Okuyama, 2008). Input–output and general equilibrium analyses allow for this more in-depth treatment and these approaches are therefore highly complementary to the econometric studies.

There is a large literature that uses input–output (IO) analysis in order to track the impact of a disaster all the way through the supply chain (Lin and Polenske, 1998). This approach has been deployed in a number of cases to analyze the impact of localized disasters that result in shocks to output or demand (Okuyama, 2008), or a port shutdown in the case of Rose and Wei (2013). MacKenzie et al. (2012) offer a recent MRIO analysis of the 2011 earthquake and tsunami in Japan.[2] In his review of modeling methods used to analyze the macro-economic consequences of terrorist attacks, Rose (2013) highlights the many limitations of IO analysis for accurately assessing these effects. Foremost among these is the absence of any role for scarcity-driven, market adjustments.

In the companion Chapter 2 of this volume, we describe in detail how IO multiplier analysis can be thought of as a special case of full CGE analysis that applies under a very particular set of (strong) assumptions. To wit, factor supplies are treated as perfectly elastic so that sectoral output can freely expand in response to the shocks. In contrast, in this chapter, we explore how factor scarcity and varying degrees of factor mobility, in the face of a shock, give rise to factor and goods price changes that mediate the kinds of adjustments that can take place.

2. METHODS

Overview

A MRIO analysis is a common approach to providing economy-wide, supply-chain analysis of shocks. An example of this methodology is portrayed in Figure 3.1. With primary factors in perfectly elastic supply, output prices are fixed and the product supply curve is horizontal. Therefore, output is demand-driven. Now, suppose income in the foreign

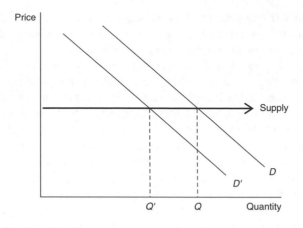

Source: Authors' construction.

Figure 3.1   Impact of a demand shock in a MRIO framework

country declines due to an exogenous event. The quantity of exports demanded falls in proportion to the foreign agents' share of the market, from D to D', and output falls by an equal amount from Q to Q' We can mimic this behavior in the CGE model by fixing primary factor prices and allowing their supply to adjust freely in the wake of the demand shock (see Chapter 2). In this case the drop in foreign incomes will result in a contraction in labor demand and an increase in unemployment in the home market.

There are several problems with this demand-driven input–output analysis. First, any increase in domestic unemployment will translate into lower domestic income and a further decrease in demand (from D' to D'' in Figure 3.2). The CGE approach, which we employ here, captures this inward shift in demand. Second, supply adjustment is likely to be costly, especially in the short run, which can be captured with an upward sloping supply curve in Figure 3.2. This could reflect capacity constraints among input suppliers, or rival uses for primary factors in other sectors of the economy, as we see below. Contrasting Figures 3.1 and 3.2, not only are the quantity responses different, but other response margins (prices, factor supplies) are accounted for, thereby lending considerable advantage to the CGE approach.

The simplest way of introducing a supply chain disruption – and the one most readily available in MRIO analysis – would be through an exogenous shock to the quantity of output in the affected sector. However, in reality, output is not an exogenous factor in the context of most disasters. A more realistic way to handle disruptions is to assume that production capacity

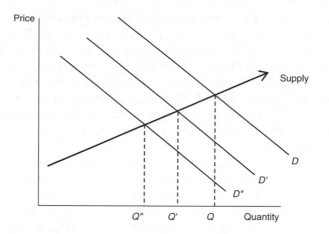

Source: Authors' construction.

Figure 3.2 Impact of a demand shock in a CGE framework

is either destroyed, or firms in the industry experience reduced efficiency. Depending on market prices and response horizons, plant operators may respond to the shock by reducing output, laying off workers, or by altering the input–output intensity of certain factors of production in an attempt to come to grips with this loss in productivity. Following this approach, output remains endogenous, with quantity and price adjustments explicitly modeled so that adjustments in both factor and commodity prices become a key part of the story. The CGE approach employed here allows us to overcome these limitations of partial equilibrium, MRIO analysis. By enforcing a link from income to expenditure, we capture the dependence of total demand on earnings in the economy. By shocking technology instead of output, we allow for affected firms to respond to the disaster by applying more capital, labor and materials, subject to availability and relevant incentives. And by endogenizing firms' output decisions, we are able to allow affected industries to respond to the natural disaster in a rational manner – a point which Rose and Wei describe as 'resilience' (Rose and Wei, 2013). However, and contrary to occasional critiques (e.g., Okuyama, 2008), *we are not assuming long run equilibrium applies* in our CGE analysis. Rather, we can vary our assumptions to allow for adjustments that may occur at different time horizons (see also Rose and Liao, 2005 on this same point).

In order to capture the short run nature of the supply chain disruptions, we invoke a special set of factor market assumptions. While one might initially think about fixing all factors of production, a bit of reflection makes it clear that this is not a reasonable assumption. With all factors of production fixed, and no short run substitution possibilities between materials and value-added, output in the model is also fixed in all sectors. With output fixed in all sectors, there can be no supply-side adjustment and any production shortfall will be met with dramatic price increases, while any reduction in demand will be accompanied by a collapse in prices. So the absence of any supply adjustment seems unrealistic and the question becomes: Where is the supply-side adjustment most likely to occur in the short run?

In our base case, we choose to fix capital stock in each sector in the short run closure. This seems reasonable, since opportunities for adjusting manufacturing capital in the wake of a natural disaster appear to be quite limited. On the other hand, we allow for the free movement of unskilled labor across sectors in response to the shock. In addition, we fix real wages for unskilled workers and allow for changes in the rate of employment. While clerks and other low-skill workers must be given notice prior to layoffs in many economies, we believe that some adjustment along these lines is likely. As part of our robustness checks, we explore the implications of restricting unskilled labor mobility in the presence of a supply shock.

The final primary factors of interest are the skilled labor categories. Here, due to the sector-specific skills of workers, we assume that there is less labor mobility. With imperfect labor mobility, skill premia are allowed to emerge across sectors over the short run. In addition, we assume firms that have invested in these workers are reluctant to lay them off, and therefore there is no change in the aggregate employment rate for skilled workers in this closure.

Experimental Design

A convenient way of thinking about the impact of different types of disruptions along the global supply chain is through the global inter-industry matrix depicted in Figure 3.3. When these flows are converted to a per-unit output basis, we refer to this as the 'A' matrix in deference to customary notation in IO analysis. The columns in the *A* matrix portray the amount of input required from every industry in every region of the world in order to produce one unit of output in a given country, where each block of rows/columns corresponds to a given country and each individual row depicts the domestic sales of an industry within that country. Due to the proclivity of industries to source products from domestic suppliers, this matrix tends to be block diagonal. The density of the off-diagonal blocks reflects the dependence of a given industry/country on foreign suppliers and export sales.

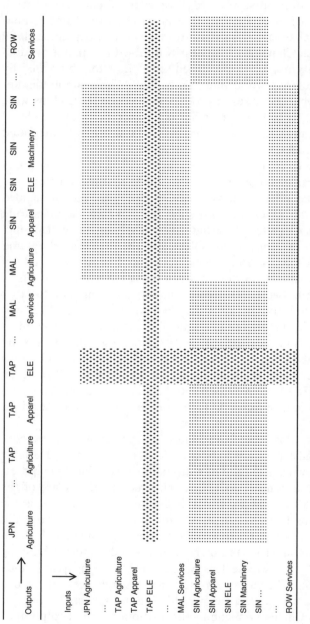

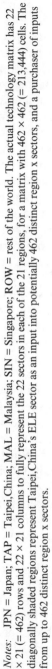

Notes: JPN = Japan; TAP = Taipei,China; MAL = Malaysia; SIN = Singapore; ROW = rest of the world. The actual technology matrix has 22 × 21 (= 462) rows and 22 × 21 columns to fully represent the 22 sectors in each of the 21 regions, for a matrix with 462 × 462 (= 213,444) cells. The diagonally shaded regions represent Taipei,China's ELE sector as an input into potentially 462 distinct region x sectors, and a purchaser of inputs from up to 462 distinct region x sectors.

Source: Authors' construction.

Figure 3.3   Global inter-industry matrix

In this chapter, we explore the impact of two different types of global supply disruptions. In the first case, we consider the situation in which a given industry (electrical equipment) in a given country (Taipei,China) experiences a natural disaster. This is motivated by the 21 September 1999 earthquake in Taipei,China that temporarily disabled two plants producing the vast majority of highly specialized semiconductor chips used by electronics manufacturers worldwide (Barry, 2005). This supply disruption resulted in global shortages in products for which these chips were critical components. It laid in stark relief the vulnerability of the global supply chain for manufactures, which has evolved into a highly integrated system in recent decades.

When viewed in terms of Figure 3.3, the first round of this supply chain disruption can be thought of as a shock to the purchasers of Taipei,Chinese semiconductor chips – represented by the narrow shaded row of the A matrix. Furthermore, any slow-down in chip manufacturing in Taipei,China will also affect those industries supplying the semiconductor industry – a set of transactions reflected in the first shaded column in Figure 3.3. And there will be second round and third round effects beyond these direct effects. For example, in many cases the products in which these chips are used are themselves intermediate inputs into other products. Therefore, in order to deduce the combination of direct and indirect effects implicit in this infinite chain of sales dependencies, we must compute the elements of the matrix: $(I - A)^{-1}$. Herein lies the heart of IO analysis. In the CGE model, these same direct and indirect elements come into play when the model is solved for a new equilibrium following an exogenous shock. However, in addition to these inter-industry dependencies, we have the income effects and factor market interactions described in Figure 3.2.

The inter-industry flows matrix in Figure 3.3 can also be used to conceptualize the second experiment to be considered in this chapter. Here, we explore the case in which a natural or man-made disaster hits Singapore – the key entrepot in Southeast Asia, through which a large share of the region's trade passes. In the case of this entrepot disruption, it is the external transactions between Singapore and her trading partners that are directly affected. These are represented by the larger shaded blocks of off-diagonal columns and rows in Figure 3.3 (rows and columns beginning with SIN). These blocks are quite dense when it comes to Singapore's trade with Southeast Asia. Therefore, anything that disrupts these flows can have a significant impact in the region, and even in the global economy. As with the Taipei,Chinese semiconductor disruption, any disruption to these flows in the A matrix will have further knock-on effects, as these traded intermediate inputs are used in other products further down the supply chain. These effects can be captured by computing $(I - A)^{-1}$ – or equivalently, by solving the CGE model.

In keeping with our desire to allow outputs to adjust endogenously in the face of a supply chain disaster, both of these experiments are implemented as shocks to the underlying technology variables. In the case of the Taipei,Chinese electronic equipment sector, we postulate a 40 percent productivity loss.[3] Thus, rather than eliminating production altogether, we assume that, if no additional inputs are applied, production would drop to 60 percent of initial levels. In fact, with this kind of adverse productivity shock, in the context of a competitive global economy, output may fall more, or less, depending on demand and supply conditions. This point will be illustrated in our robustness analysis later in the chapter.

In the case of the Singaporean trade disruption, we postulate an 80 percent reduction in productivity of international trade margin activities between Singapore and all her trading partners (both imports and exports).[4] One way of thinking about this would be that Singapore's vaunted electronic customs clearance system is disrupted such that all of these transactions must be handled by hand. Alternatively, a hurricane or tsunami might destroy some of the port facilities. In any case, the upshot is a sharp increase in the cost of trading with Singapore and hence of trading within the Southeast Asia region. Therefore, some of the shipments that had previously passed through Singapore must now be diverted along other routes, thereby raising the cost of delivered products.

3.   MODEL, DATA, PARAMETERS AND CLOSURE

CGE Model

The CGE model, which is used for this study, is a modified version of the GTAP model of global trade (Hertel, 1997). GTAP is a relatively standard, global CGE model in which products are differentiated by region of origin. For this chapter, we assume that all of the adjustment to scarcity is at the intensive margin (higher prices for existing varieties). There are other versions of the GTAP model that also feature an extensive margin of adjustment (entry and exit of new varieties and product differentiation by firm, for example by Francois, 1998 and by Hertel and Swaminathan, 1996); however, we do not believe that the extensive margin of adjustment is relevant for the short run analyses undertaken here.

Another important feature of the standard model is the treatment of international trade and transport activities. Rather than treat these activities as a pure trade barrier, akin to tariffs, bilateral merchandise trade is facilitated by the application of international transport services. The GTAP database measures the associated transport and insurance services obtained from national exports and provided to the global trade and transport sectors of which there are three distinct modes in the database (air, sea and land). Thus when entrepot trade is disrupted via productivity deterioration, trade must either contract, or transport services exports must rise in order to cover the gap left by the drop in efficiency associated with Singaporean trade flows.

Finally, and most important for the present study, *we extend the standard model to include bilateral sourcing of imports by agent.* Thus the global CGE model must embody the full '*A*' matrix shown in Figure 3.3. Therefore, for example, the intensity of Japanese imports of Taipei,Chinese electronic equipment must be allowed to vary by sector and use (consumption, government purchases, investment, and intermediate inputs).

Data

For the purposes of this study, we use the GTAP 8.1 database (Narayanan et al., 2012). This was the latest available version of the GTAP database at the time we undertook this research. It is benchmarked to the year 2007 and disaggregates global economic activity into 57 sectors and 129 countries/regions. This means that the dimensions of the '*A*' matrix in Figure 3.3 are (57x129) rows and (57x129) columns. While inverting a matrix of this dimension no longer presents a computational challenge, it does render analysis rather difficult. As a consequence, and given the focus of this chapter on manufacturing supply chains in Asia, we have aggregated the GTAP 8.1 database to 21 sectors (largely manufacturing) and to 22 economies/regions. There are 19 Asia economies/regions separately identified in this study, as well as three non-Asian regions: the European Union (EU), North America and Other.

Since the GTAP database does not track imports to individual sectors, some further adjustments were required in order to match the schematic called for in Figure 3.3; the details are provided in Chapter 2. Essentially, the procedure involves application of the UN Broad Economic Classification (or BEC concordance) at the harmonized system (HS6) trade level in order to identify which suppliers are sending products primarily to intermediate uses and which are supplying imports for final demand. It should be noted that this approach does not really employ product sourcing information. Such data can only be obtained by conducting detailed industry surveys, which are generally not available at present. The other important limitation to note is that Taipei,China is not a reporter in the HS6 trade data obtained from the United Nations. Therefore the sourcing of imports by agent for Taipei,China is done in a strictly proportional fashion. (See Chapter 2 for more details and for a comparison of BEC-based versus proportional sourcing of imports.)

Given our interest in labor markets, we also take advantage of the more refined disaggregation of labor categories, following the work of Weingarden and Tsigas (2010), as implemented by Walmsley and Carrico (2013). Rather than just two categories of labor (skilled and unskilled), we have five categories, disaggregated by occupation using source data from the International Labour Organization (ILO). These categories include: office managers and professionals, technicians and associate professionals, clerks, service and shop workers, and finally, agricultural workers and other low-skill employees. For ease of discussion below, when we refer to *skilled workers*, this category will encompass the first two groups of workers (office managers and professionals plus technicians and associate professionals). Accordingly, *unskilled workers* will refer to the final three categories (clerks; service and shop workers; and agricultural and other low-skill workers).

Parameters and Model Closure

We begin with the standard GTAP parameter file and modify these values as appropriate to this study. The constant difference of elasticities (CDE) consumer demand system parameters are based on international cross-section estimates following the approach of Reimer and Hertel (2004). Trade elasticities are based on the international cross-section estimates of Hertel et al. (2007) using bilateral imports, tariff and transport cost data for six countries in the Americas, as well as New Zealand. Production side parameters are specified in terms of elasticities of substitution among inputs in the nested constant elasticity of substitution (CES) production functions, and are based on a review of the econometric literature as reported in Hertel et al. (2009).

In addition, the GTAP model parameter file includes elasticities of transformation governing the inter-sectoral mobility of land, labor and capital. For example, in order to move labor from one sector to another, it must be 'transformed', say from manufacturing capital to services capital. These elasticities of transformation range from zero (sector-specificity, which is what we assume for capital and land) to infinite (perfect mobility, which is what we assume for unskilled labor). In the case of skilled labor, we allow for partial mobility. Specifically, we assume a value of -1.0, which means that there is incomplete labor mobility such that wages can diverge across sectors. Later, we will explore the implications of also making unskilled labor imperfectly mobile.

The final aspect of our model closure that is relevant for this study is our treatment of unemployment. Given the short run nature of this study, we allow for unemployment of unskilled labor. This is achieved in the model by imposing real wage rigidity. With real wages for unskilled workers fixed, equilibrium is restored after the shock by changing the overall employment rate. In the case of skilled labor, we assume that the aggregate employment rate is unaffected by the disaster.

4.   RESULTS FROM THE INDUSTRY-SPECIFIC SHOCK

We begin with an analysis of the adverse shock to the Taipei,Chinese electrical equipment sector. The 1999 earthquake in Taipei,China notwithstanding, it is unlikely that such an event will only affect one sector of the economy. In practice, given the spatial distribution of industries, one would expect multiple sectors to be affected. However, by focusing on a single sector, we are able to draw out more sharply the implications of a shock that is not economy-wide in nature. How will this affect other sectors in the Taipei,Chinese economy? How will it affect competing sectors in other economies? In short, this targeted shock to productivity is a useful way to think about supply disruptions that disproportionately affect a single industry.

The electrical equipment (ELE) sector in Taipei,China is disproportionate in size, accounting for roughly 10 percent of the country's gross domestic product (GDP), and more than 8 percent of global ELE exports in the year 2007. (In contrast, Japan's ELE sector accounts for less than 3 percent of GDP.) Taipei,China's ELE sector is also heavily integrated into the Asian supply chain, with two-thirds of its exports destined for Asia. The majority of these flows (43 percent of total ELE exports) are destined for the People's Republic of China (PRC).

When the ELE sector experiences this adverse productivity shock, we anticipate a variety of different impacts on the global economy. First of all, consumers will face higher priced goods due to the ensuing shortage. While this effect will likely be most sharply felt in the domestic economy, consumers in other economies that are closely integrated with Taipei,China (e.g., the PRC) will also be affected. In addition, ELE firms in other regions will be affected by this supply disruption. In their case, they stand to benefit from this event – both through higher prices for existing sales, as well as through increased sales volume to export markets. Other sectors will also be affected by this productivity shock –particularly those, such as the automotive industry, which rely on the electrical equipment sector for intermediate inputs.

Finally, we expect the rest of the Taipei,Chinese economy to be affected by this disruption. Tradable sectors may benefit from the availability of additional unskilled workers – that will hinge critically on the mobility of the labor force, as discussed above. We also anticipate this shock being accompanied by a real exchange rate depreciation. As Taipei,Chinese ELE exports shrink, other exports must rise and/or imports must contract, in order to restore balance of payments equilibrium, given a fixed capital account. This will stimulate the other tradable sectors. On the other hand, the ensuing reduction in spending due to income losses incurred in the wake of this disaster will likely harm the non-tradable sectors, which rely on consumer spending to drive sales.

Domestic Impacts

The 40 percent drop in Taipei,Chinese ELE productivity results in an 81 percent reduction in output of that sector in the short run (Table 3.1: baseline – other columns will be discussed below), as the ELE sector loses competitiveness and sheds workers (capital stock is fixed in the short run). ELE exports drop even more sharply (–85 percent: Table 3.2). In order to restore external balance, exports of other sectors must rise (Table 3.2), a development that is facilitated by a real depreciation, with the real exchange rate in Taipei,China dropping by 19 percent in the baseline case (Table 3.1). As a result, output in nearly all the other sectors of the Taipei,Chinese economy rises. The only non-ELE sectors that experience a decline in output are the two service sectors and the food industry. These sectors rely heavily on sales to domestic consumers, who experience a strong drop in real income following this disaster (–14 percent: Table 3.1, baseline). Overall the contraction in domestic demand results in a fall in short run employment of unskilled workers in the economy by 7 percent (unskilled production workers), 11 percent (clerks) and 13 percent (service workers).

As noted above, a critical piece of this analysis is the treatment of factor markets. In our baseline model, we treat capital as sector-specific, and therefore immobile in the short run. Skilled labor is partially mobile, and unskilled labor is perfectly mobile. What if unskilled labor is also imperfectly mobile? This change in assumption means less supply-side flexibility in the economy and the associated outcomes are reported under the heading 'lowmobile' in the tables of results. Comparing across the first two columns in Tables 3.1 and 3.2, we see that further restricting factor mobility results in less contraction of the ELE sector, less expansion of output and exports in the other heavily traded sectors of the economy, a stronger real depreciation, a larger decline in employment and a greater fall in

*Table 3.1   Impact of ELE disruption on Taipei, China economy
            (percentage change)*

Variable	Baseline scenario	Lowmobile scenario	Lowelast scenario	Low/low scenario
Real income	−14	−16	−18	−18
Real exchange rate	−19	−22	−26	−27
ELE output	−81	−74	−57	−52
Employment of:				
Clerks	−11	−14	−17	−18
Service workers	−13	−16	−21	−22
Unskilled production workers	−7	−9	−9	−6

Note: ELE = electronics equipment sector.

Source: Authors' calculations.

real income (two percentage points more decline). In short, the impact of this disaster on the Taipei,Chinese economy is considerably worse when unskilled workers cannot readily shift their sector of employment.

The foregoing analysis has focused on the supply-side. However, the demand side characteristics are also critical to supply-chain adjustment to an industry-specific disaster. Here, the most important parameters are the trade elasticities governing the potential to substitute away from Taipei,Chinese ELE products. If there is little potential to replace these products with substitute goods in the short run, then the adverse impact of the disruption will be much larger, and the beneficial effects for competitor economies will be smaller. The trade elasticities employed in the standard GTAP model were estimated by Hertel et al. (2007). These estimates employed data at the HS6 level, but were pooled across disaggregate commodities, with the estimated elasticities constrained to be equal within GTAP commodity categories. As such these elasticities of substitution between products sourced from different regions reflect longer run adjustments. This contrasts with short run estimates of trade elasticities, such as those by Gallaway et al. (2003) who report much smaller trade elasticities. Therefore, it seems appropriate to evaluate the impact of sharply reducing these parameter values in the context of a 'demand-side' sensitivity analysis. For purposes of the current chapter, we adopt short run values which are just one-third of the longer run values and we dub this experiment 'lowelast' for reporting purposes.

The third columns in Tables 3.1 and 3.2 report the change in selected economic variables for the Taipei,Chinese economy following the ELE

Table 3.2   Impact of ELE disruption on Taipei,China output and exports, by sector (percentage change)

Sector	Output				Exports			
	Base-line scenario	Low-mobile scenario	Low-elast scenario	Low/ low scenario	Base-line scenario	Low-mobile scenario	Low-elast scenario	Low/ low scenario
Agriculture	1	0	−2	−2	36	36	33	32
Processed food	−1	−2	−6	−6	47	52	31	33
Resources	4	2	5	2	3	5	15	11
Textiles	24	9	20	11	25	10	22	13
Apparel	12	4	4	0	53	40	33	29
Leather	19	8	11	7	26	14	18	14
Lumber	23	9	16	10	33	15	23	15
Paper products	6	2	0	0	57	47	32	31
Petro-chemicals	3	−1	0	−2	3	4	2	3
Chemical, rubber and plastics	14	6	11	7	22	14	16	12
Mineral products	5	2	2	2	44	36	26	23
Iron and steel	15	7	13	8	14	9	15	10
Nonferrous metals	20	9	17	11	29	18	20	14
Fabricated metals	19	7	14	8	42	24	30	20
Motor vehicles	6	2	−2	−2	36	33	25	25
Transport equipment	22	8	14	7	40	21	31	21
Electrical equipment	−81	−74	−57	−52	−85	−78	−61	−56
Machinery equipment	19	7	14	8	29	16	22	15
Other manufactures	15	5	8	4	28	16	21	16
Non-trade services	−5	−5	−7	−6	144	198	57	63
Services	−5	−5	−9	−8	60	75	32	36

Note: ELE = electronics equipment sector.

Source: Authors' calculations.

productivity shock in the context of these smaller trade elasticities, while retaining the baseline assumptions about the factor markets. Not surprisingly, lower trade elasticities make it harder for other firms to shift away from Taipei,Chinese ELE products and output now falls by less (−57 percent vs –81 percent in the baseline experiment). However, less intuitive is the much stronger real exchange rate depreciation and the sharper rise in unemployment. Aggregate employment of service workers now falls by 21 percent. This stems from a more indirect mechanism – namely the smaller trade elasticities in other sectors of the economy. In this 'lowelast' scenario, it is much harder for the non-ELE sectors to expand in the wake of the ELE disaster. Their ability to displace imports in the Taipei,Chinese market is greatly muted, as is their ability to penetrate foreign markets with increased exports. As a consequence, the increase in non-ELE exports is much smaller under the 'lowelast' scenario than under the baseline scenario – despite the fact that unskilled workers are perfectly mobile under this experiment. Therefore, in order to restore external balance, the real exchange rate depreciation must be much larger, and the consequences of real wage rigidity for unskilled employment are more significant when there is greater demand side rigidity in the supply chain.

It is also interesting to explore how the inelastic supply and inelastic demand scenarios interact. The final (fourth) columns in Tables 3.1 and 3.2 report results for selected Taipei,China variables when both the supply- and demand-side rigidities are imposed simultaneously. In this case, the real exchange rate depreciation is somewhat larger, as are the employment decreases for clerks and services workers. However, the employment reduction for production workers is now diminished – even relative to baseline – due to the lesser decline in Taipei,China's ELE output, as both supply- and demand-side forces conspire to retain workers in the ELE sector. In short, inelasticity on the demand and supply sides is not always mutually reinforcing – that is, the combined impact on key variables is not always as expected from a simple addition of the individual effects.

Global Impacts

Table 3.3 reports the impact of the ELE productivity shock on other regions in the global economy. The first block of columns reports the impact on domestic firms' prices for ELE products in these non-Taipei,China regions. (All price changes are reported, relative to the numeraire, which is a global index of primary factor prices.) We expect upward pressure on ELE prices for several reasons. Firstly, Taipei,Chinese ELE components represent an intermediate input to ELE manufacturing in many of these regions. So higher priced components raise the cost of the final product. *Ceteris paribus*, this will result in a decline in ELE output, as consumers purchase less in the face of higher prices. However, there is another important factor at work, which is the outward shift in demand

Table 3.3 Impact of ELE disruption on other regions' ELE output, terms of trade and real income (percentage change)

Region	ELE price				ELE output			
	Baseline scenario	Lowmobile scenario	Lowelast scenario	Low/low scenario	Baseline scenario	Lowmobile scenario	Lowelast scenario	Low/low scenario
Japan	2.3	4.3	4.5	7.2	5.2	4.1	3.4	2.4
Korea, Republic of	2.8	4.7	4.2	6.3	3.8	3.2	4.3	3.4
China, People's Republic of	2.7	4.6	3.8	5.8	5.5	4.0	4.7	3.7
Other East Asia	1.8	3.8	1.4	3.3	6.2	4.9	4.9	4.2
Singapore	2.9	4.7	4.7	6.4	1.2	1.7	1.6	1.9
Philippines	3.4	5.3	6.6	8.4	1.2	1.1	0.5	0.2
Thailand	3.2	5.1	5.0	7.1	2.3	1.8	3.3	2.3
Indonesia	2.5	4.7	2.8	5.2	8.1	5.6	8.5	6.2
Malaysia	2.9	4.7	4.1	6.0	3.5	3.0	4.0	3.3
Viet Nam	2.3	4.3	2.6	4.7	10.3	7.8	9.1	7.6
Other Southeast Asia	1.6	3.3	1.4	2.6	2.2	2.1	1.5	1.6
India	1.1	2.9	0.8	2.0	4.5	4.6	2.8	3.1
Bangladesh	2.2	4.1	2.4	4.3	2.0	1.7	2.5	2.2
Pakistan	1.5	3.2	5.8	5.6	1.5	1.5	1.0	1.0
Other South Asia	1.5	3.2	0.6	0.8	3.1	3.0	1.5	1.6
Central Asia	1.0	2.9	0.3	1.7	2.8	2.4	1.5	1.5
Pacific Islands	1.2	2.8	0.6	1.5	3.6	4.0	2.4	2.8
Australia and New Zealand	1.4	3.2	0.4	1.7	5.6	5.4	4.3	4.4
European Union	2.0	3.8	2.0	3.6	4.3	4.1	3.9	3.7
North America	1.7	3.5	1.4	2.8	5.6	5.3	4.6	4.6
Rest of world	1.7	3.4	1.1	2.4	3.2	3.2	2.6	2.6

Table 3.3 (continued)

Region	Terms of trade				Real income			
	Baseline scenario	Lowmobile scenario	Lowelast scenario	Low/low scenario	Baseline scenario	Lowmobile scenario	Lowelast scenario	Low/low scenario
Japan	0.3	0.5	2.5	3.3	0.1	0.2	0.8	1.1
Korea, Republic of	0.4	0.8	0.9	1.5	0.3	0.6	0.9	1.4
China, People's Republic of	−0.2	−0.2	−0.9	−0.9	−0.1	0.0	−0.4	−0.4
Other East Asia	−0.1	−0.2	−0.4	−0.5	0.0	−0.1	−0.2	−0.3
Singapore	0.1	0.3	0.1	0.4	0.2	0.5	0.3	0.8
Philippines	1.3	2.0	3.6	4.7	0.9	1.4	2.3	3.0
Thailand	0.3	0.5	0.4	0.6	0.3	0.6	0.5	0.8
Indonesia	0.0	0.0	−0.2	−0.3	0.0	0.0	0.0	−0.1
Malaysia	0.4	0.5	0.5	0.6	0.8	1.1	0.9	1.2
Viet Nam	0.2	0.1	0.3	−0.1	0.6	0.3	0.8	0.1
Other Southeast Asia	0.0	−0.1	−0.2	−0.5	0.0	−0.1	−0.1	−0.3
India	−0.1	−0.2	−0.2	−0.3	0.0	0.0	0.0	−0.1
Bangladesh	0.0	0.0	−0.2	−0.5	0.0	0.0	−0.1	−0.3
Pakistan	−0.2	−0.2	3.4	2.0	0.0	0.0	1.7	1.2
Other South Asia	0.0	−0.1	−1.5	−3.0	0.0	0.0	−1.0	−2.2
Central Asia	−0.2	−0.3	−0.5	−0.7	−0.1	−0.2	−0.3	−0.4
Pacific Islands	−0.1	−0.2	−0.4	−0.6	0.0	−0.1	−0.2	−0.4
Australia and New Zealand	−0.3	−0.5	−1.0	−1.3	−0.1	−0.1	−0.4	−0.5
European Union	0.0	−0.1	−0.1	−0.1	0.0	0.0	0.0	0.0
North America	−0.1	−0.1	−0.5	−0.7	0.0	0.0	−0.1	−0.2
Rest of world	−0.1	−0.3	−0.5	−0.6	−0.1	−0.1	−0.2	−0.3

Note: ELE = electronics equipment sector.

Source: Authors' calculations.

for ELE products around the world in the face of the sharp reduction in output (and accompanying price rise) in Taipei,China's ELE sector. The strongest price rises are for ELE products produced in the Southeast Asian economies, led by the Philippines (3.4 percent), Thailand (3.2 percent) and Malaysia and Singapore (2.9 percent). These are followed closely by the Republic of Korea, the PRC and Indonesia.

The second panel of columns of Table 3.3 report the percentage changes in ELE output, by region in response to the adverse productivity shock to the Taipei,Chinese industry. Recall that there are two competing forces at work here – one is the effect of higher costs, and one is the outward shift in demand for the country's ELE output. Both drive prices higher, but the first does so by raising costs and the second does so by boosting demand. In addition, the profile of ELE sales to intermediate and final demands, as well as by region, varies greatly. Therefore, it is not surprising that the pattern of output increases is somewhat different from the price changes. The strongest output rises are for Viet Nam (10.3 percent) and Indonesia (8.1 percent). Australia/New Zealand and North America also experience significant output rises as domestic producers replace Taipei,China ELE products in their domestic markets. A more nuanced view of the impact of the Taipei,Chinese ELE shock on her partner economies is offered in Figure 3.4, which reports the percentage change in non-ELE export volumes from Japan and the PRC. In the case of Japan, there is a much stronger increase in ELE exports and a consistent reduction in non-ELE exports as resources are drawn away from other sectors to permit this expansion. From this perspective, Japan looks like a competitor economy with Taipei,China. In contrast, the pattern of non-ELE export impact is different in the case of the PRC where Figure 3.4 shows that the trade effects are generally more muted, with ELE expanding much more modestly, non-ELE exports changing less as well, and, in a number of cases, non-ELE exports actually expanding. These are exports from Chinese sectors (iron and steel, non-ferrous metals) that are tied into the Taipei,Chinese economy and benefit when non-ELE tradable sectors in that economy expand. In this sense, Taipei,China and the PRC appear to be complementary economies.

The final two blocks of columns in Table 3.3 report two important economy-wide indicators for these other economies: the terms of trade (ToT) and real income. The ToT can be decomposed into three component parts (McDougall, 1993): the world price effect, the export price effect and the import price effect. Countries will benefit from the higher average *world prices* for ELE products, provided they are net exporters of ELE goods. Countries can additionally gain from the *export price effect* if their differentiated product price rises relatively more than the world average

Asia and global production networks

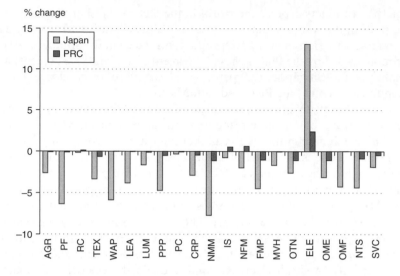

Note: AGR = agriculture; CRP = chemicals, rubber and plastics; ELE = electrical equipment; FMP = fabricated metals; IS = iron and steel; LEA = leather; LUM = lumber; MVH = motor vehicles; NFM = nonferrous metals; NMM = mineral products; NTS = nontrade services; OME = machinery equipment; OMF = other manufactures; OTN = transport equipment; PC = petro-chemicals; PF = processed food; PPP = paper products; PRC = People's Republic of China; RC = resource products; SVC = services; TEX = textiles; WAP = wearing apparel.

Source: Authors' simulation.

Figure 3.4   Impact of ELE productivity shock on non-ELE exports from Japan and the PRC (percentage change)

(e.g., the Philippines). Finally, those regions that rely disproportionately on Taipei,China for ELE imports are expected to lose from this disaster scenario due to the *import price effect*, as Taipei,China's ELE prices rise, relatively more. In light of these considerations, it is not surprising that the Philippines experiences a strong ToT gain, as do Thailand, Malaysia, Japan and the Republic of Korea. The PRC shows a ToT loss – which arises due to its heavy dependence on Taipei,China for component parts. Other Asian regions that lose on the ToT front include India, Pakistan and Central Asia.

In the absence of domestic distortions, we expect real income changes to follow the ToT, being somewhat more muted, with the relative magnitude being determined by the openness of the economy. However, the presence of numerous taxes and subsidies in the global economy complicate this story considerably. From the first column in the final panel of Table 3.3, we see that the largest gainers from the Taipei,China ELE disaster are the Philippines (0.9 percent rise in real income), followed by Indonesia, Malaysia, Thailand and the Republic of Korea. The only regions that show a decline in real income under the base case are the PRC, Central Asia, Australia/New Zealand and the rest of the world. The result that unaffected regions are likely to gain from a single region's disaster is consistent with the findings of MacKenzie et al. (2012) who analyze the impacts of the 2011 Japanese earthquake and tsunami.

The subsequent columns in Table 3.3 explore the changes in ELE prices, outputs, ToT and real incomes for non-Taipei,China regions under the low labor mobility, low substitutability in demand and combined scenarios. Here, it is clearly evident that more inelastic supply and demand curves result in significantly higher price changes. Indeed, the price rises under the combined scenario are more than twice as high as under the baseline case. Of course, the associated ELE output changes are lower under the combined low mobility and low elasticity scenarios, as it is more difficult to move unskilled labor between sectors, and firms find it harder to change their pattern of sourcing in response to the adverse productivity shock in Taipei,China. However, if we focus solely on the impact of the smaller trade elasticities, the results are somewhat more varied. The most common result is for the inelastic demands to result in smaller output expansions – since Taipei,Chinese ELE output contracts less under this parameter specification, there is less room for others to expand. However, this is not universally the case. In particular, a number of the Southeast Asian economies experience stronger output expansions under the inelastic demand cases. This suggests the presence of more complex, cross-sector effects.

With larger price changes in the more inelastic supply and demand scenarios, it is not surprising to see larger ToT effects. Indeed, under the combined inelastic supply/demand scenario, the Philippines' ToT gain reaches 4.7 percent and Japan's gain rises to 3.3 percent. There are several cases where a negligible effect becomes significantly negative under the inelastic scenario (Indonesia, Bangladesh, Other South Asia). And there are even a few cases of sign reversals. In Pakistan, for example, the ToT effect is negative in the first two cases, but turns positive in the context of low elasticities of substitution in use. For the most part, the larger (in absolute value) ToT effects translate into larger real income effects, as would be expected.[5] The largest loss is felt by Other South Asia (–2.2 percent), whereas the largest gain accrues to the Philippines (3 percent).

5.   RESULTS FROM THE ENTREPOT SHOCK

Singapore is a key trading hub in Southeast Asia, with a very large share of regional trade passing through its ports. Our experiment involves sharply reducing the efficiency with which this trade occurs, as would arise in the context of a natural disaster, which disrupted the port, or a cyber-attack, which disabled the country's customs clearance system. The entrepot shock contrasts with the preceding experiment in that it affects the productivity with which goods are traded, rather than the productivity with which they are produced. This experiment affects all the incoming and outgoing merchandise trade flows for Singapore. As with the previous experiment, we explore the impact of this shock in the context of a baseline experiment in which capital is immobile, skilled labor is partially mobile with fixed aggregate employment, and unskilled labor is perfectly mobile, with rigid real wages and variable short run employment levels. As before, these baseline impacts will be contrasted with scenarios in which, alternately, supply, demand and then both supply and demand are rendered more inelastic by either reducing unskilled labor mobility, reducing substitution across import sources, or both.

In all of these entrepot experiments, the 80 percent drop in efficiency of merchandise trading results in higher bilateral merchandise trading costs with Singapore, which rise by 400 percent. The impact of this increase on bilateral prices depends on the share of global trade and transport services in the cost, insurance, and freight-inclusive (cif) price of imports. For products such as natural resources and agricultural commodities, this has a significant impact on prices, while the impact is more moderate for low margin goods. In any case, the need to offset the reduced efficiency of Singaporean trade requires additional global trade and transport services, as does the re-routing of trade around the Singapore entrepot. Given our treatment of the international trade and transport sector as a single pool, from which the supply of shipping services are drawn to meet the global demand for international transport margins, these services must ultimately be supplied from the pool of national services exports. The increase in global trade and transport services required to accommodate this supply chain shock is reported at the bottom of Table 3.4 and ranges from 4 percent in the baseline to 6 percent when the ability of firms and households to alter their sourcing patterns is more restricted. (Note that limiting labor mobility on the supply side does not substantially alter this figure.)

The main two panels of Table 3.4 summarize the impact on the Singapore economy of this disruption in trade facilitation. With 'sand in the gears' of Singapore's usually efficient trading system, the economy

Table 3.4   Impact of entrepot disruption on Singapore economy
(percentage change)

Variable	Baseline scenario	Lowmobile scenario	Lowelast scenario	Low/low scenario
Real income	−21	−21	−28	−28
Real exchange rate	−19	−19	−29	−29
Exports	−11	−10	−0.1	−0.1
Employment of:				
Clerks	−21	−21	−29	−30
Service workers	−15	−15	−27	−27
Unskilled production workers	−25	−26	−30	−30
	Global trade and transport services			
	4	4	6	6

Source: Authors' calculations.

experiences a sharp real exchange rate depreciation, large reductions in unskilled employment, and a 21 percent decline in real income under the baseline scenario. Since the shock cuts across the board in the Singaporean economy, this outcome is little affected by the reduction in labor mobility (column two). All sectors are hurt by this entrepot disruption, and unlike the Taipei,China ELE shock, adjustment is less reliant on shifting labor between sectors. However, when trade elasticities are reduced, the macro-economic outcome is far worse for Singapore. In this case, the real exchange rate depreciation, and the reductions in employment and real income approach 30 percent. The difficulty in changing the sourcing of products affects not only her trading partners, but also Singaporean producers and therefore there is little scope for avoiding the burden of higher trade costs. This makes the economy much less competitive, thereby requiring an even greater real depreciation. In short, this is an example of a supply chain disruption for which the ability to alter the sourcing of imports is paramount.

Table 3.5 reports the impact of this entrepot disruption on global merchandise and services trade by commodity. It is hardly surprising that services exports rise, as the reduction in Singapore's trade efficiency requires additional effort to move the same amount of goods. The largest percentage reduction in global trade volume is for petro-chemicals (−1.12 percent). Singapore is an important refiner of petroleum and related products and this industry suffers from the higher cost of importing crude petroleum and exporting refined products. Transport equipment,

Table 3.5   Impact of entrepot disruption on global trade volume (percentage change)

Commodity	Global exports by commodity			
	Baseline scenario	Lowmobile scenario	Lowelast scenario	Low/low scenario
Agriculture	−0.05	−0.05	0.04	0.04
Processed food	−0.23	−0.23	−0.07	−0.06
Resources	−0.27	−0.27	−0.11	−0.11
Textiles	−0.07	−0.07	−0.04	−0.05
Apparel	−0.08	−0.07	0.02	0.01
Leather	−0.11	−0.11	−0.02	−0.02
Lumber	−0.01	−0.03	0.00	−0.04
Paper products	−0.33	−0.33	−0.15	−0.17
Petro-chemicals	−1.12	−1.13	−0.54	−0.55
Chemical, rubber and plastics	−0.28	−0.28	−0.17	−0.17
Mineral products	−0.33	−0.33	−0.21	−0.24
Iron and steel	−0.21	−0.21	−0.18	−0.18
Nonferrous metals	−0.11	−0.10	−0.13	−0.13
Fabricated metals	−0.46	−0.46	−0.31	−0.33
Motor vehicles	−0.08	−0.08	−0.20	−0.22
Transport equipment	−0.98	−0.96	−1.16	−1.14
Electrical equipment	−0.29	−0.28	−0.22	−0.23
Machinery equipment	−0.46	−0.45	−0.46	−0.45
Other manufactures	−0.18	−0.18	−0.19	−0.21
Non-trade services	0.01	0.01	−0.03	0.00
Services	0.80	0.79	1.05	1.04

Source: Authors' calculations.

machinery and equipment and fabricated metal products are also relatively hard hit. As with the earlier results, restricting factor mobility does not change the results significantly. And in the case of global commodity exports, the smaller trade elasticities have less effect than might be expected. While the smaller trade elasticities generally reduce the change in trade volume, as expected, this is not always the case, as shown by the other transport equipment sector, where the impact of lesser substitutability across sources dominates and trade falls even more under the inelastic demand scenarios.

Table 3.6 reports the impact of this entrepot disruption on the non-Singaporean economies. In the first block of columns, under the baseline parameter settings, exports for many of these economies rise, as trade

Table 3.6 *Global impact of entrepot disruption (percentage change)*

Region	Regional exports				Real exchange rate			
	Baseline scenario	Lowmobile scenario	Lowelast scenario	Low/low scenario	Baseline scenario	Lowmobile scenario	Lowelast scenario	Low/low scenario
Japan	−0.12	−0.14	−1.42	−1.62	0.24	0.30	1.49	1.96
Korea, Republic of	0.15	0.14	−0.36	−0.33	0.49	0.57	1.41	1.62
China, People's Republic of	0.00	−0.01	0.05	0.04	0.06	0.06	0.01	0.02
Taipei,China	0.03	0.02	−0.02	−0.03	0.13	0.15	−0.01	0.02
Other East Asia	0.07	0.09	0.05	0.08	0.07	0.04	0.04	0.01
Philippines	0.23	0.21	0.54	0.46	−0.18	−0.18	−0.98	−0.97
Thailand	0.16	0.10	0.28	0.25	−0.15	−0.10	−0.71	−0.70
Indonesia	−0.52	−0.48	0.78	0.73	−0.91	−1.00	−2.61	−2.87
Malaysia	−0.84	−0.84	0.03	0.00	−0.93	−0.90	−1.97	−2.02
Viet Nam	0.46	0.54	1.45	1.68	−1.48	−1.76	−4.14	−5.31
Other Southeast Asia	0.02	0.10	0.43	0.46	−0.41	−0.54	−1.28	−1.49
India	−0.02	−0.12	−0.20	−0.33	0.09	0.12	0.38	0.52
Bangladesh	0.07	0.07	0.69	0.66	−0.06	−0.09	−0.67	−0.87
Pakistan	0.11	0.10	−3.41	−1.86	0.03	0.02	3.65	2.22
Other South Asia	0.35	0.35	5.91	7.22	−0.2	−0.22	−6.45	−8.45
Central Asia	0.17	0.19	0.20	0.23	−0.08	−0.16	−0.23	−0.37
Pacific Islands	−0.20	−0.18	0.97	1.04	−0.29	−0.36	−1.58	−1.83
Australia and New Zealand	0.19	0.21	1.05	1.12	−0.36	−0.42	−1.89	−2.13
European Union	0.01	0.01	−0.15	−0.19	0.14	0.16	0.53	0.66
North America	0.05	0.06	0.39	0.50	0.04	0.04	−0.32	−0.48
Rest of world	0.16	0.18	0.26	0.30	−0.02	−0.06	−0.22	−0.31

Table 3.6 (continued)

Region	Terms of trade				Real income			
	Baseline scenario	Lowmobile scenario	Lowelast scenario	Low/low scenario	Baseline scenario	Lowmobile scenario	Lowelast scenario	Low/low scenario
Japan	0.15	0.18	1.04	1.19	0.07	0.07	0.34	0.37
Korea, Republic of	0.24	0.27	0.68	0.71	0.26	0.28	0.65	0.68
China, People's Republic of	-0.06	-0.05	-0.10	-0.10	-0.01	0.00	-0.04	-0.03
Other East Asia	0.02	0.04	-0.09	-0.07	0.03	0.04	-0.08	-0.06
Singapore	0.01	-0.03	0.04	-0.01	-0.02	-0.03	0.03	0.01
Philippines	-0.29	-0.28	-0.59	-0.54	-0.15	-0.15	-0.36	-0.32
Thailand	-0.20	-0.17	-0.51	-0.50	-0.28	-0.25	-0.55	-0.52
Indonesia	-1.61	-1.64	-2.72	-2.73	-0.80	-0.79	-1.27	-1.24
Malaysia	-1.16	-1.14	-1.74	-1.74	-1.73	-1.68	-2.36	-2.29
Viet Nam	-1.05	-1.12	-2.05	-2.25	-1.65	-1.75	-3.66	-4.14
Other Southeast Asia	-0.91	-1.03	-1.31	-1.39	-0.67	-0.72	-0.88	-0.89
India	0.09	0.14	0.38	0.49	0.03	0.03	0.16	0.20
Bangladesh	-0.17	-0.17	-0.47	-0.46	-0.08	-0.09	-0.26	-0.28
Pakistan	-0.01	0.00	1.98	1.10	0.00	0.00	0.94	0.56
Other South Asia	-0.30	-0.31	-3.92	-4.80	-0.23	-0.23	-2.96	-3.71
Central Asia	-0.16	-0.23	-0.24	-0.34	-0.07	-0.12	-0.14	-0.20
Pacific Islands	-0.81	-0.86	-1.46	-1.58	-0.15	-0.19	-0.96	-1.03
Australia and New Zealand	-0.60	-0.64	-1.46	-1.55	-0.25	-0.27	-0.67	-0.70
European Union	0.06	0.07	0.22	0.26	0.05	0.06	0.17	0.19
North America	0.01	0.01	-0.21	-0.29	0.01	0.01	-0.06	-0.08
Rest of world	-0.13	-0.17	-0.26	-0.33	-0.04	-0.06	-0.11	-0.14

Source: Authors' calculations.

106

by-passes Singapore. Indeed the only significant regional export volume declines are for the most closely related economies of Indonesia, Malaysia and the Pacific Islands, as well as for Japan. This picture is little altered by supply-side rigidity in the form of immobile labor (second column of results). However, once import sourcing is more tightly constrained (final two columns), there are some sharp differences, with exports from the Republic of Korea, India, Pakistan and the EU all turning negative as it becomes more difficult to change sourcing patterns.

The next blocks of columns in Table 3.6 report the impact of this supply disruption on the real exchange rate, ToT and real incomes for each economy across the baseline and alternate rigidity scenarios. These variables are closely related, and an improvement in any one of them reflects increased export prices, relative to import costs as trade with the entrepot becomes more costly and trade flows are diverted from Singapore. Not surprisingly, the Southeast Asian economies – closely linked to Singapore – are hardest hit by the entrepot shock, with ToT losses, real exchange rate depreciations and real income losses. In contrast, Japan and the Republic of Korea gain as their ToT improve. These welfare impacts of Singapore's entrepot shock are robust to changes in the supply side of the economy – for the same reason noted above – namely the shock does not give a strong incentive to reallocate factors of production across sectors. However, the macro-economic outcome is extremely sensitive to the trade elasticities. When sourcing of imports becomes more difficult to change (inelastic demand), the inability to avoid this entrepot shock by readily substituting imports from other sources significantly raises the costs for many of the Southeast Asian economies. The 'Other South Asia' region – dominated by Sri Lanka – is extremely hard hit under this parameter setting. Meanwhile, the inelastic demand scenario significantly enhances the gains of Japan and the Republic of Korea.

6. DISCUSSION AND CONCLUSIONS

In conclusion, we find that the GTAP-SC framework is a useful vehicle for analyzing the impact of sector and entrepot disruptions on the global supply chain, and indeed, on the global economy. Unlike the econometric approaches employed elsewhere in this volume, we are able to fully investigate the general equilibrium determinants of changes in global trade and production. And unlike the input–output approaches often used in supply chain analyses, this CGE framework allows us to explore the implications of rigidities on both the supply and demand sides for transmission of localized disasters throughout the global economy.

We find that the supply chain impacts of local disasters are rather robust to labor market rigidities when the external shock affects the entire economy, as is the case with the entrepot disruption. This is due to the fact that all sectors are adversely affected, and there is less of an incentive to dramatically change the employment of labor and capital across sectors. However, this is not the case when the disaster hits a particular industry, as is the case when Taipei,China's ELE sector experiences a 40 percent reduction in productivity. In this sector-focused, supply chain disruption, the impact, both on the Taipei,Chinese economy, as well as on the global economy, hinges critically on the mobility of labor out of the damaged sector and into other sectors of the affected economy, as well as labor mobility in the trading partners' economies.

One of the potentially surprising results from the chapter is that even a major disruption to a critical world supplier of inputs (Taipei,China's electronics industry) has modest effects on incomes elsewhere – especially under our baseline parameter settings. How does this square with our notion that disruptions to supply chains create havoc worldwide?

In contrast to supply-side rigidities, the impact of both types of disasters discussed in this chapter is heavily dependent on individual firms' abilities to substitute away from products affected by the supply chain disruption. When we reduce the associated import sourcing elasticities to one-third of their baseline values, the consequences of the disaster for the affected region are invariably much worse. And the scope for terms of trade changes and the associated real income changes in other regions is magnified. Still, it might seem that for some critical inputs there are no substitutes, at least in the short run. If input supply is disrupted, downstream firms will simply shut down.

To understand this case in light of our model it is important to think about the role of aggregation. The use of industry data, rather than firm-level data on inputs can mask two very different realities at the level of individual firms. One is the case where firms in a given industry share the same technology, and require all inputs (from all sources) used in that industry. Disruptions to a particular input are important to the extent that the input represents a large cost-share for the industry, and that close substitutes are difficult to come by.

The other case is where individual firms within the industry are extremely heterogeneous in their technologies and use of inputs. In this case, it may be that only a small subset of firms needs any particular input, but these inputs are absolutely critical to their operation. Disruption in input supply shuts these firms down entirely, but since affected firms represent only a small percentage of all firms in the industry, the impact on aggregate sector output is modest. To be clear, the composition of output changes looks different in this second case. For example, we might have 90 percent of firms unaffected by the disruption and 10 percent of firms shutting down; as opposed to all firms reducing output by 10 percent. But the aggregate effects at the sector level – and indeed the consequences for labor markets and regional income – are the same in both cases.

Of course, it could be that an input is both critical for every firm, and that all these firms lack substitutes. Where this is the case, the input would likely represent a very large share of input costs prior to the shock.[6] By using the detailed information on input shares by source country in the pre-shock equilibrium, we are taking into account whether an input is very important to a lot of firms or not. Since it is rare to find inputs that have both large cost shares and no substitutes, we believe that it will be unusual for supply disruptions to have very large aggregate effects.

NOTES

[*] This chapter has been commissioned as part of the Asian Development Bank study on Supply Chains in Asia, led by David Hummels and Benno Ferrarini. The authors would like to thank Ari Van Assche, Anson Soderbery, and Laura Puzzello for valuable comments on an earlier draft of this work.
1. For example, they find that adverse shocks to human capital result in a decreased growth rate, with no eventual return to the previous growth trajectory, while loss of physical capital seems to have no discernible long-term impact on growth.
2. MacKenzie et al. (2013) explore, alternatively, shocks based on output disruption and shocks based on demand disruption. The former are an order of magnitude more damaging, largely due to the mitigating role of foreign suppliers and inventory adjustment in the latter. Overall, they conclude that foreigners likely gained from this disruption, and that a similar disaster in other countries would be even more beneficial to the competition, due to the relatively large share of intermediates sourced domestically in the Japanese auto industry.
3. In GTAP notation, this is given by ao(ELE, TWN) = −40.
4. In GTAP notation, this is given by ats("Singapore") = −80, and atd("Singapore") = −80.
5. Of course, where there are significant efficiency gains and losses, these will likely be more muted under the low mobility/low elasticity scenarios.
6. Imagine a firm that is a monopoly supplier of some input, without which every firm in Asia shuts down, and for which no substitutes exist. You can be sure that key input is supplied at very high prices.

REFERENCES

Antras, P. and E. Helpman (2004), 'Global sourcing', *Journal of Political Economy*, **112**, 552–580.
Barry, L. (2005), *End of the Line*, New York: Doubleday.

Francois, J. (1998), 'Scale economies and imperfect competition in the GTAP model', GTAP Technical Paper No. 14, Purdue University, available at: https://www.gtap.agecon.purdue.edu/resources/res_display.asp?RecordID=317.

Gallaway, M.P., C.A. McDaniel and S.A. Rivera (2003), 'Short-run and long-run industry-level estimates of U.S. Armington elasticities', *The North American Journal of Economics and Finance*, **14**, 49–68.

Hertel, T.W. (ed.) (1997), *Global Trade Analysis: Modeling and Applications*, New York: Cambridge University Press.

Hertel, T.W. and P. Swaminathan (1996), 'Introducing monopolistic competition into the GTAP model', GTAP Technical Paper No. 6, Purdue University, available at: https://www.gtap.agecon.purdue.edu/resources/res_display.asp?RecordID=309.

Hertel, T.W., D. Hummels, M. Ivanic and R. Keeney (2007), 'How confident can we be in CGE-based analysis of free trade agreements?', *Economic Modelling*, **24**, 611–635.

Hertel, T.W., R. McDougall, B. Narayanan and A. Aguiar (2009), 'Behavioral parameters', in B. Narayanan and T.L. Walmsley (eds), *Global Trade Assistance and Protection: The GTAP 7 Data Base*, Center for Global Trade Analysis, Purdue University, available at: https://www.gtap.agecon.purdue.edu/data-bases/v7/v7_doco.asp.

Leiter, A.M., H. Oberhofer and P.A. Raschky (2009), 'Creative disasters? Flooding effects on capital, labour and productivity within European firms', *Environmental and Resource Economics*, **43**, 333–350.

Lin, X. and K.R. Polenske (1998), 'Input–output modeling of production processes for business management', *Structural Change and Economic Dynamics*, **9**, 205–226.

MacKenzie, C.A., J.R. Santos and K. Barker (2012), 'Measuring changes in international production from a disruption: case study of the Japanese earthquake and tsunami', *International Journal of Production Economics*, **138**, 293–302.

McDougall, R.A. (1993), 'Two small extensions to SALTER', SALTER Working Paper Series, No. 12, Canberra: Industry Commission.

Narayanan, G., A.A. Badri and R. McDougall (eds) (2012), *Global Trade, Assistance, and Production: The GTAP 8 Data Base*, Center for Global Trade Analysis, Purdue University.

Noy, I. and A. Nualsri (2007), 'What do exogenous shocks tell us about growth theories', SCCIE Working Paper Series, No. 07-16, Santa Cruz Center for International Economics, available at: http://sccie.ucsc.edu/.

Okuyama, Y. (2008), 'Critical review of methodologies on disaster impact estimation', mimeo, Global Facility for Disaster Risk Reduction, available at: http://gfdrr.org/sites/gfdrr.org/files/New%20Folder/Okuyama_Critical_Review.pdf.

Reimer, J.J. and T.W. Hertel (2004), 'Estimation of international demand behavior for use with input–output based data', *Economic Systems Research*, **16**, 347–366.

Rose, A. (2013), 'Macroeconomic consequences of terrorist attacks: estimation for the analysis of policies and rules', in V.K. Smith and C. Mansfield (eds), *Benefit Transfer for the Analysis of DHS Rules and Regulations*, Cheltenham, UK and Northampton, MA, USA: Edward Elgar.

Rose, A. and S. Liao (2005), 'Modeling resilience to disasters: computable general equilibrium analysis of a water service disruption', *Journal of Regional Science*, **45**, 75–112.

Rose, A. and D. Wei (2013), 'Estimating the economic consequences of a port shutdown: the special role of resilience', *Economic Systems Research*, **25**, 212–232.

Walmsley, T.L. and C. Carrico (2013), 'Disaggregating labor payments by skill level in GTAP', unpublished manuscript, Center for Global Trade Analysis.

Weingarden, A. and M. Tsigas (2010), 'Labor statistics for the GTAP database', presented at 13th Annual Conference on Global Economic Analysis Papers, Malaysia, Penang.

4. Global supply chains and natural disasters: implications for international trade*

Laura Puzzello and Paul Raschky

1. INTRODUCTION

Every once in a while news reports show the disastrous impact of natural disasters on local communities. In some cases, the losses in terms of property and lives are so big that economies struggle for months, sometimes years, before bouncing back. Local production is often affected and so is the transport of local goods to other areas. There are plenty of examples of such disasters in the 1990s and more recently: the Kobe Earthquake (Japan, 1995), the 921 earthquake (Taipei,China, 1999), Hurricanes Katrina and Rita (United States, 2004), the Japanese Great Tohoku earthquake and tsunami and the Thai floods (2011).[1] Anecdotal evidence suggests that the distinguishing feature of these recent disasters is the global scope of their effects. It is not uncommon for firms abroad to report production delays and profit losses because suppliers in source countries struck by natural disasters fail to provide parts in time. For example, the disruptions in the supply chain caused by the Great Tohoku earthquake and tsunami events in March 2011, not only forced Japanese car manufacturers to shut down their plants for a short period, but also resulted in temporary closures of a General Motors truck plant in the United States (US).[2] However, the question arises whether these global supply chain effects are just limited to a small group of extreme cases of disaster events, or are a more systematic feature of (large) natural disasters.

In this chapter we provide insights into this matter by examining the effect of disruptions to global supply chains due to natural disasters on countries' exports. Our focus is on natural disasters that have a "large" impact on the local population or economy. These, in fact, are the disasters whose extent is capable of delaying a country's production and exports, and, through supply linkages, of stretching across national borders.

In order to test whether large disasters affect countries' exports through input trade, we first construct measures of supply chain vulnerability to natural disasters. For each country and product, these measures capture the proportion of inputs provided by suppliers located in countries struck by at least one large natural disaster in a given year. We use input–output (IO) structures from the GTAP database and import data from Base pour l'analyse du commerce international (BACI) to calculate the total amount of each input, by origin country, used in the production of each good. We identify which inputs are produced in countries subject to large natural disasters in any given year using data from the International Disaster Database (EM-DAT).

Our measures of supply chain vulnerability capture interesting facts. For instance, we find that manufacturing products tend to have large shares of inputs exposed to natural disasters abroad, and small input shares exposed to domestic disasters. This is exactly what one would expect given the high incidence of input trade in the manufacturing sector. We also find that Asia and North America are the regions most vulnerable to large natural disasters both at home and abroad. That is consistent with the higher incidence of disasters in these regions and the key role they play in global production.

Our empirical results suggest that higher supply chain vulnerability to large natural disasters significantly reduces exports. Intuitively, this is because the production of goods with high supply chain vulnerability is more likely to be disrupted by large natural disasters. We also find that the negative effects on a country's exports of supply chain disruptions are bigger when large disasters happen at home. These results are robust to the identification of large disasters and disappear if one focuses on all natural disasters. We find that earthquakes, tsunamis and storms striking at home and floods abroad pose the biggest threat to global supply chains and trade. Our results further imply that more complex industries are relatively more resilient if supply shocks are due to large disasters hitting home, but not other supplier countries.

This chapter relates to a recent literature, which examines the effect of natural disasters on trade. Gassebner et al. (2010) estimate a gravity model to identify the causal effect on bilateral trade of disasters in either one of the trading countries. Their findings suggest that large disasters, whether natural or technological, decrease a country's exports, but not necessarily its imports. Countries' size and level of democracy turn out to be key determinants of the overall effect of disasters on trade. Andrade da Silva and Cernat (2012), using a gravity approach, find that domestic natural disasters affect most negatively the exports of small developing countries. Jones and Olken (2010) examine the effect of a country's weather on exports

growth, and find that higher temperatures reduce substantially the growth
of exports for poor countries, but not for rich countries. We add to this
strand of the literature by focusing on the effects on a country's exports of
large natural disasters occurring both at home and abroad, emphasizing
failures in supply chains as the potential transmission mechanism.

Our chapter also relates to a few studies that account for the international transmission of natural disasters through input trade. MacKenzie
et al. (2012) use a multiregional IO model to show that, following the
earthquake and tsunami of 2011 in Japan, the unavailability of Japanese
inputs decreased substantially both domestic and international production. Japanese output decreased the most in the transportation and office
equipment industries, which indirectly affected production in many service
and manufacturing sectors. Abroad, the People's Republic of China (PRC)
suffered, indirectly, the largest output losses. Despite these findings, the
authors conclude that, overall, other economies might have benefitted
from the Japanese disasters, as their production increased to substitute for
Japanese products both in the domestic markets and in Japan. Martin et
al. (2011) analyze the effect on the United Kingdom (UK) manufacturing
firms' productivity of extreme weather events at home and abroad. They
account for the fact that climate shocks abroad affect firms from both the
supply side, through input trade, and the demand side, through favorable
shifts in foreign consumer demand. They find evidence that importing
from countries experiencing exceptional heat decreases UK firms' productivity, while exporting to these destinations increases it. In contrast to both
these studies, we take a global perspective; our focus is on exports and the
transmission of natural disasters' effects through supply linkages.

The rest of the chapter is organized as follows. Section 2 presents some
facts on natural disasters, and discusses their potential to disrupt global
production and trade. Section 3 presents the estimating equation. Section
4 describes the data and provides details on our measures of supply chain
vulnerability. Section 5 discusses our estimates. Section 6 concludes.

2. NATURAL DISASTERS AND GLOBAL PRODUCTION: A FIRST LOOK AT THE DATA

In this section we use data from the EM-DAT database, collected by the
Centre for Research on Epidemiology of Disasters (CRED), to describe
the incidence of different types of disasters, and uncover the geographic
distribution of natural disasters, in general, and large-scale natural disasters, in particular. A disaster is recorded in the EM-DAT database if
at least one of the following occurs: (1) it kills at least ten people, (2) it

affects at least 100 people, (3) a state of emergency is declared, or (4) a call for international assistance is made. Natural disasters included in our analysis are listed in Table 4.1.[3] For each disaster, the EM-DAT database reports information on when the disaster happened, how long it lasted for, the number of people killed, the total number of people affected,[4] and the total amount of estimated damage in US dollars.

In this section we also verify whether key input suppliers in global production tend to be more often subject to natural disasters. Owing to data availability constraints, our analysis focuses on the period between 1995 and 2010.

2.1 On Natural Disasters

A natural disaster is an unforeseen natural phenomenon such as an earthquake, hurricane, or flood that causes extensive damage, destruction of properties and loss of lives. Between 1995 and 2010 the world experienced 5479 such disasters, which killed more than a million people and affected the lives of about 3.6 billion people. In the same period, natural disaster-related monetary losses tallied $1.5 trillion. Panel A in Table 4.1 reports detailed information on the number of people killed and affected, and the estimated damages related to each of the disaster types included in our sample. Panel B in Table 4.1 reports similar statistics for large natural disasters only. In the spirit of Gassebner et al. (2010) we classify a disaster as large if at least one of the following occurs: (1) it kills at least 1000 people, or (2) it affects at least 100 000 people in total, or (3) it causes damages worth at least one billion (2005) dollars.[5,6]

A glance at the first column of Table 4.1 reveals that floods and windstorms are the most frequent types of disasters and those classified as large disasters. They are also among the most costly and affect high numbers of people. The deadliest disasters, not surprisingly, are earthquakes and tsunamis. A very interesting implication of Table 4.1 is that, even though large disasters account for only 20 percent of all natural disasters, they are responsible for the vast majority of lives lost, people affected and economic costs due to natural disasters. This reinforces our belief that one is more likely to find any effect of disasters on a country's trade by considering supply chain disruptions caused by large disasters. Hence, from this point forward our discussion focuses on large natural disasters.

Table 4.2 reports statistics on the incidence and consequences of large natural disasters by country or region[7] in our sample. The 15 regions most often struck by large disasters are highlighted in grey. The country that experienced the highest number of large disasters between 1995 and 2010 is the PRC, which also reports the highest number of people killed and

Table 4.1   Incidence and consequences of natural disasters

Disaster type	Number	Number killed ('000)	Number affected (millions)	Estimated damages (2005 bn $)
Panel A All natural disasters, 1995–2010				
Drought	261	2.17	894.12	38.29
Earthquake	411	493.60	105.67	384.57
Extreme temperature	298	154.64	87.40	50.51
Flood	2 325	129.91	1 980.36	369.98
Insect infestation	23	0.00	0.50	0.27
Mass movement (Dry)	4	0.16	0.00	0.00
Mass movement (Wet)	73	4.56	2.51	1.29
Slides	238	11.67	2.91	2.72
Storm	288	145.76	74.98	105.03
Volcano	88	0.61	1.69	0.21
Wave/Surge	27	230.01	2.53	10.38
Wild fires	211	1.31	1.77	35.69
Wind storm	1 232	74.34	435.43	520.14
Total	5 479	1 248.75	3 589.87	1 519.08
Panel B Large natural disasters, 1995–2010				
Drought	154	2.04	892.78	31.53
Earthquake	80	488.98	102.62	373.89
Extreme temperature	33	134.98	86.93	48.92
Flood	431	96.71	1 959.39	321.23
Insect infestation	1	0.00	0.50	0.00
Mass movement (Dry)	0	0.00	0.00	0.00
Mass movement (Wet)	3	1.89	2.29	0.69
Slides	9	2.74	2.46	1.14
Storm	67	143.02	72.85	86.19
Volcano	5	0.53	0.92	0.16
Wave/Surge	6	228.32	2.39	8.15
Wild fires	15	0.57	1.51	30.13
Wind storm	235	60.02	429.49	462.20
Total	1 039	1 159.78	3 554.13	1 364.23

Note: A natural disaster is classified as large if at least one of the following occurs: (1) it kills at least 1 000 people, or (2) it affects at least 100 000 people, or (3) it causes damages for at least one billion (real) dollars.

Source: Authors' calculation using EM-DAT data.

Table 4.2   Regional incidence and consequences of large natural disasters (1995–2010)

	Number	Killed ('000)	Total affected (millions)	Total damages (2005 bn $)
Oceania				
Australia	11	0.21	1.57	14.48
New Zealand	1	0.00	0.30	5.87
Rest of Oceania	3	2.24	0.77	0.00
Asia				
People's Republic of China	174	115.58	2 044.57	280.36
Hong Kong, China	0	na	na	na
Japan	15	5.62	1.91	205.00
Korea, Rep. of	3	0.60	0.50	6.59
Rest of East Asia	14	1.05	14.78	30.10
Taipei,China	5	3.02	3.47	18.68
Rest of Southeast Asia	24	139.16	16.74	4.07
Indonesia	21	175.85	11.85	22.06
Sri Lanka	18	35.75	6.71	1.40
Malaysia	2	0.02	0.20	0.05
Philippines	69	10.57	68.90	3.46
Singapore	0	na	na	na
Thailand	23	9.73	59.08	2.16
Viet Nam	33	8.03	37.30	6.32
Bangladesh	37	5.87	104.32	10.30
India	78	76.03	757.65	32.40
Rest of South Asia	34	90.20	52.33	16.55
North America				
Canada	1	0.03	0.00	1.75
United States of America	69	3.40	23.59	397.78
Mexico	19	1.11	8.55	24.00
Rest of North America	0	na	na	na
South America				
Colombia	11	2.22	7.51	3.04
Peru	9	1.87	6.28	0.35
Venezuela	1	30.00	0.48	3.64
Rest of Andean Pact	9	0.22	2.07	1.36
Argentina	4	0.11	1.65	3.20
Brazil	13	0.55	16.26	4.59
Chile	4	0.60	3.14	27.35
Uruguay	1	0.00	0.12	0.04
Rest of South America	6	0.04	1.53	0.53

Table 4.2   (continued)

	Number	Killed ('000)	Total affected (millions)	Total damages (2005 bn $)
Rest of the Americas				
Central America	21	21.40	11.32	10.54
Rest of Free Trade Area of The Americas and Caribbean	23	228.52	16.76	34.65
Europe				
Austria	1	0.01	0.06	2.22
Belgium and Luxembourg	2	1.18	0.00	1.15
Denmark	2	0.01	0.00	4.30
Finland	0	na	na	na
France	10	21.10	4.03	29.46
Germany	6	9.41	0.43	19.16
United Kingdom	5	0.03	0.64	16.77
Greece	1	0.14	0.12	4.84
Ireland	0	na	na	na
Italy	4	20.42	0.14	21.33
Netherlands	2	1.00	0.25	1.45
Portugal	5	2.77	0.15	6.09
Spain	5	15.12	0.00	9.41
Sweden	1	0.01	0.00	2.80
Switzerland	3	1.06	0.00	4.12
Rest of EFTA	0	na	na	na
Rest of Europe	3	0.00	1.38	0.00
Albania	2	0.01	0.53	0.00
Bulgaria	0	na	na	na
Croatia	0	na	na	na
Cyprus	0	na	na	na
Czech Republic	2	0.05	0.30	2.19
Hungary	0	na	na	na
Malta	0	na	na	na
Poland	2	0.07	0.32	6.93
Romania	1	0.02	0.12	0.13
Slovakia	0	na	na	na
Slovenia	0	na	na	na
Estonia	0	na	na	na
Lithuania	0	na	na	na
Latvia	0	na	na	na
Russian Federation	11	58.00	2.68	5.35
Rest of Former Soviet Union	16	0.05	17.75	2.23

Table 4.2 (continued)

	Number	Killed ('000)	Total affected (millions)	Total damages (2005 bn $)
Middle East				
Turkey	9	18.50	5.42	33.22
Rest of Middle East	14	30.62	41.27	10.12
Africa				
Morocco	1	0.00	0.28	1.04
Tunisia	0	na	na	na
Rest of North Africa	1	2.27	0.21	5.31
South Africa (SA)	3	0.02	15.40	0.01
Malawi	7	0.57	9.75	0.01
Mozambique	17	1.03	10.72	0.55
Tanzania	3	0.00	5.15	0.00
Zambia	7	0.04	6.60	0.02
Zimbabwe	3	0.07	7.95	0.08
Rest of SA Development Community and Sub-Saharan Africa	104	5.15	126.51	0.63
Madagascar	13	1.07	5.97	0.38
Uganda	7	0.31	4.05	0.00
Botswana*	1	0.00	0.14	0.01
Rest of SA Custom Unions*	9	0.10	3.59	0.00
Total	*1039*	*1160*	*3554*	*1364*

Note: * = not included in the empirical analysis as unmatched in the trade data; na = not available.

Source: Authors' calculation using EM-DAT data.

affected by large natural disasters. Glancing over the table, other countries highly vulnerable to large natural disasters are in Asia (India, Philippines, Bangladesh, Viet Nam, Thailand, Indonesia, and Sri Lanka) and in North America (the US and Mexico). The US records the largest amount of estimated damages, followed by the PRC. In general, countries subject to a higher number of large disasters report higher numbers of people affected and estimated damages. The exception in this respect is Africa, where regions more vulnerable to disasters report higher numbers of people affected but not necessarily higher damages.[8]

Interestingly, the countries we found most vulnerable to large disasters are among the most active in the international trade of inputs (Baldwin and Lopez-Gonzales, 2013). To verify whether this correlation holds systematically in our data, we construct two measures of each supplier's importance in global production, using IO data from the GTAP database. The first measure we consider is the quantity of each supplier's inputs directly used in the production of one unit of world gross output, which we compute as follows:

$$\text{World per unit use of } j\text{'s inputs} = \sum_h \sum_i \frac{\sum_g B_{ji}(g, h)}{GO^W} \qquad (4.1)$$

Where $B_{ji}(g, h)$ is the amount of good g sourced by region j and used to produce one unit of country i's output of good h, and GO^W is the world's gross output. This quantity takes on larger values the more a region supplies to large producers in large sectors.[9] The second measure we construct captures the extent of a supplier's production network by counting the average number of destinations using each of that supplier's inputs.[10] Formally we compute:

$$\text{Average number of destinations per input of } j = \frac{1}{G} \sum_g \left[\sum_i I(B_{ji}(g) > 0) \right]$$

$$(4.2)$$

where $I(B_{ji}(g) > 0)$ takes on the value of 1 if region i uses input g from j in at least one sector, and G is the total number of inputs g. Figures 4.1 and 4.2 plot the quantities in (4.1) and (4.2), against the number of large natural disasters in the corresponding supplier region. For readability of the graphs all the quantities are averaged over the period 1995–2010, but results are similar if each year is considered separately. In both diagrams the relationship is positive. In other words, international suppliers that are large and that have more extended production networks tend to experience a larger number of large natural disasters. This implies that large natural disasters might pose a real threat to global production and trade through their disruptive effect on supply chains.

3.   EMPIRICAL MODEL

Natural disasters can be thought of as a combination of natural events and human activity. Worldwide, a large number of human settlements and production facilities are subject to at least one type of natural hazard exactly because the location chosen offers benefits to production and economic activities. For example, the primary sector heavily depends on access to freshwater for irrigation or direct access to the actual resource that is harvested (e.g. fisheries). Manufacturing plants are often located in

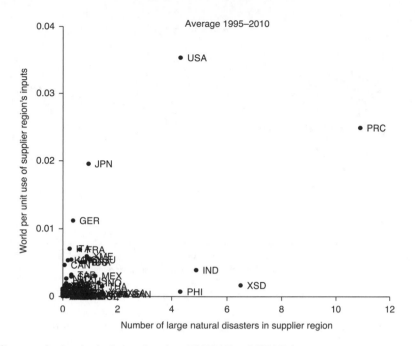

Source: Authors' calculations based on EM-DAT and GTAP data.

Figure 4.1   Suppliers' size and large natural disasters

the proximity of rivers because freshwater is used as an input factor (i.e., cooling) and riverine systems are used as a means of inland transport. Transport in general is a reason why the vast majority of today's urban agglomerations are either in coastal areas or next to riverine systems, making them vulnerable to floods, hurricanes or other climatic hazards.

More specifically, if a large disaster happens domestically, the production of exporting firms might be disrupted because of damage to physical capital and production facilities, or injuries to workers. Even firms whose production is not directly affected by the disaster might not be able to export because of the damage to domestic transport infrastructure.[11] Indeed, the destruction of roads or the temporary closure of ports can cause major export delays. If a large disaster happens abroad, the production of domestic exporting firms might be boosted or depressed depending on whether the foreign shock translates in higher or lower demand for their own products.

The existing literature on natural disasters and trade has explored the empirical relevance of these channels using information on the occurrence

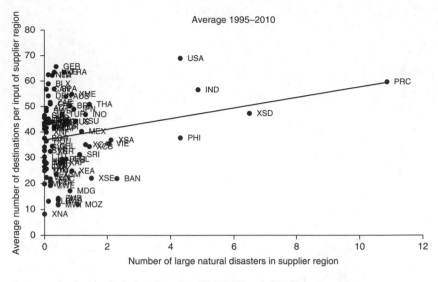

Source: Authors' calculations based on EM-DAT and GTAP data.

Figure 4.2   *Extent of suppliers' production network and large natural
                disasters*

of disasters at home or in partner countries. In contrast, our focus in this
chapter is on determining the effect on exports of disruptions to supply
chains due to large natural disasters. Independent of whether a large disaster happens at home or abroad, the production of a country's exporting
firms might be disrupted because inputs from domestic or foreign suppliers are received with delay, if at all. This might happen if domestic or
foreign suppliers are located in areas hit by the natural disaster, but also
if their suppliers or their suppliers' suppliers fail to provide (on time) key
inputs to production due to the disaster.

    In order to capture this additional transmission mechanism of disasters
on exports, we construct a measure of supply chain vulnerability, *SCV*,
which captures for each country, industry and year the share of inputs
directly and indirectly provided by suppliers located in countries hit by
large natural disasters. The intuition behind this measure is that exporters
that source a higher share of their inputs from suppliers located in areas hit
by disasters are more vulnerable and likely to experience production and
exports losses at any given point in time.

    Formally, to test the effect of large natural disasters on region i's
exports of good h, X_{ih}, we estimate the following equation:

$$\ln X_{iht} = \beta_1 SCV_{iht} + \beta_2 NLD_{it} + \beta_3 NLD^*_{iht} + \beta_4 \ln GDP_{it} + \beta_5 \ln GDPpc_{it}$$
$$+ \beta_6 \ln Remoteness_{it} + \beta_7 GATT_{it} + \varphi_h + \lambda_t + \varepsilon_{iht} \qquad (4.3)$$

where SCV_{iht} is a measure of vulnerability to large natural disasters of the supply chain of good h produced in region i; NLD_{it} is the number of large natural disasters occurred in i at time t; NLD^*_{iht} is good h's output weighted number of large natural disasters occurred abroad;[12] GDP_{it} and $GDPpc_{it}$ are i's GDP and GDP per-capita; $Remoteness_{it}$ is the trade-weighted distance of exporter i to its importers at time t; $GATT_{it}$ is a continuous variable that takes values between zero and one depending on the proportion of countries within a region that are GATT/WTO members at time t;[13] φ_h and λ_t denote industry fixed effects and time fixed effects.

We are mostly interested in the estimates of β_1. A negative coefficient indicates that countries with supply chains more vulnerable to large natural disasters tend to export less. In equation (4.3) we control for the number of large disasters that occurred at home and abroad to capture any effect of these events on trade through channels different from supply chain disruptions. Consistent with the literature, we expect β_2 to be negative. The estimates for β_3 might be positive if exporting firms benefit from disasters abroad by becoming relatively more competitive in the world market. But negative estimates for β_3 are plausible too: if large producers of good h abroad are affected by natural disasters, their demand for intra-industry inputs might decrease impacting negatively on country i's exports in that sector.

One should be cautious about the estimates of β_1 from (4.3) as they might be endogenous if variables correlated with SCV are omitted. For instance, large exporters might have a lot of domestic and international experience, which further strengthens their competitiveness. At the same time, they might be less vulnerable to large disasters if their experience allows them to better manage their supply chains. Omitting variables related to the experience of exporters induces a downward bias on β_1. In the same vein, large producers are often also large exporters. If large producers source relatively more of their inputs domestically, their supply chains might be systematically more vulnerable to large disasters because of their higher exposure to domestic natural hazards. In this case, omitting variables related to the size of exporters induces an upward bias on β_1. In our empirical analysis we carefully address this endogeneity issue. Reverse causation does not seem to be a problem in equation (4.3), as large natural disasters happen unexpectedly along the supply chain.

Our approach differs from that of previous studies on natural disasters and trade. Gassebner et al. (2010), and Andrade da Silva and Cernat (2012) estimate gravity models to explain the effect on bilateral trade of disasters. In addition to standard gravity controls, their specifications control for the incidence of disasters in the exporting country and importing country separately.[14] Jones and Olken (2010), instead, estimate the effect on the growth of a country's disaggregated exports of the temperature and precipitation in the exporting country. Even though the estimates from these studies capture the effect on trade of failures in the exporting or importing country's supply chains once disasters hit the domestic economy, this effect is not noted or modelled explicitly. More important, past studies ignore the fact that disasters hitting countries outside a trading pair can affect that pair's bilateral trade, as failures anywhere along the supply chain affect an exporter's ability to produce.

Before presenting the estimation results, the next section discusses the data, and provides details on the construction and features of our measures of supply chain vulnerability.

4.   THE DATA

In addition to the data on natural disasters we use trade data for the period 1995 to 2010 from the BACI World trade database. These data have been assembled by Gaulier and Zignano (2010) and made available online through the Centre d'Etudes Prospectives et d'Informations Internationales (CEPII). The BACI database provides disaggregated bilateral trade data for more than 200 countries. It increases the information available in the COMTRADE database by combining information reported by exporters and importers, and adjusting import values for estimated cost, insurance and freight (cif) rates.

Countries' domestic and import IO structures are taken from four different versions of the GTAP database: versions 5.4, 6, 7 and 8 with base years 1997, 2001, 2004, and 2007, respectively. Even though these versions of the database have the same sectoral disaggregation, the regional aggregation differs. We use the regional representation of version 6 to concord the data.[15] Regional IO coefficients between 1995 and 2000 are based on GTAP 5.4 for all the regions that have a match in GTAP 6; for the remaining regions we proxy the 1997 IO data with those available in GTAP 6. IO coefficients for 2001–2003, 2004–2006 and 2007–2010 are based on GTAP 6, 7 and 8, respectively.

The concordance of the BACI data with the GTAP sectoral and regional classifications leaves us with 44 sectors and 82 regions. A list of regions and sectors included in our analysis is reported in Appendix 4A.1.

Data for GDP and population are from the World Development Indicators (WDI). Each region's trade-weighted distance from its partners is constructed using bilateral distance measures from the CEPII. GATT membership data are from the CEPII gravity database.

4.1 Construction of a Measure of Supply Chain Vulnerability

The key variable in our analysis is an index of supply chain vulnerability (SCV) to natural disasters that is country and industry specific. To construct this index we first combine the GTAP IO tables with import data from BACI to determine the total amount of each input, by origin region, used in the production of each good. Using the EM-DAT data, we identify which inputs are produced in regions subject to large natural disasters at any given time.

In more detail, from the GTAP IO tables we obtain values for the amount of each domestic or imported input g directly employed in the production of one unit of each region i's good h. Let us denote these quantities by $B_{ji}(g, h)$ if input $g = 1, \ldots, G$ is sourced domestically, and by $B^*_i(g, h)$ if input g is imported. We then use the proportionality assumption, commonly adopted in the literature, to impute the distribution of IO import coefficients by source region $j = 1, \ldots, N$, in any given year. According to this assumption, if 10 percent of Chinese imports of steel are from Japan, then 10 percent of any Chinese sector's use of imported steel originates from Japan.[16] Formally, the amount of good g sourced by region $j = 1, \ldots, N$ and used to produce one unit of country i's output of good h, $B_{ji}(g, h)$, is imputed as follows:

$$B_{ji}(g, h) = \frac{M_{ij}(g)}{M_i(g)} * B^*_i(g, h) \text{ with } j \neq i \text{ and } j = 1, \ldots, N \quad (4.4)$$

where $M_{ij}(g)$ denotes the amount of good g region i imports from j, and $M_i(g)$ denotes region i's total imports of g. Let the matrix B be the $(NG \times NG)$ world input–output matrix collecting all the possible $B_{ji}(g, h)$.[17] The total amount of input region j's input g used in i's production of h, $A_{ji}(g, h)$, is obtained by taking the $ji - gh^{th}$ element of the Leontief inverse $A = (I - B)^{-1}$, where I is the $(NG \times NG)$ identity matrix.

Combining the elements in matrix A with the EM-DAT data, we construct, for each industry-region pair, the proportion of inputs potentially subject to large natural disasters at time t, SCV_{iht}, as follows:

$$SCV_{iht} = \sum_{j=1}^{N} \sum_{g=1}^{G} \frac{A_{jit}(g, h)}{A_{it}(h)} * I_{jt} \quad (4.5)$$

where $A_{it}(h)$ is the total per unit use of inputs in region i's sector h at time t, and I_{jt} is an indicator variable that takes on the value 1 if country j is subject to at least one large natural disaster in t.

The index in equation (4.5) can be further decomposed to account, separately, for a *SCV* to large natural disasters that happen at home or abroad. We define the *SCV* index to domestic disasters as:

$$SCV_{iht}^{home} = \sum_{g=1}^{G} \frac{A_{iit}(g,h)}{A_{it}(h)} * I_{it} \qquad (4.5a)$$

and the *SCV* to disasters abroad as:

$$SCV_{iht}^{*} = \sum_{j \neq i}^{N} \sum_{g=1}^{G} \frac{A_{jit}(g,h)}{A_{it}(h)} * I_{jt} \qquad (4.5b)$$

Panel A and Panel B of Figure 4.3 plot the distribution for the *SCV* indexes defined in (4.5), and (4.5a) and (4.5b), respectively. For legibility of the graph, the plots of Panel B exclude values of *SCV^home* and *SCV** equal to zero. Focusing on Panel A, there are two striking features of the *SCV* distribution: first, it is bimodal; second, more of its density is concentrated at the lower end of the support. A glance at Panel B shows that the bimodal nature of the *SCV* distribution is explained by the origin of the shock to the supply chains. A large domestic natural disaster potentially compromises the delivery of all domestic inputs used in the production of any given good. Given that domestic inputs constitute the largest share of total input purchases in any production process, *SCV* and *SCV^home* take on large values if a big disaster strikes at home. When the shock is due to natural disasters happening abroad a smaller share of total inputs is affected, so *SCV* and *SCV** take on small values. The higher concentration of the *SCV* distribution at the lower end of the support indicates that most often the origin of (potential) shocks to supply chains is foreign. This is further confirmed by the fact that *SCV^home* equals 0 in 67 percent of all possible 57 728 ($44 \times 82 \times 16$) industry-region-year combinations.

In order to explore the vulnerability of different sectors to large natural disasters, Figure 4.4 shows the *SCV* index distribution by aggregate product categories, with the 44 original sectors included in one of the following four categories: Food products, Manufacturing, Energy and Raw agriculture.[18] The *SCV* distributions are bimodal in each product category. Most interestingly, relative to the *SCV* distributions of other sectors, the manufacturing one is shifted to the right at the lower end of the support and to the left at the upper end of the support. This tells us that in the manufacturing sector, regions have a larger share of inputs that is exposed to natural disasters happening abroad. At the same time,

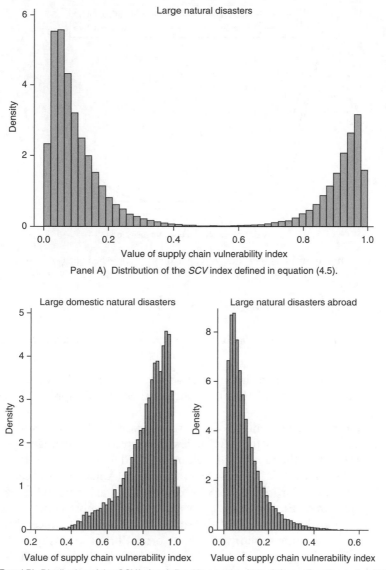

Panel A) Distribution of the *SCV* index defined in equation (4.5).

Panel B) Distribution of the *SCV* index defined in equation (4.5a, left panel) and equation (4.5b)

Note: In panel B, values of *SCV^{home}* and *SCV** equal to zero have been dropped for legibility of the plots.

Source: Authors' calculations based on EM-DAT and GTAP data.

Figure 4.3   Distribution of SCV indexes

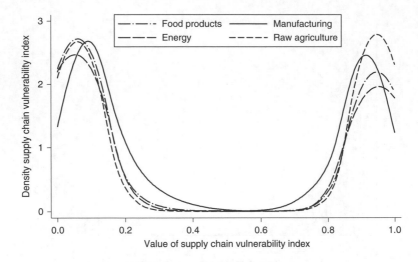

Note: Each industry-region observation is weighted by the corresponding export share in industry exports. The list of sectors included in each product category is reported in Appendix 4A.1.

Source: Authors' calculations based on EM-DAT and GTAP data.

Figure 4.4   Distribution of the SCV *index by aggregate product categories*

a lower percentage of their inputs is exposed to domestic disasters. Both findings are consistent with the higher incidence of global supply chains in manufacturing.

To explore the vulnerability of different regions to large natural disasters, Figure 4.5 shows the *SCV* index distribution by aggregate geographic areas, with the 82 original regions included in one of the following six areas: Oceania, Asia, North America, Other Americas, Africa and Middle East, and Europe.[19] The *SCV* distributions are bimodal in each geographic group. Europe stands out as having the most concentrated *SCV* density at the lower end of the support and the least concentrated at the upper end of the support. In other words, Europe is mostly vulnerable to disasters happening abroad. This is consistent with our findings in Table 4.2, which show countries in Europe were not struck by many large disasters during the sample period. Asia and North America, instead, are characterized by the highest values of the *SCV* density in the upper end of the support. This is consistent with the fact that many regions in Asia and North America received a high number of large disasters during the sample period. Interestingly, at the lower end of the support, the probability of *SCV* taking on relatively high values, between 0.2 and 0.5, is the

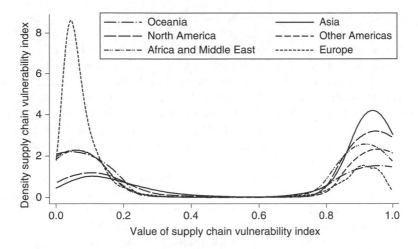

Note: Each industry-region observation is weighted by the corresponding export share in industry exports. The list of regions included in each geographical area is reported in Appendix 4A.1.

Source: Authors' calculations based on EM-DAT and GTAP data.

Figure 4.5   Distribution of the SCV *index by aggregate geographic areas*

highest in Asia and North America. Put another way, countries in Asia and North America are quite vulnerable to large disasters abroad as well. This is not surprising given that many of them are extensively involved in global production networks.[20]

5.   ESTIMATION RESULTS

5.1   Supply Chain Vulnerability and Exports

Table 4.3 reports the estimation results for equation (4.3). We report robust standard errors in parentheses, and standard errors clustered at the region-industry level in square brackets. The significance of our estimates is not affected by the residuals variance structure unless noted.

Focusing on Column (1) of Table 4.3, the estimates for the country-specific control variables are as expected when significant. Economically bigger and less remote regions tend to export more. However, a region's income per capita and its GATT membership status do not significantly affect its exports. The estimates for the weighted average number of disasters abroad, NLD^*, imply that a region's exports in a given sector decrease with the average number of large natural disasters experienced by other producers abroad. In other words, the benefits of weaker international competition are more than compensated by the loss of foreign intra-industry demand for domestic inputs. In contrast to the literature, the estimates for the number of large disasters at home, NLD, suggest that the greater the number of large natural disasters a country experiences, the higher its exports are. Consistent with our intuition, instead, the estimated coefficient for SCV is negative and significant, implying that the higher is the vulnerability of a supply chain to large natural disasters, the lower the corresponding exports.

To ensure that our estimates on SCV are not biased due to the omission of variables related to the experience and size of exporters, in Column (2) of Table 4.3 we add as control variables lagged values of the exporter's share in world trade and its size. Our estimate of the SCV coefficient is only slightly affected. This is not surprising if one considers that large exporters are big and potentially more experienced. While more experience allows exporters to improve their supply chain management, their size makes them rely relatively more on domestic inputs increasing their vulnerability to (domestic) natural disasters. These biasing effects almost cancel each other out. Interestingly, controlling for the exporter's share and size changes substantially all the other coefficients. While the magnitude of the GDP estimate shrinks, it turns out that richer regions and members of the GATT do export significantly more. The puzzling positive coefficient on NLD shown in Column (1) decreases in magnitude and becomes insignificant in Column (2). This finding put together with the fact that the estimate on SCV is not affected by the additional controls suggests that the main channel through which domestic disasters affect trade is through failures of producers' supply chains. The coefficient of NLD^* switches sign in Column (2), implying that the benefits of weaker foreign competition do, in fact, more than make up for the loss of foreign intra-industry demand for domestic inputs.

In Column (3) of Table 4.3 we control for annual changes in the trade weighted GDP of importers to ensure that the negative estimated effect of SCV on exports is not driven by changes in the demand for domestic goods from countries affected by large disasters. Our estimated effect of SCV on exports is robust to this addition.

In order to make sure our estimated effect of SCV on exports is not affected by any omitted region-time specific effect, we estimate a modified specification of equation (4.3) where all the region-time specific variables are replaced by region-time fixed effects. The last column of Table 4.3 shows our results. The size of the SCV coefficient increases in absolute value, implying that one standard deviation increase in SCV decreases

Table 4.3   Large natural disasters and exports

	(1)	(2)	(3)	(4)
Supply chain	−0.1333***	−0.1392***	−0.1403***	−0.6051***
vulnerability to large	(0.0326)	(0.0277)	(0.0278)	(0.1731)
disasters: SCV_{iht}	[0.0575]**	[0.0454]***	[0.0454]***	[0.2301]***
Number of large natural	0.0329***	0.0013	0.0014	
disasters at origin o:	(0.0060)	(0.0052)	(0.0052)	
NLD_{it}	[0.0159]**	[0.0128]	[0.0128]	
Gross output weighted	−0.1127***	0.0773***	0.0776***	0.0358**
average number of large	(0.0177)	(0.0163)	(0.0163)	(0.0177)
natural disasters abroad:	[0.0165]***	[0.0192]***	[0.0193]***	[0.0168]**
NLD^*_{iht}				
Income: GDP_{it}	0.9323***	0.2676***	0.2677***	
	(0.0074)	(0.0099)	(0.0099)	
	[0.0244]***	[0.0295]***	[0.0295]***	
Income per capita: $GDPpc_{it}$	0.0076	0.1504***	0.1509***	
	(0.0100)	(0.0093)	(0.0093)	
	[0.0334]	[0.0283]	[0.0282]***	
Log trade	−0.4473***	−0.4017***	−0.4015***	
weighted distance:	(0.0166)	(0.0146)	(0.0146)	
$\ln(Remoteness)_{it}$	[0.0567]***	[0.0457]***	[0.0457]***	
GATT membership:	−0.0375	0.2144***	0.2139***	
$GATT_{it}$	(0.0317)	(0.0281)	(0.0281)	
	[0.1029]	[0.0838]**	[0.0838]**	
Lag export share: $(\frac{X_{ih}}{X_h})_{t-1}$		19.6374***	19.6330***	19.6111***
		(0.5439)	(0.5439)	(0.8409)
		[1.7828]***	[1.7827]***	[1.9336]***
Lag gross output:		0.4841***	0.4844***	0.4896***
$GO_{ih,t-1}$		(0.0074)	(0.0074)	(0.0100)
		[0.0202]***	[0.0202]***	[0.0200]***
Change in weighted			−0.2249**	
income of importers: D			(0.0994)	
$\Delta WGDP\ importers_{it}$			[0.0715]***	
Industry fixed effects	Yes	Yes	Yes	Yes
Year fixed effects	Yes	Yes	Yes	No
Exporter-year fixed effects	No	No	No	Yes
R-squared	0.6494	0.7558	0.7558	0.7100
N	54 663	51 288	51 288	51 288

Note: Dependent variable is the log of country *i*'s exports of good *h* at time *t*: $\ln(X_{iht})$. Robust standard errors are in parentheses. Standard errors clustered by country-industry are in square brackets. *** Significant at the 1% level; ** significant at the 5% level; * significant at the 10% level.

Source: Authors' calculations based on data from the following databases: BACI, EM-DAT, GTAP, WDI and CEPII gravity.

exports by 21 percent. This is our preferred specification, which we refer to as baseline specification henceforth.

Table 4.4 reports the baseline results in Column (1). Column (2) of Table 4.4 displays the estimation results for the baseline specification with *SCV* split in SCV^{home} and *SCV**. This allows us to explore how sensitive exports are to supply chain disruptions due to large natural disasters at home and abroad, separately. We now find that, independent of the origin of disasters, higher supply chain vulnerability lowers exports. Specifically, we find that while a one standard deviation increase in SCV^{home} decreases exports by about 24 percent, a one standard deviation increase in *SCV** decreases exports by 4 percent. However, the latter estimate loses significance once standard errors are clustered at the region-industry level.

In sum, disruptions to supply chains due to large natural disasters decrease a country's exports, more so if these disasters strike at home.[21]

5.2   Impact of Natural Disasters, Supply Chain Vulnerability and Exports

Our focus so far has been on large natural disasters, as we believe not all natural disasters affect a country's production facilities or transport infrastructures to an extent capable of delaying production and affecting exports. To test this belief, we construct the *SCV* measures focusing on *all* natural disasters instead of on large natural disasters only. Columns (3) and (4) of Table 4.4 show how once we use these modified *SCV* measures supply chain vulnerability does not matter for trade.

One can argue that we fail to find any effect of *SCV* to *all* natural disasters, as we do not account for the impact of each disaster. We address this concern by constructing an alternative measure of vulnerability, *WSCI*, where we weight each input exposed to a natural disaster by a measure of that disaster's impact as follows:

$$WSCI_{iht} = \sum_{j=1}^{N} \sum_{g=1}^{G} \frac{A_{jit}(g,h)}{A_{it}(h)} * Impact_{jt}$$

with $Impact_{jt}$ being the simple average of the economic loss in GDP terms and the percentage of population affected associated to disasters hitting supplier j at time t.[22] We refer to this measure as supply chain weighted impact of all disasters, and we report results for our baseline specifications where we replace *SCV* with *WSCI* in Columns (5) and (6) of Table 4.4. Our estimates suggest that higher values for the supply chain weighted impact of natural disasters correspond to lower exports. In particular, one standard deviation increase in the supply chain weighted impact of all disasters, of all domestic disasters and of all disasters abroad decreases exports

Table 4.4 Impact of natural disasters and exports

	Large disasters	Large disasters	All disasters	All disasters			Large disasters	Large disasters
	(1)	(2)	(3)	(4)	(5)	(6)	(7)	(8)
Supply chain vulnerability to disasters: SCV_{iht}	−0.6051*** (0.1731) [0.2301]***		−0.0290 (0.2139) [0.3018]				−0.5192*** (0.1823) [0.2365]**	−0.5161*** (0.1826) [0.2359]**
Supply chain vulnerability to domestic disasters: SCV^{home}_{iht}		−0.7098*** (0.2023) [0.2827]**		−0.0819 (0.2263) [0.3077]				
Supply chain vulnerability to disasters abroad: SCV^{*}_{iht}		−0.4587** (0.1998) [0.3424]		−0.2526 (0.2211) [0.3590]				
Supply chain weighted impact of all disasters: $WSCI_{iht}$					−9.0718** (3.8231) [3.5805]**		−4.8020 (4.0172) [3.5028]	
Supply chain weighted impact of all domestic disasters: $WSCI^{home}_{iht}$						−8.2556* (4.2753) [4.5488]*		−4.2366 (4.4371) [4.5073]

133

Table 4.4 (continued)

	Large disasters (1)	Large disasters (2)	All disasters (3)	All disasters (4)	(5)	(6)	Large disasters (7)	Large disasters (8)
Supply chain weighted impact of all disasters abroad: $WSCI^{*}_{iht}$						−11.7993* (6.0889) [8.6744]		−6.8017 (6.2599) [8.5676]
Industry fixed effects	Yes	Yes	Yes	Yes	Yes	Yes	Yes	Yes
Exporter-year fixed effects	Yes	Yes	Yes	Yes	Yes	Yes	Yes	Yes
Other Controls	Yes	Yes	Yes	Yes	Yes	Yes	Yes	Yes
N	51 288	51 288	51 288	51 288	51 288	51 288	51 288	51 288
R-squared	0.7100	0.7098	0.7076	0.7081	0.7099	0.7099	0.7110	0.7109

Note: Dependent variable is the log of country i's exports of good h at time t: $\ln(X_{iht})$. The heading of each column refers to the disasters considered in calculating SCV for the relevant specification. All specifications include the following 'Other Controls': $(X_{iht}/X_{ht})_{t-1}$, $GO_{iht,t-1}$, and NLD^{*}_{iht}. Robust standard errors are in parentheses. Standard errors clustered by country-industry are in square brackets. *** Significant at the 1% level; ** significant at the 5% level; * significant at the 10% level.

Source: Authors' calculations based on data from the following databases: BACI, EM-DAT and GTAP.

by 17.0 percent, 21.0 percent and 2.6 percent, respectively. However, as shown in the last two columns of Table 4.4, these results lose significance as soon as we control for our original *SCV* measure, where only large disasters are considered. Put another way, not all natural disasters pose a real threat to global production and trade, but the large ones do.

Our *SCV* measures critically depend on the identification of large disasters. To this point we have identified large natural disasters based on non-normalized measures of impact. We do so following Gassebner et al. (2010), but recognize that the numbers of people affected or amount of damages have different implications for small and large countries or economies. So, in Table 4.5, we report estimates for our baseline specifications when the large disasters underlying our calculations are identified based on normalized measures of impact.

In Columns (3)–(4) of Table 4.5, we classify a disaster as large if at least one of the following occurs: (a) the number of people killed as a percentage of the population falls in the top 1 percent of the relevant empirical distribution; (b) the number of people affected as a percentage of the population falls in the top 10 percent of the relevant empirical distribution; (c) the economic damages as a percentage of GDP fall in the top decile of the damage to GDP distribution. Because data on economic damage are only available in a limited number of cases, in Columns (5)–(6) and (7)–(8) of Table 4.5 we define a disaster as large if it meets any of the conditions in (a) and (b), or if it generates economic damage as a percentage of GDP that falls in the top quintile and the top 5 percent of the damage to GDP distribution, respectively.[23]

Our estimates on the effect of *SCV* on exports are robust to the alternative definitions even though they tend to become smaller and weaker.[24] Across Table 4.5, a one standard deviation increase in *SCV* is estimated to decrease exports by between 13 percent and 17 percent. A one standard deviation in the supply chain vulnerability to large domestic disasters and to large disasters abroad decreases exports by between 15 and 24 percent, and 0 and 4 percent, respectively. If one considers that when a large disaster hits home, on average about 80 percent of all input purchases are affected, our estimates imply decreases in exports by between 27 percent and 43 percent.

In conclusion, large disasters, independent of how we define them, are detrimental to a country's trade, especially when they strike at home.

5.3 Supply Chain Vulnerability and Exports: Additional Results

The effect of a natural disaster on a country's exports through supply linkages might vary depending on the number of inputs used in the production

Table 4.5 *Large natural disasters and exports: robustness to alternative definitions of large disasters*

	Baseline		Bin 1		Bin 2		Bin 3	
	(1)	(2)	(3)	(4)	(5)	(6)	(7)	(8)
Supply chain vulnerability to large disasters: SCV_{iht}	−0.6051*** (0.1731) [0.2301]***		−0.3409* (0.1743) [0.1762]*		−0.3739** (0.1671) [0.1964]*		−0.4998*** (0.1875) [0.2145]**	
Supply chain vulnerability to domestic large disasters: SCV^{home}_{iht}		−0.7098*** (0.2023) [0.2827]**		−0.3929** (0.1851) [0.2151]*		−0.4993*** (0.1824) [0.2174]**		−0.4769** (0.1995) [0.2542]*
Supply chain vulnerability to large disasters abroad: SCV^{*}_{iht}		−0.4587** (0.1998) [0.3424]		−0.2146 (0.2246) [0.3265]		−0.1866 (0.1897) [0.3101]		−0.5781** (0.2611) [0.3866]
Industry fixed effects	Yes	Yes	Yes	Yes	Yes	Yes	Yes	Yes
Exporter-year fixed effects	Yes	Yes	Yes	Yes	Yes	Yes	Yes	Yes
Other Controls	Yes	Yes	Yes	Yes	Yes	Yes	Yes	Yes
N	51288	51288	51288	51288	51288	51288	51288	51288
R-squared	0.7100	0.7098	0.7092	0.7094	0.7066	0.7064	0.7108	0.7106

Note: Dependent variable is the log of country *i*'s exports of good *h* at time *t*: $\ln(X_{iht})$. All specifications include the following 'Other Controls': $(X_{ih}/X_h)_{t-1}, GO_{iht-1}$, and NLD^{*}_{iht}. In Bin 1, a natural disaster is classified as large if it causes damages as a percentage of GDP in the top decile of the damage to GDP distribution, or the number of people killed as a percentage of the population falls in the top 1 percent of the relevant empirical distribution, or the number of people affected as a percentage of the population falls in the top decile of the relevant empirical distribution. The conditions for a disaster to be considered large in Bin 2 and 3 are the same as in Bin 1 except that it must cause damage as a percentage of GDP in the top quintile and top 5 percent of the damage to GDP distribution, respectively. Robust standard errors are in parentheses. Standard errors clustered by country-industry are in square brackets. *** Significant at the 1% level; ** significant at the 5% level; * significant at the 10% level.

Source: Authors' calculations based on data from the following databases: BACI, EM-DAT and GTAP.

136

of the goods being traded, i.e., on goods' complexity. As the number of inputs used in production goes up, the higher are the chances of at least a supplier's failure. However, depending on whether inputs are complements or substitutes the same supplier's failure has, respectively, a large or a small impact on production and trade.

To explore whether more complex goods are more or less vulnerable to large disasters, we augment our baseline specifications with both a measure of complexity that is region and industry specific, and its interaction with our measures of supply chain vulnerability to large disasters. We calculate complexity in two ways using the GTAP IO data. First, we count the number of distinct inputs used in production of each good. Higher numbers correspond to more complex goods. Second, we construct the Herfindahl-Hirschman Index (HHI) of input purchases for each exported good. In this case, higher numbers imply more concentrated input purchases and lower complexity. Columns (1)–(2) and (3)–(4) in Table 4.6 display our estimates when the count of inputs and the HHI are used as a measure of complexity, respectively.

The estimates on the interaction term in Columns (1) and (3) suggest that exports of more complex goods are less vulnerable to large natural disasters. This is consistent with recent literature, which supports that more complex production chains cope better with shocks and their production is less volatile (Koren and Tenreyro, 2013; Krishna and Levchenko, forthcoming).

In Columns (2) and (4), we explore whether the effect of the interaction between a good's complexity and its vulnerability to large disasters depends on whether a disaster happens at home or abroad. The estimates in Column (4) are the most robust and imply that exports of more complex goods are less vulnerable to large natural disasters at home, but more vulnerable to natural disasters abroad. These findings imply that domestically sourced inputs are relatively easy to substitute but imported inputs are not.

The last set of results, in Table 4.7, explores a supply chain's vulnerability to large disasters by the category of the disaster. We distinguish two main categories of disasters: geological and climatic. The former includes: earthquakes, mass movements (wet and dry), slides, volcano eruptions and tsunamis. The latter consists of: floods, storms, droughts, wild fires and extreme temperature.

The results in Column (1) of Table 4.7 suggest that large disasters of climatic origin do threaten global production chains and trade. To explore further the effect of climatic disasters on exports through supply linkages, in Column (2) we analyze the effect of *SCV* to large floods and storms, separately. According to our estimates a one standard deviation increase

Table 4.6   Large natural disasters, exports and complexity

	Count distinct inputs (1)	Count distinct inputs (2)	HHI of input purchases (3)	HHI of input purchases (4)
Supply chain vulnerability to large disasters: SCV_{iht}	−1.2491*** 0.4352 [0.5192]**		−0.4880*** (0.1695) [0.2429]**	
Supply chain vulnerability to domestic large disasters: SCV_{iht}^{home}		−1.2776*** (0.4631) [0.5844]**		−0.6233*** (0.1951) [0.2853]**
Supply chain vulnerability to large disasters abroad: SCV_{iht}^{*}		−3.6057*** (1.3147) [2.1726]*		−2.0745*** (0.3441) [0.6454]***
Complexity: $Compl_{iht}$	−0.0137*** (0.0046) [0.0169]*	−0.0210*** (0.0059) [0.0094]**	0.2757*** (0.0712) [0.1507]*	−0.0277 (0.0861) [0.1839]
Interaction SCV with Complexity: $SCV_{iht}*Compl_{iht}$	0.0153* (0.0089) [0.0105]		−0.4084*** (0.1223) [0.2259]*	
Interaction SCV^{home} with Complexity: $SCV_{iht}^{home}*Compl_{iht}$		0.0129 (0.0091) [0.0112]		−0.4916*** (0.1255) [0.2296]**
Interaction SCV^{*} with Complexity: $SCV_{iht}^{*}*Compl_{iht}$		0.0791** (0.0318) [0.0528]		2.8226*** (0.5233) [1.0179]***
Industry fixed effects	Yes	Yes	Yes	Yes
Exporter-year fixed effects	Yes	Yes	Yes	Yes
Other controls	Yes	Yes	Yes	Yes
N	51 288	51 288	51 288	51 288
R-squared	0.7098	0.7096	0.7099	0.7094

Note: Dependent variable is the log of country i's exports of good h at time t: $\ln(X_{iht})$. The heading of each column refers to the measure of complexity considered in the relevant specification. All specifications include the following 'Other Controls': $(X_{ih'}/X_h)_{t-1}, GO_{ih,t-1}$, and NLD_{iht}^{*}. Robust standard errors are in parentheses. Standard errors clustered by country-industry are in square brackets. *** Significant at the 1% level; ** significant at the 5% level; * significant at the 10% level.

Source: Authors' calculations based on data from the following databases: BACI, EM-DAT and GTAP.

in a *SCV* to floods and storms decreases exports by 12 percent and 20 percent, respectively.

Finally, the last two columns of Table 4.7 display the estimated effect on exports of a supply chain's vulnerability to large disasters striking at home and abroad, separately, by disasters category. Higher supply chain vulnerability to both large geological disasters and storms hitting home leads to lower exports, while only higher supply chain vulnerability to large floods abroad lowers export.

Table 4.7 Types of large natural disasters and exports

	(1)	(2)	(3)	(4)
SCV to large geo disasters: $SCVgeo_{iht}$	−0.4513 (0.3149) [0.3534]	−0.3155 (0.3231) [0.3471]		
SCV to large climatic disasters: $SCVclim_{iht}$	−0.4861*** (0.1759) [0.2258]**			
SCV to large floods: $SCVflood_{iht}$		−0.3942* (0.2042) [0.2611]		
SCV to large storms: $SCVstorm_{iht}$		−0.7456*** (0.2486) [0.3215]**		
SCV to domestic large geo disasters: $SCVgeo_{iht}^{home}$			−1.1129** (0.4404) [0.3976]***	−1.0028** (0.4255) [0.3952]**
SCV to large geo disasters abroad: $SCVgeo_{iht}^{*}$			0.2257 (0.4121) [0.4919]	0.1695 (0.4202) [0.4653]
SCV to domestic large climatic disasters: $SCVclim_{iht}^{home}$			−0.5147** (0.2101) [0.2864]*	
SCV to domestic large floods: $SCVflood_{iht}^{home}$				−0.1780 (0.2442) [0.3320]
SCV to domestic large storms: $SCVstorm_{iht}^{home}$				−1.5375*** (0.3134) [0.4230]***
SCV to large climatic disasters abroad: $SCVclim_{iht}^{*}$			−0.4617** (0.2106) [0.3325]	
SCV to large floods abroad: $SCVflood_{iht}^{*}$				−1.0301*** (0.2995) [0.4270]**

Table 4.7   (continued)

	(1)	(2)	(3)	(4)
SCV to large storms abroad: $SCVstorm^{*}_{iht}$				0.4472 (0.3199) [0.4898]
Industry fixed effects	Yes	Yes	Yes	Yes
Exporter-year fixed effects	Yes	Yes	Yes	Yes
Other controls	Yes	Yes	Yes	Yes
N	51 288	51 288	51 288	51 288
R-squared	0.7094	0.7071	0.7058	0.6958

Note: Dependent variable is the log of country i's exports of good h at time t: $\ln(X_{iht})$. All specifications include the following 'Other Controls': $(X_{ih}/X_{h})_{t-1}$, $GO_{ih,t-1}$, and NLD^{*}_{iht}. Robust standard errors are in parentheses. Standard errors clustered by country-industry are in square brackets. *** Significant at the 1% level; ** significant at the 5% level; * significant at the 10% level.

Source: Authors' calculations based on data from the following databases: BACI, EM-DAT and GTAP.

6. CONCLUSIONS

This chapter estimates the effect of large natural disasters on countries' exports, emphasizing failures in supply chains as the potential transmission mechanism. We construct supply chain vulnerability measures that capture, for each country, industry and year, the share of inputs provided by suppliers located in countries hit by large natural disasters. We find robust evidence that higher levels of *SCV* imply significantly lower exports, especially so when large disasters happen at home. Domestic large disasters that affect a country's supply chains and its trade include earthquakes, tsunamis and storms. Foreign large disasters that pose the biggest threat to global supply chains and trade include floods.

Our findings are problematic given that countries that are subject to large disasters frequently include the PRC, the US, India and other Asian countries, which are key players in global production networks. On a brighter note, our results also suggest that not all natural disasters pose a threat to international trade, but the large ones do.

We find evidence that more complex industries are more resilient to supply chain shocks due to large disasters at home but not abroad. Recent studies show that developing countries tend to specialize in low-complexity, high-volatility goods. Thus, our results imply that large domestic natural disasters contribute to the higher volatility of production in developing countries through disruptions of supply chains. Importing inputs might increase volatility further if international suppliers are located in regions vulnerable to disasters.

On the one hand, direct disaster damage to physical assets, infrastructure and human lives could be reduced by increased investment in appropriate protective measures (i.e., dikes). However, due to diminishing returns to investment in protection against natural disasters, technological constraints and limited public funds, it is very often not feasible to provide protection against certain types of large-scale disasters for all exposed production facilities, infrastructure and people. On the other hand, financial risk-transfer (i.e., insurance) can compensate for the financial damages to physical assets and infrastructure. While financial risk-transfer provides necessary liquidity for rebuilding and repairing damaged assets, it cannot prevent the actual destruction of production facilities and the resulting disruptions in the supply chain. At its best, it can speed up the recovery period and decrease the length of the supply chain disruptions. Considering the limited potential of traditional risk-management methods to mitigate supply chain effects of natural disasters, an alternative could be a greater geographical diversification of suppliers, multiple sourcing and changes in stock-management.

NOTES

* We would like to thank David Hummels, Benno Ferrarini, Pedro Gomis-Porqueras, and participants of the ADB Global Supply Chain Conference for helpful comments and suggestions.
1. See Sherin and Bartoletti (2000) and Kumins and Bamberger (2005) for discussions related to the disruptive effects of the Taipei,China 921 earthquake, and hurricanes Katrina and Rita, respectively.
2. See 'Lacking parts, G.M. will close plant', New York Times, 17 March 2011.
3. The database records both natural and technological disasters. Technological disasters include industrial, transport and miscellaneous accidents. Our data cover technological disasters only between 1995 and 2007, so we exclude them from our analysis. We believe this does not affect our results for two main reasons. First, the correlation between the number of natural disasters and the number of technological disasters at the regional level is very high (0.85). Second, even though between 1995 and 2007 there were 3716 technological disasters, only 12 of them were *large*. Following Gassebner et al. (2010) we also exclude epidemics from our analysis. In contrast with the rest of the disasters we consider, the extent of epidemics can be contained as people avoid contact.
4. The total number of affected people include those people injured in the disaster and medically treated, people needing assistance for shelter/homeless, and people requiring immediate assistance during the period of emergency (these include people displaced or evacuated).
5. Because our definition of large natural disasters uses multiple criteria, we are able to identify large-scale disasters happening both in developed countries (where the

      economic damage is high) and developing countries (where the economic damage is not as high, if reported at all, but where many lives are affected or lost).

6.   We choose this definition of large disasters following the related literature. In Section 5.2 we discuss alternative definitions of large disasters, which take into consideration normalized measures of a disaster's impact.

7.   We use the term country and region interchangeably in the text, as our sample consists of both single countries and aggregated regions. See Appendix 4A.1 for details on the regional aggregation.

8.   This is mostly explained by missing data for estimated damages in Africa.

9.   This is evident if one notes that

$$\sum_h \sum_i \frac{\sum_g B_{ji}(g,h)}{GO^W} = \sum_h \sum_i \frac{GO^W(h)}{GO^W} \frac{GO_i(h)}{GO^W(h)} \frac{B_{ji}(h)}{GO_i(h)},$$

where $GO_i(h)$ is country i's output in sector h. Calculating (4.1) using total instead of direct input uses does not affect the results, which are available upon request to the authors.

10. One could also compute the average number of distinct region-industry pairs using each of a supplier's inputs. However, because, as detailed in section 4, we use the proportionality assumption to split import IO structures by source country, calculating that would not provide additional insights.

11. Disentangling the impact of disasters on supply chains into the effect of destroyed production capacity and destroyed transport infrastructure is difficult because of data limitations. With the exception of a few well-studied cases, data collections of natural disaster events, if at all, only contain estimates about the total damage, but do not distinguish between damage to plants and infrastructure.

12. Technically, NLD^*_{iht} is given by: $\sum_{j \neq i} \frac{GO_j(h)}{GO^W(h)} * (NLD_{jt})$, where $GO_j(h)$ and $GO^W(h)$ are region j and the world gross output of good h, and NLD_{ji} is the number of large disasters occurred in j at time t.

13. At the country level $GATT_{jt}$ can only take values zero and one.

14. Gassebner et al. (2010) use the number of disasters in the exporting and the importing country, separately, as controls. In their preferred specifications both measures are normalized by the relevant country's land area. Andrade da Silva and Cernat (2012) control for the occurrence of specific natural disasters in the exporting country only using a dummy variable.

15. There are two reasons why we do not use the regional aggregation of version 5.4. First, France and the US would be included in an aggregate 'Rest of the World' (ROW). Second, Asia has a better country disaggregation in GTAP version 6. Given the importance of France and the US in world trade, and the incidence of disasters and production networks in Asia we believe that the regional disaggregation in GTAP version 6 improves our identification.

16. See Winkler and Milberg (2009), Puzzello (2012), and Feenstra and Jensen (2012) for assessments of the proportionality assumption.

17. The elements of the world matrix B are important for three interrelated strands of the literature. The first calculates the factor content of trade in the presence of international differences in production techniques and trade in inputs (Reimer, 2006; Trefler and Zhu, 2010; Puzzello, 2012). The second aims to quantify the extent of global production networks and their effect on an economy's wage structure (Hummels et al. 2001; Feenstra and Hanson, 1996, 1999). The third examines the value added content of trade, which depends on a country's participation in global production chains, and direct and indirect absorption of domestic output (Johnson and Noguera, 2012).

18. Appendix 4A.1 lists the sectors included in each of the four product categories.

19. Appendix 4A.1 lists the regions included in each of the six geographical areas.

20. Changes in the SCV index over time can occur because of changes in either the input use or the incidence of large natural disasters across supplier regions. Empirically, changes

in *SCV* turn out to be explained mostly by changes in the incidence of disasters across supplier regions between years. If in two consecutive years a country is either hit or not hit by a large disaster changes in *SCV* are explained almost completely by changes in the incidence of disasters in foreign suppliers' countries. In all other cases, big switches in our *SCV* measure are observed and depend almost entirely on the change in the incidence of disasters at home.

21. Any particular exporter or year does not drive these results. Estimates for the baseline specifications when observations for either an exporter or a year are dropped are available upon request.
22. We do not measure impact only using the percentage of population affected because doing so would understate the impact of disasters in wealthy countries where, typically, the number of people affected is small but the reported economic damage is large and more likely to be reported.
23. The conclusions drawn from Tables 4.1 and 4.2, and Figures 4.1–4.5 hold independent of the definition of large disasters, with two main exceptions. First, as we increase the cutoff for the damage to the GDP distribution, the number of large disasters in the richer countries decreases. Second, the correlation in Figure 4.2 becomes flatter and insignificant.
24. Given that the presence of rich countries varies across Bins, the findings imply our *SCV* estimates are robust to the exclusion of large disasters in rich countries.

REFERENCES

Andrade da Silva, J., and L. Cernat (2012), 'Coping with loss: the impact of natural disasters on developing countries' trade flows', Trade Chief Economist Note – European Commission, **1**.

Baldwin, R., and J. Lopez-Gonzalez (2013), 'Supply-chain trade: a portrait of global patterns and several testable hypotheses', NBER Working Paper Series, No. 18957.

Feenstra, R.C., and G.H. Hanson (1996), 'Globalization, outsourcing and wage inequality', *American Economic Review*, **86**, 240–245.

Feenstra, R.C., and G.H. Hanson (1999), 'The impact of outsourcing and high-technology capital on wages: estimates from the United States, 1979–1990', *Quarterly Journal of Economics*, **114**, 907–940.

Feenstra, R.C., and J.B. Jensen (2012), 'Evaluating estimates of materials offshoring from US manufacturing', *Economics Letters*, **117**, 170–173.

Gassebner, M., A. Keck, and R. Teh (2010), 'Shaken, not stirred: the impact of disasters on international trade', *Review of International Economics*, **18**, 351–368.

Gaulier, G., and S. Zignano (2010), 'BACI: International trade database at the product-level, the 1994–2007 version', CEPII Working Paper Series, No. 23.

Hummels, D.L., J. Ishii, and K.-M. Yi (2001), 'The nature and growth of vertical specialization in world trade', *Journal of International Economics*, **54**, 75–96.

Johnson, R.C., and G. Noguera (2012), 'Accounting for intermediates: production sharing and trade in value added', *Journal of International Economics*, **86**, 224–236.

Jones, B., and B.A. Olken (2010), 'Climate shocks and exports', *American Economic Review: Papers and Proceedings*, **100**, 454–459.

Koren, M., and S. Tenreyro (2013), 'Technological diversification', *American Economic Review*, **103**, 378–414.

Krishna, P., and A. Levchenko (forthcoming), 'Complexity, comparative advantage and volatility', *Journal of Economic Behavior and Organization*.

Kumins, L., and R. Bamberger (2005), 'Oil and gas disruptions from hurricanes Katrina and Rita', Congressional Research Report for Congress.

MacKenzie, C.A., J.R. Santos, and K. Barker (2012), 'Measuring changes in international production from a disruption: case study of the Japanese earthquake and tsunami', *International Journal of Production Economics*, **138**, 293–302.

Martin, R., M. Muûls, and A. Ward (2011), 'The sensitivity of UK manufacturing firms to extreme weather events', mimeo.

Puzzello, L. (2012), 'A proportionality assumption and measurement biases in the factor content of trade', *Journal of International Economics*, **87**, 105–111.

Reimer, J.J. (2006), 'Global production sharing and trade in the services of factors', *Journal of International Economics*, **68**, 384–408.

Sherin, B., and S. Bartoletti (2000), 'Taiwan's 921 quake and what it means to the semiconductor industry', available at http://www.semiconductorsafety.org/proceedings00/sherinbrian.pdf.

Trefler, D., and S.C. Zhu (2010), 'The structure of factor content predictions', *Journal of International Economics*, **82**, 195–207.

Winkler, D., and W. Milberg (2009), 'Errors from the "proportionality assumption" in the measurement of offshoring: application to German labor demand', SCEPA Working Paper Series, No. 2009–12.

APPENDIX 4A.1   REGIONAL AND SECTORAL AGGREGATION

The concordance of BACI data with the GTAP sectoral and regional classifications leaves us with 82 regions and 44 sectors. We list them below.

Region Aggregation

Oceania
AUS (Australia, Cocos Islands, Christmas Island, Heard Island and McDonald Island), NZL (New Zealand), XOC (Rest of Oceania: American Samoa, Cook Islands, Fiji, Micronesia Federated States of, Guam, Kiribati, Marshall Islands, Northern Mariana Islands, New Caledonia, Niue, Nauru, Palau, Papua New Guinea, French Polynesia, Solomon Islands, Tokelau, Tonga, Tuvalu, Vanuatu, Wallis and Futuna, Samoa, and United States Minor Outlying Islands);

Asia
PRC (People's Republic of China), HKG (Hong Kong, China), JPN (Japan), KOR (Republic of Korea), XEA (Rest of East Asia: Mongolia, Korea, Democratic People's Republic of, Macao), TAP (Taipei,China), XSE (Rest of Southeast Asia: Brunei Darussalam, Cambodia, Lao People's Democratic Republic, Myanmar, Timor-Leste), INO (Indonesia), MAL (Malaysia), PHI (Philippines), SIN (Singapore), THA (Thailand), VIE (Viet Nam), BAN (Bangladesh), IND (India), SRI (Sri Lanka), XSA (Rest of South Asia: Afghanistan, Bhutan, Maldives, Nepal, Pakistan);

North America
CAN (Canada), USA (United States of America), MEX (Mexico), XNA (Rest of North America: Bermuda, Greenland, Saint Pierre and Miquelon);

Other Americas
COL (Colombia), PER (Peru), VEN (Venezuela), XAP (Rest of Andean Pact: Bolivia, Ecuador), ARG (Argentina), BRA (Brazil), CHL (Chile), URY (Uruguay), XSM (Rest of South America: Falkland Islands, French Guiana, Guyana, Paraguay, Suriname), XCA (Central America: Belize, Costa Rica, El Salvador, Guatemala, Honduras, Nicaragua, Panama), XCB (Rest of Free Trade Area of the Americas and Rest of the Caribbean: Antigua and Barbuda, Bahamas, Barbados, Dominica, Dominican Republic, Grenada, Haiti, Jamaica, Puerto Rico, Saint Kitts and Nevis, Saint Lucia, Saint Vincent and the Grenadines, Trinidad and Tobago,

Virgin Islands – US; Anguilla, Aruba, Cayman Islands, Cuba, Montserrat, Netherlands Antilles, Turks and Caicos, Virgin Islands – British);

Europe
AUT (Austria), BLX (Belgium and Luxembourg), DEN (Denmark), FIN (Finland), FRA (France), GER (Germany), UKG (United Kingdom), GRC (Greece), IRE (Ireland), ITA (Italy), NET (Netherlands), POR (Portugal), SPA (Spain), SWE (Sweden), SWI (Switzerland), XEF (Rest of Efta: Iceland, Liechtenstein, Norway), XER (Rest of Europe: Andorra, Bosnia and Herzegovina, Faroe Islands, Gibraltar, Macedonia, the former Yugoslav Republic of, Monaco, San Marino, Serbia and Montenegro), ALB (Albania), BGR (Bulgaria), HRV (Croatia), CYP (Cyprus), CZE (Czech Republic), HUN (Hungary), MLT (Malta), POL (Poland), ROU (Romania), SVK (Slovakia), SVN (Slovenia), EST (Estonia), LVA (Latvia), LTU (Lithuania), RUS (Russian Federation), XSU (Rest of Former Soviet Union: Armenia, Azerbaijan, Belarus, Georgia, Kazakhstan, Kyrgyz Republic, Moldova, Republic of, Tajikistan, Turkmenistan, Ukraine, Uzbekistan), TUR (Turkey);

Africa and Middle East
XME (Rest of Middle East: Bahrain, Iran, Iraq, Israel, Jordan, Kuwait, Lebanon, Oman, Palestinian Territory, Occupied, Qatar, Saudi Arabia, Syrian Arab Republic, United Arab Emirates, Yemen), MAR (Morocco), TUN (Tunisia), XNF (Rest of North Africa: Algeria, Egypt, Libyan Arab Jamahiriya), ZAF (South Africa), MWI (Malawi), MOZ (Mozambique), TZA (Tanzania), ZMB (Zambia), ZWE (Zimbabwe), XSD (Rest of Southern African Development Community and Rest of Sub-Saharan Africa: Angola, Congo, the Democratic Republic of the, Mauritius, Seychelles; Benin, Burkina Faso, Burundi, Cameroon, Cape Verde, Central African Republic, Chad, Comoros, Congo, Cote d'Ivoire Djibouti, Equatorial Guinea, Eritrea, Ethiopia, Gabon, Gambia, Ghana, Guinea, Guinea-Bissau, Kenya, Liberia, Mali, Mauritania, Mayotte, Niger, Nigeria, Rwanda, Saint Helena, Sao Tome and Principe, Senegal, Sierra Leone, Somalia, Sudan, Togo), MDG (Madagascar), UGA (Uganda), BWA (Botswana), XSC (Rest of South African Customs Union: Lesotho, Namibia, Swaziland).

Sector Aggregation

Raw agriculture
PDR (Paddy rice), WHT (Wheat), GRO (Cereal grains not elsewhere classified (nec, henceforth)), V_F (Vegetables, fruit, nuts), OSD (Oil seeds),

C_B (Sugar cane, sugar beet), PFB (Plant-based fibers), OCR (Crops nec), CTL (Bovine cattle, sheep and goats, horses), OAP (Animal products nec), RMK (Raw milk), WOL (Wool, silk-worm cocoons), FOR (Forestry), FSH (Fishing);

Food products
OMN (Minerals nec), CMT (Bovine meat products), OMT (Meat products nec), VOL (Vegetable oils and fats), MIL (Dairy products), PCR (Processed rice), SGR (Sugar), OFD (Food products nec), B_T (Beverages and tobacco products);

Manufacturing
TEX (Textiles), WAP (Wearing apparel), LEA (Leather products), LUM (Wood products), PPP (Paper products, publishing), P_C (Petroleum, coal products), CRP (Chemical, rubber, plastic products), NMM (Mineral products nec), I_S (Ferrous metals), NFM (Metals nec), FMP (Metal products), MVH (Motor vehicles and parts), OTN (Transport equipment nec), ELE (Electronic equipment), OME (Machinery and equipment nec), OMF (Manufactures nec);

Energy
COL (Coal), OIL (Oil), GAS (Gas), ELY (Electricity), GDT (Gas manufacture, distribution).

5. Vertical specialization, tariff shirking and trade

Alyson C. Ma and Ari Van Assche

1. INTRODUCTION

The organization of production has changed in the past few decades. Groundbreaking advances in transportation and communications technology have enabled firms to separate value chain tasks in space and time (Grossman and Rossi-Hansberg, 2008). Recent studies have extensively investigated how this added organizational flexibility allows firms to arbitrage factor cost and institutional differences across countries, leading to the emergence of global value chains (see Van Assche, 2012 for an overview).

An additional benefit related to the slicing up of value chains, which has received less attention, is that it allows firms to more easily circumvent trade policy barriers. To avoid a country-specific trade barrier, a company no longer has to relocate its entire value chain to another country, but only a single value chain stage, often final assembly. Fung et al. (2007, pp. 58–59), for example, describe how the trading company Li & Fung scrambled to restructure its value chain in response to an unexpected trade policy shock:

> [O]n a Friday in early September 2006, the South African government announced that it would be imposing strict quotas on Chinese imports in two weeks. Li & Fung had orders already in production for South African retailers that would be affected by these changes. Managers began to look at contingency plans to move production to factories in different countries and even to move the last stage of existing orders to different end countries to satisfy non-China country-of-origin rules.

The trading company's urge to restructure its value chain to circumvent trade barriers implies that *tariff shirking* may be a powerful force affecting trade patterns. A firm's ability to circumvent trade policy, in turn, may have important implications for the effectiveness of trade policy to protect domestic firms and for the transmission of trade policy shocks along different parts of the value chain.

In this chapter, we present an analytical framework that allows us to investigate the effects of tariff shirking on trade. We build on the heterogeneous firm models by Melitz (2003) and by Chaney (2008), but allow Northern firms to manufacture their goods either in their home country (local value chain) or in the South (global value chain). We show that this added organizational flexibility makes it profitable for some Northern firms (at the margin) to circumvent country-specific tariff hikes by relocating their manufacturing. For example, if tariffs increase on Southern exports, some Northern firms will reshore their manufacturing to their home country, leading to an extensive margin effect. Several strong results emerge from the model. First, tariff shirking reduces the effectiveness of trade policy to protect a domestic industry since it provides foreign companies with an extra tool to circumvent country-specific tariffs. Second, vertical specialization increases the elasticity of bilateral exports to country-specific tariff hikes. Third, Southern exports that are part of global value chains are more sensitive to a country-specific tariff hike than Southern exports that are part of local value chains. Fourth, the effect of trade policy is distributed unevenly along the value chain. While tariff shirking dampens the vulnerability of headquarters services to trade policy shocks, it amplifies the vulnerability of manufacturing to trade policy shocks.

Guided by the theory, we empirically investigate the prediction that Southern exports that are part of global value chains are more sensitive to a country-specific tariff hike than Southern exports that are part of local value chains. For this purpose, we draw on both firm-level and provincial level data from the customs statistics of the People's Republic of China (PRC). We do so by making a distinction between Chinese exports under two separate customs regimes: processing trade and ordinary trade. As both Kee and Tang (2013) and Koopman et al. (2012) have illustrated, processing exports are predominantly part of global value chains, while ordinary exports more extensively use domestic value chains. In line with our theoretical predictions, we find strong evidence that processing exports are more sensitive to the imposition of antidumping measures than ordinary exports. This is mostly due to the extensive margin effect identified in the theoretical model.

The rest of the chapter is organized as follows. In Section 2, we survey the related literature on trade policy and global value chains. In Section 3, we present the theoretical model and discuss our central predictions. Section 4 then presents the data and methods used for our empirical analysis, and the results. Section 5 talks about the implications for policy and we finally conclude.

2. VERTICAL SPECIALIZATION AND TRADE POLICY

The growing ability of companies to separate value chain tasks in space and time is intrinsically related to the modularization of product architectures. Ulrich (1995) defines a product as a combination of components – or modules – that interact with one another according to the design rules of its product architecture. Products' architectures can vary on a continuum from integral to modular depending on the number of inter-dependencies between modules (Schilling, 2000). If the product architecture is integral, modules are highly interdependent and require constant monitoring and tacit interactions. In that case, geographically separating value chain activities is hard to do since it requires significant coordination efforts (Fort, 2011). In contrast, if the product architecture is modular, then the modules interact through codified (and often digitized) interfaces, which make them relatively independent from one another. In that case, modules can be geographically separated at a relatively low coordination cost.

The emergence of e-mail, the Internet and common communications protocols, as well as the increased availability of high-capacity computing power, has made it easier for firms to modularize their product architecture. Currently, many companies rely on sophisticated computer-aided design (CAD) technologies and business-to-business (B2B) systems to share codified information between geographically separated locations. These technologies allow them to perform tasks in geographically dispersed locations with limited risk of miscommunication and with a relatively modest cost of monitoring (Blinder, 2006; Leamer and Storper, 2001; Levy and Murnane, 2003). Indeed, Fort (2011) estimates that US companies that use CAD technology to coordinate shipments have fragmented their international production processes more extensively than have companies without CAD technology.

A now vast literature in international trade has investigated how the added organizational flexibility related to the modularization of product architectures allows firms to arbitrage cost differences across countries. Beyond the traditional sources of comparative advantage such as technological differences and relative endowments, scholars have pinpointed new sources of comparative advantage for task trade. Focusing on the fact that global value chains often involve multiple companies that sign contracts with each other, one stream of literature has identified the quality of a country's judiciary system as a source of comparative advantage (Acemoglu et al., 2007; Costinot, 2009; Levchenko, 2007; Nunn, 2007). Other studies have focused on the quality of a country's transportation infrastructure (Gamberoni et al., 2010) and labor markets (Helpman and Itskhoki, 2010) as a source of comparative advantage.

Less attention has been paid to trade policy barriers as a cost factor that can be arbitraged through the restructuring of the value chain.[1] The literature has largely considered trade policy barriers as a factor that reduces a firm's incentive to slice up its value chains. Focusing on worldwide tariffs, Yi (2003) shows that they have a higher impact on the cost of trade within global value chains as compared with regular trade (i.e. trade of final goods fully produced in a single country), since the same component needs to cross borders multiple times. As a result, he predicts that a relatively small rise in worldwide tariffs or other trade barriers will deter many firms from fragmenting production internationally, therefore leading to a large drop in trade.[2]

In Yi's (2003) model, the ability to fragment production internationally does not provide firms with added flexibility to circumvent tariffs, since tariffs world-wide are assumed to uniformly move up or down. The literature on *tariff jumping*, then again, provides insights into the effect of tariff changes on the spatial structure of production. Belderbos and Sleuwaegen (1998) and Blonigen (2002) provide evidence that many firms react to a country-specific tariff increase or antidumping measure by moving their production to the destination country, thereby avoiding the trade barrier. Blonigen et al. (2004) show that such tariff jumping foreign direct investment (FDI) reduces the effectiveness of trade policy to protect domestic firms.

Surprisingly, the international trade literature has paid limited attention to tariff shirking as a strategy to avoid country-specific changes in trade policy. Distinct from tariff jumping, where the firm moves production to the destination country or region, a firm under tariff shirking would try to circumvent the trade policy barrier by moving manufacturing to a third country that does not face the trade policy barrier.[3] Arguably, vertical specialization has made tariff shirking easier since firms only need to move a part of their value chain instead of their entire value chain. In the next section we move to set up a theoretical model that allows us to analyze the mechanism of tariff shirking and the effect on trade.

3. MODEL

Our model builds on the firm heterogeneity models of Melitz (2003) and Chaney (2008), but allows firms to manufacture their final goods either in their home country (local value chain) or in a Southern country (global value chain). Consider a world with many small Northern countries and a small Southern country. In each country j, households spend the fixed amount $Y^j > 0$ on a specific differentiated goods sector. The demand function for a variety v in this sector produced in country i and sold in country j equals:

$$y^{ij}(v) = A^j p^{ij}(v)^{-\varepsilon}, \qquad (5.1)$$

where $\varepsilon = \frac{1}{1-\alpha} > 1$ is the elasticity of substitution between any pair of differentiated goods and the demand level A^j is exogenous from the point of view of the individual firm and the individual country (due to the small country assumption).[4]

Exports from country i to country j are subject to an *ad valorem* tariff t^{ij}, where $\tau^{ij} = 1 + t^{ij}$. Tariffs are country-specific and vary across countries. The tariff implies that the consumer price in country j is higher than the domestically charged price (i.e. in country i):

$$p^{ij}(v) = p^i(v)(1 + t^{ij}) = p^i(v)\tau^{ij}, \qquad (5.2)$$

where $p^i(v)$ is the domestic price.

In each country, a continuum of firms has the know-how to produce a single variety. We assume that each firm draws a productivity φ from a cumulative Pareto distribution $G(\varphi)$ with shape parameter $z > \varepsilon - 1$ (Helpman et al., 2004):

$$G(\varphi) = 1 - \varphi^{-z}. \qquad (5.3)$$

An inverse measure of the heterogeneity in a sector is given by z. If z is high, firms are more homogeneous, in the sense that more output is concentrated among the smallest and least productive firms. We assume that all countries face an identical Pareto distribution function.

The value chain of a product consists of three stages: knowledge-intensive headquarters service production, labor-intensive manufacturing and final sale. A firm is required to produce its headquarters services in its home country. Manufacturing, in contrast, is footloose and can be conducted either in a Northern country at a fixed unit labor cost of ω^N or in the South at a fixed unit labor cost of ω^S. If manufacturing is not co-located with headquarters services, the firm faces a fixed cost g of coordinating its global value chain activities across borders. Finally, to sell its product variety to consumers in the destination country j, a firm faces a fixed cost f.

In our model, we assume that wages are fixed and are lower in the South than in the Northern countries, $\omega^S < \omega^N$. Furthermore, we assume that the following condition holds:[5]

$$\left(\frac{\omega^N}{\omega^S}\right)^{\varepsilon-1}\left(\frac{\tau^N}{\tau^S}\right)^{\varepsilon} > 1. \tag{5.4}$$

Under this condition, any firm has a marginal cost advantage of manufacturing its products in the South compared to the North. In other words, the wage advantage of manufacturing in the South is sufficiently large to outweigh a potential tariff advantage of exporting the final good from the North.

Without loss of generality, we will focus on the strategies of firms from a single Northern country $l = N$ and from the South $l = S$ that sell their products to a specific Northern destination country j. For notational clarity, we will drop the subscript j that identifies the destination country.

We solve the model in two steps. In Section 3.1, we analyze the benchmark scenario of "no vertical specialization" where Northern and Southern firms are required to spatially co-locate headquarters services and manufacturing. In Section 3.2, we then study the scenario of "vertical specialization" where it becomes optimal for some Northern firms to slice up their value chain and offshore their manufacturing to a Southern country. By comparing the equilibrium outcomes of both scenarios we can investigate how the extra organizational ability of slicing up the value chain affects the elasticity of exports to country-specific tariff changes.

3.1 No Vertical Specialization

Consider the benchmark case where g approaches infinity so that all firms are better off co-locating manufacturing with headquarters services.[6] This is in line with the scenario where the product architecture is integral so that it is difficult to spatially disperse value chain activities. From equations (5.1) and (5.2), firms from $l \in \{N, S\}$ choose y to maximize $\pi^l = (p^l - \frac{\omega^l}{\varphi})y^l - f$. It is straightforward to check that this program yields the optimal price, $p^l = \frac{\omega^l}{\alpha\varphi}$, the optimal firm-specific exports:

$$x^l = \frac{B}{1-\alpha}\left(\frac{\varphi}{\omega^l}\right)^{\varepsilon-1}\tau^{l-\varepsilon}, \tag{5.5}$$

and the optimal firm-specific profit:

$$\pi^l = \left(\frac{\varphi}{\omega^l}\right)^{\varepsilon-1}\tau^{l-\varepsilon}B - f, \tag{5.6}$$

where $B = (1 - \alpha)A\alpha^{\varepsilon-1}$. Intuitively, equations (5.5) and (5.6) suggest that a firm's exports and profits decline with the rise of its home country l's wages ω^l and the country-specific tariffs it faces τ^l.

Not all firms are able to generate enough profits to cover the fixed cost f of exporting to the destination country. Define φ^l as the threshold productivity at which $\pi^l = 0$. Using equation (5.6), the cut-off productivity coefficient for firms in country l equals:

$$\varphi^l = \omega^l\left(\frac{f}{B}\right)^{\frac{1}{\varepsilon-1}}\tau^{l\frac{\varepsilon}{\varepsilon-1}}. \tag{5.7}$$

From equation (5.6), it is clear that less productive firms with $\varphi < \varphi^l$ do not export to the destination country, while firms with $\varphi > \varphi^l$ become exporters.

Country l's aggregate exports to the destination country equal the sum of exports by firms with $\varphi > \varphi^l$. Using the firm-level export equation (5.5), the aggregate export equation equals:

$$X^l = \int_{\varphi^l}^{\infty} x^l(\varphi)\,dG(\varphi) = \frac{B}{1-\alpha}\tau^{l-\varepsilon}\int_{\varphi^l}^{\infty}\left(\frac{\varphi}{\omega^l}\right)^{\varepsilon-1}dG(\varphi). \tag{5.8}$$

We can use equation (5.8) to investigate the elasticity of aggregate exports X^l with respect to a country-specific tariff change τ^l. As illustrated by Chaney (2008) the effect can be decomposed into two different margins:

$$-\frac{dX^l/d\tau^l}{X^l/\tau^l} = -\frac{\tau^l}{X^l}\left(\int_{\varphi^l}^{\infty}\frac{\partial x^l(\varphi)}{\partial \tau^l}dG(\varphi)\right) + \frac{\tau^l}{X^l}\left(x^l(\varphi^l)\,G'(\varphi^l)\frac{\partial\varphi^l}{\partial\tau^l}\right), \tag{5.9}$$

where the first term is the *intensive margin* and the second is the *extensive margin*. The intensive margin determines by which amount existing exporters (or incumbents) change the size of their exports. The extensive margin defines the amount that aggregate exports change due to firm entry and exit. In Appendix 5A.1, we solve equation (5.9) to obtain the elasticity of a country's exports to a country-specific tariff change:

$$-\frac{dX^l}{X}\frac{\tau^l}{d\tau^l} = \varepsilon + (z - (\varepsilon - 1))\frac{\varepsilon}{\varepsilon - 1}. \tag{5.10}$$

There are two important aspects to note about this elasticity. First, the elasticity differs from Chaney (2008) because we model trade barriers as *ad valorem* tariffs and not as iceberg transport costs. As Cole and Davies (2011) show, the use of *ad valorem* tariffs implies that, unlike in Chaney (2008), the elasticity of trade with respect to trade barriers is a function of the elasticity of substitution between product varieties. It is important to emphasize, however, that the central predictions of our model would be unaffected if we had used iceberg transport costs. Second, due to our assumption that the productivity dispersion is identical across countries, the elasticity of aggregate exports with respect to a country-specific tariff change is the same for both Northern countries and South. In the remainder of the chapter, we will use equation (5.10) as a benchmark to investigate how vertical specialization alters the impact of country-specific trade policy shocks on trade.

3.2 Vertical Specialization

Consider next the scenario where the fixed coordination costs g are within the parameter range. $f[(\frac{\tau^N}{\tau^S})^\varepsilon (\frac{\omega^N}{\omega^S})^{\varepsilon-1} - 1] < g < +\infty$. In that case, it is only optimal for the most productive Northern firms to locate their manufacturing in the South.[7] As Figure 5.1 illustrates, three organizational forms coexist in the industry under this condition: (1) Southern firms with local

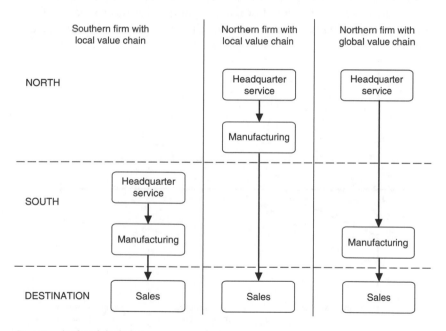

Source: Authors' depiction.

Figure 5.1   Types of organizational forms exporting to the destination country

value chains, (2) Northern firms with local value chains, and (3) Northern firms with global value chains. In the remainder of this section, we estimate the elasticity of exports with respect to country-specific tariffs for these three organizational forms.

3.2.1 Southern firms

Due to the marginal cost advantage of manufacturing in the South, there is no benefit for Southern firms to manufacture their goods in the North. As a result, all Southern firms co-locate manufacturing with headquarters services in the South and the analysis is identical to Section 3.1. The elasticity of Southern firms' exports with respect to a country-specific tariff change thus equals:

$$-\frac{dX^S}{X^S}\frac{\tau^S}{d\tau^S} = \varepsilon + (z - (\varepsilon - 1))\frac{\varepsilon}{\varepsilon - 1}. \tag{5.11}$$

3.2.2 Northern firms

As is illustrated in Figures 5.1 and 5.2, two types of Northern firms sell their products to the destination country: less productive firms ($\varphi^N < \varphi < \varphi^{NO}$) which manufacture in the North, and more productive

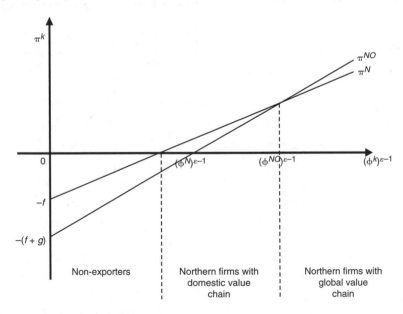

Source: Authors' calculations.

Figure 5.2 *Productivity and Northern firms' organizational form*

firms ($\varphi > \varphi^{NO}$) which manufacture in the South. We consider their optimization problems in turn.

For Northern firms with a *domestic value chain* ($\varphi^N < \varphi < \varphi^{NO}$), the profit maximization problem is identical to section 3.1. Firm-specific profits amount to $\pi^N = (\frac{\varphi}{\omega^N})^{\varepsilon-1}\tau^{N-\varepsilon}B - f$, which imply that firms with a productivity below $\varphi^N = \omega^N(\frac{f}{B})^{\frac{1}{\varepsilon-1}}\tau^{\frac{N-\varepsilon}{\varepsilon-1}}$ do not export to the destination country. Firm-specific exports amount to $x^N = \frac{B}{1-\alpha}(\frac{\varphi}{\omega^N})^{\varepsilon-1}\tau^{N-\varepsilon}$.

Northern firms with a *global value chain* ($\varphi > \varphi^{NO}$) perform their manufacturing in the South and choose y to maximize $\pi^{NO} = (p - \frac{\omega^S}{\varphi})y - f - g$. For these firms, their optimal price equals $p^{NO} = \frac{\omega^S}{\alpha\varphi}$, their firm-specific exports equal:

$$x^{NO} = \frac{B}{1-\alpha}\left(\frac{\varphi}{\omega^S}\right)^{\varepsilon-1}\tau^{S-\varepsilon}, \tag{5.12}$$

and their firm-specific profits equal:

$$\pi^{NO} = \left(\frac{\varphi}{\omega^S}\right)^{\varepsilon-1}\tau^{S-\varepsilon}B - f - g. \tag{5.13}$$

Using equations (5.5) and (5.13), the threshold at which $\pi^N(\varphi^{NO})=\pi^{NO}(\varphi^{NO})$ equals:

$$\varphi^{NO} = \left(\frac{g}{B(\omega^{S^{1-\varepsilon}}\tau^{S-\varepsilon} - \omega^{N^{1-\varepsilon}}\tau^{N-\varepsilon})}\right)^{\frac{1}{\varepsilon-1}}. \tag{5.14}$$

The Northern firms with a productivity $\varphi > \varphi^{NO}$ manufacture in the South, while firms with a productivity $\varphi^N < \varphi < \varphi^{NO}$ manufacture in the North.

3.3 Aggregate Exports by Firm Type

Aggregate exports from the North by firms with domestic value chains, X^N, equals the integral of firm-level exports x^N for firms with a productivity $\varphi^N < \varphi < \varphi^{NO}$. Using equation (5.5):

$$X^N = \int_{\varphi^N}^{\varphi^{NO}} x^N(\varphi)\,dG(\varphi). \tag{5.15}$$

Aggregate exports from the South by Northern firms with global value chains, X^{NO}, equals the integral of firm-level exports x^{NO} for Northern firms with a productivity $\varphi > \varphi^{NO}$. Using equation (5.12):

$$X^{NO} = \int_{\varphi^o}^{\infty} x^{NO}(\varphi) \, dG(\varphi). \tag{5.16}$$

We can use these aggregate export equations to investigate if vertical specialization affects the elasticity of exports with respect to country-specific tariffs.

3.3.1 Impact of an increase in τ^S on X^{NO}

We first investigate the impact of an *ad valorem* bilateral tariff increase τ^S on X^{NO}. In Appendix 5A.2, we use equation (5.16) to calculate that the elasticity of X^{NO} with respect to τ^S equals:

$$-\frac{dX^{NO}/d\tau^S}{X^{NO}/\tau^S} = \varepsilon + (z - (\varepsilon - 1))\frac{\varepsilon}{\varepsilon - 1}\chi, \tag{5.17}$$

where

$$\chi = \frac{\left(\dfrac{\omega^N}{\omega^S}\right)^{\varepsilon-1}\left(\dfrac{\tau^N}{\tau^S}\right)^{\varepsilon}}{\left(\dfrac{\omega^N}{\omega^S}\right)^{\varepsilon-1}\left(\dfrac{\tau^N}{\tau^S}\right)^{\varepsilon} - 1} > 1.$$

Due to our assumption in equation (5.4) that there is a marginal cost advantage of manufacturing in the South compared to the North, the following inequality holds: $\chi > 1$. As a result, if we compare to the equation (5.10), Northern firms' exports from South, X^{NO}, are more elastic with respect to an increase in τ^S than their exports were under no vertical specialization. This result is driven by an extra extensive margin effect related to tariff shirking. If τ^S increases, it induces an extra number of firms to stop exporting from country S since they move assembly back to N to circumvent the tariff hike. Note that the extra elasticity denoted by χ is larger if the marginal cost advantage of manufacturing in the South is smaller. In other words, the smaller is the marginal cost advantage of manufacturing in the South, the more X^{NO} would be affected by tariff shirking.

Compared to equation (5.11), Northern firms' exports from South, X^{NO}, are also more elastic than Southern firms' exports from South, X^S, with respect to an increase in τ^S. This is once again because some Northern firms (at the margin) have the extra flexibility to circumvent the tariff increase by reshoring manufacturing back to the North. An implication of the difference in elasticities between Southern exports conducted by Northern and Southern firms is that an increase in τ^S will reduce the share of Southern exports conducted by Northern firms. Define s^{NO} as the share of Southern exports conducted by Northern firms:

$$s^{NO} = \frac{X^{NO}}{X^{NO} + X^S}. \tag{5.18}$$

By taking the derivate of equation (5.18) and using the elasticities in equations (5.11) and (5.17), it is straightforward to show that the share s^{NO} is negatively affected by a rise in τ^S:

$$\frac{\partial s^{NO}}{\partial \tau^S} = -\frac{1}{\tau^S} s^{NO}(1 - s^{NO})(z - (\varepsilon - 1))\frac{\varepsilon}{\varepsilon - 1}(\chi - 1) < 0. \tag{5.19}$$

In our empirical analysis, we will further investigate this specific prediction of the model.

3.3.2 Impact of an increase in τ^N on X^N

We next investigate the effect of an *ad valorem* bilateral tariff increase τ^N on X^N. In Appendix 5A.2, we use equation (5.15) to calculate that the elasticity equals:

$$-\frac{dX^N/d\tau^N}{X^N/\tau^N} = \varepsilon + (z - (\varepsilon - 1))\frac{\varepsilon}{\varepsilon - 1}\left(1 + \frac{X^{NO}}{X^N} * \frac{1}{\left(\frac{\omega^N}{\omega^S}\right)^{\varepsilon - 1}\left(\frac{\tau^N}{\tau^S}\right)^{\varepsilon} - 1}\right). \tag{5.20}$$

If we compare with the scenario of no vertical specialization in equation (5.10), it is clear that X^N is more elastic with respect to τ^N under vertical specialization than under no vertical specialization since

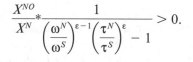

This result is once again due to an extra extensive margin effect. The logic is the following. Compared to *no vertical specialization*, a tariff hike not only induces a number of Northern firms to become non-exporters, but also causes a number of firms to divert their exports through the South in order to circumvent the tariff increase. This extra tariff shirking effect at the extensive margin, which is driven by the ability to fragment assembly from input production, increases the elasticity of X^N with respect to τ^N.

The extra elasticity once again depends on the size of the marginal cost advantage of manufacturing in the South. The smaller this marginal cost advantage is, the more sensitive is X^N to a country-specific tariff hike.

3.3.3 Sensitivity of production stages to trade policy shocks

Finally, we investigate whether vertical specialization affects the impact of a tariff increase differentially along the two vertical stages of the value chain: (non-footloose) headquarters services and (footloose) manufacturing.

It is straightforward to show that vertical specialization *reduces* the vulnerability of sector-wide headquarters services in the North to a country-specific tariff increase τ^N or τ^S. The intuition is the following. Since a number of companies (at the margin) are able to dampen the effect of the tariff hike by relocating their manufacturing, the demand for products sold by firms from N is less affected by the tariff hike than under the no-vertical-specialization scenario. As a result, non-footloose headquarters service production in country N is also less vulnerable to the tariff hike.

In contrast, vertical specialization *increases* the vulnerability of manufacturing activities in both country N and S to a country-specific tariff increase τ^N or τ^S. As Northern companies (at the margin) relocate their manufacturing to circumvent tariffs, footloose manufacturing activities become particularly vulnerable to trade policy shocks. Manufacturing in country N, for example, is extra vulnerable to an increase in τ^N since it induces a number of firms to cease manufacturing in N and offshore it to S. Similarly, manufacturing in country S is extra vulnerable to an increase in τ^S since it induces a number of Northern firms to cease production in S and reshore it to country N.

4. EMPIRICAL ANALYSIS

A key prediction from the model is that Southern exports that are part of global value chains are more elastic with respect to a country-specific tariff hike than Southern exports that are part of local value chains. As a result, a country-specific tariff hike should reduce the share of exports that are part of global value chains. In this section, we draw on both province-level (1997–2009) and firm-level (2000–2006) data from Chinese customs statistics to investigate this claim.

To classify Chinese exports that are part of global versus local value chains, we distinguish between two customs regimes: processing trade and ordinary trade. These two trade forms differ in terms of tariff treatment and the ability of firms to sell on the domestic market:

- Under the processing trade regime, firms enjoy the right of duty-free imports of intermediate goods and capital equipment that are used in their export processing activity, but face restrictions in selling to the domestic market.
- Under the ordinary trade regime, firms pay import duties on imported inputs but can sell their output locally.

Due to these distinct characteristics the processing trade regime is used primarily by exporting firms that are part of a global value chain, while the ordinary trade regime is used by exporting firms that have more extensive domestic value chains. Two stylized facts back this up. First, recent estimates suggest that processing exports embody less than half as much domestic value added than ordinary exports (Kee and Tang, 2013; Koopman et al., 2012). Second, as is shown in Figure 5.3, foreign-owned firms play a much more dominant role in the processing trade regime than in the ordinary trade regime. Between 1997 and 2009, the share of processing exports conducted by foreign-owned enterprises increased from 64 percent to 85 percent. In comparison, this share throughout the sample period remained under 30 percent in the ordinary trade regime. We use

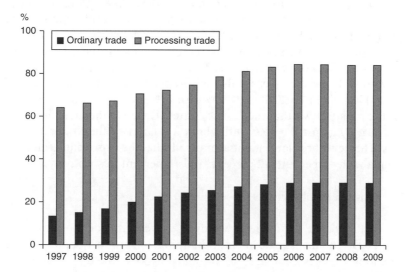

Source: Authors' calculations using data from the People's Republic of China's Customs Statistics.

Figure 5.3   *Share of the People's Republic of China's exports conducted by foreign-owned enterprises, by customs regime, 1997–2009 (%)*

this distinction to evaluate the theoretical prediction that exports are more sensitive to country-specific trade policy shocks under the processing trade regime than under the ordinary trade regime.

As our measure of country-specific trade policy shocks, we use antidumping cases against the PRC as identified in the Global Antidumping Database (GAD) published by the World Bank (Bown, 2009). The benefit of using antidumping as a measure for a country-specific trade policy shock is that it is generally imposed by a country on firms of a specific country, and not across the board. The GAD has detailed information on each antidumping case, such as product information (6-digit HS codes), the investigating country, the target country, the preliminary determination date and the year it was revoked. For our analysis, we collect information on all antidumping cases against the PRC during the period 1997–2009. We match the GAD data with the Chinese customs data at the HS6 digit level, the most disaggregated level at which the two datasets are comparable.

From 1997 to 2009 there were a total of 1042 cases of which 1011 were in the manufacturing sector. We focus our study on the manufacturing sector, which is more in line with the theory presented on vertical specialization. Over the 12-year period in the data set, the average number of cases was 78 per year with a median of 61 cases. The antidumping charges were imposed on \$131 billion of Chinese exports, which represented 1.75 percent of total Chinese exports in manufacturing. Table 5.1 shows that the number of cases increased by 162 percent from 55 to 144 between 2000 and 2001. The number of cases also spiked in 2006 with 127 cases (up by 22 percent) and again in 2008 and 2009 with 110 and 158 cases, respectively. The table also shows that the United States (US) held the most antidumping charges against the PRC with about a quarter of the total number of cases. The next three largest initiators are India, the European Union, and Canada with 15 percent, 12 percent, and 10 percent, respectively.

4.1   Province-level Analysis

In a first step, we use aggregate province-level data for the time period 1997–2009 to investigate if antidumping disproportionately affects processing exports compared to ordinary exports. In our analysis, our dependent variable is the share in value of bilateral exports that is organized through processing trade in a specific HS 6-digit industry and year:

$$Share_{ijkt} = \frac{PX_{ijkt}}{PX_{ijkt} + OX_{ijkt}},$$ (5.21)

Table 5.1 Summary statistics of preliminary antidumping decisions imposed against the People's Republic of China, by year and country

	Year of preliminary antidumping decision													
	1997	1998	1999	2000	2001	2002	2003	2004	2005	2006	2007	2008	2009	Total
India	1	8	3	9	21	8	24	2	9	11	6	11	36	149
Indonesia	8	3	0	0	0	0	0	0	0	0	0	0	0	11
Israel	0	0	2	0	0	0	0	0	1	3	4	0	0	10
Malaysia	0	0	0	0	0	1	0	0	0	0	0	0	0	1
Pakistan	0	0	0	0	0	0	0	0	1	4	0	0	4	9
Philippines	0	0	0	1	0	0	0	0	0	0	0	0	0	1
Republic of Korea	3	2	0	1	0	0	9	2	2	3	4	7	0	33
Turkey	0	0	0	0	0	2	0	0	0	0	0	0	0	2
Taipei,China	0	0	0	0	0	0	0	0	0	14	0	0	0	14
South Africa	13	4	0	1	2	1	0	1	3	4	2	3	1	35
European Union	11	20	2	6	3	1	3	2	20	20	5	7	21	121
Argentina	8	0	2	0	11	6	1	4	1	5	2	17	38	95
Brazil	0	2	0	0	0	0	0	0	0	5	3	2	16	28
Colombia	0	0	0	0	0	0	0	2	1	47	2	7	3	62
Mexico	1	1	1	0	5	1	3	1	2	2	2	3	0	22
Peru	0	1	6	0	11	4	1	1	0	0	0	0	0	24
Trinidad and Tobago	0	0	0	1	0	0	0	6	0	0	0	0	0	7
Venezuela	0	0	13	0	0	0	0	0	0	0	0	0	0	13
Canada	2	0	0	11	43	2	3	8	1	2	1	10	17	100
United States	13	0	2	25	46	50	5	42	3	5	5	42	15	253
Australia	1	0	0	0	2	3	0	3	1	2	0	1	7	20
New Zealand	0	0	0	0	0	0	0	1	0	0	0	0	0	1
Total	61	41	31	55	144	79	49	75	45	127	36	110	158	1011

Source: Authors' calculations using the Global Antidumping Database.

where PX_{ijkt} is the value of Chinese processing exports from province i to country j in industry k and year t, and OX_{ijkt} is the value of Chinese ordinary exports from province i to country j in industry k and year t. To test the prediction of the theoretical model, we estimate the following regression equation:

$$Share_{ijkt} = \alpha_i + \alpha_k + \alpha_t + \beta * AD_{jkt} + \varepsilon_{ijkt}, \qquad (5.22)$$

where α_i, α_k and α_t are province, industry and year fixed effects; AD_{jkt} is a dummy variable that takes on a value of 1 when a HS 6-digit export industry k faces an antidumping measure imposed by country j in a year t and 0 otherwise; and ε_{ijkt} is an error term. There will be evidence that an antidumping measure disproportionately affects processing trade if the OLS estimate $\hat{\beta}$ is negative and significant.

The results of the benchmark analysis are presented in Column 1 of Table 5.2. The negative and significant coefficient on the antidumping indicator suggests that the share of processing exports declines after the imposition of antidumping duties. Specifically, an antidumping imposition reduces the share of processing exports by 7.6 percent. We can infer

Table 5.2   Province-level estimation results

Dependent variable: $Share_{ijkt}$

	Benchmark	Foreign PT/ Domestic OT	Foreign PT/Domestic OT/only AD sectors
	(1)	(2)	(3)
AD	−7.590***	−8.371***	−11.118***
	(0.606)	(0.720)	(0.736)
Year FE	Yes	Yes	Yes
Sector FE	Yes	Yes	Yes
Province FE	Yes	Yes	Yes
Observations	931 293	713 761	410 630
R^2	0.16	0.19	0.18

Notes:
AD = antidumping; FE = fixed effects; OT = ordinary trade regime; PT = processing trade regime.
Coefficients are reported with robust standard errors that are clustered at the province level. Standard errors are given in parentheses. The individual coefficient is statistically significant at the *10%, **5% or ***1% level.

Source: Authors' calculations using the Global Antidumping Database and data from the People's Republic of China's Customs Statistics.

from this that processing exports are considerably more sensitive to the imposition of antidumping duties than ordinary exports.

In Column 2 of Table 5.2, we test whether the results are sensitive to excluding Chinese firms that conduct processing exports and foreign firms that conduct ordinary exports. This restriction aligns the empirical estimation better to the theory that Southern exports within global value chains are conducted by Northern firms, while Southern exports within local value chains are conducted by Southern firms. The results are similar to the benchmark analysis, with a slightly larger reduction of 8.4 percent in the share of processing exports.

In Column 3 of Table 5.2, as an additional robustness test, we exclude all industries from our data sample in which no antidumping was imposed during the entire sample period (1997–2009). The results are once again similar to the benchmark analysis, with a larger reduction of 11.1 percent.

4.2 Firm-level Analysis

The province-level data do not allow us to examine the impact of antidumping impositions on the intensive and extensive margin separately. To distinguish these two effects, we therefore utilize more disaggregated firm-level data from Chinese customs statistics that are only available for the subsample 2000 to 2006.

We define *intensive margin* as exports by incumbent firms. To be considered as an incumbent, a firm must have at least one year of positive exports in an industry affected by antidumping prior to the imposition of the antidumping charges and at least one year of positive exports after the imposition. For example, a firm exporting a girl's 16-inch bike to the US in years 2001 to 2004 would be considered an incumbent if the US imposed an antidumping charge on the PRC for the item in year 2002.[8]

We define *extensive margin* as exports by non-incumbent firms (Morrow and Brandt, 2013). In other words, the extensive margin captures exports by firms that did not export in a year prior to the imposition of antidumping charges or did not export in a year after the imposition of antidumping charges.

To investigate if antidumping disproportionately affects processing exports compared to ordinary exports at the intensive margin, we use the following dependent variable:

$$Share\_Int_{jkt} = \frac{PX\_Int_{jkt}}{PX\_Int_{jkt} + OX\_Int_{jkt}}, \qquad (5.23)$$

where PX_Int_{jkt} is the value of processing exports to country j by incumbents in industry k and year t, and OX_Int_{jkt} is the value of ordinary exports to country j by incumbents in industry k and year t. Similar to above, we test our central prediction by estimating the following regression equation:

$$Share\_Int_{jkt} = \alpha_k + \alpha_t + \beta * AD_{jkt} + \varepsilon_{jkt}, \qquad (5.24)$$

where α_k and α_t are industry and year fixed effects; AD_{jkt} is a dummy variable that takes on a value of 1 when an HS 6-digit export industry k faces an antidumping measure imposed by country j in a year t and 0 otherwise; and ε_{jkt} is an error term. There will be evidence that an anti-dumping measure disproportionately affects processing trade at the intensive margin if the OLS estimate $\hat{\beta}$ is negative and significant.

To investigate if antidumping disproportionately affects processing trade compared to ordinary trade at the extensive margin, we use the following dependent variable:

$$Share\_Ext_{jkt} = \frac{PX\_Ext_{jkt}}{PX\_Ext_{jkt} + OX\_Ext_{jkt}}, \qquad (5.25)$$

where PX_Ext_{jkt} is the value of processing exports to country j by non-incumbents in industry k and year t, and OX_Ext_{jkt} is the value of ordinary exports to country j by non-incumbents in industry k and year t. Similar to above, we estimate the following regression equation:

$$Share\_Ext_{jkt} = \alpha_k + \alpha_t + \beta * AD_{jkt} + \varepsilon_{jkt}. \qquad (5.26)$$

There will be evidence that an antidumping measure disproportionately affects processing exports at the extensive margin if the OLS estimate $\hat{\beta}$ is negative and significant.

In Columns 1–3 of Table 5.3, we present the benchmark results for the share of processing exports in total Chinese exports. The results for the pooled estimation, intensive margin, and extensive margin are provided in Columns 1, 2, and 3, respectively. All three specifications include year and sector fixed effects. We find that antidumping has a negative impact on the share of processing exports across all three specifications, although it is only significant at the 10 percent level for the intensive margin. When incumbent and non-incumbent firms are pooled together, antidumping reduces the share of processing exports by 3.1 percent. When only incumbents are considered (intensive margin), antidumping reduces the share of processing exports by 2.1 percent. For non-incumbents (extensive margin), antidumping reduces the share of processing exports by 2.4 percent.

Table 5.3 *Firm-level estimation results and decomposition using value of exports*

Dependent: Share of processing exports in total value of export

	Benchmark			Domestic OT/ Foreign PT		Domestic OT/Foreign PT/Import Cut off		Domestic OT/Foreign PT/Import Cut off/AD	
	(1) Pooled	(2) Intensive	(3) Extensive	(4) Intensive	(5) Extensive	(6) Intensive	(7) Extensive	(8) Intensive	(9) Extensive
AD	−3.13***	−2.07*	−2.41**	−3.247**	−3.271**	−4.021**	−3.569**	−2.451*	−4.449***
	(0.834)	(1.147)	(1.176)	(1.402)	(1.351)	(1.420)	(1.373)	(1.468)	(1.401)
Year FE	Yes	Yes	Yes	Yes	Yes	Yes	Yes	Yes	Yes
Sector FE	Yes	Yes	Yes	Yes	Yes	Yes	Yes	Yes	Yes
Observations	370871	91692	279179	76637	217223	76250	216889	28029	124457
R^2	0.28	0.44	0.32	0.44	0.33	0.44	0.33	0.46	0.34

Notes:
AD = antidumping; FE = fixed effects; OT = ordinary trade regime; PT = processing trade regime.
Coefficients are reported with robust standard errors that are clustered at the firm level. Standard errors are given in parentheses. The individual coefficient is statistically significant at the *10%, **5% or ***1% level.

Source: Authors' calculations using the Global Antidumping Database and data from the People's Republic of China's Customs Statistics.

Similar to the provincial-level estimation, we also conducted a number of robustness tests of our firm-level results. First, in Columns 4–5 of Table 5.3, we solely considered processing exports conducted by foreign-owned firms and ordinary exports by Chinese-owned firms. The results are similar to the benchmark findings, but with larger negative magnitudes of 3.2 percent and 3.3 percent at the intensive and extensive margin, respectively.

The decision to impose antidumping could be considered endogenous since the foreign firms that originate from the imposing country may actively lobby for or against their imposition. To address this possible endogeneity, we have therefore as a robustness test eliminated from our data sample any firm that imports more than 5 percent of its imports from a country that imposes antidumping.[9] The findings in Columns 6–7 of Table 5.3 suggest that it leads to slightly larger decreases in exports.

Finally, in Columns 8–9, we exclude all industries from our data sample in which no antidumping was imposed during the entire sample period. In this case, we find that the coefficient on the antidumping indicator for the intensive margin is negative as in the benchmark but at only the 10 percent significance level. The result predicts that the share of processing exports in total exports by incumbents decreases by 2.5 percent in the presence of an antidumping measure. The coefficient on the antidumping indicator for the extensive margin is highly significant and with a larger magnitude than the benchmark. Specifically, the share of processing exports at the extensive margin is reduced by 4.5 percent in reaction to antidumping.

In Table 5.4, we estimate our empirical specification using quantities instead of values. In other words, we use as our dependent variable the share of processing exports in the total quantity exported for years 2001 to 2005. The results confirm the previous results that antidumping charges negatively affect the share of processing exports in total exports, at both the intensive and the extensive margin.

5. CONCLUDING REMARKS

The core idea behind the chapter is that trade policy matters for the organization of global value chains, a notion that seems to have been neglected by trade economists, but has major implications for our understanding of trade and the international transmission of trade policy shocks. To gain new insights into this research area, we have developed a theoretical model in which a firm's ability to spatially separate manufacturing from headquarters services gives it the flexibility to circumvent a country-specific tariff increase by relocating its manufacturing elsewhere, a phenomenon

Table 5.4 Firm-level estimation results and decomposition using quantity of export

Dependent: Share of processing exports in total quantity of exports

	Benchmark			Domestic OT/ Foreign PT		Domestic OT/Foreign PT/Import Cut off		Domestic OT/Foreign PT/Import Cut off/AD	
	Pooled	Intensive	Extensive	Intensive	Extensive	Intensive	Extensive	Intensive	Extensive
	(1)	(2)	(3)	(4)	(5)	(6)	(7)	(8)	(9)
AD	−2.83***	−2.00*	−2.36**	−3.072**	−2.746**	−3.651**	−2.459*	−3.217**	−3.724**
	(0.819)	(1.146)	(1.186)	(1.393)	(1.365)	(1.415)	(1.366)	(1.484)	(1.391)
Year FE	Yes	Yes	Yes	Yes	Yes	Yes	Yes	Yes	Yes
Sector FE	Yes	Yes	Yes	Yes	Yes	Yes	Yes	Yes	Yes
Observations	370 224	91 571	278 653	76 537	216 691	76 156	216 358	27 994	124 167
R^2	0.28	0.45	0.32	0.45	0.33	0.45	0.33	0.47	0.34

Notes:
AD = antidumping; FE = fixed effects; OT = ordinary trade regime; PT = processing trade regime.
Coefficients are reported with robust standard errors that are clustered at the firm level. Standard errors are given in parentheses. The individual coefficient is statistically significant at the *10%, **5% or ***1% level.

Source: Authors' calculations using the Global Antidumping Database and data from the People's Republic of China's Customs Statistics.

that we have termed tariff shirking. We have illustrated a number of general equilibrium implications of tariff shirking. First, we have shown that it increases the elasticity of exports within global value chains to country-specific trade policy shocks by creating an extra extensive margin effect. Second, we have illustrated that tariff shirking differentially affects the vulnerability of headquarters services and manufacturing to country-specific trade policy shocks. Whereas tariff shirking dampens the vulnerability of headquarters services to trade policy shocks, it amplifies the vulnerability of manufacturing to trade policy shocks. This last result is complementary to Bergin et al.'s (2011) finding that offshored assembly activities in Mexico are more vulnerable to US business cycle shocks than corresponding US industries.

We used firm-level and province-level export data from the PRC to see if there is evidence that Chinese exports that are part of global value chains are more sensitive to antidumping measures than Chinese exports that rely on domestic value chains. The answer is yes: processing exports that rely heavily on imported inputs are consistently more sensitive to antidumping duties than ordinary exports. This result is found to be primarily driven by an extensive margin effect.

While our empirical results apply only to the PRC, the economic logic is broader and suggests that tariff shirking may be an important driver of trade and the international organization of production, and an important determinant of the effectiveness of trade policy. The policy implications of our analysis are complex. Policymakers may be inclined to try to prevent tariff shirking and restore the effectiveness of country-specific trade policy barriers by linking them to rules of origin. Such a move, however, would further increase the administrative complexity of trade and may even end up being detrimental for a country. As Deardorff (2013) shows, rules of origin can reduce or even eliminate completely the gains from trade. A policy reaction that would be more in line with the spirit of the World Trade Organization would be to step away from discriminatory trade policy barriers, which are less effective due to tariff shirking, and to focus on non-discriminatory trade policy barriers that limit the potential of tariff shirking.

NOTES

1. Konings and Vandenbussche (2013) provide evidence that antidumping measures on imported inputs negatively affect firms' exports. However, they do not analyze whether firms react to this through tariff shirking.
2. Escaith and Diakantoni (2012) and Miroudot and Rouzet (2013) use international input–output matrices to estimate the effective protection rates when components cross borders multiple times.

3. There is a recent literature on export platform FDI that investigates the drivers of a firm's decision to conduct FDI in a third country (Ekholm et al., 2007; Grossman et al., 2006; Ito, 2013; Mrázová and Neary, 2013). However, these studies have mainly focused on the effect of uniform changes in trade costs across countries, and not on the effect of country-specific changes in trade costs, therefore ruling out tariff shirking. Furthermore, they have not considered the implications for the effectiveness of trade policy.
4. As is well known from previous studies, $A^i = Y^i/[\int_0^{n_i} p^i(v)^{1-\varepsilon} dv]$, where n_i is the measure of varieties available in country i and $p_i(v)$ is the price of variety v in country i. Firms treat A_i as fixed since they are too small to individually affect A_i.
5. Under this condition, the marginal profit of manufacturing a unit in the South exceeds the marginal profit of manufacturing a unit in the North. One can obtain this condition by using equation (5.6).
6. Alternatively, we could cut off the productivity at a maximum value.
7. If, $g < f[(\frac{\tau_s^N}{\tau_s^S})^\varepsilon (\frac{\omega^N}{\omega^S})^{\varepsilon-1} - 1]$, it is optimal for all Northern firms to manufacture in the South. In this unrealistic case, there will be no extra extensive margin effect and the elasticity of bilateral exports with respect to a country-specific tariff change reverts to that of the case of no vertical specialization.
8. Given our definition of an incumbent, firms would not be considered in this category for years 2000 and 2006. As such, we dropped these years in our estimation.
9. We would like to thank Laura Puzzello for suggesting this robustness test. The results are similar for other cut off levels.

REFERENCES

Acemoglu, D., P. Antràs, and E. Helpman (2007), 'Contracts and technology adoption', *The American Economic Review*, **97**, 916–943.

Belderbos, R. and L. Sleuwaegen (1998), 'Tariff jumping DFI and export substitution: Japanese electronics firms in Europe', *International Journal of Industrial Organization*, **16**, 601–638.

Bergin, P.R., R.C. Feenstra, and G.H. Hanson (2011), 'Volatility due to offshoring: theory and evidence', *Journal of International Economics*, **85**, 163–173.

Blinder, Alan S. (2006), 'Offshoring: the next industrial revolution', *Foreign Affairs*, **85**, 113.

Blonigen, Bruce A. (2002), 'Tariff-jumping antidumping duties', *Journal of International Economics*, **57**, 31–49.

Blonigen, B.A., K. Tomlin, and W.W. Wilson (2004), 'Tariff-jumping FDI and domestic firms' profits', *Canadian Journal of Economics/Revue Canadienne d'Économique*, **37**, 656–677.

Bown, C.P. (2009), 'Global antidumping database (Current Version 5.0)', Brandeis University working paper, available online at www.brandeis.edu/~cbown/global_ad.

Chaney, T. (2008), 'Distorted gravity: the intensive and extensive margins of international trade', *The American Economic Review*, **98**, 1707–1721.

Cole, M.T. and R.B. Davies (2011), 'Strategic tariffs, tariff jumping, and heterogeneous firms', *European Economic Review*, **55**, 480–496.

Costinot, A. (2009), 'On the origins of comparative advantage', *Journal of International Economics*, **77**, 255–264.

Deardorff, A.V. (2013), 'Rue the ROOs: Rules of Origin and the gains (or losses) from trade agreements', University of Michigan mimeo.

Ekholm, K., R. Forslid, and J.R. Markusen (2007), 'Export-platform foreign direct investment', *Journal of the European Economic Association*, **5**, 776–795.

Escaith, Hubert, and A. Diakantoni (2012), 'Reassessing effective protection rates in a trade in tasks perspective: evolution of trade policy in 'Factory Asia', World Trade Organization Economic Research and Statistics Division, Staff Working Paper ERSD-2012-13.

Fort, T. (2011), 'Breaking up is hard to do: Why firms fragment production across locations', University of Maryland mimeo.

Fung, V.K., W.K. Fung, and Y.R. Wind (2007), *Competing in a Flat World: Building Enterprises for a Borderless World*, Pearson Prentice Hall.

Gamberoni, E., R. Lanz, and R. Piermartini (2010), 'Timeliness and contract enforceability in intermediate goods trade', World Bank Policy Research Working Paper Series 5482.

Grossman, G.M., E. Helpman, and A. Szeidl (2006), 'Optimal integration strategies for the multinational firm', *Journal of International Economics*, **70**, 216–238.

Grossman, G.M., and E. Rossi-Hansberg (2008), 'Trading tasks: A simple theory of offshoring', *American Economic Review*, **98**, 1978.

Helpman, E., and O. Itskhoki (2010), 'Labour market rigidities, trade and unemployment', *The Review of Economic Studies*, **77**, 1100–1137.

Helpman, E., M.J. Melitz, and S.R. Yeaple (2004), 'Export versus FDI with heterogeneous firms', *The American Economic Review*, **94**, 300–316.

Ito, T. (2013), 'Export-platform foreign direct investment: theory and evidence', *The World Economy*, **36**, 563–581.

Kee, H.L., and H. Tang (2013), 'Domestic value added in Chinese exports: firm-level evidence', mimeo, Johns Hopkins University.

Konings, J. and H. Vandenbussche (2013), 'Anti-dumping protection hurts exporters: firm-level evidence', *Review of World Economics*, **149**, 295–320.

Koopman, R., Z. Wang, and S.-J. Wei (2012), 'Estimating domestic content in exports when processing trade is pervasive', *Journal of Development Economics*, **99**, 178–189.

Leamer, E.E., and M. Storper (2001), 'The economic geography of the internet age', National Bureau of Economic Research Working Paper No. 8450.

Levchenko, A.A. (2007), 'Institutional quality and international trade', *The Review of Economic Studies*, **74**, 791–819.

Levy, F., and R.J. Murnane (2003), 'The skill content of recent technological change: an empirical exploration', *The Quarterly Journal of Economics*, **118**, 1279–1333.

Melitz, M.J. (2003), 'The impact of trade on intra-industry reallocations and aggregate industry productivity', *Econometrica*, **71**, 1695–1725.

Miroudot, S., and D. Rouzet (2013), 'The cumulative impact of trade barriers along the value chain: an empirical assessment using the OECD inter-country input–output model', mimeo, OECD.

Morrow, P., and L. Brandt (2013), 'Tariffs and the organization of trade in China', mimeo, University of Toronto.

Mrázová, M., and J. Neary (2013), 'Selection effects with heterogeneous firms', mimeo, University of Oxford.

Nunn, N. (2007), 'Relationship-specificity, incomplete contracts, and the pattern of trade', *The Quarterly Journal of Economics*, **122**, 569–600.

Schilling, M.A. (2000), 'Toward a general modular systems theory and its application to interfirm product modularity', *Academy of Management Review*, **25**, 312–334.

Ulrich, K. (1995), 'The role of product architecture in the manufacturing firm', *Research Policy*, **24**, 419–440.

Van Assche, A. (2012), 'The rise of global value chains: implications for Canadian trade and competition policies', Institute for Research on Public Policy No. 31.

Yi, K.-M. (2003), 'Can vertical specialization explain the growth of world trade?', *Journal of Political Economy*, **111**, 52–102.

APPENDIX 5A.1 NO VERTICAL SPECIALIZATION

The elasticity of aggregate exports X^l with respect to country-specific tariff τ^l under no vertical specialization can be separated into an intensive and an extensive margin effect:

$$-\frac{dX^l/d\tau^l}{X^l/\tau^l} = -\frac{\tau^l}{X^l}\left(\int_{\varphi^l}^{\infty}\frac{\partial x^l(\varphi)}{\partial\tau^l}dG(\varphi)\right) + \frac{\tau^l}{X^l}\left(x^l(\varphi^l)\,G'(\varphi^l)\frac{\partial\varphi^l}{\partial\tau^l}\right). \quad (5A.1.1)$$

Using the definition of equilibrium individual exports from equation (5.5) and using the assumption that country l is small enough so that a change in τ^l does not affect B, we get:

$$\frac{dx^l(\varphi)}{d\tau^l} = -\varepsilon\frac{x^l}{\tau^l}.$$

Inserting this into (5A.1.1) and rearranging, we obtain:

$$-\frac{dX^l/d\tau^l}{X^l/\tau^l} = \varepsilon + \frac{x^l(\varphi^l)\,G'(\varphi^l)\varphi^l}{X^l}*\frac{\tau^l}{\varphi^l}\frac{\partial\varphi^l}{\partial\tau^l} \quad (5A.1.2)$$

Using the definition of the distribution of productivity shocks $G'(\varphi) = z\varphi^{-z-1}$ from equation (5.3) and the definition of firm-level exports from equation (5.5), we can rewrite aggregate exports in the following way:

$$X^l = \int_{\varphi^l}^{\infty}x^l(\varphi)\,dG(\varphi) =$$

$$= \int_{\varphi^l}^{\infty}\frac{B}{1-\alpha}\left(\frac{\varphi}{\omega^l}\right)^{\varepsilon-1}\tau^{l-\varepsilon}z\varphi^{-z-1}d\varphi$$

$$= \frac{1}{z-(\varepsilon-1)}*x^l(\varphi^l)\,G'(\varphi^l)\varphi^l.$$

Inserting this into (5A.1.2), we obtain:

$$-\frac{dX^l/d\tau^l}{X^l/\tau^l} = \varepsilon + (z-(\varepsilon-1))*\frac{\tau^l}{\varphi^l}\frac{\partial\varphi^l}{\partial\tau^l}. \quad (5A.1.3)$$

From equation (5.7), we can derive that $\frac{\tau^l}{\varphi^l}\frac{\partial\varphi^l}{\partial\tau^l} = \frac{\varepsilon}{\varepsilon-1}$ so that:

$$-\frac{dX^l}{X^l}\frac{\tau^l}{d\tau^l} = \varepsilon + (z - (\varepsilon - 1))\frac{\varepsilon}{\varepsilon - 1} = \frac{z\varepsilon}{\varepsilon - 1}. \tag{5A.1.4}$$

APPENDIX 5A.2 VERTICAL SPECIALIZATION

Elasticity of Aggregate Exports X^{NO} with Respect to Tariff τ^S

We first calculate the elasticity of aggregate exports by Northern firms that manufacture in the South, X^{NO}, with respect to tariff τ^S. The elasticity can once again be separated into an intensive and an extensive margin effect:

$$-\frac{dX^{NO}/d\tau^S}{X^{NO}/\tau^S} = -\frac{\tau^S}{X^{NO}}\left(\int_{\varphi^{NO}}^{\infty}\frac{\partial x^{NO}(\varphi)}{\partial\tau^S}dG(\varphi)\right) + \frac{\tau^S}{X^{NO}}\left(x^{NO}(\varphi^{NO})\,G'(\varphi^{NO})\frac{\partial\varphi^{NO}}{\partial\tau^S}\right).$$

$$\tag{5A.2.1}$$

Using equation (5.12) and using the assumption that country l is small enough so that a change in τ^S does not affect B, we get:

$$\frac{dx^{NO}(\varphi)}{d\tau^S} = -\varepsilon\frac{x^{NO}}{\tau^S}$$

Inserting this into (5A.2.1) and rearranging, we obtain:

$$-\frac{dX^{NO}/d\tau^S}{X^{NO}/\tau^S} = \varepsilon + \frac{x^{NO}(\varphi^{NO})\,G'(\varphi^{NO})\varphi^{NO}}{X^{NO}} * \frac{d\varphi^{NO}}{\varphi^{NO}}\frac{\tau^S}{d\tau^S} \tag{5A.2.2}$$

We can use the definition of firm-level exports from equation (5.12) and the definition of the distribution of productivity shocks in equation (5.3) to rewrite aggregate exports in the following way:

$$X^{NO} = \int_{\varphi^{NO}}^{\infty} x^{NO}(\varphi)\,dG(\varphi) = \frac{1}{z - (\varepsilon - 1)} * x^{NO}(\varphi^{NO})\,G'(\varphi^{NO})\varphi^{NO}. \tag{5A.2.3}$$

Inserting (5A.2.3) into (5A.2.2), we obtain:

$$-\frac{dX^{NO}/d\tau^S}{X^{NO}/\tau^S} = \varepsilon + (z - (\varepsilon - 1)) * \left(\frac{\tau^S}{\varphi^{NO}}\frac{\partial\varphi^{NO}}{\partial\tau^S}\right) \tag{5A.2.4}$$

We can use equation (5.14) to derive the elasticity of the cut-off condition φ^{NO} with respect to tariffs:

$$\frac{d\varphi^{NO}}{\varphi^{NO}}\frac{\tau^S}{d\tau^S} = \frac{\varepsilon}{\varepsilon - 1}\chi$$

where

$$\chi = \frac{\left(\dfrac{\omega^N}{\omega^S}\right)^{\varepsilon-1}\left(\dfrac{\tau^N}{\tau^S}\right)^{\varepsilon}}{\left(\dfrac{\omega^N}{\omega^S}\right)^{\varepsilon-1}\left(\dfrac{\tau^N}{\tau^S}\right)^{\varepsilon} - 1}.$$

Inserting this elasticity into (5A.2.4) gives:

$$-\frac{dX^{NO}/d\tau^S}{X^{NO}/\tau^S} = \varepsilon + (z - (\varepsilon - 1))\frac{\varepsilon}{\varepsilon - 1}\chi. \qquad (5A.2.5)$$

Elasticity of Aggregate Exports X^N with Respect to Tariff τ^N

We can next calculate the elasticity of aggregate exports X^N with respect to tariff τ^N under vertical specialization. The elasticity can once again be separated into an intensive and an extensive margin effect:

$$-\frac{dX^N/d\tau^N}{X^N/\tau^N} = -\frac{\tau^N}{X^N}\left(\int_{\varphi^N}^{\varphi^{NO}}\frac{\partial x^N(\varphi)}{\partial \tau^N}dG(\varphi)\right) + \frac{\tau^N}{X^N}\left[x^N(\varphi^N)\,G'(\varphi^N)\frac{\partial \varphi^N}{\partial \tau^N}\right.$$

$$\left. - x^N(\varphi^{NO})\,G'(\varphi^{NO})\frac{\partial \varphi^{NO}}{\partial \tau^N}\right]$$

Using the definition of equilibrium individual exports from equation (5.4) and using the assumption that country l is small enough so that a change in τ^N does not affect B, we get:

$$\frac{dx^N(\varphi)}{d\tau^N} = -\varepsilon\frac{x^N}{\tau^N}.$$

Inserting this into the above equation and rearranging, we obtain:

$$-\frac{dX^N/d\tau^N}{X^N/\tau^N} = \varepsilon + \left(\frac{x^N(\varphi^N)\,G'(\varphi^N)\varphi^N}{X^N}*\frac{\partial \varphi^N}{\partial \tau^N}\frac{\tau^N}{\varphi^N} - \frac{x^N(\varphi^{NO})\,G'(\varphi^{NO})\varphi^{NO}}{X^N}*\frac{\partial \varphi^{NO}}{\partial \tau^N}\frac{\tau^N}{\varphi^{NO}}\right).$$

$$(5A.2.6)$$

We have shown above that $\frac{\partial \varphi^N}{\partial \tau^N} \frac{\tau^N}{\varphi^N} = \frac{\varepsilon}{\varepsilon - 1}$. Furthermore, it is straightforward to derive from equation (5.14) that:

$$\frac{d\varphi^{NO}}{\varphi^{NO}} \frac{\tau^N}{d\tau^N} = -\frac{\varepsilon}{\varepsilon - 1}(\chi - 1) < 0,$$

where

$$\chi = \frac{\left(\frac{\omega^N}{\omega^S}\right)^{\varepsilon - 1}\left(\frac{\tau^N}{\tau^S}\right)^{\varepsilon}}{\left(\frac{\omega^N}{\omega^S}\right)^{\varepsilon - 1}\left(\frac{\tau^N}{\tau^S}\right)^{\varepsilon} - 1} > 1.$$

Inserting these cut-off elasticities into (5A.2.6) and rearranging:

$$-\frac{dX^N/d\tau^N}{X^N/\tau^N} = \varepsilon + \frac{\varepsilon}{\varepsilon - 1}\left(\frac{x^N(\varphi^N)\,G'(\varphi^N)\varphi^N - x^N(\varphi^{NO})\,G'(\varphi^{NO})\varphi^{NO}}{X^N}\right)$$

$$\left(\frac{x^N(\varphi^N)\,G'(\varphi^N)\varphi^N - x^N(\varphi^{NO})\,G'(\varphi^{NO})\varphi^{NO}}{X^N} + \chi^*\frac{x^N(\varphi^{NO})\,G'(\varphi^{NO})\varphi^{NO}}{X^N}\right)$$

$$(5\text{A}.2.7)$$

Using the definition of firm-level exports from equation (5.5) and the definition of the distribution of productivity shocks in equation (5.3), we can rewrite aggregate exports in the following way:

$$X^N = \int_{\varphi^N}^{\varphi^{NO}} x^N(\varphi)\,dG(\varphi) = \frac{1}{z - (\varepsilon - 1)} * [x^N(\varphi^N)\,G'(\varphi^N)\varphi^N - x^N(\varphi^{NO})\,G'(\varphi^{NO})\varphi^{NO}].$$

Inserting this equation into (5A.2.7) and rearranging, we obtain:

$$-\frac{dX^N/d\tau^N}{X^N/\tau^N} = \varepsilon + (z - (\varepsilon - 1))\frac{\varepsilon}{\varepsilon - 1}$$

$$\left(1 + \chi^*\frac{x^N(\varphi^{NO})}{x^{NO}(\varphi^{NO})} * \frac{x^{NO}(\varphi^{NO})\,G'(\varphi^{NO})\varphi^{NO}}{x^N(\varphi^N)\,G'(\varphi^N)\varphi^N - x^{NO}(\varphi^{NO})\,G'(\varphi^{NO})\varphi^{NO}}\right). \quad (5\text{A}.2.8)$$

Inserting equations (5.5), (5.12), (5A.2.3) and the definition of χ into (5A.2.8), we can rearrange the equation to:

$$-\frac{dX^N/d\tau^N}{X^N/\tau^N} = \varepsilon + (z-(\varepsilon-1))\frac{\varepsilon}{\varepsilon-1}\left(1 + \frac{X^{NO}}{X^N} * \frac{1}{\left(\frac{\omega^N}{\omega^S}\right)^{\varepsilon-1}\left(\frac{\tau^N}{\tau^S}\right)^{\varepsilon} - 1}\right). \quad (5A.2.9)$$

6. Changes in the production stage position of People's Republic of China trade

Deborah Swenson

1. INTRODUCTION

In the discussion of developments in global value chains, the People's Republic of China (PRC) has featured front and center due to the effects of its market reforms, and the country's 2001 World Trade Organization (WTO) entry. The PRC's participation in global value chains has also attracted note due to the sheer scale of its involvement in international trade. This attention is certainly warranted due to the heavy involvement of the country's imports and exports in the relocation and reorganization of production through global value chains. However, while the nature of the PRC's contributions and connections has been recorded in great detail in a small number of cases, such as for the Apple iPod, detailed knowledge of its production structures and the related trade connections for most products at the same level is rarely available.

In the absence of detailed data on the production of all products, economists have managed to use other methods for drawing inferences about shifts in global production by tracking trade in parts and components, or through the use of input–output tables.[1] Due to the operation of special processing export policies, PRC trade has yielded further insights into the developments of global value chains.[2] However, an ongoing assessment of changes in its production activity is warranted due to major changes in the country's economic environment, which include increases in the cost of labor and changes in technology, as well as changes in production chain opportunities following its 2001 WTO entry.[3] Further, since Johnson and Noguera (2012b) and Baldwin and Lopez-Gonzalez (2013) document large declines in the value added content of trade in recent years, it is important to evaluate how the trends have been manifested in the PRC's engagement in production.

To provide complementary insights about shifts in the trade

connections between the PRC and Asia, as well as the rest of the world, this chapter applies new product-level measures describing the position of products in the production process to PRC trade. The idea that production is conducted through a sequence of steps is easy to visualize, and has long been embedded as a feature in economic models of international production.[4] More recently, the idea of sequential production has been taken to the data, in the work of Antras and Chor (forthcoming), Fally (2012a), and Antras et al. (2012). In this work, data on United States (US) production is used to develop measures that characterize an industry or product's place in the production sequence. With this data in hand, I am able to use this production metric to observe how the characteristics of PRC trade, and trade in intermediates in particular, have changed in recent years.[5]

Analysis of PRC trade growth at the product level between 2001 and 2011 indicates that the *stages* (number of plant-level steps) embedded in imports have increased, while the number of stages implicitly contained in exports have declined. However, this aggregate change reflects both changes in the composition of trade, as well as changes in sourcing within industries or within trade-partner relationships. In general, the overall shift appears to relate tightly to shifts in the industry composition of Chinese trade.

Naturally, while product level trade grew in the majority of cases, not all of the country's trade relationships observed at the product-province-country-ownership level survived over the decade of observation. For this reason, I also analyze how the probability of transaction exit was related to the stages implicitly contained in PRC imports of intermediates. Here, I find the probability that an import transaction exit is related to slower levels of export growth. Further, as with expansion of existing transactions, industry plays a large role in the change in stages. Between 2001 and 2011, the exit of trade transactions was heavily concentrated in high-stage products for some industries. Similarly, the degree of exit was heavily concentrated in low-stage products for other industries. Thus, while we have notions of how technology, income, distance and other factors contribute to the relocation of production chains, this suggests that the influences of these factors on sequential stage characteristics or PRC participation in production chains are anything but uniform across industries.

The remainder of the chapter is organized as follows. First, to provide some background the next section introduces the data set and discusses recent developments in PRC trade. Next, I describe recent measures of production position – *Upstreamness* and *Stages* – and provide a summary of changes in these measures for PRC trade. The fourth section describes product trade variety, across countries and industries. The analysis in sections 5 and 6 is in two parts: the first analysis tests how trade growth was related to measures of production position, while the second set of regressions tests how the measures of production position were related to transaction exit.

2. DEVELOPMENTS IN PRC TRADE

The core data in this project are Chinese import and export transactions for the years 1997 to 2011, which are collected by the General Administration of Customs. A key strength of these data is the fact that they include a number of identifiers that enable researchers to observe the agents, and forms of activity that underpin the trade activities conducted by firms in the PRC. Further, since the government offers trade policies that facilitate processing trade, each trade transaction reports the customs regime under which products enter or exit. While there are a handful of custom regimes reported in the data, the two forms of organization that account for the majority of Chinese trade activity are ordinary trade and processing trade. The latter is especially interesting, since firms engaged in processing trade by definition procure some of their inputs from abroad and export all of their output. While the activities of global value chains are not limited to the use of the processing trade regime, rules governing the use of the processing trade benefit firms through a number of channels, including the exemption from tariffs on imported inputs used in the production of export goods. The operation of the processing trade regime provides a data trail for research, since the administration of processing trade requires processing firms to provide separate reports on their imports of inputs and subsequent export. Thus data from processing firms shed light on the operation of global value chains.[6] Firms that are not exclusively engaged in export may nonetheless provide or use inputs or assembly services that are integrated with global value chains. However, this activity does not qualify firms for tariff reductions on imported inputs, and at least in the earliest years of this analysis, may have left firms with less autonomy in their choice and use of imported inputs.

A second important identifier in the Chinese trade data is the marker for ownership, which allows researchers to distinguish whether the trade was conducted by foreign owned enterprises, state owned enterprises, or private firms. As has been shown by Koopman et al. (2008), as well as by others, throughout the 2000s the overwhelming majority of processing trade volume was handled by foreign owned firms, while private firms and state owned enterprises (SOEs) were responsible for the majority of ordinary trade.

The last noteworthy identifier in the trade data is the information on the location of the entity that produces the export, or the location that was responsible for import purchases. While these data are recorded at a fine geographic level – not just city, but zone within the city – this chapter aggregates the data and studies geographic differences in import or export at the provincial level. As with many national customs collection systems, the PRC chooses to report transactions at a level of detail that goes beyond the 6-digit harmonized system (HS) set of codes. However, since the PRC modified its 8-digit identifiers over the sample period, the product level component of this project aggregates the transactions data to the 6-digit level for analysis.

Changes in the Composition of PRC Exports

One notable development has been the shift in industry composition of exports since the late 1990s. To illustrate the changing industrial composition, the HS6 product transactions in the data set were assigned to 13 industries based on their 2-digit HS code, and the data were aggregated to the industry-year level.[7] As the upper panel of Table 6.1 shows, in both 1997 and 2011 the textile and electronic machinery sectors were the two sectors that were responsible for the highest shares in total exports. However, their relative representation flipped during the time interval: while textiles exports in 1997 were substantially larger than electronics exports in 1997, the relative importance of the two industries reversed, with electronics taking a substantial and ongoing lead for the latter years of the sample period. Since processing exports are known participants in global value chains, the lower panel of Table 6.1 displays the industry sector export shares only for processing exports. Similar to the upper panel for all exports, processing exports also recorded a dramatic reversal in the relative importance of textiles and electronics. While the textile and electronics industries were almost at parity, each responsible for roughly 20 percent of processing exports in 1997, by 2011 the share of textiles in processing exports declined below 5 percent, while the share of processing exports comprised of electrical machinery products rose to almost 35 percent.

The contrast between the importance of textiles and electronics in overall export as compared with processing export raises an important issue in the use of processing trade as a lens for observing Chinese participation in global value chains. The fact that the PRC still had substantial textile exports while processing exports of textiles declined

Table 6.1   Industry shares of Chinese exports and processing exports

	1997	2001	2007	2011
Export shares (%)				
Textiles	23.7	18.8	13.6	12.7
Electrical machinery	13.5	19.3	24.7	23.5
Non-manufacturing	12.6	9.5	4.9	5.0
Miscellaneous manufacturing	10.5	10.1	9.0	9.0
Non-electrical machinery	7.5	12.6	18.8	9.0
Metals	7.4	6.1	9.5	7.6
Footwear and headgear	5.6	4.6	2.5	2.8
Chemicals and allied industries	5.2	4.8	4.2	5.1
Raw hides, leather and fur	3.4	3.2	1.3	1.6
Plastics and rubber	3.2	3.1	3.0	1.8
Transportation	2.8	3.6	4.5	5.8
Stone, clay and glass	2.8	2.5	2.2	3.2
Wood and wood products	1.9	1.8	1.7	1.6
Total	100.0	100.0	100.0	100.0
Processing export shares (%)				
Electrical machinery	21.2	29.0	37.5	34.6
Textiles	20.0	13.7	5.9	4.8
Miscellaneous manufacturing	13.7	12.1	9.6	8.9
Non-electrical machinery	10.3	17.6	27.3	27.6
Footwear and headgear	7.2	4.8	1.8	1.6
Metals	6.8	3.9	2.8	2.3
Plastics and rubber	4.2	4.0	3.6	4.0
Raw hides, leather and fur	4.1	3.1	0.9	0.6
Transportation	3.9	4.0	4.5	7.6
Non-manufacturing	3.7	2.5	2.2	2.1
Stone, clay and glass	2.0	2.0	1.2	3.1
Chemicals and allied industries	1.5	1.8	1.5	1.5
Wood and wood products	1.4	1.3	1.1	1.1
Total	100.0	100.0	100.0	100.0

Source: Author's calculation.

precipitously may be attributed to at least two factors. First, since later in the period textile exports were increasingly provided by the new entry of private firms in the textile industry, the decline in processing exports of textiles can be partially explained by the fact that private firms are less frequently engaged in processing trade than were foreign invested firms. The other factor that explains the trends in processing trade participation is the general decline in usage of processing trade. When studying the decline in the share of processing trade in PRC exports, Brandt and Morrow (2013) document the role of input tariff reductions that reduced a cost advantage that differentially benefited processing export-ers relative to ordinary exporters, and the growth in domestic markets.[8] Alternatively, as the variety of domestic inputs increased, and as local demand expanded, processing trade could have shrunk in importance as local demand was met by local firm entry rather than processing trade expansion by foreign owned firms. Thus, while earlier processing trade data may have provided a relatively comprehensive view of PRC par-ticipation in global value chains, it is likely that an increasing share of production sharing activities was moving outside of the processing trade regime in the later years.

More generally, Table 6.1 shows that the majority of manufacturing industries had fairly stable export shares over the sample period. However, the one industry that draws attention for its buoyancy is the transpor-tation sector, which moved from 2.8 percent to 5.8 percent of overall exports, and from 3.9 percent to 7.6 percent of processing exports between 1997 and 2011.

For another view of changes in trade composition, the data can be aggregated by product type, rather than industry composition. Thus to gain insight into developments in the PRC's activities within global value chains, UN Broad Economic Classification (BEC) codes that provide a mapping between HS6 product codes and good type were used to distin-guish trade in final goods from trade in intermediate inputs and primary goods. Further, while parts of the analysis track changes in trade in intermediate goods, the UN BEC codes can be used further to distinguish between product trade in parts and components and product trades in semi-finished goods.

By aggregating processing trade imports and exports by product type, we can examine the types of products flow into and out of Chinese processing trade operations to describe how the composition of processing trade has changed over time. Figure 6.1a, which shows the developments in processing imports and exports for the five goods categories (capital goods, consumer goods, parts and components, semi-finished goods and primary goods), reveals that aside from the downturn during the global recession, the PRC has managed a sustained growth in its exports of final goods – growth that is particularly pronounced in the case of capital goods as compared with the growth in the export of consumer final goods. Through the entire period, the country was both an importer and an exporter of intermediate goods; however it was a net importer of both parts and components and semi-finished goods.

For comparison Figure 6.1b displays the developments in the PRC's

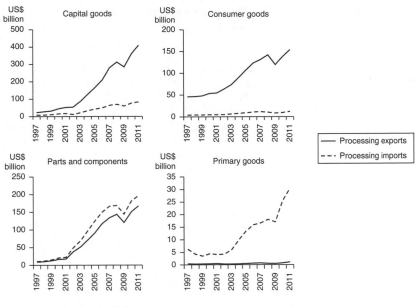

Source: Author's calculation.

Figure 6.1a   People's Republic of China processing trade, 1997–2011

overall imports and exports of the five goods groups. On the export side, the growth in overall consumer products exports is more pronounced than was the growth in consumer products exports by processing trade firms. One factor for this change, noted by Brandt and Morrow (2013), was a decline in importance of the processing trade in industry sectors where input tariffs declined. More important, the data show that the PRC involvement with intermediate inputs trade extended outside of processing trade. As with processing trade, import and export of parts and components and of semi-finished goods all increased, though the country transitioned from a net importer to a modest net exporter in the semi-finished goods category, while it retained its status as a net importer in the parts and components sector. Thus, because the activities of global value chain type production were not limited to the activities of firms engaged in processing trade, it appears important when describing the developments in the country's participation in global value chains to analyze changes in both processing and ordinary trade.[9]

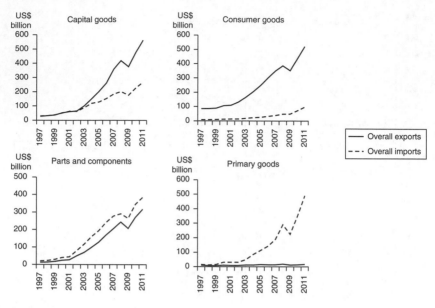

Source: Author's calculation.

Figure 6.1b   People's Republic of China overall trade, 1997–2011

3.   PRODUCTION STAGES – UPSTREAMNESS AND STAGES

To search for evidence of shifts in the country's position in global supply chains, I turn to new measures of product position developed by Fally (2012a, 2012b). Conceptually, we can visualize production as involving a number of steps, as final goods are created through the completion of a number of tasks. Within this sequential process, a good can be characterized by the number of stages or steps that precede or follow the handling of a particular product. Based on this idea, Fally generates measures of *Upstreamness* and *Stages*. For example, each input handled in a production chain will ultimately be handled in a number of steps prior to completion and sale as a final good. The count of future stages is deemed *upstreamness*. Similarly, the creation of each input implies that the input has already passed through a number of prior steps. When weighted by the value-added of each step, Fally terms the count of prior steps, *stages*.[10] Through the use of the US Bureau of Economic Analysis concordances, Fally links his measures of upstreamness and stages to HS6 products.

In this project, I use HS6 product identifiers to match Fally's measures of stages and upstreamness with Chinese customs data on imports and exports. While production techniques may not be identical in the US and the PRC, the connection is used to answer two questions. First, how does the production chain position of the products traded by the PRC – traded intermediate products in particular – compare with the production chain position of US-based activities? Second, when the measures are applied to Chinese trade across the 2000s, is there evidence that the production chain position of the country's trade has shifted over time – overall, by industry or across countries? Both of these questions are descriptive empirical inquiries. In particular, while Antras and Chor (forthcoming) test a property rights model of the firm by examining the connection between their related measure of *downstreamness* to ownership and the elasticity of demand, the connection between product position and trade outcomes is still a new research endeavor. Further, since Nunn (2007) has shown how lock-in due to relationship specific investments is especially important in intermediate inputs, it is not clear whether one would expect to see noticeable changes in the production position of PRC trade.[11] Thus, this work will provide some initial evidence on this question.

In contrast with Fally's observation that US production data in recent decades has been characterized by a decline in the number of stages, the PRC's intermediate imports are characterized by increases in both stages and upstreamness between 2001 and 2011. For example, if I calculate PRC stage measures by weighting each HS6 intermediate input import transaction by its dutiable value, the PRC's measure of stages rose from 2.49 to 2.61 in the decade running from 2001 and 2011. This trend is interesting, since it suggests that the PRC, in contrast with the US, is participating in industries that are increasing in stages, rather than declining in stages. This change could arise from one of two sources. First, changes in relative production capability could cause Chinese firms to move away from the processing of low stage items to the processing of higher stage items that are characterized by handling by a larger number of prior plants. This would imply that the upstreamness measure should have declined over the period, since the later receipt of the inputs along the production chain implies that the completion of the production will require fewer subsequent steps to arrive at the end of the production sequence. However, if I take the same approach, and calculate the weighted average of upstreamness for PRC intermediate imports using transaction dutiable values as weights, these too rose, beginning at a value of 2.84 and ending at 3.18 during the period. Taken together, this evidence suggests that the PRC was moving into production processes that involved production chains of increasing length.[12]

Next, to better understand the trends in PRC values of the stages and

Table 6.2   *Import upstreamness and stages by trade type*

	Upstreamness				Stages			
	1997	2001	2007	2011	1997	2001	2007	2011
All Imports								
Processing trade	2.52	2.58	2.55	2.53	2.45	2.45	2.42	2.39
Processing trade (weighted)	2.69	2.73	2.55	2.52	2.48	2.41	2.35	2.31
Ordinary trade	2.26	2.42	2.42	2.39	2.37	2.32	2.30	2.29
Ordinary trade (weighted)	2.69	2.79	3.11	3.21	2.39	2.34	2.26	2.42
Intermediate input imports								
Processing trade	2.66	2.59	2.78	2.58	2.47	2.34	2.44	2.42
Processing trade (weighted)	2.81	2.84	3.12	2.83	2.51	2.35	2.45	2.41
Ordinary trade	2.59	2.59	3.09	2.57	2.34	2.47	2.31	2.31
Ordinary trade (weighted)	2.78	3.30	3.44	3.42	2.41	2.35	2.26	2.23

Note: For each product group, the first row represented the unweighted average, while the second row denoted (weighted) is the mean value for Upstreamness or Stages, when dutiable import transaction values are used as weights.

Source: Author's calculation.

upstreamness measures, I provide more systematic disaggregation of Chinese imports, noting differential trends across different groups of trade. I apply Fally's measures to import data, and examine how they differ by type of importer (processing firms versus ordinary firms), and by industry. In Table 6.2, I begin by presenting information on aggregate shifts in the measures for processing and ordinary imports between 1997 and 2011. As the first two rows show, the average stages of all processing imports declined between 1997 and 2011, whether the average is computed as the average across all transactions, or the average across all transactions weighted by the dutiable values of import. In a similar evaluation of average upstreamness, the evidence is mixed. However, when the processing trade observations are weighted by dutiable transaction value, the data show that the number of stages subsequent to the receipt of the import declined between 1997 and 2011.

However, one problem with upstreamness or stages measures based on the universe of imports is the fact that they combine both intermediate inputs and raw materials. Alternatively, the measures may also change over time due to the inclusion of capital goods imports. Thus, to isolate changes related to the use of intermediates, the bottom rows of Table 6.2 recalculate average upstreamness and stages, using data only on imported intermediates. Under this new metric, the data now suggest that imported

Table 6.3   Upstreamness and stages for intermediates trade by source region

| | All intermediate imports | | | |
| | Upstreamness | | Stages | |
	2000	2011	2000	2011
Japan	2.73	**2.74**	2.45	2.42
ASEAN 5	2.95	**3.10**	2.51	**2.68**
Republic of Korea and Taipei,China	2.96	**3.00**	2.62	2.59
NAFTA	2.87	**2.89**	2.48	**2.50**
European Union 28	2.47	**2.61**	2.36	**2.39**
Australia and New Zealand	2.94	**3.20**	2.41	**2.46**
	Processing intermediate imports			
Japan	2.59	**2.66**	2.41	2.37
ASEAN 5	2.81	**2.82**	2.38	**2.54**
Republic of Korea and Taipei,China	2.74	**2.77**	2.56	2.49
NAFTA	2.77	**2.92**	2.31	**2.49**
EU28	2.53	**2.74**	2.36	**2.47**
Australia and New Zealand	3.05	**3.23**	2.46	2.44
	Ordinary intermediate imports			
Japan	2.97	2.80	2.55	2.42
ASEAN 5	3.08	**3.27**	2.67	**2.78**
Republic of Korea and Taipei,China	3.33	3.00	2.75	2.59
NAFTA	2.92	2.91	2.55	2.52
European Union 28	2.49	**3.20**	2.37	**2.46**
Australia and New Zealand	2.90	**3.05**	2.38	**2.45**

Notes:
ASEAN 5 = Indonesia, Malaysia, the Philippines, Singapore and Thailand.
Regional values are weighted averages that use trade transaction values as weights. Values in 2011 columns are listed in bold if the value increased between 2000 and 2011.

Source: Author's calculation.

intermediates have gone through more stages prior to their import for Chinese processing. It also suggests that the products imported by PRC processors are closer to final demand than before, since the number of stages characterizing processing trade imported inputs declined between 1997 and 2011.

For a different view on upstreamness and stages, Table 6.3 presents measures based on imported intermediate inputs that were sourced from different regions. In the case of processing imports of intermediates,

Table 6.4   Industry input import stages, by trade type

	Stages					
	All intermediates import		Processing intermediates import		Ordinary intermediates import	
	2000	2011	2000	2011	2000	2011
Non-manufacturing	2.02	2.01	2.04	1.91	2.01	2.01
Chemicals and allied industries	2.70	**2.80**	2.56	**2.72**	2.76	**2.81**
Plastics and rubber	2.86	2.76	2.85	2.77	2.89	2.80
Raw hides, leather and fur	3.25	3.21	3.25	3.19	3.23	**3.25**
Wood and wood products	2.42	**2.48**	2.40	**2.43**	2.43	**2.50**
Textiles	2.67	2.65	2.67	**2.68**	2.64	**2.66**
Footwear and headgear	2.14	2.13	2.14	2.13	2.15	2.14
Stone, clay and glass	2.20	**2.28**	2.26	**2.28**	2.04	**2.28**
Metals	2.46	**2.51**	2.46	**2.49**	2.47	**2.49**
Non-electrical machinery	2.32	2.29	2.23	**2.41**	2.25	2.22
Electrical machinery	2.18	2.16	2.20	2.17	2.16	2.15
Transportation	2.41	**2.44**	2.37	**2.38**	2.45	**2.47**
Miscellaneous manufacturing	2.13	**2.17**	2.10	**2.18**	2.19	**2.21**
Overall	2.41	2.28	2.48	2.41	2.34	2.22

Note: Industry values are weighted averages that use trade transaction values as weights. Values in 2011 column are listed in bold if the value increased between 2000 and 2011.

Source: Author's calculation.

upstreamness increased for all regional groups, without exception. In contrast, stages increased between 1997 and 2011 in three of the six cases. Notably, the regional dimension for ordinary trade is somewhat different, as the increase in upstreamness and stages was present in only three of the six sources. Nonetheless, since processing and ordinary firms specialized in somewhat different industries, the differences might reflect such composition differences, rather than differences in sourcing preferences.

To determine whether processing versus ordinary firm sourcing choices differed by industry, Table 6.4 presents information on the stages characterizing import of intermediates for processing and by ordinary importers disaggregated by industry. The striking result here is the tight correspondence between the values recorded for processing and ordinary trade by industry. While the relative importance of stages for processing and ordinary exports varies by industry, this suggests that the profit maximizing organization of production chain input use did not differ significantly for processing versus ordinary firms.

If changes in upstreamness or stages were driven solely by macro or country factors, such as increases in assembly costs or changes in transportation charges, we would expect the changes in stages to be similar across industries. However, comparison of trends in Table 6.4 reveals that stages rose in six of the thirteen industries, while they declined in the remaining industries. If the trends are evaluated using only processing or ordinary trade, the industries that had rising stage imports in the case of processing intermediate input imports were the same industries that also had ordinary imports of intermediates that were characterized by rising stages. Thus, it appears that fundamental changes in technology or organizational form were more important in determining the trend in stages than general macroeconomic factors.

For a last comparison, it is worth asking how trends in upstreamness and stages for export of intermediate inputs compared with the values observed in their imports. Notably, among intermediate inputs both stages and upstreamness were declining. When weighted by the export value of each HS6 intermediate input, the number of stages fell from 2.49 in 2000 to 2.40 in 2011, while the value of upstreamness declined from 2.83 to 2.60.[13]

4. IMPORTED INPUT PRODUCT VARIETY

To provide another view on sourcing changes over time, I examine changes in input diversity and input sourcing. A simple way to measure input diversity is to count the number of unique HS6 products imported by firms in the PRC. While the trade transactions are initially recorded at the 8-digit level, the use of 8-digit PRC trade data is complicated by the fact that the HS8 code lexicon was increased over the period of study. To avoid the appearance of product introductions that were actually created by innovations or modifications in the trade classification system, it is safer to remain instead with counts based on HS6 codes.

On the import side, Table 6.5 demonstrates that between 1997 and 2011, both PRC processing and ordinary firms reduced the diversity of their imports based on HS6 codes. However, since we are interested in the operation of global value chains, it makes sense to track developments in the import of intermediates and capital goods. Again, the data in Table 6.5 show that import diversity measured by unique product counts declined between 1997 and 2011 for both processing and ordinary trade. However, one possibility is that firms reduced the range of imported intermediates and capital goods, as they moved out of unprofitable or unsuccessful export product lines. Consistent with this conjecture, counts of unique

Table 6.5   Unique transactions — processing and ordinary trade

	Unique HS6 products		Unique HS6 province	
	Processing	Ordinary	Processing	Ordinary
Imports				
1997	4 445	4 824	30 819	41 882
2001	4 309	4 865	28 787	51 478
2007	4 042	4 800	28 787	57 997
2011	3 891	4 801	27 267	61 277
Imported intermediate and capital goods				
1997	3 441	3 634	26 643	33 751
2001	3 342	3 678	24 653	41 654
2007	3 157	3 632	25 189	47 030
2011	2 950	3 471	22 921	46 767
Exports				
1997	3 996	4 835	19 278	56 191
2001	3 705	4 882	16 309	65 629
2007	3 693	4 795	18 427	77 698
2011	3 366	4 719	16 524	77 119

Source: Author's calculation.

HS6 export product lines contracted for both processing and ordinary exporters.[14]

Naturally, the use of HS6 counts at the national level is overly coarse given the scale of the PRC's economic activity. As an alternative, Table 6.5 also shows how unique counts of HS6-Province activities changed over the time period. When geographic detail is added, the spread of ordinary trade across provinces is evidenced by the 50 percent increase over the period in the number of HS6-province ordinary transactions. In the case of processing, the concentration of producers in a more limited number of provinces is evidenced in the smaller counts. Most notable is the decrease in distinct processing trade transactions, whether recorded for imports, imported intermediates and capital goods, or exports.

The earlier data characteristics presented in Table 6.1 show that the industry composition of processing trade has changed over the sample period. Since the predominance of textile exports over non-electrical machinery and electrical machinery activities was overturned by 2011, I check to see whether the change in input sourcing diversity was related to industry composition. To illustrate industry trends in the sourcing of intermediates and capital goods, Table 6.6 presents the counts of HS6 products for these

*Table 6.6   Imported intermediate and capital goods by industry –
processing and ordinary trade*

	1997	2001	2007	2011
Textiles				
Processing HS6	500	497	496	481
Ordinary HS6	464	484	500	499
Non-electrical machinery				
Processing HS6	336	314	333	319
Ordinary HS6	244	248	224	197
Electrical machinery				
Processing HS6	238	232	218	188
Ordinary HS6	244	248	224	197

Source: Author's calculation.

major industries. What is notable about the table is that there is no evidence of a shrinking range of inputs purchased by the textile industry, while the reduction in input range observed in the non-electrical machinery industry is small and the reductions for the electrical machinery industry are moderate. For this reason, the reduction in the range of HS6 products cannot be blamed on the decline in the importance of textile production. Further, to the extent that there were industry trends in the diversity of inputs sourced, the trends were similar for both ordinary and processing traders. One likely cause of the similarity is that developments in Chinese production of inputs allowed the country's firms to increase domestic content in production as documented by Kee and Tang (2012). Thus, as new parts became available domestically, it would have enabled both processing and ordinary exporting firms to replace imported varieties with local varieties.

Finally, for an alternative geographic approach, it is also possible to track unique HS6-source region counts for processing and ordinary trade in intermediates and capital goods. The counts, which are reported in Table 6.7, reveal some modest shifts in the location of sourcing. First, while the count of distinct intermediate inputs imported from Japan, Hong Kong, China, the Republic of Korea and Taipei,China decreased between 1997 and 2011, the counts for most other regions remained stable or decreased. In the case of capital goods imports, the diversity of capital goods declined across all regions. Here too, the fact that export of capital goods expanded rapidly during this time period suggests that PRC firms had the option of replacing imported capital goods with newly developed local varieties.

Table 6.7   Imported intermediate inputs and capital goods by source region, HS6 counts

	1997	2001	2007	2011
Intermediate inputs imports				
Hong Kong, China	3014	2962	1938	1546
Japan	2728	2741	2718	2556
ASEAN 5	2123	2265	2284	2135
Republic of Korea and Taipei,China	2687	2714	2662	2504
NAFTA	2503	2550	2703	2622
European Union 28	2639	2748	2808	2704
Australia and New Zealand	1205	1365	1731	1596
Rest of the world	2346	2422	2776	2684
Capital goods imports				
Hong Kong, China	648	642	395	314
Japan	629	620	598	542
ASEAN 5	507	530	459	396
Republic of Korea and Taipei,China	600	596	574	519
NAFTA	607	626	603	551
European Union 28	618	637	627	571
Australia and New Zealand	342	369	401	342
Rest of the world	543	550	546	530

Notes:
ASEAN 5 = Indonesia, Malaysia, the Philippines, Singapore and Thailand; HS = harmonized system; NAFTA = North American Free Trade Agreement.
Number of unique HS6 codes of intermediates or capital goods.

Source: Author's calculation.

5.   ANALYSIS OF PRODUCT LEVEL TRADE DATA – PRODUCTION POSITION AND PRC TRADE GROWTH

To determine whether PRC imports and exports involve products that are characterized by changing positions, as determined by Fally's stages or upstreamness measures, I implement a few simple estimating frameworks. This begins with equations (6.1A) and (6.1B).

$$\Delta \ln (Import)_{pcho} = \beta_1 \frac{Stages}{Upstreamness} + \beta_2 \ln (Import, 2000)_{pcho} + \psi_{pcho}$$

$$(6.1A)$$

$$\Delta \ln(Import)_{pcho} = \sum \sigma_p + \sum \lambda_c + \sum \xi_i + \sum \mu_o$$

$$+ \beta_1 \frac{Stages}{Upstreamness} + \beta_2 \ln(Import, 2000)_{pcho} + \psi_{pcho} \qquad (6.1B)$$

The dependent variable, $\Delta \ln(Import)$, which measures the change in import value between 2000 and 2011, has subscripts, *pcho*, referring to the province (p), country (c), hs6 good (h), and ownership type (o) of each trade transaction.[15] To determine whether import growth differed by product position in the value chain, each regression includes Fally's measure of either stages or upstreamness. For scaling, each observation of changes in import value is also related to the import value in the initial year, $\Delta \ln(Import, 2000)$.

Due to unmeasured features that may have influenced changes in import, the specifications beginning with (6.1B) also include a large set of fixed effects, the first of which, δ_p, is province. This control is intended to capture differences in provincial participation in international trade that arose from factors such as differences in provincial endowments, geography, and policy. For example, Defever and Riaño (2012) note the importance of policy interventions, such as free trade zones at the subnational level in the PRC, as factors that contributed to the unusually strong presence of *pure exporters* – firms whose exports comprised 90 percent or more of sales. Others, including Lu et al. (2012), have suggested that the PRC is a lumpy country. If so, the failure of factor price equalization within the country due to dramatic differences in local endowments will influence regional speciali-zation patterns. Further, as noted by Head et al. (2011), there is evidence of provincial differences in sourcing choices, which suggests that provincial differences in foreign direct investment (FDI) connections may establish differential choices in the sourcing of intermediates. Thus, fixed effects for provinces are meant to account for these factors and other elements that may have caused unevenness in the growth of trade across the country.

The regression specifications also include fixed effects for firm owner-ship type, μ_o. This set of fixed effects distinguishes between firms that had foreign involvement (foreign owned firms and joint ventures), as compared with the other main ownership types: state-owned enterprises and private firms. The use of these indicators is justified by the differential capabilities and opportunities that were available to firms in each of these three ownership groups.[16]

Country fixed effects λ_c, are added to capture differences in country trade opportunities over time that were related to changes in income, exchange rates, policy and other factors over the analysis period 2001–2011. Finally, to capture differences in industry trends and opportunities, the fixed effects regressions include controls for industry, ξ_i. When classifying each transaction as a member of an industry, the transactions HS6 codes were assigned to the industry categories, as described in Appendix Table 6A.1.

Table 6.8a illustrates how during 2001–2011 changes in PRC imports of intermediates and overall imports were related to Fally's stages and upstreamness measures. In the case of imports, the results show that imports of HS6 products that were characterized by higher values of stages or upstreamness grew more rapidly than did HS6 product imports that were lower on either of these scales. In the case of the stages measure, the strength of this correlation was stronger for intermediate input imports than it was for overall imports.

Next, to evaluate whether HS6 product export growth was systematically related to Fally's (2012b) measures of upstreamness or stages, analogous regression specifications were applied to changes in Chinese exports of intermediate products and overall exports.

$$\Delta \ln (Export)_{pcho} = \beta_1 \frac{Stages}{Upstreamness} + \beta_2 \ln (Export, 2000)_{pcho} + \psi_{pcho} \quad (6.2A)$$

$$\Delta \ln (Export)_{pcho} = \sum \sigma_p + \sum \lambda_c + \sum \xi_i + \sum \mu_o \quad (6.2B)$$

$$+ \beta_1 \frac{Stages}{Upstreamness} + \beta_2 \ln (Export, 2000)_{pcho} + \psi_{pcho}$$

When these specifications are used to examine the country's export growth, the results in Table 6.8b show that exports grew less rapidly in sectors that were characterized by higher values of stages or upstreamness. Thus the relationship between upstreamness or stages and export growth was directly opposite to the correlations describing import growth.

While the initial results provide an overview of general trade trends based on the full sample with ownership firm type fixed effects to control for general differences in firm trade by firm ownership, it is possible that firm ownership may have affected firm propensity to expand the import or export of higher stage items. Thus, in the first three columns of Tables 6.9a and 6.9b, the imports and exports of intermediate inputs are analyzed separately for each of the three major firm ownership types: foreign owned, SOEs and private firms.[17] Similar to the overall results in Tables 6.8a and 6.8b, the new regressions show that stages were positively related to import growth and negatively related to export growth, regardless of firm ownership. However, the correlation between stages and intermediates trade growth was stronger for both exports and imports in the case of private firms than the correlation for trade transactions that were handled by foreign firms.

Since differential trade growth could also be manifested along

Table 6.8a Stages/upstreamness and changes in Chinese imports, 2000–2011

	All imports				Imported intermediates			
	(1)	(2)	(3)	(4)	(5)	(6)	(7)	(8)
Stages	0.148***		0.357***	0.308***	0.255***	0.267***	0.401***	0.242***
	-0.027		-0.032	-0.012	-0.031	-0.015	-0.039	-0.016
Upstreamness		0.183***						
		-0.01						
ln (Import_2000)	-0.556***	-0.559***	-0.544***	-0.549***	-0.597***	-0.599***	-0.576***	-0.576***
	-0.003	-0.003	-0.003	-0.003	-0.003	-0.003	-0.003	-0.003
Controls			Industry Country Province Firm Type	Industry Country Province Firm Type			Industry Country Province Firm Type	Industry Country Province Firm Type
N	128 571	128 571	128 571	128 571	85 156	85 156	85 156	85 156
Adjusted R^2	0.262	0.264	0.364	0.366	0.283	0.285	0.385	0.386

Note: Standard errors in parentheses. * $p < 0.10$, ** $p < 0.05$, *** $p < 0.01$.

Source: Author's calculation.

197

Table 6.8b *Stages/upstreamness and changes in Chinese exports, 2000–2011*

	All exports				Exported intermediates			
	(1)	(2)	(3)	(4)	(5)	(6)	(7)	(8)
Stages	-0.280***		-0.408***		-0.486***		-0.358***	
	-0.033		-0.038		-0.038		-0.046	
Upstreamness		-0.503***		-0.389***		-0.344***		-0.240***
		-0.012		-0.014		-0.017		-0.019
ln (*Exports_2000*)	-0.865***	-0.852***	-0.865***	-0.857***	-0.826***	-0.827***	-0.820***	-0.819***
	-0.003	-0.003	-0.003	-0.003	-0.004	-0.004	-0.004	-0.004
Controls			Industry Country Province Firm Type	Industry Country Province Firm Type			Industry Country Province Firm Type	Industry Country Province Firm Type
N	110489	110489	110489	110489	70049	70049	70049	70049
Adjusted R^2	0.451	0.459	0.521	0.524	0.425	0.426	0.495	0.496

Note: Standard errors in parentheses. * $p < 0.10$, ** $p < 0.05$, *** $p < 0.01$.

Source: Author's calculation.

Table 6.9a   *Stages and changes in Chinese imports of intermediates:*
differences by firm ownership and source region, 2000–2011

	By firm ownership			By source region		
	(1) Foreign invested enterprise	(2) State- owned enterprise	(3) Private enterprise	(4) Republic of Korea and Taipei,China	(5) ASEAN	(6) Rich countries
Stages	0.116**	0.857***	0.705***	0.722***	0.953***	0.125***
	−0.049	−0.072	−0.119	−0.075	−0.136	−0.048
ln (*Imports*_2000)	−0.571***	−0.563***	−0.697***	−0.604***	−0.597***	−0.576***
	−0.005	−0.006	−0.010	−0.006	−0.013	−0.004
Controls	Industry	Industry	Industry	Industry	Industry	Industry
	Country	Country	Country	Country	Country	Country
	Province	Province	Province	Province	Province	Province
				Firm Type	Firm Type	Firm Type
N	50170	24774	10212	25397	7116	51410
Adjusted R^2	0.359	0.347	0.496	0.429	0.324	0.357

Note: Standard errors in parentheses. * p < 0.10, ** p < 0.05, *** p < 0.01.

Source: Author's calculation.

geographic lines, Tables 6.9a and 6.9b also test whether the correlation
between growth in intermediates imports and exports and the measure
of stages differed for different country regions. For this examination,
I report the regressions for three country groups: (1) the Republic of
Korea and Taipei,China, (2) Association of Southeast Asian Nations
(ASEAN) and (3) rich countries (Japan, the US, Canada, European
Union 28, Australia, and New Zealand). In the case of imported inputs,
import growth for all three country groups was most rapid for HS6
products that were characterized by higher levels of stages. However,
since the correlation is especially strong for the first two groups located
in Asia, as compared with the rich country aggregate, it appears that
nearby Asian locations were increasing their supply share of higher stage
intermediates.

   In the case of intermediate exports, Table 6.8b indicates there was a
negative correlation between stages and export growth in the full sample.
However, in Table 6.9b the separate regressions for each of the geographic
regions provide no single response. Similar to the full sample, the data show
that the export growth to rich countries was much slower in high stage intermediate products than it was in HS6 products that had lower values of the

Table 6.9b   *Stages and changes in Chinese exports of intermediates: differences by firm ownership and destination region, 2000–2011*

	By firm ownership			By destination region		
	(1) Foreign invested enterprise	(2) State- owned enterprise	(3) Private enterprise	(4) Republic of Korea and Taipei,China	(5) ASEAN	(6) Rich countries
Stages	−0.369***	−0.008	−1.009***	0.184**	−0.041	−0.716***
	−0.066	−0.077	−0.11	−0.083	−0.129	−0.063
ln (*Exports_2000*)	−0.778***	−0.852***	−0.923***	−0.756***	−0.833***	−0.855***
	−0.006	−0.007	−0.009	−0.007	−0.010	−0.005
Controls	Industry	Industry	Industry	Industry	Industry	Industry
	Country	Country	Country	Country	Country	Country
	Province	Province	Province	Province	Province	Province
				Firm Type	Firm Type	Firm Type
N	37 291	22 433	10 325	22 098	7 979	38 504
Adjusted R^2	0.419	0.527	0.596	0.422	0.51	0.502

Note: Standard errors in parentheses. * p < 0.10, ** p < 0.05, *** p < 0.01.

Source: Author's calculation.

stage measure. In contrast, there is no apparent correlation in the case of exported intermediates destined for ASEAN countries, while the correlation with exports to Taipei,China and the Republic of Korea group was positive.

The demand for imported intermediates is linked, in part, to the demand for those inputs in the production of exports. Thus, the estimating equation is further changed to include the contemporaneous, 2000 to 2011, change in export demand according to regression equation (6.3).

$$\Delta \ln(Export)_{pcho} = \sum \sigma_p + \sum \lambda_c + \sum \xi_i + \sum \mu_o + \beta_1 Stages$$

$$+ \beta_2 \ln(Import, 2000)_{pcho} + \beta_3 \Delta \ln(Export) + \psi_{pcho} \qquad (6.3)$$

Table 6.10 first demonstrates the results of estimating this new equation with different measures of the change in export, beginning with industry-province (*ip*) export changes, followed by industry-province-ownership (*ipo*) changes in export. As expected, either export measure is positively related to changes in intermediates export, and the estimated coefficient on stages is similar regardless of the export measure.

Table 6.10   *Stages and changes in Chinese intermediate imports: controlling for export demand, 2000–2011*

	(1)	(2)	(3)	(4)	(5)
ln (*Imports_2000*)	−0.576***	−0.576***	−0.576***	−0.577***	−0.580***
	−0.003	−0.003	−0.003	−0.003	−0.003
Δln (*Exports_All_ip*)	0.096***		0.015		
	−0.026		−0.029		
Δln (*Exports_All_ipo*)		0.105***	0.101***		
		−0.015	−0.017		
Δln (*Exports_Fin_ipo*)				−0.027***	−0.027***
				−0.006	−0.006
Δln (*Exports_Int_ipo*)				−0.011*	−0.003
				−0.006	−0.006
Δln (*Exports_Cap_ipo*)				0.017***	0.011**
				−0.006	−0.006
Stages	0.400***	0.403***	0.403***	0.397***	0.377
	−0.039	−0.039	−0.039	−0.039	−0.263
Chemicals					−0.351
					−0.273
Plastics					1.081***
					−0.274
Furs					0.403
					−0.558
Wood					0.926***
					−0.297
Textile					−0.611**
					−0.297
Footwear					−1.153
					−1.503
Stoneware and glass					0.541
					−0.387
Metals					−0.318
					−0.282
Machinery					−1.604***
					−0.317
Electrical machinery					−0.912***
					−0.297
Transport equipment					0.870
					−0.664
Miscellaneous manufacturing					2.741***
					−0.394
N	85 142	85 142	85 142	85 142	85 142
Adjusted R^2	0.385	0.386	0.386	0.386	0.389

Notes: Standard errors in parentheses. * $p < 0.10$, ** $p < 0.05$, *** $p < 0.01$. Regressions include fixed effects for country, ownership, industry, and province.

Source: Author's calculation.

Nonetheless, the fact that the regression fit is somewhat better when the industry-province-ownership (*ipo*) measures of export changes are included suggests that trade decisions which link imports to exports are tied to firm ownership type.

To further explore the connection between intermediates import and provincial export, I generate three industry-province export measures. The first measures changes in exports of final consumption goods (Δ*Exports_Fin_ipo*), the second measures changes in exports of intermediate goods (Δ*Exports_Int_ipo*), and the last measures changes in the export of capital goods (Δ*Exports_Cap_ipo*).[18] When the export data are delineated along these usage lines, the association between intermediates import and industry-province-ownership export reveals some interesting differences. First, the strong positive association between intermediates import and export is only apparent in the case of capital goods export. In contrast, there is a negative association in the case of final consumer goods and intermediates export. Nonetheless, while the coefficients on each form of export demand differ dramatically, the estimated coefficient on stages is almost identical to the value of stages coefficients in the earlier regressions. Thus, even when controlling for different measures of export demand, the general finding remains: Chinese imports of intermediate inputs have indeed been more rapid in higher-stage HS6 products.

The final column in Table 6.10 modifies regression equation (6.3) to allow the coefficient on stages to differ across industries. This improves the regression fit, and reveals considerable cross-industry differences in the correlation between intermediates import and the measure of stages. First, the correlations are strongly negative, and highly significant for the textiles, non-electrical machinery and electrical machinery sectors. Since these sectors were among the largest export sectors of the country, it suggests that the negative correlation might be related to industry scale. In contrast, large positive and significant correlations between intermediates import growth and stages are observed in the wood, plastics and miscellaneous manufacturing sectors.

6.   ANALYSIS OF PRODUCT LEVEL TRADE DATA – TRANSACTION EXIT

While the initial regressions show how the *stages* characteristics of PRC imports and exports, and imports of intermediates in particular, changed between 2000 and 2011, the initial analysis is focused on trade relationships that continued over the sample period. For this reason, the initial regressions provide insight into the changing composition of trade for products that were traded in all years. However, many trade transactions observed in 2000 were not present in 2011. Thus, we can gain further information on the changing composition of Chinese intermediate imports by evaluating the characteristics that predisposed some of the original transactions to end, while others continued 11 years later.

An overview of the product data suggests that PRC imports of inter-mediates and capital goods were moving from lower stage to higher stage HS6 products. For example, of the 3442 distinct HS6 intermediates and capital goods imports recorded in 1997, the average value of stages for the 563 HS6 products that were not imported in 2011 was 2.40, while the average value of stages for the 2879 products that were imported in both years was 2.45. Further, between 1997 and 2011 the PRC started to import 202 HS6 intermediate and capital goods products that it did not import in 1997. The average value of stages for this group was higher yet, at 2.56. Thus, it appears that the product composition of the country's import of intermediates and capital goods was moving toward higher stage products.

To determine whether production stage helped to predict whether a trade relationship would end, specification (6.4) examines the probability that a particular trade transaction was terminated. The dependent variable for this exercise is the dichotomous variable *EXIT*.

$$Prob(EXIT)_{pcho} = \sum \sigma_p + \sum \lambda_c + \sum \xi_i + \sum \mu_o \qquad (6.4)$$

$$+ \beta_1 \, Stages + \beta_2 \ln(Import, \, 2000)_{pcho} + \beta_3 \Delta \ln(Export)_{ipo} + \psi_{pcho}$$

Beginning with the universe of intermediate input import transactions observed in 2000 at the province-industry-firmownership-hs6 (p-i-o-hs6) level the indicator variable *EXIT* is set to 0 for p-i-o-hs6 transactions that were also observed in 2011, and 1 for all cases where the p-i-o-hs6 trans-action was not observed in 2011. However, since HS6 codes were refined over the sample period, some ongoing trade transactions were recorded under different HS6 headings in different years. Thus, to avoid the poten-tial of classifying an ongoing transaction as an exit, HS6 codes were first converted to a single HS6 classification using the World Bank concord-ance for HS6 codes.[19] The variable *stages* is included in the regression to learn whether the risk of exit was higher for some production stages than others. The remaining regressors and fixed effects in specification (6.4) are similar to those used to describe changes in import or export value.

The basic results are in Table 6.11. First, in columns 1–4, the basic regression is run first for all Chinese imports, followed by individual regressions run for import of intermediate inputs, capital goods and final

Table 6.11 Stages and the probability of exit from import

	(1) All	(2) Intermed	(3) Capgood	(4) Final	(5) Intermed	(6) Intermed	(7) Intermed
Stages	0.443***	0.581***	-0.074*	0.234***	0.633***	0.633***	-0.102*
	-0.010	-0.013	-0.041	-0.027	-0.016	-0.016	-0.058
*ASEAN					-0.112***		
					-0.021		
*Rich						0.106***	
						-0.021	
*Chemicals							0.418***
							-0.062
*Plastics							0.689***
							-0.067
*Furs							-0.018
							-0.222
*Wood							1.169***
							-0.078
*Textile							1.109***
							-0.077
*Footwear							0.394
							-0.489
*Stoneware & glass							-0.355***
							-0.115
*Metals							1.642***
							-0.068
*Machinery							1.668***
							-0.091

	(1)	(2)	(3)	(4)	(5)	(6)
*Electrical Machinery						0.207***
						-0.075
*Transport Equipment						-0.587***
						-0.217
*Miscellaneous manufacturing						-1.169***
						-0.121
ln (*Imports_2000*)	-0.078***	-0.076***	-0.069***	-0.088***	-0.076***	-0.081***
	-0.001	-0.001	-0.002	-0.003	-0.001	-0.001
Δln (*Exports_All_ipo*)	-0.052***	-0.050***	-0.033***	-0.036***	-0.050***	-0.052***
	-0.004	-0.005	-0.008	-0.010	-0.005	-0.005
N	261 233	165 795	48 809	39 140	165 795	165 795
Log likelihood	-143 000	-89 200	-26 800	-20 300	-89 200	-88 200

Notes:
Capgood = capital goods; Intermed = intermediate goods.
Standard errors in parentheses. * p < 0.10, ** p < 0.05, *** p < 0.01. Each regression has fixed effects that control for industry, country, province, and firm ownership type.

Source: Author's calculation.

Table 6.12 Industry exit from import of intermediates, by industry, 2000–2011

	(1) Machinery	(2) Electronics	(3) Transport	(4) Miscellaneous manufacturing	(5) Textiles	(6) Footwear
Stages						
*Hong Kong, China	1.136***	0.493***	0.661	−0.835***	1.885***	1.136***
	−0.205	−0.128	−0.682	−0.259	−0.130	−0.205
*ASEAN5	0.839***	−0.428**	−1.508*	−0.073	−1.158***	0.839***
	−0.270	−0.17	−0.859	−0.367	−0.171	−0.270
*Japan	0.120	−0.158	−1.722*	−0.558	−0.892***	0.120
	−0.287	−0.186	−0.984	−0.442	−0.269	−0.287
*Republic of Korea and Taipei,China	0.500*	−0.348**	−1.622	−0.203	−0.616***	0.500*
	−0.266	−0.166	−1.010	−0.351	−0.160	−0.266
	0.352	−0.763***	−2.002**	−0.651*	−0.001	0.352
	−0.276	−0.179	−0.833	−0.384	−0.271	−0.276
*NAFTA						
*European Union 28	0.720***	−0.704***	−1.593*	−1.040***	−0.593***	0.720***
	−0.270	−0.176	−0.872	−0.391	−0.194	−0.270

*Australia and New Zealand	0.385	−0.175	−1.504	−2.237**	1.650**	0.385
	(0.427)	(0.348)	(1.399)	(0.915)	(0.668)	(0.427)
*Rest of the world	0.454	−0.196	−0.672	−0.779	−1.372***	0.454
	(0.337)	(0.209)	(1.075)	(0.476)	(0.229)	(0.337)
ln (Imports_2000)	−0.095***	−0.051***	−0.119***	−0.090***	−0.129***	−0.095***
	(0.005)	(0.003)	(0.012)	(0.006)	(0.003)	(0.005)
Δln (Exports_All_ipo)	−0.030**	−0.023	−0.001	−0.056**	−0.233***	−0.030**
	(0.014)	(0.017)	(0.041)	(0.026)	(0.027)	(0.014)
N	14447	15808	1941	8274	27139	338
Log likelihood	−7052	−9139	−937	−4292	−14000	−165

Notes:
ASEAN 5 = Indonesia, Malaysia, the Philippines, Singapore and Thailand; NAFTA = North American Free Trade Agreement.
Standard errors in parentheses. * $p < 0.10$, ** $p < 0.05$, *** $p < 0.01$. Each regression has fixed effects that control for country, province, and firm ownership type.

Source: Author's calculation.

consumption goods. In each regression, the results show that import trade relationships at the province-HS6 product-country-ownership type level were less likely to end in the case of transactions that were larger in value in the initial year, 2000. In the full sample, import transactions in higher HS6 stage products were more likely to end than were transactions involving lower HS6 stage products. However, the stage characteristics of exiting products differed across good type. Notably, while there was a higher exit rate for high stage imports of intermediate goods or consumer goods, lower stage capital goods were at a greater threat of exit. To examine the geographic dimensions of these correlations, columns 5 and 6 add interactions between the variable stages and indicator variables for ASEAN countries and rich countries. In the case of intermediate imports, the interaction terms reveal that the higher stage intermediate input imports were at slightly lower risk of termination in the case of import from rich source countries, while higher stage intermediate input imports were at slightly higher risk of termination in the cases where they were imported from ASEAN country sources. However, these apparent changes are driven by changes in the industrial composition of PRC trade changes. In particular, if the estimating framework adds interactions between stages and industry indicator variables, the data reveal highly different exit risks across industries based on stages. For example, higher stage products were at particularly high exit risk in the wood, textile and machinery sectors, while high sector products faced much lower exit risk in the cases of the transportation and miscellaneous manufacturing sectors. When the industry interactions are included, the country interaction terms that were shown in columns 5 and 6 no longer have any statistically significant relationship.

Due to the large differences in the correlation of stages with exit across industries, Table 6.12 runs separate exit regressions for a number of the industries in the sample. The regression specification tests how exit from transactions is related to the import source, controlling for general country, province and ownership fixed effects. On an industry dimension, one main distinction is between industries that are characterized by exit from high stage imported inputs, regardless of source: namely machinery and footwear. In contrast, in other industries the exit is similar across all sources, with the exit concentrated in lower stage imported intermediates: namely electronics, transportation equipment, and miscellaneous manufacturing. Alone, this evidence would suggest that changes in technology have dictated the changing patterns in intermediates import. However, the fact that other industries have differential stage correlations depending on source (textiles), while the strength of the correlations differ markedly across countries, suggest that there is no uniform technological development behind the unbundling of production that governs the organization of all industries. Further, although it is hard to characterize industry level incentives for co-location, these results might also be affected by industry needs to move groups of items/activities at the same time in the relocation of modules of activity.

Since processing exports and ordinary exports were qualitatively similar at the industry level, and because firms have shifted increasingly from processing to ordinary exports, the analysis has focused primarily on the trade in intermediate inputs, regardless of the customs regime. However, to test for robustness, I experimented with some alternative samples. First, processing trade, though a large component of the country's overall trade, is not ubiquitous, as the large majority of provinces are only lightly involved in processing trade. Further, although the government sought to change this pattern with its new "Go West" policies that were introduced in 2006, examination of trade at the provincial level does not suggest that the pattern has shifted. For this reason, as a first test for robustness, I estimate the specification shown in Table 6.10, column 4 on the subset of provinces that were the most heavily involved in processing trade: Guandong, Jiangsu, Shandong, Shanghai, and Zhejian. When the estimation is limited to the smaller subsample, the coefficient on stages in Table 6.10, column 4 drops almost imperceptibly from 0.397 to 0.396.

To provide further insight into changes in industry structure, I posed the following question. If we look at the types of inputs that were introduced into PRC processing trade, can we see anything systematic about the handling of those items in later years? Implementation of this idea required the identification of products that were common to supply chains. Thus, the first step was to take processing trade data to form a list of HS6 products that were processing intermediates or capital goods between the years 1997 and 2001. To do so, BEC codes were applied to assign goods to product groups, and all goods that were categorized as final goods or primary goods were dropped from the sample. This left 3521 distinct HS6 codes that were either intermediate or capital goods. Next, the sample was limited only to transactions that were known to involve processing trade, due to their presence in the processing trade regime. This restriction reduced the number of unique HS6 codes to 3300. Notably, there is a strong overlap between intermediates and capital goods trade conducted by processing and ordinary firms, as ordinary firms handled 3448 distinct HS6 product categories during this same period. For a final screen in creating a list of supply chain trade, the list of distinct products was limited to those transactions that involved foreign invested firms. This screen reduces the scope of HS6 items to 3200, of which 2691 were intermediate inputs, while 501 involved capital goods imports. Since the data cross HS6 code groups that were classified according to the changing definitions from 1997, 2002, and 2007, the World Bank concordance, as described by Cebeci (2012), was used to form a single set of codes. Due to changes in definitions over time, this consolidates groups of HS6 codes that were later regrouped. Adopting this consolidation leaves 2405 unique consolidated groups of HS6 intermediate product imports, and 449 groups of HS6 capital goods imports. After identifying this subset of products, I ran the specification of Table 6.10, column 4 only on those goods. In this setting, the coefficient on stages rises much more dramatically to a statistically significant value of 0.87, which suggests that processing imports of intermediates were growing most rapidly for high-stage products.

7.   CONCLUSIONS

To assess changes in the position of the PRC in production this chapter studies how the production position, or stages, of the country's trade changed during the 2000s. The data show that imported intermediates grew more rapidly in high stage items – items that embodied a greater number of stages of handling prior to their import. Production position was also related to the likelihood of transaction exit, as higher stage intermediate imports were more likely to cease between 2000 and 2011 than were imports of lower stage intermediates. The data reveal shifts in composition of intermediates trade along geographic, firm ownership and industry lines. However, the strong heterogeneity in compositional changes across industries suggests that the recent reconfiguration of industry may be shaped not only by aggregate factors (such as changes in wages or export demand) that would move all industries in a similar fashion, but also by industry-level factors that allow for the unbundling of industry production, and influence the locations at which activities cluster.

NOTES

1. Hummels et al. (2001) pioneered this approach in international data. Its refinement and application to PRC trade is demonstrated in Johnson and Noguera (2012a).
2. Koopman et al. (2008); Ma et al. (2009); and Ma and Van Assche (2010) use this approach to assess the contribution of PRC value-added in production, and to demonstrate how economic factors influence the organization of global production networks. More generally, Gaulier et al. (2007) provide insights into changes in country connections and product composition of PRC trade.
3. For example, Johnson and Noguera (2012b) finding that country bilateral value added to export ratios decline when countries join regional trade agreements suggests that the organization of production sharing activities responds to trade reforms.

4. Use of sequential production can be seen in Findlay (1978), Dixit and Grossman (1982), Sanyal (1983), Yi (2003) and Baldwin and Venables (2010).
5. When Amiti and Freund (2010) apply US measures of industry skill-intensity to PRC trade, they find that the distribution of imported inputs – both processing and ordinary – shifted between 1992 and 2005 from less-skilled to more skilled sectors.
6. Koopman et al. (2008); Ma et al. (2009); and Ma and Van Assche (2010) exploit information from Chinese processing trade activities.
7. The industry groups are: Textiles, Electrical machinery, Non-manufacturing, non-electrical machinery, Metals, Footwear and headgear, Chemicals and allied industries, Raw hides, Leather and fur, Plastics and rubber, Transportation, Stone clay and glass, Wood and wood products, and miscellaneous manufacturing. The mapping between HS codes and industries is listed in Appendix Table 6A.2.
8. At the firm level, Wang and Yu (2012) show that some firms specialized in processing exports, while others engaged in both processing and ordinary exports. Notably, they show that the productivity of pure processing firms is inferior to firms that are engaged in both processing and ordinary trade.
9. Further, when Gangnes et al. (2012) study the effects of trade shocks on PRC trade, they do not uncover any systematic evidence that processing exports had different responses to OECD income changes than did nonprocessing exports, though they do observe distinct responses for durable versus nondurable goods.
10. While the concept of upstreamness or stages is based on the idea of tasks, the creation of the measures are based on US Bureau of Economic Analysis input–output tables from 2002. Thus, the measures are more closely related to the number of plants involved in the production process than they are related to the number of tasks.
11. This can explain Levchenko's (2007) finding that trade is enhanced by institutions that support the formation of contractual arrangements.
12. This cannot be interpreted as a move into more sophisticated sectors, as Fally does not uncover a positive correlation between the length of his production sequence measures and sector technological levels. Recent declines in US measures of stages are in part due to the rising importance of the service sector as a share of output.
13. The numbers in this example were calculated by applying Fally's production measures to the universe of data on Chinese export transactions, and calculating the raw average outcome as well as the outcome when weighted by export transaction values.
14. This may be due to local provision of intermediates, consistent with Kee and Tang's (2012) evidence.
15. Due to revisions in HS6 codes over time, I use a World Bank consolidated HS6 codes, documented by Cebeci (2012), to link transaction codes that changed during the sample period. In the case where codes were changed, the data are aggregated according to the linked/consolidated HS6 code. The concordance was downloaded from: http://econ.worldbank.org/WBSITE/EXTERNAL/EXTDEC/EXTRESEARCH/EXT PROGRAMS/EXTTRADERESEARCH/0,,contentMDK:23192741~pagePK:641681 82~piPK:64168060~theSitePK:544849,00.html.
16. For an overview on the relevance of firm-ownership type differences for firm operations, Hale and Long (2012) provide firm-level operational details and an overview of the PRC policies.
17. In this project, foreign owned and joint venture firms are included in the category foreign invested enterprises (FIE), while the category Private includes both private and collective firms.
18. Each form of demand is created by applying the UN BEC codes to the HS6 trade data. The intermediates group includes both parts and components and the semi-finished categories. Final consumption and capital goods categories are defined according to Appendix Table 6A.2.
19. http://documents.worldbank.org/curated/en/2012/11/17122599/concordance-among-harmonized-system-1996-2002-2007-classifications.

REFERENCES

Amiti, M. and C. Freund (2010), 'The anatomy of China's export growth', in R.C. Feenstra and S.-J. Wei (eds), *China's Growing Role in World Trade*, University of Chicago Press, pp. 35–56.

Antras, P. and D. Chor (forthcoming), 'Organizing the global value chain', *Econometrica*.

Antras, P., D. Chor, T. Fally, and R. Hillberry (2012), 'Measuring upstreamness of production and trade', *American Economic Review Papers & Proceedings*.

Baldwin, R. and J. Lopez-Gonzalez (2013), 'Supply-chain trade: a portrait of global patterns and several testable hypotheses', NBER Working Paper 18957.

Baldwin, R. and A. Venables (2010), 'Relocating the value chain: offshoring and agglomeration in the global economy', NBER Working Papers 16611.

Brandt, L. and P.M. Morrow (2013), 'Tariffs and the organization of trade in China', University of Toronto Working Paper–491.

Cebeci, T. (2012), *A Concordance Among Harmonized System 1996, 2002 and 2007 Classifications*, Washington, DC: World Bank, http://documents. worldbank.org/curated/en/2012/11/17122599/concordance-among-harmonized-system-1996-2002-2007-classifications.

Defever, F. and A. Riaño (2012), 'China's pure exporter subsidies', Centre for Economic Performance Discussion Paper No. 1182.

Dixit, A. and G. Grossman (1982), 'Trade and protection with multistage production', *Review of Economic Studies*, **49**, 583–594.

Fally, T. (2012a), 'Production staging: measurement and facts', University of Colorado, Boulder, Manuscript.

Fally, T. (2012b), 'Data on the fragmentation of production in the U.S.', University of Colorado, Boulder, Manuscript.

Findlay, R. (1978), 'An "Austrian" model of international trade and interest rate equalization', *Journal of Political Economy*, **86**, 989–1007.

Gangnes, B., A.C. Ma, and A. Van Assche (2012), 'Global value chains and the transmission of business cycle shocks', ADB Economics Working Paper Series, No. 329.

Gaulier, G., F. Lemoine, and D. Unal-Kesenci (2007), 'China's emergence and the reorganization of trade flows in Asia', *China Economic Review*, **18**, 209–243.

Hale, G. and C. Long (2012), *Foreign Direct Investment in China: Winners and Losers*, Singapore: World Scientific.

Head, K., R. Jing, and J. Ries (2011), 'Import sourcing of Chinese cities: order versus randomness', University of British Columbia, Manuscript.

Hummels, D., J. Ishii, and K.-M. Yi (2001), 'The nature and growth of vertical specialization in world trade', *Journal of International Economics*, **54**, 75–96.

Johnson, R. and G. Noguera (2012a), 'Accounting for intermediates: production sharing and trade in value added', *Journal of International Economics*, **86**, 224–236.

Johnson, R. and G. Noguera (2012b), 'Fragmentation and trade in value added over four decades', NBER Working Paper 18186.

Kee, H.L. and H. Tang (2012), 'Domestic value added in Chinese exports: firm-level evidence', Johns Hopkins School of Advanced International Studies, Manuscript.

Koopman, R., Z. Wang, and S.-J. Wei (2008), 'How much of Chinese exports is really made in China? Assessing domestic value-added when processing trade is pervasive', NBER Working Paper 14109.
Levchenko, A. (2007), 'Institutional quality and international trade', *Review of Economic Studies*, **74**, 791–819.
Lu, D. (2010), 'Exceptional exporter performance? Evidence from Chinese manufacturing firms', University of Chicago, Manuscript.
Lu, M., C. Milner, and Z. Yu (2012), 'Regional heterogeneity and China's trade: sufficient lumpiness or not?', *Review of International Economics*, **20**, 415–429.
Ma, A. and A. Van Assche (2010), 'The role of trade costs in global production networks: evidence from China's processing trade regime', World Bank Policy Research Working Paper 5490.
Ma, A., A. Van Assche, and C. Hong (2009), 'Global production networks and China's processing trade', Asian Development Bank Institute Working Paper Series Number 175.
Nunn, N. (2007), 'Relationship-specificity, incomplete contracts and the pattern of trade', *Quarterly Journal of Economics*, **122**, 569–600.
Sanyal, K.K. (1983), 'Vertical specialization in a Ricardian model with a continuum of stages of production', *Economica*, **50**, 71–78.
Wang, Z. and Z. Yu (2012), 'Trading partners, traded products and firm performances of China's exporter-importers: does processing trade make a difference?', *The World Economy*, **35**, 1795–1824.
Yi, K.-M. (2003), 'Can vertical specialization explain the growth of world trade?', *Journal of Political Economy*, **111b**, 52–102.

APPENDIX 6A.1 DATA CLASSIFICATIONS

Industry categories are in Table 6A.1. Traded products are assigned to five goods categories (Primary, Semi-finished, Parts and components, Capital, and Consumption). The assignments are based on the UN BEC (Broad Economic Categories) classifications of production stages that provide a link between products at the 6-digit Harmonized System and the production stage code (Table 6A.2).

Table 6A.1 Industry classifications

Name	HS 2-digit codes
Non-manufacturing	01–27
Chemicals and allied industries	28–38
Plastics and rubber	39–40
Raw hides, leather and fur	41–43
Wood and wood products	44–49
Textiles	50–63
Footwear and headgear	64–67
Stone, clay and glass	68–71
Metals	72–83
Machinery	84
Electrical machinery	85
Transportation	86–89
Miscellaneous manufacturing	90–97

Table 6A.2 Goods classifications

Goods category	BEC code
Primary goods	111, 21, 31
Intermediate goods	
Semi-finished goods	121, 22, 322
Parts and components	42, 53
Final goods	
Capital goods	41, 521
Consumption goods	112, 122, 51, 522, 61, 62, 63

7. External rebalancing, structural adjustment, and real exchange rates in developing Asia*

Andrei Levchenko and Jing Zhang

1. INTRODUCTION

The developing Asia region has been the fastest-growing in the world in recent decades. As is common for fast-growing countries, the region's growth has been export-led, and many of the countries in it have been running trade surpluses. As these countries develop, sustained economic growth will require a rebalancing from reliance on exports and toward greater domestic demand.

What will be the consequences of that rebalancing process, for the developing Asia countries themselves and for the rest of the world? A country running a trade surplus is spending less than the value of its output. Rebalancing – an elimination of the trade surplus – then by construction increases the country's total spending. If the country is small (i.e., does not affect the world goods prices) and all goods are freely traded, rebalancing directly increases nominal spending, but has no effect on the real exchange rate, factor prices, or the sectoral allocation of employment. A small country model with non-tradeable goods, sometimes called the "dependent economy" or the Salter–Swan model (Salter 1959; Swan 1960) predicts that a rise in domestic spending due to the elimination of the trade surplus will increase demand for non-tradeables and their prices, thereby moving factors of production into non-tradeables and appreciating the country's real exchange rate. The dependent economy model assumes a small country and a single exportable good, and thus it makes no prediction on how the patterns of international specialization or relative factor prices will change in response to rebalancing. In the two-country Ricardian model with a continuum of goods, Dornbusch et al. (1977) show that an elimination of the trade surplus in a country will raise both its relative and real wage, and reduce the set of goods that it exports. In summary, classical theory predicts that an elimination of a trade surplus in a country: (i) increases both relative and real incomes; (ii) appreciates the real exchange rate; (iii) increases the employment share in the non-traded sector; and (iv) reduces exports. All of these effects are reversed in the trade deficit countries as the trade imbalance is eliminated.

As insightful as these predictions are, classical theory leaves many unanswered questions. First and foremost, while the directions of the effects outlined above are well-established, stylized small-country or two-country models are too simplistic to reliably gauge the magnitudes involved. Second, the world is a great deal more complex than the simple models. The real world features many heterogeneous countries with highly asymmetric trade relationships between them. While this distinction is non-existent in two-country models, in the real world the elimination of the People's Republic of China's (PRC) trade surplus will likely have a very different global impact than the elimination of Japan's trade surplus, since those two countries occupy different positions in the world trading system. In addition, the world is increasingly engaged in intermediate input trade ("the global supply chains"), and thus a rebalancing in, say, the PRC will have knock-on effects on countries supplying inputs to its traded and non-traded sectors. Finally, the world has many surplus and many deficit countries at the same time. An elimination of the trade imbalance in several surplus countries simultaneously may yield heterogeneous effects in the different surplus countries. While the complexity of the real-world global economy may not overturn the basic predictions of the classical theory, in order to develop a set of quantitative results about the impact of rebalancing, we must develop a framework that goes some way toward reflecting the rich heterogeneity of countries and trading relationships observed in the world today.

This chapter uses a large-scale quantitative model of production and trade to simulate the global impact of rebalancing. The analysis is based on a Ricardian-Heckscher–Ohlin framework that features 75 countries (including 14 from developing Asia), 19 tradeable and 1 non-tradeable sector, multiple factors of production, as well as the full set of cross-sectoral input–output linkages forming a global supply chain. The model is implemented on sectoral trade and production data in such a way that it matches the sector-level bilateral trade shares in our sample of countries, as well as the countries' relative incomes. In the baseline equilibrium, we solve the model under the observed levels of trade imbalances in each country. We then compare outcomes to the counterfactual scenario in which "external rebalancing" took place, and each country is constrained to have balanced trade. This exercise thus follows the approach of Obstfeld and Rogoff (2005) and Dekle et al. (2007, 2008). We examine the impact of rebalancing on a range of outcomes, including relative wages, real exchange rates, the size of the non-tradeable sector, and finally welfare.

Our model quantifies these impacts for both developing Asia and the rest of the world. In the surplus countries in the region (the PRC, the Republic of Korea, Malaysia, among others) relative wages with respect to the United States (US) rise by double digits, 17.5 percent at the median, and the real exchange rate with respect to the US dollar appreciates by a similar, slightly smaller, amount. Interestingly, the trade-weighted real exchange rate in these countries appreciates by much less (1.5 percent at the median), with the Republic of Korea and Taipei,China actually experiencing modest real depreciations in trade-weighted terms. This difference is due to the fact that these countries trade a great deal among themselves, and thus as they are all appreciating against the US dollar, their real appreciation against one another is much more modest.

As expected, a rebalancing toward greater domestic demand in the surplus countries is accompanied by an increase in the size of the non-tradeable sector. At the median, the share of labor in the non-tradeable sector rises by 4 percentage points. This is a modest change in proportional terms: the average share of labor in the non-tradeable sector is two-thirds in this group of countries. Finally, the impact on welfare of the rebalancing is a fraction of 1 percent among the surplus countries (0.4 percent at the median). Welfare corresponds to the real income in this model. A rebalancing leads to a rise in factor prices, and an increase in the price level. The net effect on welfare is more subdued than either the change in nominal factor prices or the change in the price level.

The impact is roughly opposite for the deficit countries in developing Asia (India, Sri Lanka, Viet Nam, among others). While for four out of seven developing Asia deficit countries wages relative to the US rise, the average increase, at about 5.1 percent, is much more subdued than for the surplus countries. While the real exchange with respect to the US appreciates in most of these countries, the trade-weighted real exchange depreciates in all of them, on average by 6 percent. As rebalancing requires a reduction in domestic spending, the share of labor in the non-tradeable sector shrinks by 3 percentage points. All in all, these countries experience a significant reduction in welfare of about 2.6 percent on average.

It is intuitive that countries running surpluses tend to benefit from the reductions in their own trade surplus, and vice versa. However, the multilateral trade patterns are also important for understanding the impact of rebalancing on these economies. Countries that currently export mostly to the deficit countries (chiefly the US) tend to experience reductions in welfare due to the rebalancing. By contrast, countries exporting to the major surplus countries (chiefly the PRC) tend to benefit.

In addition to the classical contributions discussed above, our chapter is related to the more recent literature on the impact of external rebalancing. Obstfeld and Rogoff (2005) simulate rebalancing in a three-country (the US, Europe, Asia) Armington model. Dekle et al. (2007, 2008) perform a similar exercise in a Ricardian model with 42 countries and two sectors (tradeable and non-tradeable). Our chapter is the first to evaluate global rebalancing in a multi-sector framework with a full-fledged within- and cross-sectoral set of input–output linkages. This allows for a much greater degree of precision regarding each country's impact on its trading partners. In addition, our chapter is the first, to our knowledge, to apply this quantitative approach with particular emphasis on developing Asia.

The rest of the chapter is organized as follows. Section 2 lays out the quantitative framework and discusses the details of calibration and estimation. Section 3 discusses the main results, and Section 4 concludes.

2. QUANTITATIVE FRAMEWORK

Motivated by the discussion in the Introduction, our goal is to assess the impact of global rebalancing in an appropriately rich quantitative model. Classical theory emphasizes that in order to model rebalancing, it is essential for the framework to feature: (i) both traded and non-traded sectors (Salter 1959; Swan 1960); and (ii) endogenous specialization (Dornbusch et al. 1977). We also argued that a reliable assessment will require: (iii) a large number of countries; and (iv) a sufficiently rich production structure that features multiple sectors and a fully articulated set of input–output linkages between them, forming a global supply chain. It turns out that a multi-sector version of the Eaton and Kortum (2002) Ricardian model (henceforth the EK approach) provides the necessary tractability to build a quantitative framework of this scale.

2.1 The Environment

The world is comprised of $N = 75$ countries, indexed by n and i. There are $J = 19$ tradeable sectors, plus one non-tradeable sector $J + 1$. Utility over these sectors in country n is given by

$$U_n = \left(\sum_{j=1}^{J} \omega_j^{\frac{1}{\eta}} (Y_n^j)^{\frac{\eta-1}{\eta}} \right)^{\frac{\eta}{\eta-1}\xi_n} (Y_n^{J+1})^{1-\xi_n}, \tag{7.1}$$

where Y_n^{J+1} is the non-tradeable-sector composite good, and Y_n^j is the composite good in the tradeable sector j. That is, utility is Cobb–Douglas in tradeables and non-tradeables, implying that consumers have a constant expenditure share devoted to tradeable goods, equal to ξ_n in country n. In turn, the bundle of tradeables is a constant elasticity of substitution (CES) aggregate of the J tradeable sectors, with η the elasticity of substitution between the tradeable sectors, and ω_j the taste parameter for tradeable sector j.

The assumption that utility is Cobb–Douglas in tradeables and non-tradeables will have quantitative implications for the extent of labor reallocation following external rebalancing. Generally, a higher elasticity of substitution would imply greater factor reallocation, as demand will respond more to relative price changes. It is well known that Cobb–Douglas utility implies an elasticity of substitution between tradeables and the non-tradeables equal to 1. This assumption is not too far from the available estimates. Herrendorf et al. (2013) estimate the elasticity of substitution between services (which in our model is interpreted as non-tradeables) and manufacturing of 0.9. Other estimates show even smaller substitution possibilities. For instance, Święcki (2013) estimates the elasticity to be 0.2, implying very few substitution possibilities between manufacturing and services. Under that elasticity, the labor reallocation towards non-tradeables in surplus countries will be even smaller.

A related issue is the role of non-homothetic preferences. For instance, a surplus country like the PRC will experience an income increase when external rebalancing takes place. Non-homothetic preferences such that higher incomes imply greater demand for non-tradeables would translate into even greater reallocation of labor to the non-tradeable sector following rebalancing. As will become clear below, however, the change in real income due to rebalancing is rather modest – a fraction of 1 percent for the surplus developing Asia countries. Thus, we would not expect a large change in the relative demand for non-tradeables acting through a non-homotheticity channel following rebalancing.

All goods and factor markets are competitive, and all production features constant returns to scale, implying that all profits are zero. There are two factors of production, labor (with country n endowed with L_n units) and capital (K_n). Production uses labor, capital, and intermediate inputs from other sectors. The cost of an input bundle in country n and sector j is:

$$c_n^j = (w_n^{\alpha_j} r_n^{1-\alpha_j})^{\beta_j} \left(\prod_{k=1}^{J+1} (p_n^k)^{\gamma_{k,j}} \right)^{1-\beta_j},$$

where w_n is the wage of workers, r_n is the return to capital, and p_n^k is the price of intermediate input from sector k in country n. That is, the production function is Cobb–Douglas in the two primary factors K_n and L_n and the intermediate inputs. The intermediate inputs can come from any other sector.

The share of payments to labor in value added (also known as "labor intensity") is given by α_j. It varies by sector: some sectors will be very labor-intensive, others less so. The share of value added in the value of total output is given by β_j. It varies across sectors as well: some sectors will spend a lot on intermediate inputs relative to the value of gross output, others less so. Finally, $\gamma_{k,j}$ captures the usage in sector j of intermediate inputs coming from sector k. Precisely, $\gamma_{k,j}$ is the share of spending on sector k inputs in total input spending in sector j. These shares will vary by output industry j as well as input industry k. That is, we allow for the apparel sector, say, to use a great deal of textile inputs, but much fewer basic metals inputs.

Each sector $j = 1, \ldots, J + 1$ is composed of a continuum of varieties $q \in [0,1]$ unique to each sector. Perfectly competitive producers can produce each variety q in each sector j in every country n. However, productivities will differ across countries in each q and j. Producing one unit of good q in sector j in country n requires $\frac{1}{z_n^j(q)}$ input bundles. Following the EK approach, productivity $z_n^j(q)$ for each $q \in [0,1]$ in each sector j is random, and drawn from the Fréchet distribution with cumulative distribution function:

$$F_n^j(z) = e^{-T_n^j z^{-\theta}}$$

In this distribution, T_n^j is a central tendency parameter. It varies by both country and sector, with higher values of T_n^j implying higher *average* productivity draws in sector j in country n. The parameter θ captures dispersion, with larger values of θ implying smaller dispersion in draws.

The intuition for this physical environment is as follows. Each j should be thought of as a very large sector, say textiles, apparel, or electrical machinery. Within each sector, there is a large number of varieties q. If j is apparel, then blue cotton T-shirts, green cotton T-shirts, black socks, etc, are different varieties q within apparel. Each country can produce each q, but productivities will vary across countries: Japan may happen to be better at blue cotton T-shirts than Viet Nam, but Pakistan may be better than Japan at producing black socks. While we may not be able to say with confidence whether Japan or Pakistan is better at making black socks, we will be able to make statements about the *average* productivity of each country in the apparel sector, captured by T_n^j. Since there is a continuum of varieties q, and the Fréchet distribution has infinite support, even countries with a very low T_n^j relative to their trading partners will have a few q's in which they got an unusually high draw, and thus they would be able to produce individual varieties even in its (on average) comparative disadvantage sectors.

Why impose the assumptions that there is a continuum of varieties in each sector, and that productivity draws come from a Fréchet distribution? The reasons are realism and tractability. Real-world trade flows within broad sectors are characterized by substantial two-way trade: pairs of countries often ship similar products to each other. This setup allows us to model that phenomenon and thus successfully match global bilateral trade flows within each sector. The Fréchet distributional assumption helps because it yields especially simple analytical expressions for bilateral trade shares, thus making model estimation and calibration easy even for a very large number of countries.

The production cost of one unit of good q in sector j and country n is thus equal to $c_n^j/z_n^j(q)$. International trade is subject to "iceberg" costs: $d_{ni}^j > 1$ units of good q produced in sector j in country i must be shipped to country n in order for one unit to be available for consumption there. The trade costs need not be symmetric – d_{ni}^j need not equal d_{in}^j – and will vary by sector. We normalize $d_{nn}^j = 1$ for any n and j. The price at which country i supplies tradeable good q in sector j to country n is:

$$p_{ni}^j(q) = \left(\frac{c_i^j}{z_i^j(q)}\right)d_{ni}^j.$$

Buyers of each good q in tradeable sector j in country n will shop globally, and will only buy from the cheapest source country. Thus the price actually paid for this good in country n will be:

$$p_n^j(q) = \min_{i=1,\ldots,N} \{p_{ni}^j(q)\}.$$

International trade happens whenever the cheapest provider of some variety q to some market n is foreign. Note that there are several ways to be the cheapest supplier of good q in sector j in country n. A country may become the cheapest source of a good because it is productive (high $z_i^j(q)$), it has cheap inputs (low c_i^j), or it has low trade costs.

Output in sector j is produced from varieties $q \in [0,1]$ using a CES production function:

$$Q_n^j = \left[\int_0^1 Q_n^j(q)^{\frac{\varepsilon-1}{\varepsilon}} dq\right]^{\frac{\varepsilon}{\varepsilon-1}},$$

where ε denotes the elasticity of substitution across varieties q, Q_n^j is the total output of sector j in country n, and $Q_n^j(q)$ is the amount of variety q

that is used in production in sector j and country n. Note that some of the $Q_n^j(q)$'s will be imported, except in the non-tradeable sector.

Trade is not balanced. We incorporate trade imbalances following the approach of Dekle et al. (2007, 2008) and assume that at a point in time, a trade imbalance represents a transfer from the surplus to the deficit country. Specifically, the budget constraint (or the resource constraint) of the consumer is

$$\sum_{j=1}^{J+1} p_n^j Y_n^j = w_n L_n + r_n K_n - D_n,\tag{7.2}$$

where p_n^j are prices of sector j output in country n, and D_n is the trade surplus of country n. When D_n is negative, countries are running a deficit and consume more than their factor income. The deficits add up to zero globally, $\sum_n D_n = 0$, and are thus transfers of resources between countries.

2.2 Characterization of Equilibrium

Given the preferences and technology described above and the exogenous parameters of the model, we can find the global equilibrium in this economy. Factors of production (K_n and L_n) are perfectly mobile across sectors within a country, but immobile across countries. Intuitively, the global equilibrium is a set of resource allocations and prices such that all markets clear, both domestically and internationally. What follows is the formal definition of equilibrium and the detailed statement of the equilibrium conditions in this economy.

The competitive equilibrium of this model of the world economy with exogenous trade deficits consists of a set of prices, allocation rules, and trade shares such that: (i) given the prices, all firms' inputs satisfy the first-order conditions, and their output is given by the production function; (ii) given the prices, the consumers' demand satisfies the first-order conditions; (iii) the prices ensure the market clearing conditions for labor, capital, tradeable goods and non-tradeable goods; and (iv) trade shares ensure exogenous trade deficit for each country.

The set of prices includes the wage rate w_n, the rental rate r_n, the sectoral prices $\{p_n^j\}_{j=1}^{J+1}$, and the aggregate price P_n in each country n. The allocation rules include the capital and labor allocation across sectors $\{K_n^j, L_n^j\}_{j=1}^{J+1}$, final consumption demand $\{Y_n^j\}_{j=1}^{J+1}$, and total demand $\{Q_n^j\}_{j=1}^{J+1}$ (both final and intermediate goods) for each sector. The trade shares include the expenditure share π_{ni}^j in country n on goods coming from country i in sector j.

2.2.1 Demand and prices

It can be easily shown that the price of sector j's output will be given by:

$$p_n^j = \left[\int_0^1 p_n^j(q)^{1-\varepsilon} dq \right]^{\frac{1}{1-\varepsilon}}.$$

Following the standard EK approach, it is helpful to define

$$\Phi_n^j = \sum_{i=1}^N T_i^j (c_i^j d_{ni}^j)^{-\theta}.$$

This value summarizes, for country n, the access to production technologies in sector j. Its value will be higher if in sector j, country n's trading partners have high productivity (T_i^j) or low cost (c_i^j). It will also be higher if the trade costs that country n faces in this sector are low. Standard steps lead to the familiar result that the price of good j in country n is simply

$$p_n^j = \Gamma(\Phi_n^j)^{-\frac{1}{\theta}} \tag{7.3}$$

where $\Gamma = [\Gamma(\theta + \frac{1}{\theta} - \varepsilon)]^{\frac{1}{1-\varepsilon}}$, with Γ the Gamma function. The consumption price index in country n is then:

$$P_n = B_n \left(\sum_{j=1}^J \omega_j (p_n^j)^{1-\eta} \right)^{\frac{1}{1-\eta} \xi_n} (p_n^{J+1})^{1-\xi_n}, \tag{7.4}$$

where $B_n = \xi_n^{-\xi_n} (1 - \xi_n)^{-(1-\xi_n)}$.

Given the set of prices $\{w_n, r_n, P_n, \{p_n^j\}_{j=1}^{J+1}\}_{n=1}^N$, we first characterize the optimal allocations from final demand. Consumers maximize utility (7.1) subject to the budget constraint (7.2). The first order conditions associated with this optimization problem imply the following final demand:

$$p_n^j Y_n^j = \xi_n (w_n L_n + r_n K_n - D_n) \frac{\omega_j (p_n^j)^{1-\eta}}{\sum_{k=1}^J \omega_k (p_n^k)^{1-\eta}}, \text{ for all } j = \{1, .., J\} \tag{7.5}$$

and

$$p_n^{J+1} Y_n^{J+1} = (1 - \xi_n)(w_n L_n + r_n K_n - D_n).$$

2.2.2 Production allocation and market clearing

The EK structure in each sector j delivers the standard result that the probability of importing good q from country i, π_{ni}^j, is equal to the share of total spending on goods coming from country i, X_{ni}^j / X_n^j, and is given by

$$\frac{X_{ni}^j}{X_n^j} = \pi_{ni}^j = \frac{T_i^j(c_i^j d_{ni}^j)^{-\theta}}{\Phi_n^j}.$$

Let Q_n^j denote the total sectoral demand in country n and sector j. Q_n^j is used for both final consumption and intermediate inputs in domestic production of all sectors. That is,

$$p_n^j Q_n^j = p_n^j Y_n^j + \sum_{k=1}^J (1 - \beta_k)\gamma_{j,k}\left(\sum_{i=1}^N \pi_{in}^k p_i^k Q_i^k\right) + (1 - \beta_{J+1})\gamma_{j,J+1} p_n^{J+1} Q_n^{J+1}.$$

Total expenditure in sector $j = 1, \ldots, J + 1$ of country n, $p_n^j Q_n^j$, is the sum of (i) domestic final consumption expenditure $p_n^j Y_n^j$; (ii) expenditure on sector j goods as intermediate inputs in all the traded sectors $\sum_{k=1}^J (1 - \beta_k)\gamma_{j,k}(\sum_{i=1}^N \pi_{in}^k p_i^k Q_i^k)$, and (iii) expenditure on the j's sector intermediate inputs in the domestic non-traded sector $(1 - \beta_{J+1})\gamma_{j,J+1} p_n^{J+1} Q_n^{J+1}$. These market clearing conditions summarize the two important features of the world economy captured by our model: complex international production linkages, as much of world trade is in intermediate inputs, and a good crosses borders multiple times before being consumed (Hummels et al., 2001); and two-way input linkages between the tradeable and the non-tradeable sectors.

In each tradeable sector j, some goods q are imported from abroad and some goods q are exported to the rest of the world. Country n's exports in sector j are given by $EX_n^j = \sum_{i=1}^N I_{i \neq n} \pi_{in}^j p_i^j Q_i^j$, and its imports in sector j are given by $IM_n^j = \sum_{i=1}^N I_{i \neq n} \pi_{ni}^j p_n^j Q_n^j$, where $I_{i \neq n}$ is the indicator function. The total exports of country n are then $EX_n = \sum_{j=1}^J EX_n^j$, and total imports are $IM_n = \sum_{j=1}^J IM_n^j$. Exogenous trade deficit requires that for any country n, $EX_n - IM_n = D_n$.

Given the total production revenue in tradeable sector j in country n, $\sum_{i=1}^N \pi_{in}^j p_i^j Q_i^j$, the optimal sectoral factor allocations must satisfy

$$\sum_{i=1}^N \pi_{in}^j p_i^j Q_i^j = \frac{w_n L_n^j}{\alpha_j \beta_j} = \frac{r_n k_n^j}{(1 - \alpha_j)\beta_j}.$$

For the non-tradeable sector $J + 1$, the optimal factor allocations in country n are simply given by

$$p_n^{J+1} Q_n^{J+1} = \frac{w_n L_n^{J+1}}{\alpha_{J+1}\beta_{J+1}} = \frac{r_n K_n^{J+1}}{(1 - \alpha_{J+1})\beta_{J+1}}.$$

Finally, for any n the feasibility conditions for factors are given by

$$\sum_{j=1}^{J+1} L_n^j = L_n \text{ and } \sum_{j=1}^{J+1} K_n^j = K_n.$$

2.3 Welfare

Welfare in this framework corresponds to the indirect utility function. Straightforward steps using the CES functional form can be used to show that the indirect utility in each country n is equal to total income divided by the price level. Since both goods and factor markets are competitive, total income equals the total returns to factors of production. Thus total welfare in a country is given by $(w_n L_n + r_n K_n)/P_n$, where the consumption price level P_n comes from equation (7.4). Expressed in per-capita terms it becomes

$$\frac{w_n + r_n k_n}{P_n}, \tag{7.6}$$

where $k_n = K_n/L_n$ is capital per worker. This expression is the metric of welfare in all counterfactual exercises below. Importantly, we do not include the direct effect of consuming (or transferring away) D_n when calculating the welfare levels of countries. Rather, we focus on real factor incomes.

2.4 Calibration

The equations above define the equilibrium in this economy. Analytical solutions of this model are not available. However, the equilibrium can be found numerically. Essentially, the equilibrium conditions are simply a set of non-linear equations in the prices and resource allocations. Solving the model amounts to finding a solution to this set of equations.

Any numerical implementation, of course, requires us to take a stand on the values of every parameter in the model. Specifically, we must take a stand on the following sets of parameters: (i) moments of the productivity distributions T_n^j and θ; (ii) trade costs d_{ni}^j; (iii) production function parameters α_j, β_j, $\gamma_{k,j}$, and ε; (iv) country factor endowments L_n and K_n; and (v) preference parameters ξ_n, ω_j, and η. What follows is a detailed discussion of how each parameter is picked. As there are many parameters to be chosen, we follow three broad approaches in choosing them. First, in some cases we use data and model-implied relationships to estimate sets of parameters structurally. This is the most sophisticated approach. Second, some parameters can be easily computed with basic data, without the need to rely on the model structure explicitly. Finally, in a very limited set of cases, we simply adopt parameter values estimated elsewhere in the literature and commonly used. This approach is followed only in cases where the model does not provide enough guidance on how to compute these parameters based on data.

The structure of the model is used to estimate the sector-level technology parameters T_n^j for a large set of countries. The estimation procedure relies on fitting a structural gravity equation implied by the model, and using the resulting estimates along with data on input costs to back out the underlying technology. Intuitively, if controlling for the typical gravity determinants of trade, a country spends relatively more on domestically produced goods in a particular sector, it is revealed to have either a high relative productivity or a low relative unit cost in that sector. The procedure then uses data on factor and intermediate input prices to net out the role of factor costs, yielding an estimate of relative productivity. This step also produces estimates of bilateral sector-level trade costs d_{ni}^j. The parametric model for iceberg trade costs includes the common geographic variables such as distance and common border, as well as policy variables, such as regional trade agreements and currency unions. The detailed procedures for all three steps are described in Levchenko and Zhang (2011) and reproduced in Appendix 7A.1.

Estimation of sectoral productivity parameters T_n^j and trade costs d_{ni}^j requires data on total output by sector, as well as sectoral data on bilateral trade. For 52 countries in the sample, information on output comes from the 2009 UNIDO Industrial Statistics Database. For the European Union countries, the EUROSTAT database contains data of superior quality, and thus for those countries we use EUROSTAT production data. The two output data sources are merged at the roughly 2-digit International Standard Industrial Classification of All Economic Activities (ISIC) Revision 3 level of disaggregation, yielding 19 manufacturing sectors. Bilateral trade data were collected from the UN COMTRADE database, and concorded to the same sectoral classification. We assume that the dispersion parameter θ does not vary across sectors. There are no reliable estimates of how it varies across sectors, and thus we do not model this variation. We pick the value of $\theta = 8.28$, which is the preferred estimate of EK.[1] It is important to assess how the results below are affected by the value of this parameter. One may be especially concerned about how the results change under lower values of θ. Lower θ implies greater within-sector heterogeneity in the random productivity draws. Thus, trade flows become less sensitive to the costs of the input bundles (c_i^j), and the gains from intra-sectoral trade become larger relative to the gains from inter-sectoral trade. Elsewhere (Levchenko and Zhang 2011) we re-estimated all the technology parameters using instead a value of $\theta = 4$, which has been advocated by Simonovska and Waugh (2011) and is at or near the bottom of the range that has been used in the literature. Overall, the outcome was remarkably similar. The correlation between estimated T_i^j's under $\theta = 4$ and the baseline is above 0.95, and there is actually somewhat greater variability in T_i^j's under $\theta = 4$.

The production function parameters α_j and β_j are estimated using the UNIDO and EUROSTAT production data, which contain information on output, value added, employment, and wage bills. To compute α_j for each sector, we calculate the share of the total wage bill in value added, and take a simple median across countries (taking the mean yields essentially the same results). To compute β_j, we take the median of value added divided by total output.

The intermediate input coefficients $\gamma_{k,j}$ are obtained from the direct requirements table for the United States. We use the 1997 Benchmark Detailed Make and Use Tables (covering approximately 500 distinct sectors), as well as a concordance to the ISIC Revision 3 classification to build a direct requirements table at the 2-digit ISIC level. The direct requirements table gives the value of the intermediate input in row k required to produce one dollar of final output in column j. Thus, it is the direct counterpart to the input coefficients $\gamma_{k,j}$. Note that we assume these to be the same in all countries.[2] In addition, we use the US IO matrix to obtain α_{J+1} and β_{J+1} in the non-tradeable sector, which cannot be obtained from UNIDO.[3] The elasticity of substitution between varieties within each tradeable sector, ε, is set to 4 (as is well known, in the EK model this elasticity plays no role, entering only the constant Γ).

The total labor force in each country, L_n, and the total capital stock, K_n, are obtained from the Penn World Tables 6.3. Following the standard approach in the literature (see, e.g., Hall and Jones 1999, Bernanke and Gürkaynak 2001, and Caselli 2005), the total labor force is calculated from the data on the total GDP per capita and per worker.[4] The total capital is calculated using the perpetual inventory method that assumes a depreciation rate of 6 percent: $K_{n,t} = (1 - 0.06)K_{n,t-1} + I_{n,t}$, where $I_{n,t}$ is total investment in country n in period t. For most countries, investment data start in 1950, and the initial value of K_n is set equal to $I_{n,0}/(\gamma + 0.06)$, where γ is the average growth rate of investment in the first 10 years for which data are available.

The share of expenditure on traded goods, ξ_n in each country is sourced from Uy et al. (2013), who compile this information for 36 developed and developing countries. For countries unavailable in their data, values of ξ_n are imputed based on their level of development. We fit a simple linear relationship between ξ_n and log PPP-adjusted per capita GDP from the Penn World Tables on the countries in the Uy et al. (2013) dataset. The fit of this simple bivariate linear relationship is quite good, with an R^2 of 0.55. For the remaining countries, we then set ξ_n to the value predicted by this bivariate regression at their level of income. The taste parameters for tradeable sectors ω_j were estimated by combining the model structure above with data on final consumption expenditure shares in the US sourced from the US IO matrix, as described in Appendix 7A.1. The elasticity of substitution between broad sectors within the tradeable bundle, η, is set to 2. Since these are very large product categories, it is sensible that this elasticity would be relatively low. It is higher, however, than the elasticity of substitution between tradeable and non-tradeable goods that is set to 1 by the Cobb–Douglas assumption.

2.5   Basic Patterns

All of the variables that vary over time are averaged over the period 2005–2007 (the latest available year on which we can implement the quantitative model). To assess the impact of rebalancing we use values of D_n for 2011, which is the latest available year total trade data are available for a large sample of countries. The trade balance D_n is defined as goods exports minus goods imports, and the data to compute trade balances are sourced from the World Bank's World Development Indicators. Appendix Table 7A.1 lists the 20 sectors along with the key parameter values for each sector: α_j, β_j, the share of non-tradeable inputs in total inputs $\gamma_{J+1,j}$, and the taste parameter ω_j.

Table 7.1 reports the sample of developing Asian countries and their trade balances, both in absolute terms and as a share of each country's GDP. In absolute terms, the largest trade surplus ($224 billion) belongs to the PRC, and the largest trade deficit ($110 billion) to India. Of course, those are the largest countries in absolute terms, and thus their trade balances as a share of GDP (3 percent of GDP for PRC, –6 percent of GDP for India) are actually some of the lowest in this group of countries. Relative to GDP, Kazakhstan and Malaysia have the largest trade surplus (22 percent and 16 percent, respectively), and Fiji and Sri Lanka the largest deficits (23 percent and 11 percent, respectively).

Table 7.2 reports the same data for the rest of the sample, broken down by country group/region. As is well known, the US has the largest trade deficit in absolute terms ($711 billion), and Germany, the largest trade surplus ($199 billion).

Table 7.1   Developing Asia: country sample and deficits

Country	3-letter code	Trade balance	
		US$ billion	Percent of GDP
Bangladesh	BAN	−7.31	−6.89
Fiji	FIJ	−0.79	−22.54
India	IND	−110.54	−6.17
Indonesia	INO	31.07	4.00
Kazakhstan	KAZ	37.25	22.17
Malaysia	MAL	42.49	15.89
Pakistan	PAK	−12.35	−6.39
People's Republic of China	PRC	223.70	3.38
Philippines	PHI	−15.03	−7.08
Republic of Korea	KOR	29.35	2.75
Sri Lanka	SRI	−5.75	−10.57
Taipei,China	TAP	21.26	4.74
Thailand	THA	20.74	6.24
Viet Nam	VIE	−3.94	−3.43

Note: This table reports, for countries in the developing Asia region, the trade balances in US$ billion and as percent of GDP, as well as the 3-letter codes used to denote the countries.

Source: World Development Indicators.

3. COUNTERFACTUAL: IMPACT OF EXTERNAL REBALANCING

This section traces out the impact of external rebalancing on outcomes in developing Asia and the rest of the world. We proceed by first solving the model under the baseline values of all the estimated parameters and observed trade imbalances, and present a number of checks on the model fit with respect to observed data. Then, we compute counterfactual welfare and sectoral factor allocations under the assumption that all trade imbalances disappear ($D_n = 0$ for all n). We present the impact of external rebalancing on relative wages, real exchange rates, welfare, as well as the sectoral structure of these countries.

Note that in our framework trade deficits take the form of transfers and thus external rebalancing amounts to simply removing those transfers. The exercise follows the treatments of external rebalancing in Obstfeld and Rogoff (2005) and Dekle et al. (2007, 2008).

The model is static, and thus does not allow us to think about

Table 7.2   Rest of the world: country sample and deficits

Country	3-letter code	Trade balance	
		US$ billion	Percent of GDP
Organisation for Economic Co-operation and Development			
Australia	AUS	20.31	1.61
Austria	AUT	−4.89	−1.23
Belgium-Luxembourg	BLX	−12.23	−2.49
Canada	CAN	−10.56	−0.64
Denmark	DEN	8.61	2.66
Finland	FIN	5.75	2.31
France	FRA	−82.75	−3.11
Germany	GER	198.81	5.77
Greece	GRC	−38.31	−13.17
Iceland	ISL	0.85	6.39
Ireland	IRE	56.88	26.92
Italy	ITA	−29.5	−1.39
Japan	JPN	42.20	0.74
Netherlands	NET	53.60	6.66
New Zealand	NZL	2.12	1.41
Norway	NOR	60.58	13.41
Portugal	POR	−23.35	−10.05
Spain	SPA	−63.57	−4.45
Sweden	SWE	12.05	2.40
Switzerland	SWI	24.33	4.02
United Kingdom	UKG	−163.53	−6.96
United States	USA	−711.41	−4.84
Central and Eastern Europe			
Bulgaria	BGR	−3.67	−7.25
Czech Republic	CZE	1.71	0.82
Hungary	HUN	2.95	2.19
Poland	POL	−15.41	−3.13
Romania	ROM	−12.96	−7.32
Russian Federation	RUS	167.14	9.99
Slovak Republic	SVK	0.79	0.87
Slovenia	SVN	−1.51	−3.13
Ukraine	UKR	−14.64	−9.71
Latin America and Caribbean			
Argentina	ARG	12.79	3.14
Bolivia	BOL	1.00	4.58
Brazil	BRA	22.09	0.96
Chile	CHL	12.13	5.22
Colombia	COL	3.21	1.04

Table 7.2   (continued)

Country	3-letter code	Trade balance	
		US$ billion	Percent of GDP
Latin America and Caribbean			
Costa Rica	CRI	−6.25	−16.22
Ecuador	ECU	−1.10	−1.77
El Salvador	SLV	−4.48	−20.13
Guatemala	GTM	−4.78	−10.82
Honduras	HND	−4.13	−25.19
Mexico	MEX	−6.37	−0.58
Peru	PER	8.10	4.90
Trinidad and Tobago	TTO	4.62	−21.28
Uruguay	URY	−1.08	−2.50
Venezuela RB	VEN	35.82	10.09
Middle East and North Africa			
Egypt Arab Rep.	EGY	−20.24	−9.03
Iran Islamic Rep.	IRN	48.03	−
Israel	ISR	−5.61	−2.44
Jordan	JOR	−7.96	−28.80
Kuwait	KWT	64.24	42.69
Saudi Arabia	SAU	196.47	38.24
Turkey	TUR	−74.93	−9.95
Sub-Saharan Africa			
Ethiopia	ETH	−5.16	−18.17
Ghana	GHA	−3.17	−8.88
Kenya	KEN	−7.42	−22.56
Mauritius	MUS	−2.13	−20.36
Nigeria	NGA	29.68	12.56
Senegal	SEN	−1.97	−14.52
South Africa	ZAF	1.93	0.50
Tanzania	TZA	−3.87	−16.56

Notes:
− = data not available; RB = República Bolivariana.
This table reports the country sample outside of the developing Asia region, trade balances in US$ billion and as percent of GDP as well as the 3-letter codes used to denote the countries.

Source: World Development Indicators.

what the surplus countries are getting in return for running a surplus. Presumably, in the real world they are accumulating foreign assets that they can draw on to raise consumption at some future date. Thus, our welfare comparisons should not be thought of as capturing the full present discounted value of eliminating trade imbalances. Rather, they should be seen as capturing utility from current period consumption, relative to the counterfactual current period consumption in the world without imbalances. Note that while our welfare results are subject to this caveat, predictions about real exchange rates and factor allocations are more straightforward to understand, since both refer to static prices and resource allocations, and thus for those it is not crucial what happens in future periods.

Since the model is static and there is no capital accumulation, our exercise also does not feature the impact of rebalancing on the capital stock. At the extreme, if all trade imbalances were turned into capital stock, then a deficit country would experience not just a static loss of income but also a dynamic loss of capital per worker. It would not be feasible to model this channel in our model, because it cannot be identified empirically how much of the trade deficit in each country is consumed or invested, much less what consumption and investment would have been in the rebalancing counterfactual.

3.1   Model Fit

Table 7.3 compares the wages, returns to capital, and trade shares in the baseline model and in the data. The top panel shows that mean and median wages implied by the model are very close to the data. The correlation coefficient between model-implied wages and those in the data is 0.99. The second panel performs the same comparison for the return to capital. Since it is difficult to observe the return to capital in the data, we follow the approach adopted in the estimation of T_n^j's and impute r_n from an aggregate factor market clearing condition: $r_n/w_n = (1 - \alpha)L_n/(\alpha K_n)$, where α is the aggregate share of labor in GDP, assumed to be two-thirds. Once again, the average levels of r_n are very similar in the model and the data, and the correlation between the two is about 0.97.

Next, we compare the trade shares implied by the model to those in the data. The third panel of Table 7.3 reports the spending on domestically produced goods as a share of overall spending, π_{nn}^j. These values reflect the overall trade openness, with lower values implying higher international trade as a share of absorption. The averages are quite similar, and the correlation between the model and data values is 0.84. Finally, the bottom panel compares the international trade flows in the model and the data.

Table 7.3   The fit of the baseline model with the data

		Model	Data
Wages:			
	mean	0.407	0.413
	median	0.147	0.154
	corr(model, data)	0.990	
Return to capital:			
	mean	0.966	1.074
	median	0.757	0.758
	corr(model, data)	0.947	
π^j_{nn}	.		
	mean	0.586	0.565
	median	0.631	0.607
	corr(model, data)	0.839	
$\pi^j_{ni}, i \neq n$			
	mean	0.006	0.006
	median	0.0002	0.0002
	corr(model, data)	0.747	

Notes: This table reports the means and medians of wages relative to the US (top panel); return to capital relative to the US (second panel), share of domestically produced goods in overall spending (third panel), and share of goods from country *i* in overall spending (bottom panel) in the model and in the data. Wages and return to capital in the data are calculated as described in Appendix 7A.1.

Source: Authors' calculations.

The averages are very close, and the correlation between model and data is nearly 0.75.

We conclude from this exercise that our model matches quite closely the relative incomes of countries, as well as bilateral and overall trade flows observed in the data. We now use the model to carry out a number of counterfactual scenarios to assess the impact of external rebalancing.

3.2   Main Results

Table 7.4 presents the impact of rebalancing in developing Asia. To ease interpretation, we split that group of countries into those with surpluses and deficits. Conveniently, there are seven in each group. The table reports the change in the wage (relative to the US wage), the change in the real exchange rate (RER) with respect to the US, the change in the trade-weighted real exchange rate, the absolute change in the share of labor employed in the non-tradeable sector, and the percentage change

Table 7.4 Developing Asia: impact of external rebalancing

	(1) Δw_n	(2) ΔRER (with respect to US)	(3) ΔRER (trade- weighted)	(4) Δ Share of L_n in NT	(5) Δ Welfare
Surplus countries					
Indonesia	17.47	13.33	1.48	0.04	0.07
Kazakhstan	71.36	36.45	25.25	0.36	1.36
Malaysia	25.57	15.69	4.67	0.14	1.88
People's Republic of China	16.67	12.87	1.39	0.03	0.34
Republic of Korea	14.11	11.57	−2.24	0.01	−0.03
Taipei,China	16.22	12.25	−0.14	0.03	0.46
Thailand	18.72	13.78	1.47	0.05	0.41
Mean	25.73	16.56	4.56	0.10	0.64
Median	17.47	13.33	1.47	0.04	0.41
Deficit countries					
Bangladesh	6.80	8.34	−1.65	−0.03	−2.57
Fiji	−1.84	4.27	−5.55	−0.08	−4.58
India	−0.25	1.17	−12.63	−0.04	−1.78
Pakistan	6.31	8.26	−8.29	−0.03	−2.86
Philippines	5.09	5.80	−5.97	−0.03	−1.34
Sri Lanka	−12.13	−1.99	−10.46	−0.16	−8.14
Viet Nam	7.18	8.02	−2.25	−0.02	−1.98
Mean	1.59	4.84	−6.68	−0.06	−3.32
Median	5.09	5.80	−5.97	−0.03	−2.57

Notes:
NT = non-tradeable; RER = real exchange rate; US = United States of America.
Units are in percentage points, with the exception of column (2), which is the absolute
change in the share of labor in the non-tradeable sector. This table reports the changes in
wages relative to the US, the real exchange rate (both relative to the US price level and
trade-weighted), the absolute change in the share of labor in the non-tradeable sector, and
the change in welfare, due to the closing of trade imbalances world-wide.

Source: Authors' calculations.

in welfare. The units are in percentage points, with the exception of the
change in the labor share, which is expressed in absolute terms.

The RERs are defined as follows. The RER with respect to the United
States is the ratio of the price levels:

$$RER_{n,US} = \frac{P_n}{P_{US}}.$$

Thus, by convention, an increase in $RER_{n,US}$ represents a real appreciation for country n. The trade-weighted RER is defined similarly, except that in the denominator is the trade-weighted geometric average of all the countries with which n trades:

$$RER_{n,tw} = \frac{P_n}{\prod_i P_i^{tw_{ni}}},$$

where tw_{ni} is the share of trade with country i (imports plus exports) in total country n's trade (imports plus exports).

A number of results stand out. The surplus countries experience a large increase in wages relative to the US, about 20 percent on average. The magnitude of the shift in the RER relative to the US is of similar, but somewhat smaller, magnitude. This is to be expected, given that the US is the largest deficit country in the world. As the US is forced to consume less, its labor demand falls, and so do wages.[5]

Interestingly, the appreciation in the trade-weighted RER for the surplus countries in developing Asia is much more subdued, 1.47 percent at the median compared to 13.3 percent for the US-based RER. This is to be expected: much of these countries' trade is with each other, and thus even as they are all appreciating relative to the US, their trade-weighted appreciation is much smaller. The Republic of Korea and Taipei,China even experience modest RER depreciations.

In all of the surplus countries, external rebalancing leads to an increase in the share of labor employed in the non-tradeable sector, as expected. Now that these countries are not transferring income abroad, domestic demand rises, and with it demand for non-tradeables. The change is modest on average: at the median there is a 4 percentage point increase in the share of labor in the non-tradeable sector. On average in this group of countries, the share of labor in the non-tradeable sector is two-thirds. For the PRC, for instance, the labor share in non-tradeables increases by 3 percentage points.

Finally, the impact of external rebalancing on welfare is much smaller than on either relative wages or RERs. At the median, these countries experience a rise in welfare of 0.41 percent, 2 orders of magnitude less than the average increase in the relative wage. This is sensible: as these countries' relative wages rise dramatically, so do domestic prices. The net impact is positive (with the sole exception of the Republic of Korea), but much smaller than the gross changes in either wages or price levels. Note that our metric for welfare is real factor income (7.6). Thus, we ignore any direct impact of changes in D_n on consumption.

The bottom half of Table 7.4 presents the results for the deficit countries in developing Asia. Starting with the relative wage, for four out of seven countries in this sample the relative wage (compared to the US) actually rises. This is because while these countries do have deficits, the deficit of the US is still larger. By the same token, six out of seven of these countries actually experience a real appreciation relative to the US, even though they also have to close their deficits. The picture becomes much clearer when we move to the trade-weighted exchange rates. By this metric, every single one of these countries experiences a real depreciation, with an average of 6–7 percent.

Predictably, the share of labor devoted to the non-tradeable sector falls in these countries due to the rebalancing. The absolute magnitudes are similar to the surplus countries, but with the opposite sign. Finally, all of the countries in this sample experience a fall in welfare, of about 3 percent on average. This is a much more sizeable welfare change than for the surplus countries.

Table 7.5 presents the outcomes of the rebalancing for the rest of the world. For the US, welfare falls by 0.85 percent. Looking at the summary statistics across regions, we see that by and large welfare falls due to the rebalancing, which reflects the net trade surplus Asia runs with the rest of the world.

3.2.1 Interpretation

As expected, countries that currently run deficits spend less after the rebalancing, and their welfare falls. Countries with observed surpluses spend more, and their welfare rises. The relationship between welfare changes and the initial trade balance is thus positive, and is depicted in Figure 7.1. The initial trade balance explains quite well the subsequent welfare change. The correlation between these two for developing Asia is 0.81. Note that our welfare numbers do not include the direct effect of consuming the trade surplus (see Section 2.3). The positive welfare impact of rebalancing comes from the general equilibrium effect of changes in domestic spending on the demand for factors of production, and thus on real wages and the return to capital.

While changes in domestic spending have an impact on countries, in a world integrated through trade we would also expect changes in the trade balances of one's trading partner to affect welfare. Intuitively, an increase in spending in one's trading partner is expected to stimulate a country's exports and therefore increase the demand for that country's

Table 7.5   Rest of the world: impact of external rebalancing

	(1) Δw_n	(2) ΔRER (with respect to US)	(3) ΔRER (trade-weighted)	(4) Δ Share of L_n in NT	(5) Δ Welfare
Organisation for Economic Co-operation and Development					
Australia	16.88	12.92	2.15	0.02	0.41
Austria	10.71	8.96	−1.88	−0.01	−0.23
Belgium-Luxembourg	9.36	8.17	−1.65	−0.01	−0.43
Canada	5.89	4.26	0.27	0.00	−0.27
Denmark	14.82	11.69	1.03	0.01	0.12
Finland	14.29	11.54	−1.26	0.01	0.04
France	7.48	6.34	−3.63	−0.01	−0.38
Germany	16.00	12.25	2.20	0.02	0.36
Greece	−11.14	−6.64	−17.30	−0.07	−3.40
Iceland	17.63	13.52	2.13	0.02	0.40
Ireland	33.55	20.29	12.82	0.15	1.71
Italy	9.41	7.82	−2.36	−0.01	−0.28
Japan	13.41	11.03	−1.81	0.00	−0.04
Netherlands	18.37	13.40	2.49	0.03	0.59
New Zealand	13.75	10.87	−0.79	0.01	−0.02
Norway	26.27	18.36	8.61	0.07	1.22
Portugal	−3.11	−1.13	−9.36	−0.05	−1.84
Spain	4.17	3.96	−5.79	−0.02	−0.79
Sweden	14.43	11.61	0.23	0.01	0.05
Switzerland	16.08	12.39	2.56	0.03	0.25
United Kingdom	4.61	4.66	−5.07	−0.02	−0.99
United States	0.00	0.00	−9.54	−0.03	−0.85
Mean	11.49	8.92	−1.18	0.01	−0.20
Median	13.58	10.95	−1.02	0.01	−0.03
Central and Eastern Europe					
Bulgaria	−2.32	1.87	−6.97	−0.09	−3.12
Czech Republic	12.86	10.26	−0.44	0.01	0.04
Hungary	13.71	10.64	0.08	0.01	0.20
Poland	7.97	7.54	−3.41	−0.02	−0.73
Romania	4.40	5.18	−4.31	−0.04	−1.31
Russian Federation	48.2	30.07	18.58	0.15	1.24

Table 7.5   (continued)

	(1) Δw_n	(2) ΔRER (with respect to US)	(3) ΔRER (trade-weighted)	(4) Δ Share of L_n in NT	(5) Δ Welfare
Central and Eastern Europe					
Slovak Republic	12.91	10.27	−0.56	0.01	0.07
Slovenia	9.08	7.92	−1.79	−0.02	−0.41
Ukraine	−3.84	3.44	−11.86	−0.10	−5.08
Mean	11.44	9.69	−1.19	−0.01	−1.01
Median	9.08	7.92	−1.79	−0.02	−0.41
Latin America and Caribbean					
Argentina	16.43	11.78	1.33	0.02	0.67
Bolivia	13.03	10.70	0.20	0.01	0.41
Brazil	14.20	11.32	0.11	0.01	0.13
Chile	17.15	12.25	2.98	0.03	0.80
Colombia	12.71	9.84	3.30	0.01	0.09
Costa Rica	−17.65	−9.17	−12.48	−0.12	−6.78
Ecuador	8.91	7.75	0.43	−0.01	−0.60
El Salvador	−4.84	−1.20	−2.23	−0.09	−3.41
Guatemala	−21.90	−11.24	−14.43	−0.14	−8.75
Honduras	−13.93	−3.87	−5.57	−0.16	−7.98
Mexico	5.93	4.44	0.96	0.00	−0.49
Peru	22.83	15.40	6.43	0.07	1.20
Trinidad and Tobago	42.53	22.05	15.67	0.14	1.63
Uruguay	6.83	7.02	−4.02	−0.03	−1.06
Venezuela, RB	51.46	25.05	19.67	0.20	1.91
Mean	10.25	7.48	0.82	0.00	−1.48
Median	12.71	9.84	0.43	0.01	0.09
Middle East and North Africa					
Egypt, Arab Rep.	−4.06	3.54	−8.03	−0.08	−5.55
Iran, Islamic Rep.	52.80	37.61	25.26	0.16	0.82
Israel	6.10	5.34	−1.42	−0.02	−0.68
Jordan	−27.74	−5.33	−23.57	−0.21	−18.50
Kuwait	62.02	34.61	22.50	0.37	2.27
Saudi Arabia	475.00	94.41	79.80	4.60	−34.55

Table 7.5 (continued)

	(1) Δw_n	(2) ΔRER (with respect to US)	(3) ΔRER (trade-weighted)	(4) Δ Share of L_n in NT	(5) Δ Welfare
Middle East and North Africa					
Turkey	−2.90	1.69	−9.61	−0.09	−3.68
Mean	80.17	24.55	12.13	0.68	−8.55
Median	6.10	5.34	−1.42	−0.02	−3.68
Sub-Saharan Africa					
Ethiopia	7.59	10.73	−5.77	−0.03	−3.90
Ghana	6.73	7.51	−4.06	−0.03	−1.60
Kenya	1.21	2.02	−9.71	−0.03	−1.68
Mauritius	−12.99	−5.25	−11.59	−0.13	−6.33
Nigeria	76.01	52.98	43.97	0.26	0.39
Senegal	6.62	7.08	−4.18	−0.02	−1.62
South Africa	12.40	10.11	−2.05	0.00	−0.04
Tanzania	−9.77	−2.06	−10.63	−0.07	−6.67
Mean	10.98	10.39	−0.50	0.00	−2.68
Median	6.68	7.29	-4.98	-0.03	−1.65

Notes:
NT = non-tradeable; RB = República Bolivariana; RER = real exchange rate; US = United States of America.
Units are in percentage points, with the exception of column (2), which is the absolute change in the share of labor in the non-tradeable sector. This table reports the changes in wages relative to the US, the real exchange rate (both relative to the US price level and trade-weighted), the absolute change in the share of labor in the non-tradeable sector, and the change in welfare, due to the closing of trade imbalances world-wide.

Source: Authors' calculations.

factors of production. It turns out that a country's welfare changes due to global rebalancing are strongly positively correlated with whether it exports mostly to the deficit or to surplus countries. Figure 7.2 presents a scatterplot of welfare changes on the y-axis against the export-share-weighted deficit of a country's trading partners. That is, if a country exports disproportionately to countries currently running deficits, it will have negative values on the x-axis, and vice versa. There is a pronounced positive relationship: countries exporting mostly to deficit countries tend to experience a fall in welfare, while countries exporting more to surplus countries tend to increase their welfare. The correlation between the two variables is 0.82. This scatterplot demonstrates the importance of

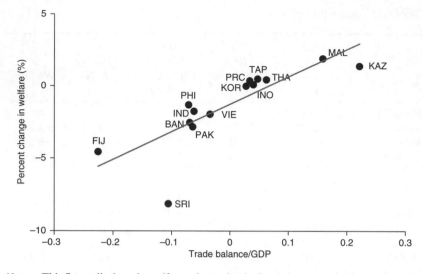

Note: This figure displays the welfare gains to developing Asian countries from external rebalancing against their trade balance as a share of GDP, along with the least-squares fit.

Source: Authors' calculations.

Figure 7.1   Developing Asia: initial trade balances and change in welfare

multilateral trade relationships for fully understanding the importance of rebalancing.

To be more concrete, we can compare the major export destinations of Sri Lanka and Bangladesh to those of Kazakhstan and Taipei,China. Thirty-seven percent of Sri Lanka's and 30 percent of Bangladesh's exports go to the US and the UK, the major deficit countries in the world. Thus, a rebalancing hurts the demand for their exports, and leads to reductions in their welfare. By contrast, 21 percent of Kazakhstan's and 35 percent of Taipei,China's exports go to the PRC, the major trade surplus country. This difference in the identity of the major export destination corresponds well to the difference in the welfare impact of rebalancing in these four countries.

4.   CONCLUSION

Fast-growing countries often run sustained trade surpluses. A natural question going forward is what would be the long-run impact of external rebalancing – narrowing or elimination of trade imbalances – on the

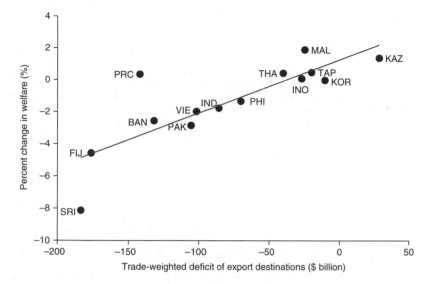

Note: This figure displays the welfare gains to developing Asian countries from external rebalancing against the export-share weighted trade imbalances of their trading partners, along with the least-squares fit. The units on the x-axis are US$ billions.

Source: Authors' calculations.

Figure 7.2   Developing Asia: trade balances in export destinations and change in welfare

economies of developing Asia and the rest of the world. In this chapter, we evaluate this question using a quantitative multi-country, multi-sector model of world production and trade that includes 14 economies of developing Asia as well as 61 other major economies from the rest of the world.

In our developing Asia sample, there are seven surplus countries and seven deficit ones. For the surplus countries (the PRC, Malaysia, and others), the global external rebalancing brings about a significant rise in relative wages, a real appreciation, an increase in the size of the non-traded sector, and an increase in welfare of a fraction of 1 percent on average. For the deficit countries, the impacts are the opposite: a real depreciation, a shrinking of the non-traded sector, and a 2–3 percent reduction in welfare. We show that multilateral trade relationships are important for developing the full account of the impact of global rebalancing: countries currently exporting mostly to deficit countries tend to lose from rebalancing, whereas countries exporting to the surplus countries tend to gain in welfare.

NOTES

* We are grateful to the participants of the ADB Global Supply Chain Conference for helpful suggestions.
1. Shikher (2005, 2011, 2012), Burstein and Vogel (2012), and Eaton et al. (2011), among others, follow the same approach of assuming the same θ across sectors. Caliendo and Parro (2010) use tariff data and triple differencing to estimate sector-level θ. However, their approach may suffer from significant measurement error: at times the values of θ they estimate are negative. In addition, in each sector the restriction that θ > ε − 1 must be satisfied, and it is not clear whether Caliendo and Parro (2010) estimated sectoral θ's meet this restriction in every case. Our approach is thus conservative by being agnostic on this variation across sectors.
2. Di Giovanni and Levchenko (2010) provide suggestive evidence that at such a coarse level of aggregation, input–output matrices are indeed similar across countries. To check robustness of the results, we collected country-specific I–O matrices from the GTAP database. Productivities computed based on country-specific IO matrices were very similar to the baseline values. In our sample of countries, the median correlation was 0.98, with all but 3 out of 75 countries having a correlation of 0.93 or above, and the minimum correlation of 0.65.
3. The US IO matrix provides an alternative way of computing α_j and β_j. These parameters calculated based on the US IO table are very similar to those obtained from UNIDO, with the correlation coefficients between them above 0.85 in each case. The US IO table implies greater variability in α_j's and β_j's across sectors than does UNIDO.
4. Using the variable name conventions in the Penn World Tables, $L_n = 1000 * pop * rgdpch / rgdpwok$.
5. Note that this is not a necessary outcome. Rebalancing in the US requires a shift of domestic factors of production from the non-tradeable to the tradeable sectors. If the tradeable sectors were more labor-intensive than the non-tradeable sectors, this may actually raise labor demand in the US, since in that case factors would be reallocating from capital- to labor-intensive sectors. In practice, it is if anything the opposite: tradeable sectors are on average less labor intensive than non-tradeable ones, though the difference is not drastic (Table 7A.1).

REFERENCES

Bartelsman, E.J. and W. Gray (1996), 'The NBER manufacturing productivity database', NBER Technical Working Paper 205.

Bernanke, B. and R. Gürkaynak (2001), 'Is growth exogenous? Taking Mankiw, Romer, and Weil seriously', *NBER Macroeconomics Annual*, **16**, 11–57.

Berthelon, M. and C. Freund (2008), 'On the conservation of distance in international trade', *Journal of International Economics*, **75**, 310–320.

Burstein, A. and J. Vogel (2012), 'International trade, technology, and the skill premium', Mimeo, UCLA and Columbia University.

Caliendo, L. and F. Parro (2010), 'Estimates of the trade and welfare effects of NAFTA', Mimeo, University of Chicago.

Caselli, F. (2005), 'Accounting for cross-country income differences', in S. Durlauf and P. Aghion (eds), *Handbook of Economic Growth*, **1**, Elsevier-North Holland, 679–741.

Dekle, R., J. Eaton, and S. Kortum (2007), 'Unbalanced trade', *American Economic Review: Papers and Proceedings*, **97**, 351–355.

Dekle, R., J. Eaton, and S. Kortum (2008), 'Global rebalancing with gravity: measuring the burden of adjustment', IMF Staff Papers, **55**, 511–540.

di Giovanni, J. and A.A. Levchenko (2010), 'Putting the parts together: trade, vertical linkages, and business cycle comovement', *American Economic Journal: Macroeconomics*, **2**, 95–124.

Do, Q.-T. and A.A. Levchenko (2007), 'Comparative advantage, demand for external finance, and financial development', *Journal of Financial Economics*, **86** (3).

Dornbusch, R., S. Fischer, and P. Samuelson (1977), 'Comparative advantage, trade, and payments in a Ricardian model with a continuum of goods', *American Economic Review*, **67**, 823–39.

Eaton, J. and S. Kortum (2002), 'Technology, geography, and trade', *Econometrica*, **70**, 1741–1779.

Eaton, J., S. Kortum, B. Neiman, and J. Romalis (2011), 'Trade and the global recession', NBER Working Paper No. 16666.

Finicelli, A., P. Pagano, and M. Sbracia (2013), 'Ricardian selection', *Journal of International Economics*, **89**, 96–106.

Hall, R. and C. Jones (1999), 'Why do some countries produce so much more output per worker than others?', *Quarterly Journal of Economics*, **114**, 83–116.

Herrendorf, B., R. Rogerson, and A. Valentinyi (2013), 'Two perspectives on preferences and structural transformation', *American Economic Review*, **103**, 2752–2789.

Hummels, D., J. Ishii, and K.-M. Yi (2001), 'The nature and growth of vertical specialization in world trade', *Journal of International Economics*, **54**, 75–96.

Levchenko, A.A. and J. Zhang (2011), 'The evolution of comparative advantage: measurement and welfare implications', NBER Working Paper No. 16806.

Obstfeld, M. and K.S. Rogoff (2005), 'Global current account imbalances and exchange rate adjustments', *Brookings Papers on Economic Activity*, **36**, 67–146.

Salter, W.E.G. (1959), 'Internal and external balance: the role of price and expenditure effects', *Economic Record*, **35**, 226–238.

Shikher, S. (2005), 'Accounting for international trade', Mimeo, Suffolk University.

Shikher, S. (2011), 'Capital, technology, and specialization in the neoclassical model', *Journal of International Economics*, **83**, 229–242.

Shikher, S. (2012), 'Putting industries into the Eaton-Kortum model', *Journal of International Trade and Economic Development*, **21**, 807–837.

Simonovska, I. and M.E. Waugh (2011), 'The elasticity of trade: estimates and evidence', University of California Davis Working Paper No. 11-2.

Swan, T.W. (1960), 'Economic control in a dependent economy', *Economic Record*, **36**, 51–66.

Święcki, T. (2013), 'Intersectoral distortions, structural change and the welfare gains from trade', Mimeo, Princeton University.

Uy, T., K.-M. Yi, and J. Zhang (2013), 'Structural change in an open economy', *Journal of Monetary Economics*, **60**, 667–682.

Waugh, M. (2010), 'International trade and income differences', *American Economic Review*, **100**, 2093–2124.

APPENDIX 7A.1 PROCEDURE FOR ESTIMATING T_n^j, D_{ni}^j, AND ω_j

This appendix reproduces from Levchenko and Zhang (2011) the details of the procedure for estimating technology, trade costs, and taste parameters required to implement the model. Interested readers should consult that paper for further details on estimation steps and data sources.

7A.1 Tradeable Sector Relative Technology

We now focus on the tradeable sectors. Following the standard EK approach, first divide trade shares by their domestic counterpart:

$$\frac{\pi_{ni}^j}{\pi_{nn}^j} = \frac{X_{ni}^j}{X_{nn}^j} = \frac{T_i^j(c_i^j d_{ni}^j)^{-\theta}}{T_n^j(c_n^j)^{-\theta}},$$

which in logs becomes:
Let the (log) iceberg costs be given by the following expression:

$$\ln d_{ni}^j = d_k^j + b_{ni}^j + CU_{ni}^j + RTA_{ni}^j + ex_i^j + v_{ni}^j,$$

where d_k^j is an indicator variable for a distance interval. Following EK, we set the distance intervals, in miles, to [0, 350], [350, 750], [750, 1500], [1500, 3000], [3000, 6000], [6000, maximum). Additional variables are whether the two countries share a common border (b_{ni}^j), belong to a currency union (CU_{ni}^j), or to a regional trade agreement (RTA_{ni}^j). Following the arguments in Waugh (2010), we include an exporter fixed effect ex_i^j. Finally, there is an error term v_{ni}^j. Note that all the variables have a sector superscript j: we allow all the trade cost proxy variables to affect true iceberg trade costs d_{ni}^j differentially across sectors. There is a range of evidence that trade volumes at sector level vary in their sensitivity to distance or common border (see, among many others, Do and Levchenko 2007, Berthelon and Freund 2008).

This leads to the following final estimating equation:

$$\ln\left(\frac{X_{ni}^j}{X_{nn}^j}\right) = \underbrace{\ln(T_i^j(c_i^j)^{-\theta}) - \theta ex_i^j}_{\text{Exporter Fixed Effect}} \underbrace{-\ln(T_n^j(c_n^j)^{-\theta})}_{\text{Importer Fixed Effect}}$$

$$\underbrace{-\theta d_k^j - \theta b_{ni}^j - \theta CU_{ni}^j - \theta RTA_{ni}^j}_{\text{Bilateral Observables}} \underbrace{-\theta v_{ni}^j}_{\text{Error Term}},$$

This equation is estimated for each tradeable sector $j = 1,...J$. Estimating this relationship will thus yield, for each country, an estimate of its technology-cum-unit-cost term in each sector j, $T_n^j(c_n^j)^{-\theta}$, which is obtained by exponentiating the importer fixed effect. The available degrees of freedom imply that these estimates are of each country's $T_n^j(c_n^j)^{-\theta}$ relative to a reference country, which in our estimation is the United States. We denote this estimated value by S_n^j:

$$S_n^j - \frac{T_n^j}{T_{us}^j}\left(\frac{c_n^j}{c_{us}^j}\right)^{-\theta},$$

where the subscript *us* denotes the United States. It is immediate from this expression that estimation delivers a convolution of technology parameters T_n^j and cost parameters c_n^j. Both will of course affect trade volumes, but we would like to extract technology T_n^j from these estimates. In order to do that, we follow the approach of Shikher (2012). In particular, for each country n, the share of total spending going to home-produced goods is given by

$$\frac{X_{nn}^j}{X_n^j} = T_n^j\left(\frac{\Gamma c_n^j}{p_n^j}\right)^{-\theta}$$

Dividing by its US counterpart yields:

$$\frac{X_{nn}^j/X_n^j}{X_{us,us}^j/X_{us}^j} = \frac{T_n^j}{T_{us}^j}\left(\frac{c_n^j}{c_{us}^j}\frac{p_{us}^j}{p_n^j}\right)^{-\theta} = S_n^j\left(\frac{p_{us}^j}{p_n^j}\right)^{-\theta},$$

and thus the ratio of price levels in sector j relative to the US becomes:

$$\frac{p_n^j}{p_{us}^j} = \left(\frac{X_{nn}^j/X_n^j}{X_{us,us}^j/X_{us}^j}\frac{1}{S_n^j}\right)^{\frac{1}{\theta}}. \tag{7A.1}$$

The entire right-hand side of this expression is either observable or estimated. Thus, we can impute the price levels relative to the US in each country and each tradeable sector.

The cost of the input bundles relative to the US can be written as:

$$\frac{c_n^j}{c_{us}^j} = \left(\frac{w_n}{w_{us}}\right)^{\alpha_j\beta_j}\left(\frac{r_n}{r_{us}}\right)^{(1-\alpha_j)\beta_j}\left(\prod_{k=1}^{J}\left(\frac{p_n^k}{p_{us}^k}\right)^{\gamma_{k,j}}\right)^{1-\beta_j}\left(\frac{p_n^{J+1}}{p_{us}^{J+1}}\right)^{\gamma_{J+1,j}(1-\beta_j)}.$$

Using information on relative wages, returns to capital, price in each tradeable sector from (7A.1), and the non-tradeable sector price relative to the US, we can thus impute the costs of the input bundles relative to the US in each country and each sector. Armed with those values, it is straightforward to back out the relative technology parameters:

$$\frac{T_n^j}{T_{us}^j} = S_n^j \left(\frac{c_n^j}{c_{us}^j}\right)^{-\theta}.$$

7A.2   Trade Costs

The bilateral, directional, sector-level trade costs of shipping from country i to country n in sector j are then computed based on the estimated coefficients as:

$$\ln \hat{d}_{ni}^j = \theta \hat{d}_k^j + \theta \hat{b}_{ni}^j + \theta \widehat{CU}_{ni}^j + \theta \widehat{RTA}_{ni}^j + \theta \widehat{ex}_{ni}^j + \theta \hat{v}_{ni}^j$$

for an assumed value of θ. Note that the estimate of the trade costs includes the residual from the gravity regression $\theta \hat{v}_{ni}^j$. Thus, the trade costs computed as above will fit bilateral sectoral trade flows exactly, given the estimated fixed effects. Note also that the exporter component of the trade costs $\theta \widehat{ex}_{ni}$ is part of the exporter fixed effect. Since each country in the sample appears as both an exporter and an importer, the exporter and importer estimated fixed effects are combined to extract an estimate of $\theta \widehat{ex}_{ni}^j$.

7A.3   Complete Estimation

So far we have estimated the levels of technology of the tradeable sectors relative to the United States. To complete our estimation, we still need to find (i) the levels of T for the tradeable sectors in the United States; (ii) the taste parameters ω_j, and (iii) the non-tradeable technology levels for all countries.

To obtain (i), we use the NBER-CES Manufacturing Industry Database for the US (Bartelsman and Gray 1996). We start by measuring the observed total factor productivity (TFP) levels for the tradeable sectors in the US. The form of the production function gives

$$\ln Z_{us}^j = \ln \Lambda_{us}^j \ln + \beta_j \alpha_j \ln L_{us}^j + \beta_j (1 - \alpha_j) \ln K_{us}^j$$

$$+ (1 - \beta_j) \sum_{k=1}^{J+1} \gamma_{k,j} \ln M_{us}^{k,j} \qquad (7A.2)$$

where Λ^j denotes the measured TFP in sector j, Z^j denotes the output, L^j denotes the labor input, K^j denotes the capital input, and $M^{k,j}$ denotes the intermediate input from sector k. The NBER-CES Manufacturing Industry Database offers information on output, and inputs of labor, capital, and intermediates, along with deflators for each. Thus, we can estimate the observed TFP level for each manufacturing tradeable sector using the above equation.

If the United States were a closed economy, the observed TFP level for sector j would be given by $\Lambda_{us}^j = (T_{us}^j)^{\frac{1}{\theta}}$. In the open economies, the goods with inefficient domestic productivity draws will not be produced and will be imported instead. Thus, international trade and competition introduce selection in the observed TFP level, as demonstrated by Finicelli et al. (2013). We thus use the model to back out the true level of T_{us}^j of each tradeable sector in the United States. Here we follow Finicelli et al. (2013) and use the following relationship:

$$(\Lambda_{us}^j)^\theta = T_{us}^j + \sum_{i \neq us} T_i^j \left(\frac{c_i^j d_{us,i}^j}{c_{us}^j} \right)^{-\theta}$$

Thus, we have

$$(\Lambda_{us}^j)^\theta = T_{us}^j \left[1 + \sum_{i \neq us} \frac{T_i^j}{T_{us}^j} \left(\frac{c_i^j d_{us,i}^j}{c_{us}^j} \right)^{-\theta} \right] = T_{us}^j \left[1 + \sum_{i \neq us} S_i^j (d_{us,i}^j)^{-\theta} \right]. \quad (7A.3)$$

This equation can be solved for underlying technology parameters T_{us}^j in the US, given estimated observed TFP Λ_{us}^j, and all the S_i^j's and $d_{us,i}^j$'s estimated in the previous subsection.

To estimate the taste parameters $\{\omega_j\}_{j=1}^J$, we use information on final consumption shares in the tradeable sectors in the US. We start with a guess of $\{\omega_j\}_{j=1}^J$ and find sectoral prices p_n^k as follows. For an initial guess of sectoral prices, we compute the tradeable sector aggregate price and the non-tradeable sector price using the data on the relative prices of non-tradeables to tradeables. Using these prices, we calculate sectoral unit costs and Φ_n^j's, and update prices according to equation (7.3), iterating until the prices converge. We then update the taste parameters according to equation (7.5), using the data on final sectoral expenditure shares in the US. We normalize the vector of ω_j's to have a sum of one, and repeat the above procedure until the values for the taste parameters converge.

Finally, we estimate the non-tradeable sector TFP using the relative prices. In the model, the non-tradeable sector price is given by

$$p_n^{J+1} = \Gamma (T_n^{J+1})^{-\frac{1}{\theta}} c_n^{J+1}.$$

Since we know the aggregate price level in the tradeable sector p_n^T, c_n^{J+1}, and the relative price of non-tradeables (which we take from the data), we can back out T_n^{J+1} from the equation above for all countries.

Table 7A.1   Sectors

ISIC code	Sector Name	α_j	β_j	$\gamma_{J+1,j}$	ω_j
15	Food and beverages	0.290	0.290	0.303	0.169
16	Tobacco products	0.272	0.490	0.527	0.014
17	Textiles	0.444	0.368	0.295	0.019
18	Wearing apparel, fur	0.468	0.369	0.320	0.109
19	Leather, leather products, Footwear	0.469	0.350	0.330	0.015
20	Wood products (excl. furniture)	0.455	0.368	0.288	0.008
21	Paper and paper products	0.351	0.341	0.407	0.012
22	Printing and publishing	0.484	0.453	0.407	0.005
23	Coke, refined petroleum products, nuclear fuel	0.248	0.246	0.246	0.141
24	Chemical and chemical products	0.297	0.368	0.479	0.009
25	Rubber and plastics products	0.366	0.375	0.350	0.014
26	Non-metallic mineral products	0.350	0.448	0.499	0.073
27	Basic metals	0.345	0.298	0.451	0.002
28	Fabricated metal products	0.424	0.387	0.364	0.013
29C	Office, accounting, computing, and other machinery	0.481	0.381	0.388	0.051
31A	Electrical machinery, communication equipment	0.369	0.368	0.416	0.022
33	Medical, precision, and optical instruments	0.451	0.428	0.441	0.038
34A	Transport equipment	0.437	0.329	0.286	0.220
36	Furniture and other manufacturing	0.447	0.396	0.397	0.065
4A	Non-tradeables	0.561	0.651	0.788	–
	Mean	0.400	0.385	0.399	0.053
	Min.	0.248	0.246	0.246	0.002
	Max.	0.561	0.651	0.788	0.220

Notes:
– = data not available; ISIC = International Standard Industrial Classification of All Economic Activities.
This table reports the sectors used in the analysis. The classification corresponds to the ISIC Revision 3, 2-digit, aggregated further due to data availability. α_j is the value-added based labor intensity; β_j is the share of value added in total output; $\gamma_{J+1,j}$ is the share of non-tradeable inputs in total intermediate inputs; ω_j is the taste parameter for tradeable sector j, estimated using the procedure described in Section A7.3.
Variable definitions and sources are described in detail in the text.

8. Global supply chains and macroeconomic relationships in Asia

Menzie Chinn*

1. INTRODUCTION

One of the key challenges to the analysis of open economy macroeconomic interactions involves the understanding of how flows in goods and services, capital and asset prices respond in a world where trade is not limited to final goods, but includes (potentially many) stages of intermediate production. That is particularly true in parts of the world deeply involved in trade in global supply chains – the phenomenon wherein a final good is produced in separate countries. Nowhere has this process of production fragmentation extended as far as in East Asia: hence, the need for an examination of the macroeconomic implications for the region.

In this chapter, I survey the various channels by which economic interactions might evolve with increasing integration. First, I assess the implications for the measurement of macroeconomic variables; in particular the real exchange rate – the relative price of traded goods and services – will become more difficult to measure. One can no longer merely apply the final good prices to deflate the nominal exchange rate; rather one would need to keep track of the value added at each stage of production – and where it took place.

Second, I assess the ramifications for the measurement of the relationship between exchange rates and trade flows, when relative prices and trade flows are properly measured.

Third, the impact of greater vertical specialization on exchange rate pass-through into traded goods prices is examined.

Fourth, I assess the evidence on business cycle synchronization. With production fragmented across economies, in principle an additional channel has been added to the other means by which shocks are propagated across economies.

Finally, I investigate the conjecture that increasing integration by

249

way of global supply chains will lead to increasing motivation for poli-cymakers to stabilize nominal exchange rates, insofar as exchange rate volatility complicates planning and production in integrated production chains.

The following conclusions stem from the survey.

First, the conventional means of measuring international competitive-ness are going to be less and less adequate, as production becomes more fragmented. Relatedly, it will become less and less tenable to estimate the traditional partial equilibrium trade equations in order to obtain macro-level trade elasticities, as mis-measurement of trade flows becomes more pronounced, and appropriate deflators for real exchange rates diverge further from the typically used deflators.

Second, the increasing role of intermediate inputs will likely drive down exchange rate pass-through. This is true even if the increase is due to increasing arms-length transactions. However, to the extent that pass-through is less pronounced the greater the amount of intra-firm trade, a further decrease in exchange rate pass-through is likely to occur.

Third, business cycle correlations are rising throughout the region. The more prominent increases are often associated with the People's Republic of China (PRC), a finding consistent with the country's growing role in the global supply chain. Furthermore, the propagation of shocks throughout the East Asia system is consistent with the PRC driving movements in output, at least in the Republic of Korea and Taipei,China.

Finally, there is evidence that the central banks of the region are paying more heed to the Chinese currency's value, at the high frequency (daily) and at lower frequency (monthly), with respect to rates of depreciation, as well as levels of exchange rates. Since these relationships are not struc-tural, there is no guarantee that they will remain in place. At the same time, continued integration by way of production fragmentation should make central bankers pay extra attention to stabilizing currency values against each other.

2. THE MEASUREMENT OF THE REAL EFFECTIVE EXCHANGE RATE[1]

The real exchange rate occupies a central role in international finance as the key relative price between home and foreign goods. In a world where trade is in final goods, and all goods are traded, the real exchange rate definition is relatively clear:

$$q_t \equiv s_t - p_t + p_t^* \qquad (8.1)$$

where s is the log nominal exchange rate expressed in home currency units per foreign, and p is the log price level for home final goods, and p^* for foreign final goods. Then q denotes the number of home units of final goods necessary to obtain one unit of foreign.

This simple expression can be complicated in a number of ways, depending upon whether there are nontraded goods, or whether final goods are the only goods traded.[2] The fact that there are multiple countries should not complicate the expression terribly. Then the real exchange rate is a weighted average of the exchange rates and price levels corresponding to the various trade partners. The complication involves what weights to attribute to each bilateral real exchange rate.[3]

The correct definition of the real exchange rate is altered when there is trade in intermediate goods. Then one can ask either of two questions. The first is whether agents have preferences over the value added originating in different countries, or preferences over final goods. This distinction is sometimes characterized as the difference between trade in tasks versus trade in goods.

Let's consider the first approach. Then, the appropriate definition of the relative price of traded output is the relative price of value added expressed in common currency terms. In practical terms, this greatly complicates the calculation of the relative price. Now one has to keep track of where inputs come from, and measure the appropriate price deflators for the amount of value added actually incorporated into the good in a given country.

Bems and Johnson (2012) argue that the conventional real effective exchange rates incorporating prices of gross sales do not conform to any theoretically justified measure – not even one in which goods are produced without imported intermediates. In addition, the popular expedient of using consumer price indices instead of price indices of the goods traded introduces another possible difference. Of course the relevant question is whether in practice the conventional measures deviate substantially from the theoretically more correct measures.

In practice, Bems and Johnson find that in many cases the appropriate effective exchange rates do differ from the conventionally used ones. However, the differences are most pronounced for exactly those instances wherein one would expect the biggest differences – the PRC, Germany, other East Asian economies. Figures 8.1a–c depict the conventional (IMF) real effective exchange rates and the Bems–Johnson value added counterparts for the PRC, Japan and Republic of Korea (all graphed so that a rise denotes an *appreciation*).

Interestingly, the big differences in the real exchange rate values are not driven by the adjustment in trade weights. Rather the main factor is in the

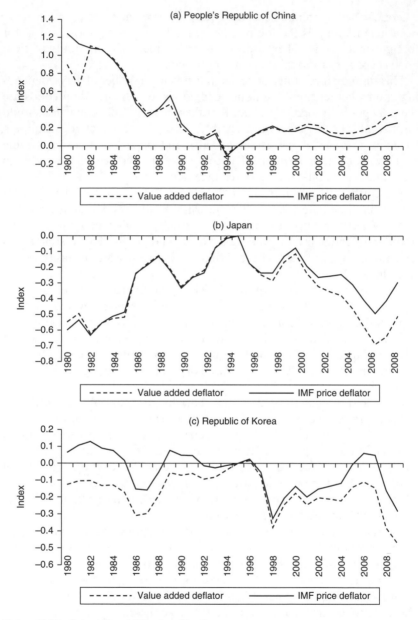

Note: IMF – International Monetary Fund.

Source: Bems and Johnson (2012) and IMF.

Figure 8.1   Real effective exchange rates (1995 = 100)

use of a value-added deflator, rather than the consumer price index (CPI). It has always been known that the use of the CPI is likely to lead to mistaken inferences regarding relative prices due to the heavy weight adduced to services and other nontraded goods in CPIs.[4]

For instance, over the 1995–2009 period, the Chinese effective exchange rate appreciated 11.4 percentage points more than was implied using the conventional (CPI, trade weighted) measured using log changes (Figure 8.1a).[5] Relative to 2000, the differential is 8.8 percentage points. Had this result been known in 2005–2006, the controversy over yuan (CNY) exchange rate misalignment might have been less heated. Most of the difference is attributable not to the difference in trade weights, but rather to the difference in use of the deflator.[6]

Japan is another case of a country deeply involved in the East Asian global supply chain. In this instance, as of 2009, the cumulative gap between the conventional and value added series, both based on year 1995, amounted to 21.7 percentage points more after taking into account intermediate goods and the correct deflator than was indicated using the conventional measure (Figure 8.1b). This result casts in a different light the increase in the trade balance in the years leading up to the global financial crisis; apparently the improvement was driven by a greater than measured yen depreciation. The Korean value added measure also shows a less pronounced appreciation than the conventional measure (Figure 8.1c).

Notice the correct deflator is not the deflator for all of gross domestic product (GDP), but for the value added component imbedded in traded goods. The two might move together, but there are no guarantees. CPIs are likely to deviate even further from the ideal deflator.

The Bems–Johnson approach focuses on value added. An alternative approach is to view trade as driven by preferences over final goods – that is, the price of the final good, but taking into account the price savings due to outsourcing of production is key. This approach is taken up by Bayoumi et al. (2013).

In this approach, one wants to take into account the costs along the entire production chain, i.e., taking into account outsourcing of production. As mentioned before, this approach makes more sense if preferences are expressed over goods, rather than value-added. Bayoumi et al. implement this alternative approach and show that the impact vis-à-vis the Bems–Johnson formulation is in several cases minor. On the other hand, in the case of the PRC, use of outsourcing means that the appreciation in the value of final goods is less than the appreciation in terms of tasks. This approach is consistent with the Thorbecke (2011) measurement of the integrated exchange rate measure for the PRC, which incorporates information on inputs from other East Asian countries in the production of Chinese exports.

On the other hand, for the United States (US), the difference is negligible. Finally there are intermediate cases such as Germany, where the trade-in-tasks and trade-in-goods measure deviates sometimes, and at other times, does not.[7]

To the extent that competitiveness is appropriately defined over the value added component of exports and imports, this issue of measurement is quantitatively important in the East Asian region.

3. ASSESSING THE IMPLICATIONS FOR TRADE FLOWS

3.1 Background

One of the reasons that one would want to measure correctly exchange rates is so that one could obtain accurate measures of competitiveness, and hence of the responsiveness of trade flows to price changes.

The typical macroeconomist's approach is to assume that one can estimate trade elasticities in a partial equilibrium framework following the "imperfect substitutes" methodology outlined in, for instance, Goldstein and Khan (1985). That is, one can write out export and import equations (assuming log-linear functional forms, where lowercase letters denote log values of upper case):

$$ex_t = \delta_0 + \delta_1 q_t + \delta_2 y_t^{RoW} + \delta_3 z_t^i + \varepsilon_{1t} \qquad (8.2)$$

$$im_t = \beta_0 + \beta_1 q_t + \beta_2 y_t^i + \beta_3 z_t^{RoW} + \varepsilon_{2t} \qquad (8.3)$$

where y is income, z is a supply (shift) variable, and $\beta_1 < 0, \beta_2 > 0, \beta_3 > 0$ and, $\delta_1 > 0, \delta_2 > 0$ and $\delta_3 > 0$.

Notice that exports are the residual of production over domestic consumption of exportables; similarly imports are the residual of foreign production over foreign consumption of tradables. The difference between this specification and the standard is the inclusion of the exportables supply shift variable, z. In standard import and export regressions, this term is omitted, implicitly holding the export supply curve fixed; in other words, it constrains the relationship between domestic consumption of exportables and production of exportables to be constant. A bout of consumption at home that reduces the supply available for exports would induce an apparent structural break in equation (8.2) if the z term is omitted. Similarly, omission of the rest-of-world export supply term from the import equation makes the estimated relationships susceptible to structural breaks.[8]

The preceding estimation procedure assumes that the export and import equations can be estimated separately. This would be most appropriate if trade was in final goods, but clearly this is a less and less tenable proposition over time. Johnson (2014) summarizes the prevailing estimates: exports of value added are equal to about 70 percent–75 percent of gross exports, down from about 85 percent in the 1970s–1980s.

The foregoing is a reduced form approach. As documented in Hillberry and Hummels (2012), estimation of such reduced form equations is typically plagued by endogeneity issues (as well as measurement error). To the extent that the relative price variable is the real exchange rate, which incorporates the nominal exchange rate, the problem is mitigated. In the typical econometric exercise, the real exchange rate is weakly exogenous for trade flows.[9]

In the macroeconomic literature, most attempts to deal with the issue of vertical specialization have been ad hoc in nature. In addressing US trade for instance, Chinn (2010) takes an indirect approach. He adduces the high income elasticities to production fragmentation, which in turn is increasing as tariffs are reduced, following Hummels et al. (2001), Yi (2003) and Chen et al. (2005). At this juncture it is useful to recognize that services exhibit less of this fragmentation.[10]

Chinn (2010) finds that the tariff factor and the square both enter with statistical significance, indicating that lower tariffs increase trade flows. However, as expected, higher energy costs, as proxied by the relative price of oil, also enter in. These findings are indirectly supportive of the view that vertical specialization is important. So too is the fact that income elasticities differ substantially for durables and nondurables, particularly on the US export side.

Clearly, the results pertaining to the US, with relatively low levels of vertical specialization in trade flows, are of some, but limited, relevance.[11] Perhaps the most important instance would be the Chinese case. In their study of Chinese imports and exports, Cheung et al. (2010, 2012) follow previous studies by incorporating an ad hoc correction. This involves adding processing imports into the export equation, and exports into the processing imports equation.

Cheung et al. (2012) consider Chinese trade flows with respect to the rest-of-the-world using the Chinese version of equations (8.2) and (8.3). Then q is the real value of the RMB, and z_t^{RoW} replaced with w in the import equation. The variable w is a shift variable accounting for other factors that might increase import demand. Because of the PRC's role in the global supply chain, it is assumed that a fraction of imports is intermediate goods and its demand is driven by export activity; hence *w* could include exports.[12] Also, to account for the PRC's role in the global supply chain, they include exports as an independent variable.[13] Exports enter in with the expected sign (and a near unit elasticity). However, the real exchange rate retains a negative and significant coefficient.

Another way Cheung et al. (2012) address the supply chain effect is to disaggregate the trade flows. The Chinese customs agency categorizes exports and imports into those goods that are to be used for processing purposes, and those to be used as ordinary exports or imports. For instance, processing imports are usually for manufacturing finished products in the country for (re-) exporting, and these imports are usually subjected to more favorable tariff rates. In contrast, processing exports are exports that are used by the importing country for processing and assembly.

For both ordinary and processing exports, the typical result is that the value of the yuan (CNY) enters in with the right sign and statistical significance. One large difference is the fact that ordinary exports do not exhibit a statistically significant sensitivity to rest-of-world GDP (unless a post-World Trade Organization trend is included). In contrast, processing exports always exhibit income elasticities in excess of unity.

Next, they investigate whether the corresponding disaggregation yields more promising results for imports. For ordinary imports, the income elasticity is positive but not statistically significant, while the exchange rate has the wrong effect. If one includes exports (which is not well motivated for ordinary imports), the results are largely negative as well, since no economic variable enters with significance.

For processing imports, both income and the real exchange rate enter significantly, but the latter enters with the wrong sign. Including exports results in properly signed coefficients for the exchange rate and export variables. Income now enters with a negative, and significant, sign. These results demonstrate that obtaining a correctly signed price elasticity depends on accounting, however imperfectly, for imported inputs.

3.2 Using the "Correct" Real Exchange Rate Measure

An ideal approach would estimate a relationship between the trade flows and the real exchange rate, measured in consistent terms. As Johnson (2014) observes, there are two ways to proceed. The first is to work with a model couched in terms of value added. Another is to remain in the final goods framework, and work backward to calculate the amount of value added at various stages of production. In the absence of that data, one can return to the ad hoc procedure used by Cheung et al. (2010). If one estimates a relationship with imports as a function of income, real exchange rate, exports and a time trend over the 2000Q1–2009Q4 period using the conventional real exchange rate measure, one obtains an estimated (and statistically significant) import elasticity of 1.5; that is, an appreciation of the CNY induces a decrease in imports, even after controlling (imperfectly) for the export motivation. Using the Bems–Johnson real exchange rate measure the point estimate drops to 0.6, and is no longer statistically significant.

In the case of the PRC, the use of a value added real exchange rate helps to eliminate a strongly perverse finding. This suggests that, contrary to some findings (including Cheung et al., 2010, 2012), trade flows (even mismeasured) do respond to real exchange rate changes.

Whether in fact the true underlying trade elasticities have changed is a separate matter that cannot be determined from these data. With exchange rate changes operating only on value added, rather than on gross sales, it is tempting to conclude that the *measured* impact on trade flows will be less. The canonical example is the case wherein imported inputs are used to produce an exported good. In that case, an exchange rate depreciation raises the price of export (for simplicity one-for-one), but also increases the price of the imported input (for simplicity, one-for-one again). Then the exchange rate depreciation only affects the relative price of the value added. The true impact (on value added) should be unchanged, but will appear to be smaller over time as vertical specialization proceeds, holding all else constant. Thorbecke and Smith (2010) and Thorbecke (2011) estimate the impact of exchange rate changes on gross trade flows, taking into account intermediate trade flows.[14]

What about evaluating bilateral trade elasticities? Here, the analysis becomes more complicated, as one cannot simply examine the bilateral trade, activity and price variables.[15] The response of one country's exports to a change in the nominal exchange rate will have different effects if, for instance, three countries are involved in production sharing. If the CNY appreciates against a currency of a country from which it imports intermediate goods to be used in exports to the US, the gross price of Chinese goods exported to the US will likely fall even if the bilateral dollar–yuan rate has not changed. This will then have an impact on demand for Chinese value added, even if the original shock did not involve a change in Chinese value added.[16]

4.   EXCHANGE RATE PASS-THROUGH

4.1   Background

Exchange rate pass-through is the relationship between trade prices (or consumer prices) and exchange rates. Increased vertical specialization is likely to reduce pass-through, according to various models, although the effect is likely to be difficult to detect in the welter of other effects.

The standard approach to explaining exchange rate pass-through (e.g., Hooper and Mann, 1989) appeals to imperfect competition, but without explicit micro-foundations. Let P_x^* be the price of exports from the foreign (*) country, denominated in foreign currency; and C^* be the marginal cost of production (also in foreign currency terms).

$$P_x^* = \mu C^* \tag{8.4}$$

where μ is the cost-markup. The US import price (PM^i) is obtained by multiplying through by the exchange rate (E, in currency i/foreign currency unit, e.g., Korean won/US$):

$$PM^i = E(PX^*) = E\mu C^* \tag{8.5}$$

Where the markup, μ, depends on the degree of substitutability between US and imported goods, and capacity utilization in the foreign country, as in:

$$\mu = \left(\frac{P^i}{C^* E} \right)^{\alpha} (CU^*)^{\beta} \tag{8.6}$$

where P^i is the average local price level in local currency of the good in question. Solving, and taking logs yields:

$$pm^i = (1 - \alpha)e + \alpha p^i + (1 - \alpha)c^* + \beta cu^* \tag{8.7}$$

Note that $\partial pm^i / \partial e \equiv (1 - \alpha) \equiv$ exchange rate pass-through (where ∂ denotes partial derivative).

Further observe that the expression has implications for foreign firms' (log) markup:

$$pm^\$ - e - c^* = \alpha(p^\$ - e - c^*) + \beta cu^* \tag{8.8}$$

so that the log markup or profit margin on sales to the US is a function of gap between the US price and foreign cost. When α is near unity (or pass-through is low) then a rise in *e* causes a decline in foreign profit margins.[17]

Note three limitations. First, the exposition above relies upon all value added originating in a given country. Second, most of the studies of exchange rate pass-through have focused on industrialized countries. Third, these studies focused on macroeconomic determinants (most importantly, inflation). Within this literature, the evidence in the years before the financial crisis documented a decline in industrial country exchange rate pass-through. These studies included a comprehensive analysis by the Federal Reserve of US import prices (Marazzi et al., 2005), and industrial countries generally (Sekine, 2006). Bailliu and Fujii (2004) attribute the drop to the decline in trend inflation.

The development of open economy, New Keynesian models has focused attention on the relationship between exchange rate pass-through and whether pricing is undertaken in producer currency or local currency. Local currency pricing is consistent with incomplete pass-through into import prices. The fact that export price pass-through is also less than complete suggests to Choudhri and Hakura (2012) that there is a mixture of producer currency and local currency pricing occurring for both exports and imports.

There is, of course, an endogeneity issue. Gopinath et al. (2010) show that the selection of pricing currency depends upon the desired level of exchange rate pass-through. This is the topic of some recent analyses, which have focused on the microeconomic aspects of exchange rate pass-through. In particular, increasing vertical specialization should on average reduce exchange rate pass-through. That's because, with imported inputs, an exchange rate change will change marginal costs, as illustrated in the example in the previous section. Hellerstein and Villas-Boas (2010) and Neiman (2010) document the fact that exchange rate pass-through varies inversely with the intensity of vertical specialization for US imports. Of the $16 trillion of gross world trade in 2010, roughly $6.3 trillion is intra-firm in nature, so presumably this phenomenon extends to other currencies and trade flows (UNCTAD, 2013).

4.2 Application to East Asia

Ghosh and Rajan (2007) survey the literature on exchange rate pass-through in Asia, and find a wide dispersion of estimates, ranging from relatively high for developing Asian economies such as Thailand and Indonesia, and substantially lower for industrial Japan. The dispersion of estimates is not unexpected given the wide diversity of exchange rate regimes (and relatedly, inflation outcomes).

Choudhri and Hakura (2012) provide some recent estimates of import and export exchange rate pass-through, obtained using vector autoregressions (VARs) over the 1979–2010 period. Estimates for selected East Asian economies are presented in Figures 8.2a–b, for import and export pass-through, respectively.[18] While the estimates for Hong Kong, China and Singapore indicate very low import pass-through coefficients, in accord with the predictions, those for Thailand and Singapore exceed the average for emerging market economies. This suggests that, for now at least, macroeconomic factors (inflation, exchange rate regime) trump micro factors.

Amiti et al. (2012) provide a microeconomic-based explanation for exchange rate pass-through to be particularly muted. They note that large exporters are often large importers. In such instances, in the presence of strategic complementarities and high market shares, exchange rate pass-through will tend to be small. To the extent that this characterization applies to East Asian firms, then one would expect the relatively low exchange rate pass-through coefficients to make sense, holding all else constant. However, with the exceptions of both Hong Kong, China and Singapore, pass-through coefficients appear fairly high, which suggests that other macroeconomic factors that have been determined to be important (inflation, exchange rate regime) trump micro factors. Nonetheless, to the extent that the process of vertical specialization continues, then pass-through coefficients should decline over time.[19]

5.   SYNCHRONIZATION OF BUSINESS CYCLES

5.1   Business Cycles

During the Great Recession, output in East Asia was hit particularly hard as trade flows dropped precipitously. Several hypotheses were put forward for why trade fell so much more than output, including the drying up of trade financing, a composition effect (hard hit durables are much more procyclical than nondurables), and the importance of vertical specialization.[20] On this point there is no complete agreement, but it at least seems to be a plausible argument that high degrees of vertical specialization will induce greater business cycle comovement.

Kose and Yi (2001) are an early expositor of the view that greater vertical specialization leads to greater business cycle synchronization. More recently Burstein et al. (2008) have argued that vertical specialization is an important determinant of synchronization. Arkolakis and Ramanarayanan (2009) show that GDP growth will become more synchronized if imperfect competition prevails.

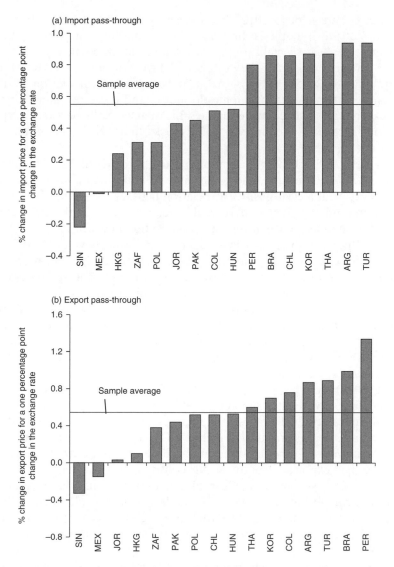

Note: ARG = Argentina, BRA = Brazil; CHL = Chile; COL = Colombia; HKG = Hong Kong, China; HUN = Hungary; JOR = Jordan; KOR = Republic of Korea; MEX = Mexico; PAK = Pakistan; PER = Peru; POL = Poland; SIN = Singapore; THA = Thailand; TUR = Turkey; ZAF = South Africa.

Source: Choudhri and Hakura (2012).

Figure 8.2 One quarter exchange rate pass-through for (a) emerging market imports; (b) emerging market exports

Carare and Mody (2012) have recently undertaken an empirical analysis of this hypothesis. In it, they relate volatility spillovers and the extent of vertical specialization, for a sample of 18 countries, over the 1977–2007 period. First, they estimate a factor structural VAR (Stock and Watson, 2005). The FSVAR allows for a decomposition of the variance of the shocks into domestic shocks and common international shocks that affect all countries in the same quarter. Spillovers have a specific interpretation – country-specific shocks that affect other countries after one quarter.

The degree of vertical specialization is taken from the OECD's *Measuring Globalization* publication, and is the share of imported inputs in exports. They document a clear positive association between the change in growth spillovers and the change in vertical specialization over the 1995–2000 period; when the change in vertical specialization between 1995 and 2000 rises by 1 percent, the change in the share of spillovers in volatility rises by 0.92 units. The bivariate relationship between vertical specialization and spillovers is stronger than that between trade intensity and spillovers (the partial effect is not discernable due to multicollinearity).

One drawback of this approach is that the link is between vertical specialization in the form of imports used for overall exports, and overall sensitivity to spillovers from the rest of the world. That is, there is no direct relationship between bilateral vertical specialization and the spillover from a particular trading partner.[21]

Ng (2010) examines a sample of 30 OECD countries over the 1970–2004 period, but investigates the relationship between bilateral correlation and bilateral trade linkages. He regresses bilateral GDP correlation coefficients, derived from HP-filtered GDP, on two measures of vertical specialization – the imported input share of gross output (weighted using either exports or output). Ng controls for intra-industry trade, trade intensity, similarity in industrial structure, and financial integration (all bilateral). While the standard variables, such as trade intensity and intra-industry trade, matter, the latter loses significance when the vertical specialization measures are included; in addition, trade intensity takes on the wrong sign.

Di Giovanni and Levchenko (2012) examine a larger, more detailed dataset that encompasses 55 countries and 28 manufacturing sectors, over the 1970–1999 period. They use a decomposition of the correlation of output growth correlation into correlations between sector growth correlations. They find that for this sample, vertical linkages account for 32 percent of the impact of bilateral trade on aggregate comovement of GDP growth, a share that is consistent with previous studies such as Burstein et al. (2008).

In interpreting these results in the context of East Asia, several caveats are necessary. Ng's sample only includes four East Asian countries: Japan, the Republic of Korea, the PRC, and Taipei,China – plus Indonesia. The di Giovanni and Levchenko study added Hong Kong, China in East Asia, and they also include Malaysia and Singapore; however they omit the PRC. Perhaps more importantly, the vertical integration statistics apply to either before 2000, or up to 2000. In other words, most of the relationship between vertical specialization and business cycle correlation that is documented pertains to the extent of linkages in place over a decade ago.

This suggests that it might be useful to examine more recent trends in business cycle dynamics, under the presumption that the links have become stronger over time.

5.2   Recent Trends in East Asian Business Cycle Dynamics

In this section, I document the changes in business cycle dynamics over the past thirty years. In the absence of recent data on the extent of bilateral vertical specialization for all the relevant countries in the region, I limit myself to documenting the business cycle dynamics

To this end, I examine the time series properties of real GDP in the region, utilizing quarterly data over the 1980Q1–2012Q4 period. The use of quarterly data allows for a more detailed view of business cycle dynamics. I focus on the four newly industrialized countries (NICs), of Hong Kong, China, the Republic of Korea, Singapore and Taipei,China; and the emerging Asian economies of the PRC, Indonesia, Malaysia, Philippines and Thailand. I check the correlations with Japan, the US, and, for comparison's sake, Mexico.

In order to isolate the business cycle components, I employ several statistical techniques: a Hodrick–Prescott (HP) filter, quadratic detrending and log-differencing.[22] The resulting bilateral correlations of HP-filtered deviations of log GDP are then calculated for the 1990Q1–1997Q4 and 1999Q1–2012Q4 periods. The change in the correlation coefficients between the two sub periods is reported in Table 8.1.

The results indicate that correlation coefficients among the East Asian countries rise, sometimes significantly. In particular, the PRC's correlation rises with most of the East Asian countries rise, and substantially so with Singapore and Japan – the latter is important to the extent that it matches the narrative of increasing linkages between the two economies.[23] Note the exception is Indonesia, but in this case the result is probably an artifact of the sharp and permanent drop in the trend in Indonesian GDP in 1997. This event distorts the estimated business cycle obtained using the HP filter (as well as linear detrending). In fact, once one takes out the

Table 8.1 *Change in business cycle correlations, using Hodrick–Prescott detrending*

Correlation	PRC	JPN	KOR	TAP	HKG	INO	MAL	PHI	SIN	THA	USA	MEX
PRC	0.000											
JPN	0.821	0.000										
KOR	0.088	0.262	0.000									
TAP	0.409	0.734	0.046	0.000								
HKG	−0.003	0.919	0.048	0.131	0.000							
INO	−0.250	0.086	−0.263	−0.418	−0.131	0.000						
MAL	0.457	0.393	0.136	0.456	0.474	−0.251	0.000					
PHI	0.838	0.287	−0.126	0.112	0.118	−0.035	0.002	0.000				
SIN	0.510	0.613	0.074	0.721	0.455	−0.421	−0.042	−0.047	0.000			
THA	0.143	0.265	−0.165	0.268	0.298	−0.051	−0.077	−0.069	−0.157	0.000		
USA	0.123	0.564	0.288	0.490	0.533	−0.313	0.526	0.650	0.724	0.227	0.000	
MEX	0.779	0.443	0.807	0.726	0.767	0.054	0.515	0.545	0.777	0.366	0.711	0.000

Notes:
PRC = People's Republic of China; HKG = Hong Kong, China; INO = Indonesia; JPN = Japan; KOR = Republic of Korea; MEX = Mexico; MAL = Malaysia; PHI = Philippines; SIN = Singapore; TAP = Taipei,China; THA = Thailand; USA = United States. Dark-shaded cell values are greater than 0.30, light-shaded cell values are smaller than −0.15.

Source: Author's calculations.

Indonesian entries, the dominant impression one obtains is that business cycle correlations have risen, often substantially.[24, 25]

The HP filter is but one way of identifying business cycles; it tends to identify smaller cyclical deviations than those obtained using quadratic detrending. If one uses quadratic detrending, once again one obtains broadly similar results (as long as one ignores the Indonesian results). The intra-East Asia correlations typically rise in the more recent period. This characterization holds regardless of whether the sample ends in 2006 or 2012.

Using non-overlapping four quarter growth rates as a measure of business cycles, one obtains results similar to those obtained using the HP filter to define business cycles. Business cycle correlations have tended to rise, as summarized in Table 8.2. The exceptions involve Indonesia, or involve very modest declines. If the later subsample is extended to 2012, then the pattern is more pronounced.

It is notable that the PRC's correlation rises in a noticeable fashion with Japan and Republic of Korea, using this definition of the business cycle. So too do correlations between Japan and Taipei,China, as well as Singapore and Taipei,China.

Typically, researchers have examined the static correlations as a way of explaining the strength of economic interactions. An alternative is to use an econometric methodology that allows for dynamics. I use a simple non-structural VAR to characterize the dynamics relating key variables to individual economies. Ideally, one would want to model all the economies simultaneously; however, there are not enough observations to undertake such an analysis using this approach. Hence, I use a more ad hoc approach, examining each East Asian country's dynamics separately.[26]

In each case I estimate a two lag VAR including the US, Japan, the PRC and each respective East Asian country, using the indicated ordering. This means that I assume that all economic activity variables – in this case the HP filter defined output gaps – are endogenous, but the US business cycle is more exogenous than Japan's, Japan's is more exogenous than the PRC's, and the PRC's is more exogenous than the cycle of the individual small East Asian economy.[27]

In order to conserve space, I present the detailed results for two of the larger economies of interest (Republic of Korea and Taipei,China), and discuss the other economies' results in general terms. Republic of Korea and Taipei,China are two countries that account for large shares of global imports used for exports.[28] The resulting impulse response functions (IRFs) show the response of a variable to a one standard deviation shock to a particular variable. Plus/minus one standard error bands are included

Table 8.2 Change in business cycle correlations, using non-overlapping four-quarter growth rates

Correlation	PRC	JPN	KOR	TAP	HKG	INO	MAL	PHI	SIN	THA	USA	MEX
PRC	0.000											
JPN	0.514	0.000										
KOR	0.465	-0.103	0.000									
TAP	0.201	0.338	0.264	0.000								
HKG	0.721	0.222	-0.431	0.356	0.000							
INO	-0.046	0.579	-0.036	-0.462	0.289	0.000						
MAL	0.260	-0.074	0.347	0.276	0.163	-0.478	0.000					
PHI	0.129	-0.094	-0.279	0.082	0.019	0.480	-0.567	0.000				
SIN	0.215	0.060	-0.071	1.073	0.542	-0.138	0.302	0.139	0.000			
THA	0.199	-0.003	-0.525	0.318	0.149	-0.121	-0.378	0.048	0.229	0.000		
USA	-0.531	-0.019	0.324	0.775	0.426	-0.095	0.091	0.132	-0.007	0.011	0.000	
MEX	-0.455	0.433	0.444	-0.008	0.177	-0.729	-0.281	-0.271	0.153	-0.008	0.008	0.000

Notes:
PRC = People's Republic of China; HKG = Hong Kong, China; INO = Indonesia; JPN = Japan; KOR = Republic of Korea; MEX = Mexico; MAL = Malaysia; PHI = Philippines; SIN = Singapore; TAP = Taipei,China; THA = Thailand; USA = United States. Dark-shaded cell values are greater than 0.30, light-shaded cell values are smaller than -0.15.

Source: Author's calculations.

266

to illustrate the degree of statistical precision – or lack of – in each set of estimates.

In Figure 8.3a, the graph in the first row of the first column denotes the response of the US GDP output gap to a shock to the US output gap, over time, during the 1981Q1–1997Q4 period. The hump shaped pattern indicates that after an initial positive impact, the response increases before decaying toward zero. The impulse response is statistically significant. The second figure in the first column shows the response of the Japanese output gap to the US output gap shock. As in the third and fourth figures (the Chinese and Korean output gaps), the output gap does not respond with statistical significance to US output shocks.

The second column shows the impulse response functions for shocks to the Japanese output gap, while the third and fourth show the corresponding functions for Chinese and Korean output gaps. One general characteristic of these figures is that only the impulse response functions in the diagonal elements display much statistical significance.

These results can be interpreted as indicating that whatever macroeconomic business cycle links there are between the US, Japan, the PRC and the Republic of Korea they are not typically easy to detect in the pre-1997 sample.

For the 1999Q1–2007Q4 period (Figure 8.3b), the IRFs provide a substantially different story. The Japanese output gap responds to the US output gap, as does the Korean. Now, Japanese and Korean output gaps respond to the Chinese output gap (borderline significance). In other words, the PRC's business cycle has a noticeable impact on two other economies with which the vertical specialization links are particularly strong.

Given the strongly synchronized downturn in trade flows and economic activity in 2008–2009, attributed by some to increasing vertical specialization, my prior was that extending the sample to incorporate the global recession would have strengthened these results. Surprisingly, the aforementioned effects largely disappear when the sample is extended up to 2012Q4 (results not shown). One interpretation of this phenomenon is that the effect of the vertical specialization linkages have been obscured by the divergence in macro policies, with Chinese GDP delinking from the rest of the global supply chain. The alternative view would allow that the measurement of the business cycle (i.e., output gap) has become much more problematic at the end of the sample period.

Next I consider Taipei,China. In the early period (Figure 8.4a), there are rarely any significant effects detected – most economies' output gaps appear to be affected by their own lagged output gaps. In this respect, the

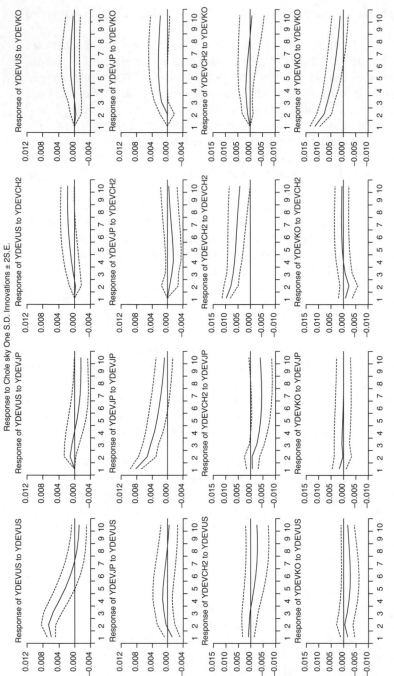

Response to Cholesky One S.D. Innovations ± 2S.E.

Note: VAR = vector autoregression.

Source: Author's calculations.

Figure 8.3a   Impulse response functions for Republic of Korea VAR, 1981Q1–1997Q4

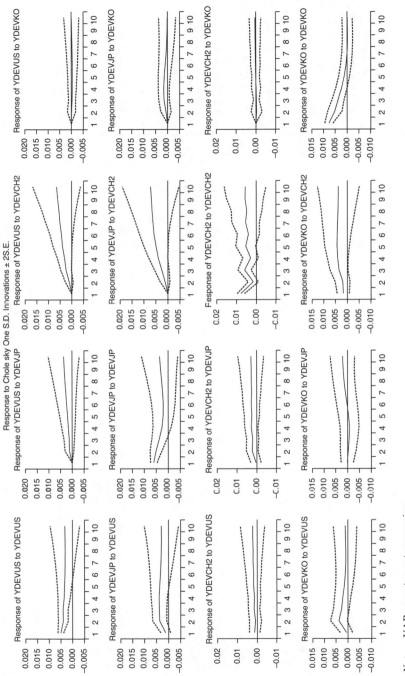

Note: VAR = vector autoregression.

Source: Author's calculations.

Figure 8.3b   Impulse response functions for Republic of Korea VAR, 1999Q1–2007Q4

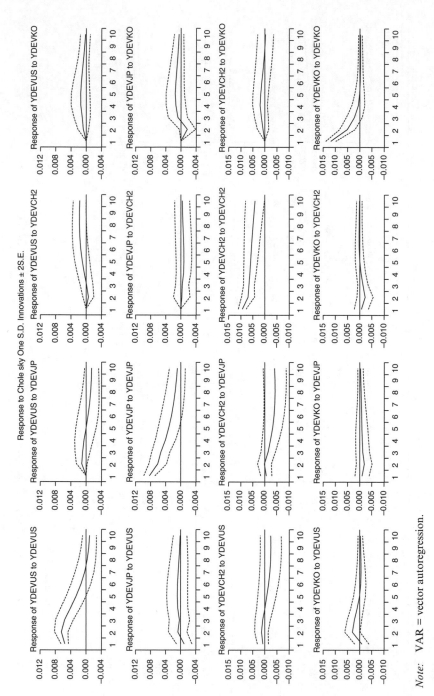

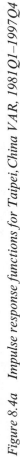

Note: VAR = vector autoregression.

Source: Author's calculations.

Figure 8.4a Impulse response functions for Taipei,China VAR, 1981Q1–1997Q4

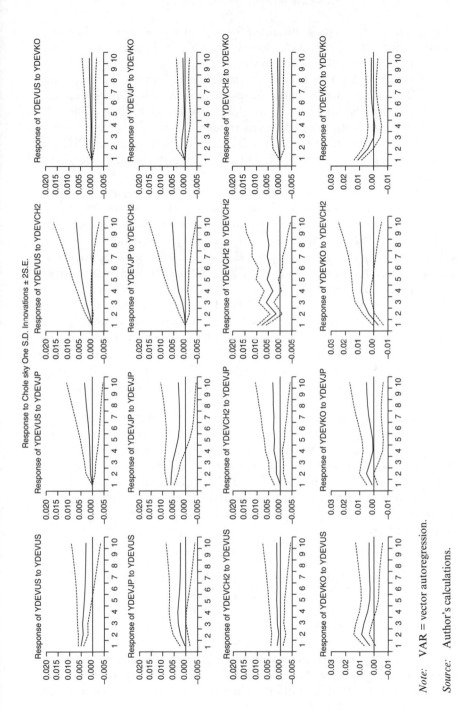

Note: VAR = vector autoregression.

Source: Author's calculations.

Figure 8.4b   Impulse response functions for Taipei,China VAR, 1999Q1–2007Q4

findings are similar to those obtained for Republic of Korea. In the more recent 1999Q1–2007Q4 period, both Japanese and Taipei,China output gaps respond to the US output gap shock.

In contrast to the results for the earlier period, in the latter period (Figure 8.4b), Taipei,China output responds positively to Chinese output, and with statistical significance at the 3–4 quarter horizon. The US appears to respond to the PRC, even though it is treated as more exogenous than the PRC; however the results are borderline significant.[29] Once again, these results largely disappear once one extends the latter sample to 2012Q4.

A similar pattern of contrasting results holds for Singapore, Thailand and Malaysia. In the early period, most output gaps are largely explained by lagged own-economy output gaps. In the latter period, the output gaps respond to the PRC's output gap, with borderline statistical significance (after accounting for US and Japan effects). The enhanced sensitivity of these countries' business cycles to the PRC's is also detected in alternative global models (Bussiere et al., 2012).

On the other hand, Indonesia and the Philippines do not exhibit any substantial change in IRFs, particularly of own output gap to the Chinese output gap, moving from the early period to the later. It is conceivable that other factors obscure the relationship. For instance, Indonesia's intermediate exports to PRC are substantial, but involve mostly energy exports. The Philippines experienced numerous political shocks during the 1980s and 1990s.

In sum, during this period when arguably global supply chains have become increasingly important, business cycle correlations have risen, and risen in a fashion mostly consistent with the pattern of linkages. Moreover, using an HP-filtered measure of the business cycle, it appears that in the period up to the onset of the global financial crisis, the PRC's role in determining business cycles in East Asia grew.[30] However, that evidence is less visible in the period spanning the global recession and the subsequent recovery.

6.   EXCHANGE RATE STABILIZATION AND THE CHINESE DOMINANCE THESIS

6.1   Previous Assessments

As vertical integration proceeds, it is likely that government reaction functions – in particular those of central banks – will evolve. One conjecture is that to the extent that exchange rate movements complicate decision making within the global supply chain, one would anticipate that policymakers experience pressure to stabilize exchange rates.[31]

On the other hand, it is unclear whether policymakers will want to stifle one key avenue of macroeconomic adjustment. For instance, Bems (2012) shows that increasing vertical specialization does not have unambiguous effects on the amount of exchange rate adjustment necessary to effect a given change in trade inflows. That's because accounting for intermediates means that countries are more closed than conventionally understood; but accounting for domestic intermediates means that economies are more open as services (which are typically thought of as untraded) are incorporated in exports.

Nonetheless, the conventional wisdom holds that policymakers will welcome more stable exchange rates when there is much production sharing. If they are to stabilize against each other, which currency will they stabilize against? There are several candidates –historically, the US dollar is the obvious candidate, due to its use as a financing and invoicing currency. But with the PRC's outsize role in trade transactions (and supply chains), it seems reasonable to ask whether the regional central banks will coordinate to an ever greater extent on the Chinese yuan, much as European countries anchored their currencies to the Deutsche mark some thirty years ago.

This hypothesis gains even more plausibility as Chinese authorities embark on a project to internationalize the renminbi (RMB). The measures include allowing for RMB swaps, and encouraging invoicing in CNY.[32]

Figures 8.5 and 8.6 show the evolution of the regional currencies, including the Chinese yuan (CNY), expressed in terms of IMF Special Drawing Rights (SDRs), in the wake of the reform of the Chinese exchange rate regime in July 2005, and after the financial crisis starting in July 2010. Notice that the currencies of the region appear to follow the Chinese yuan, suggesting that central banks in the region pay close attention to Chinese currency interventions.

One way of making this assessment is to examine how daily currency movements are related to movements in the major currencies – the United States dollar (USD), the euro (EUR), the Japanese yen (JPY) and the CNY (all expressed against the SDR). The regression coefficients are then interpretable as the weight ascribed to each currency in the currency basket targeted by the central bank.

$$\Delta e_t^{\frac{i}{SDR}} = \alpha_0 + \alpha_1 \Delta e_t^{\frac{USD}{SDR}} + \alpha_2 \Delta e_t^{\frac{CNY}{SDR}} + \alpha_3 \Delta e_t^{\frac{EUR}{SDR}}$$

$$+ \beta_4 \Delta e_t^{JPY/SDR} + \alpha_5 \Delta e_t^{GBP/SDR} + u_t \qquad (8.9)$$

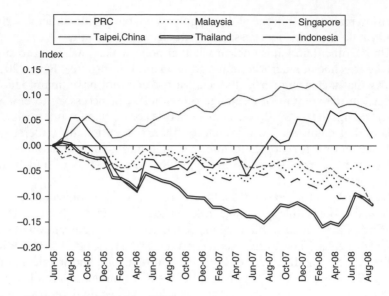

Note:　PRC = People's Republic of China.

Source:　Author's calculations.

Figure 8.5　Log exchange rates against special drawing rights, 2005M06 = 0

Where $e^{i/SDR}$ is the number of currency units per SDR, in logs, the i superscript denotes the specific East Asian currency of interest, and Δ is the first difference operator.

For instance, if $\alpha_1 = 1$ for i = KRW (Korean won), then the interpretation would be that the Bank of Korea targeted the US dollar.

Huang et al. (2013) examine daily data from January 1999 to July 2005, and July 2005 to June 2013, for the Hong Kong dollar (HKD), Indian rupee (INR), Indonesian rupiah (IDR), Korean won (KRW), Malaysian ringgit (MYR), Singapore dollar (SGD), and Thai baht (THB), using equation (8.8). In all cases, the weight ascribed to the USD declines going from the first sample to the second, save the SGD and THB. Moreover, the estimated weight on the CNY becomes statistically significant. Those results confirm that at high frequencies (daily), the central banks have paid much more attention to movements in the CNY than they did before July 2005.

Fratzscher and Mehl (2011) use a variant of this approach. In their study, they assess the tripolar thesis – the idea that the USD, EUR and CNY are becoming the anchors for currency management – using daily

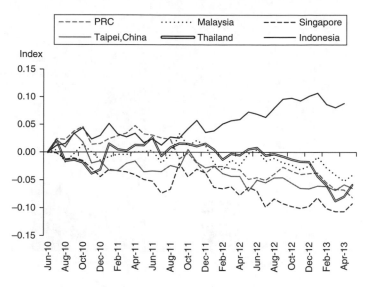

Note: PRC = People's Republic of China.

Source: Author's calculations.

Figure 8.6   Log exchange rates against special drawing rights, 2010M06 = 0

data on nearly fifty exchange rates over the 1996 to 2011 period. They undertake two types of analyses; the first is an unconditional factor analysis, and the second, an extension of the first, augmented with policy announcements.

In the unconditional analysis, the authors regress changes in the exchange rates against the SDR on a US, euro area and regional factor, and other conditioning variables. The US factor (the US dollar–SDR exchange rate) is taken as exogenous, the euro factor is the residual from the regression of the euro exchange rate on the dollar rate, and the regional factor is a GDP-weighted average of the regional currencies (excluding the CNY), orthogonalized by taking the residuals from a regression on the dollar and euro rates.[33]

Fratzscher and Mehl find that the regional factor is increasing in importance over time. The US factor is dominant both pre- and post-reform (July 2005). The results for emerging Asia are reported in Figure 8.7. For the currencies of that region, the coefficient on the US factor is 0.74 and 0.60, respectively. This means that after July 2005, a depreciation of 10 percent in the US dollar induces a depreciation of 6 percent in a currency. The Asian regional factor coefficient increases from 0.19 to 0.25.

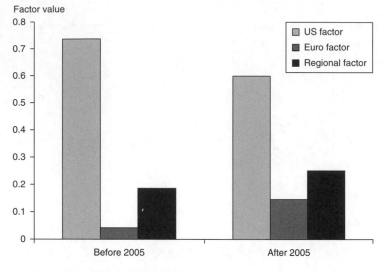

Source: Fratzscher and Mehl (2011), Table 6.

Figure 8.7   Determinants of East Asian currency movements, 1997–2011

The interesting question is whether the CNY drives the regional factor. Using Granger causality tests, the authors find that pre-2005, one typically cannot reject the hypothesis that the CNY does not Granger-cause the regional factor; post-2005, one rejects the null. In addition, replacing the regional factor with the CNY rate yields similar results.

Fratzscher and Mehl then extend the analysis to include dummy variables for Chinese statements regarding increased flexibility or reserve diversification. The general pattern of factor loading estimates remains intact, while Chinese official announcements have a greater impact in the latter period.[34]

6.2   Longer Term Trends and Exchange Rate Adjustment

The preceding section outlined approaches that examined the behavior of exchange rates at high (daily) frequency. However, for macroeconomic interactions, one needs to know how the exchange rates behave over the longer term – monthly and quarterly. Not only are changes of interest, so too are levels.

In this section I attempt to redress this deficiency by examining how East Asian exchange rates have been managed in response to major currencies.

$$\Delta e_t^{\frac{i}{SDR}} = \beta_0 + \beta_1 e_{t-1}^{\frac{i}{SDR}} + \beta_2 e_{t-1}^{\frac{USD}{SDR}} + \beta_3 e_{t-1}^{\frac{CNY}{SDR}}$$

$$+ \beta_4 e_{t-1}^{\frac{JPY}{SDR}} + \beta_5 F_{t-1} + \beta_6 \Delta e_{t-1}^{\frac{i}{SDR}} + \beta_7 \Delta e_{t-1}^{\frac{USD}{SDR}}$$

$$+ \beta_8 \Delta e_{t-1}^{CNY/SDR} + \beta_9 \Delta e_{t-1}^{JPY/SDR} + \beta_{10}\Delta F_t + u_t \quad (8.10)$$

where F is the financial stress index for the US.

This specification is an error correction model, which allows for a long run cointegrating relationship between the log levels of the six exchange rates against the SDR. The long run cointegrating relationship is given by the expression $-\beta_k/\beta_1$, while β_1 is an estimate of the rate of reversion to long run equilibrium. Note the inclusion of the contemporaneous first difference of the financial stress index is consistent with weak exogeneity of US financial stress.[35]

I estimate the specification in equation (8.10) over two samples, 1999M01 to 2005M06, and 2005M07 to 2013M04, and examine the evolution of weights attached to the USD and the CNY going between the two subsamples.[36] This break matches with the reform in the Chinese exchange rate regime. I do not include the HK\$ (since at this frequency it is collinear with the USD), but add in the currency for Taipei,China (NT\$).

Note that the estimation of the error correction specifications is appropriate if the series are cointegrated. While the series do not appear to be cointegrated over the entire 1999M01–2013M04 period, they do appear cointegrated over the subsamples, thus validating the estimation procedure implemented.

Table 8.3 reports the results of estimating equation (8.10); the top half presents results pertaining to the early subsample, before the reform of the Chinese exchange rate regime. The bottom half applies to the later subsample.

Because the CNY is effectively pegged to the USD during the early period, it is not possible to identify a separate CNY effect. Hence, the only currencies included in the estimation in the early period are the USD and JPY. Nonetheless, it is still surprisingly difficult to identify a long run relationship between the currency values in the early sub-period. By and large the proportion of variation explained is nil, while there is some slight evidence of mean reversion, as evidenced by negative estimated β_1 coefficients. Because the fit is so poor, there is only weak evidence of a long run relationship between the various currencies and the USD and JPY (denoted by the US(LR) and JP(LR) entries).

In the bottom half of Table 8.3, the results suggest a much better fit. In all cases, there is evidence of reversion to long run relationships between

Table 8.3　Coefficients from error correction model

	KRW	SGD	NTD	IDR	MYR	THB
Period: 1999M01–2005M06						
B_1	−0.117†	−0.110	0.141†	−0.105†	−9.593	−0.054
	(0.075)	(0.095)	(0.075)	(0.069)	(9.703)	(0.064)
US	−0.055	0.036	−0.173**	0.129†	9.557	0.006
	(0.039)	(0.052)	(0.069)	(0.082)	(9.705)	(0.035)
JP	0.045	0.040	−0.038	−0.112	0.052**	−0.005
	(0.073)	(0.031)	(0.064)	(0.132)	(0.024)	(0.065)
Adj R^2	0.03	0.02	0.14	0.02	0.01	−0.05
US(LR)	−0.47	na	na	1.23	na	na
JP(LR)	0.38	na	na	−1.07	na	na
Period: 2005M07–2013M04						
B_1	−0.160***	−0.167**	−0.156**	−0.212***	−0.204**	−0.151***
	(0.063)	(0.074)	(0.064)	(0.064)	(0.081)	(0.053)
CN	−0.019	0.176*	0.029	−0.099	0.144*	0.171**
	(0.086)	(0.091)	(0.048)	(0.099)	(0.082)	(0.083)
US	0.247**	−0.092**	0.016	−0.018	−0.025	−0.046
	(0.108)	(0.045)	(0.058)	(0.109)	(0.043)	(0.057)
JP	−0.051	−0.005	0.032†	0.025	−0.009	−0.023
	(0.051)	(0.029)	(0.024)	(0.046)	(0.027)	(0.029)
Adj R^2	0.55	0.15	0.3	0.32	0.07	0.04
CN(LR)	−1.19	**1.05**	0.19	−0.47	**0.71**	1.13
US(LR)	**1.54**	−0.55	0.10	−0.08	0.12	−0.30
JP(LR)	−0.32	0.03	0.21	−0.12	−0.04	−0.15

Notes:
IDR = Indonesian rupiah; KRW = Korean won; MYR = Malaysian ringgit; NTD = New Taiwan dollars; SGD = Singapore dollar; THB = Thai baht.
na =not available; significant at † 20%; * 10%; ** 5%; *** 1%.
Coefficient estimates from equation (8.9). B_1 is coefficient on lagged level of dependent variable. *CN, US, JP* are coefficients on respective currency values. *CN(LR)*, *US(LR)*, and *JP(LR)* are implied long run elasticities. Bold face entries indicate that both the long run and reversion coefficient used to calculate the long run elasticities are statistically significant at the 10% marginal significance level.

Source:　Author's calculations.

the individual currencies and the CNY, USD and JPY. For instance, the estimated β_1 ranges between 0.16 and 0.21. This means the half-life of a deviation of the exchange rate from the long run relationship ranges from 3 to 4 months, ignoring short run dynamics.

For the cases where the coefficients are statistically significant, the CNY has taken on a more important role. For the SGD, the MYR and the THB, the Chinese currency is the dominant factor, as measured by the long run coefficient. In the case of the NTD, no currency seems to have an important impact; however, a slight variation in the specification (assuming US financial stress is not weakly exogenous with respect to the Taipei,China currency) leads to a significant role for the Chinese currency.

One interesting counterexample is the KRW; in this case, the USD remains the most important factor. This is somewhat surprising, given the strong economic links to Japan and the PRC. However, this outcome is consistent with results for daily data given in Huang et al. (2013).

Bringing together the results from other studies and the preceding empirical exercise, it appears fairly clear that more currencies are becoming anchored to the CNY, particularly since the reform of the Chinese exchange rate regime in 2005. Why this phenomenon is occurring cannot be determined within the context of these empirical studies, but one of the reasons is likely because in the context of an integrated supply chain, large exchange rate movements are unwelcome. With a lot of production costs located in the PRC, it makes sense that the Chinese currency would serve as one of the nominal anchors for the region's currencies.

7. CONCLUSION

The increasing importance of global supply chains in East Asia has sparked substantial research tracing out the microeconomic and trade implications. The macroeconomics profession has been a relative latecomer to examining the implications for the transmission of price and output effects. Moreover, the ramifications for how policy reaction functions will evolve in response to the changing nature of trade linkages have only been touched upon. This survey suggests several conclusions.

First, the conventional means of measuring international competitiveness are going to be less and less adequate, as production becomes more fragmented. Relatedly, it will become less and less tenable to estimate the traditional partial equilibrium trade equations in order to obtain macro-level trade elasticities, as mis-measurement of trade flows becomes more pronounced, and appropriate deflators for real exchange rates diverge further from the typically used deflators.

Second, the increasing role of vertical specialization will likely drive down exchange rate pass-through. This is true even if the increase is due to increasing arms-length transactions. However, to the extent that pass-through is less pronounced the greater the amount of intra-firm trade, a decrease in exchange rate pass-through is likely to occur.

Third, business cycle correlations are rising throughout the region. The more prominent increases are often associated with the PRC, a finding consistent with the country's growing role in the global supply chain. Furthermore, the propagation of shocks throughout the East Asia system is consistent with the PRC driving movements in output, at least in the Republic of Korea and Taipei,China.

Finally, there is evidence that the central banks of the region are paying more heed to the Chinese currency's value. This is true at the high frequency (daily) and at lower frequency (monthly); it is true with respect to rates of depreciation, as well as levels of currency values. Since these relationships are not structural, there is no guarantee that they will remain in place. At the same time, continued integration by way of production fragmentation should make central bankers pay extra heed to stabilizing currency values against each other.

NOTES

*   Paper prepared for the ADB Conference on Global Supply Chains and Trade in Value Added. I thank David Hummels for very helpful comments. All remaining errors remain solely my responsibility.
1.   Data sources for each section are listed in Appendix 8A.1.
2.   See Chinn (2006) for a discussion of the various different concepts of the real exchange rate. In general, intermediates are not directly accounted for.
3.   The conventional approach uses trade weights for traded goods, assuming goods are differentiated by location.
4.   There is a tradeoff between the use of the theoretically correct measures and the conventional ones. The former requires detailed data on trade flows and from input–output tables. Substantial measurement error is likely to be introduced as a consequence of using conventional measures that use prices of final goods.
5.   The sharp move in 1994 should be treated with caution, as the series is calculated using official rates. Fernald et al. (1999) document the fact that pre-1994, many transactions were taking place at a different "swap" rate.
6.   This leads to the question of whether simply using GDP deflators would mitigate the problem substantially.
7.   Koopman et al. (2012) approach the issue of measuring vertical specialization, defined in various ways, in a manner that nests some of the other approaches. Their approach incorporates measurement of domestic value added that is incorporated in imports used in exports.
8.   The problem, of course, is obtaining good proxies for these supply terms. In some previous studies, a measure of the US capital stock has been used. Obvious candidates, such as US industrial production for US exports, exhibit too much collinearity with rest-of-world GDP to identify the supply effect precisely. That is why this supply factor has typically been identified in panel cross section analyses (Gagnon, 2003).
9.   For instance, as in Chinn (2005).
10.   Barrell and Dées (2005) and Camarero and Tamarit (2003) address the issue of very high income elasticities by incorporating FDI into the specifications. IMF (2007) incorporates exports of intermediates in the import equation, and imports of intermediates in the export equation, to account for vertical specialization. This procedure reduces the estimated income elasticities.
11.   Although even for the United States, the impact of vertical specialization is measurable;

the conventional and value added measures deviate by about 10 percent from 1995 to 2009.

12. One particularly difficult issue involves price deflators to use to convert nominal magnitudes into real. Until 2005, the Chinese did not report price indices for imports and exports; this limits the sample to one far too short to use in the analysis. Hence, we rely upon a variety of proxy measures, each with some drawbacks. Since the trade flows are reported in US dollars, the price measures we consider include the US producer price index for finished goods, price indices from the World Bank, and Hong Kong, China re-export unit value indices. We only report results based upon the last deflator; the remaining results are qualitatively similar to those reported, and are available upon request.

13. It could be argued that we should use processing exports instead of total exports. Substituting one for the other does not lead to any consequential changes in the results. We conjecture that this is the case because the two series share the same trajectory. See Figure 3 in Cheung et al. (2012).

14. See Thorbecke (2006) for an examination of the impact of a yuan appreciation on the US-PRC trade balance, taking into account imported intermediate goods.

15. Obviously, at a minimum, this approach would require correct measurement of bilateral trade flows. Koopman et al. (2012) show that in many instances, particularly involving East Asia, gross and value added trade balances can differ substantially.

16. This example is a modification of an example in Johnson (2014).

17. Estimates of exchange rate pass-through for industrial countries are around 0.5, according to Campa and Goldberg (2005). Long run pass-through of 50 percent implies that long-run profit margins for foreign exporting firms sustain extremely large shifts if wages are sticky in the local currency.

18. Regression-based estimates are of similar magnitudes.

19. Ito and Chinn (2013) document the rapid rise in CNY invoicing in Chinese trade. To the extent this is a largely exogenously driven process, exchange rate pass-through should be expected to decline over time, holding all else constant.

20. See Baldwin (2009) for a summary of competing views.

21. In addition, most of the sample involves OECD countries, and includes only two East Asian countries (Japan and the Republic of Korea).

22. An end-point problem arises in the context of the HP-filter, which is a two sided filter. I have implemented the standard procedure, which is to extend the sample (in this case by seven quarters) using an ARIMA (1,1,1) so the two-sided filter can be implemented up to 2012Q4. A more economically substantive problem is that the recent observations are likely to be based upon preliminary data, while data earlier in the sample are likely to have undergone repeated benchmarking revisions.

23. If one expands the latter subsample to 2012, the business cycle correlations are typically higher, attributable to the common shock associated with the global recession.

24. The fairly large change in the PRC-Philippines correlation probably reflects the end of shocks to the Philippine economy arising from political events. The PRC-Philippines correlation is actually negative in the earlier sample period.

25. Tempering the results, it is of note that the correlations also rise for Mexico and all other countries in the sample. On the other hand, most of the Mexico pre-crisis correlations were negative, or slightly positive (with Japan and United States), so that in the latter sub-period, the Mexico correlations are still modest.

26. An alternative approach would be to use a VAR incorporating more macro variables, such as interest or exchange rates, or employ a structural VAR. Given the brevity of the available subsamples, and the large number of parameters that would have to be estimated, I have opted for more parsimonious specifications. For an alternative approach, see Bussiere et al. (2012).

27. This means a standard Cholesky decomposition is used, rather than the restriction imposed by theory involving zero constraints.

28. Baldwin and Lopez-Gonzalez (2013), Table 23. This characterization applies to 2009.

29. The results regarding US-PRC interactions differ because the impulse response functions depend upon all the estimated parameters in the system of equations. In any case, the *quantitative* impacts are very similar.
30. For an assessment based upon imports for production, see Ahuja and Nabar (2012).
31. For a practitioner's view on how exchange rate movements complicate the management of production chains, see Mahidhar (2006).
32. See Chinn (2012) for a discussion of what prerequisites need to hold for internationalization of a currency, with special reference to emerging market currencies. Ito and Chinn (2013) examine the determinants of the use of the yuan as an invoicing currency.
33. The other conditioning factors are the three-month USD Libor-US Treasury (TED) spread and the equity volatility index (VIX). These variables control for credit and liquidity risk.
34. Spencer (2013) takes issue with the yuan bloc thesis. He undertakes a more limited analysis, regressing exchange rates on four anchor currencies (US dollar, euro, yen, and Chinese yuan), and finds that post-2005, the dollar retains a high factor loading. There is a problem of interpretation, since the yuan is managed against the dollar, so movements adduced to the yuan might be more properly adduced to the dollar. Nonetheless, the importance of the dollar persists even after the yuan is orthogonalized against the other major currencies (although for the Korean won and the Malaysian ringgit, the yuan coefficient is larger than the corresponding dollar coefficient, so there does appear to be some evidence of a more prominent yuan bloc, even in this analysis).
35. The financial stress index is suppressed in the early subsample.
36. I suppress inclusion of the US financial stress index in the early subsample, since it does not vary much.

REFERENCES

Ahuja, A., and M. Nabar (2012), 'Investment-led growth in China: global spillovers', IMF Working Paper No. 12/267.

Amiti, M., O. Itskhoki, and J. Konings (2012), 'Importers, exporters, and exchange rate disconnect', mimeo.

Arkolakis, C., and A. Ramanarayanan (2009), 'Vertical specialization and international business cycle synchronization', *The Scandinavian Journal of Economics*, **111**, 655–680.

Bailliu, J., and E. Fujii (2004), 'Exchange rate pass-through and the inflation environment in industrialized countries: an empirical investigation', Bank of Canada Working Paper No. 2004–21.

Baldwin, R. (ed.) (2009), *The Great Trade Collapse: Causes, Consequences and Prospects*, London: CEPR.

Baldwin, R. and J. Lopez-Gonzalez (2013), 'Supply-chain trade: a portrait of global patterns and several testable hypotheses', NBER Working Paper No. 18957, Cambridge, MA: National Bureau of Economic Research.

Barrell, R. and S. Dées (2005), 'World trade and global integration in production processes: a re-assessment of import demand equations', ECB Working Paper No. 503, Frankfurt: European Central Bank.

Bayoumi, T., M. Saito, and J. Turunen (2013), 'Measuring competitiveness: trade in goods or tasks?', IMF Working Paper No. 13/100, Washington, DC: IMF.

Bems, R. (2012), 'Intermediate inputs, external rebalancing and relative price adjustment', mimeo.

Bems, R., and R.C. Johnson (2012), 'Value-added exchange rates', NBER Working Paper No. 18498, Cambridge, MA: National Bureau of Economic Research.

Burstein, A., C. Kurz, and L. Tesar (2008), 'Trade, production sharing, and the international transmission of business cycles', *Journal of Monetary Economics*, **55**, 775–795.

Bussiere, M., A. Chudik, and G. Sestieri (2012), 'Modelling global trade flows: results from a GVAR model', Globalization and Monetary Policy Institute Working Paper No. 119, Dallas: Federal Reserve Bank of Dallas.

Camarero, M. and C. Tamarit (2003), 'Estimating the export and import demand for manufactured goods: the role of FDI', Leverhulme Center Research Paper Series No. 2003/34, Nottingham: University of Nottingham.

Campa, J.M., and L.S. Goldberg (2005), 'Exchange rate pass-through to import prices', *Review of Economics and Statistics*, **87**, 679–690.

Carare, A., and A. Mody (2012), 'Spillovers of domestic shocks: will they counteract the "Great Moderation"?', *International Finance*, **15**, 69–97.

Chen, H., M. Kondratowicz, and K.-M. Yi (2005), 'Vertical specialization and three facts about U.S. international trade', *North American Journal of Economics and Finance*, **16**, 35–59.

Cheung, Y.-W., M. Chinn, and E. Fujii (2010), 'China's current account and exchange rate', in R. Feenstra and S.-J. Wei (eds), *China's Growing Role in World Trade*, University of Chicago Press for NBER.

Cheung, Y.-W., M. Chinn, and X.W. Qian (2012), 'Are Chinese trade flows different?', *Journal of International Money and Finance*, **31**, 2127–2146.

Chinn, M. (2005), 'Doomed to deficits? Aggregate U.S. trade flows revisited', *Review of World Economics*, **141**, 460–485.

Chinn, M. (2006), 'A primer on real effective exchange rates: determinants, overvaluation, trade flows and competitive devaluations', *Open Economies Review*, **17**, 115–143.

Chinn, M. (2010), 'Supply capacity, vertical specialization and trade costs: the implications for aggregate U.S. trade flow equations', mimeo.

Chinn, M. (2012), 'A note on reserve currencies with special reference to the G-20 countries', paper written for the International Growth Centre (IGC), India Central Programme.

Choudhri, E. and D. Hakura (2012), 'The exchange rate pass-through to import and export prices: the role of nominal rigidities and currency choice', IMF Working Paper No. 12226, Washington, DC: IMF.

Di Giovanni, J., and A. Levchenko (2012), 'Putting the parts together: trade, vertical linkages, and business cycle comovement', *American Economic Journal: Macroeconomics*, **2**, 95–124.

Fernald, J., H. Edison, and P. Loungani (1999), 'Was China the first domino? Assessing links between China and other Asian economies', *Journal of International Money and Finance*, **18**, 515–535.

Fratzscher, M., and A. Mehl (2011), 'China's dominance hypothesis and the emergence of a tri-polar global currency system', ECB Working Paper No. 1392.

Gagnon, J.E. (2003), 'Long-run supply effects and the elasticities approach to trade', FRB International Finance Discussion Paper 754.

Ghosh, A., and R.S. Rajan (2007), 'A survey of exchange rate pass-through in Asia', *Asian-Pacific Economic Literature*, **21**, 13–28.

Goldstein, M., and M. Khan (1985), 'Income and price effects in foreign trade', in R. Jones and P. Kenen (eds), *Handbook of International Economics*, Vol. 2, Amsterdam: Elsevier.

Gopinath, G., O. Itskhoki, and R. Rigobon (2010), 'Currency choice and exchange rate pass-through', *American Economic Review*, **100**, 304–336.

Hellerstein, R., and S.B. Villas-Boas (2010), 'Outsourcing and pass-through', *Journal of International Economics*, **81**, 170–183.

Hillberry, R. and D. Hummels (2012), 'Trade elasticity parameters for a CGE model', in P.B. Dixon and D.W. Jorgenson (eds), *Handbook of Computable General Equilibrium Modeling*, Elsevier.

Hooper, P., and C. Mann (1989), 'Exchange rate pass-through in the 1980s: the case of US imports of manufactures', *Brookings Papers in Economic Activity*, **1**, 297–337.

Huang, Y., D.L. Wang, and G. Fan (2013), 'Paths to a reserve currency: internationalization of RMB and its implications', paper prepared for ADBI workshop Currency Internationalization: Lessons for the RMB, Tokyo.

Hummels, D., J. Ishii, and K.-M. Yi (2001), 'The nature and growth of vertical specialization in world trade', *Journal of International Economics*, **54**, 75–96.

International Monetary Fund (2007), 'Chapter 3: Exchange rates and the adjustment of external imbalances', *World Economic Outlook*, Washington, DC: IMF.

Ito, H. and M. Chinn (2013), 'The rise of the "Redback" and China's capital account liberalization: an empirical analysis on the determinants of invoicing currencies', paper prepared for Asian Development Bank Institute workshop on Currency Internationalization: Lessons for the RMB, Tokyo.

Johnson, R.C. (2014), 'Five facts about value-added exports and implications for macroeconomics and trade research', *Journal of Economic Perspectives*, **28** (2), 119–142.

Koopman, R., Z. Wang, and S.-J. Wei (2012), 'Tracing value-added and double counting in gross exports', NBER Working Paper No. 18579, Cambridge, MA: National Bureau of Economic Research.

Kose, M.A., and K.-M. Yi (2001), 'International trade and business cycles: is vertical specialization the missing link?', *The American Economic Review*, **91**, 371–375.

Mahidhar, V. (2006), 'Managing in the face of exchange-rate uncertainty: a case for operational hedging', A Deloitte Research Study.

Marazzi, M., N. Sheets, R.J. Vigfusson, J. Faust, J.E. Gagnon, J. Marquez, R.F. Martin, T.A. Reeve, and J.H. Rogers (2005), 'Exchange rate pass-through to U.S. import prices: some new evidence', International Finance and Discussion Papers No. 833.

Neiman, B. (2010), 'Stickiness, synchronization, and pass through in intrafirm trade prices', *Journal of Monetary Economics*, **57**, 295–308.

Ng, E.C.Y. (2010), 'Production fragmentation and business-cycle comovement', *Journal of International Economics*, **82**, 1–14.

Sekine, T. (2006), 'Time-varying exchange rate pass-through: experiences of some industrial countries', BIS Working Paper No. 202.

Spencer, M. (2013), 'A "yuan bloc" in Asia? Not yet', *Global Economic Perspectives*, New York: Deutsche Bank.

Stock, J., and M.W. Watson (2005), 'Implications of dynamic factor models for VAR analysis', NBER Working Paper No. 11467, Cambridge, MA: National Bureau of Economic Research.

Thorbecke, W. (2006), 'How would an appreciation of the renminbi affect the US trade deficit with China?', *BE Journal of Macroeconomics*, **6**, 1–17.
Thorbecke, W. (2011), 'The effect of exchange rate changes on trade in East Asia', Asian Development Bank Institute Working Paper No. 263.
Thorbecke, W. and G. Smith (2010), 'How would an appreciation of the RMB and other East Asian currencies affect China's exports?', *Review of International Economics*, **18**, 95–108.
United Nations Conference on Trade and Development (2013), *World Investment Report*, UN: New York and Geneva.
Yi, K.-M. (2003), 'Can vertical specialization explain the growth of world trade?', *Journal of Political Economy*, **111**, 53–102.

APPENDIX 8A.1

Section 2

Exchange rates: VAREER and REER_INS from Bems and Johnson (2012).

Section 3

Data on exchange rates, GDP, trade flows, from Cheung et al. (2012).

Section 4

Quarterly real GDP in local currency, from IMF, *International Financial Statistics*, except Euro area GDP from European Central Bank, and Korean GDP from Organisation for Economic Co-operation and Development via FRED, and Chinese GDP pre-2000 from Cheung et al. (2010).

Malaysian GDP starts in 1988, Thai GDP in 1993, Singapore GDP begins in 1983Q2, Indonesian GDP starts in 1997, Taipei,China GDP data in 1981. Annual data from IMF, *World Economic Outlook* (April 2013) spliced to all series except Taipei,China using regressions in logs, where annual data is interpolated via quadratic match average. All GDP series except US, Japan, Republic of Korea, Euro area, and United Kingdom, seasonally adjusted using ARIMA X-12 applied to logged values.

HP detrending uses default $\lambda=1600$ for quarterly data; end point problem addressed by using ARIMA(1,1,1) to project out seven quarters, before HP filter is applied. For Indonesia, the ARIMA is applied only to the 1997–2013Q1 sample.

Section 5

Exchange rates: Bilateral SDR exchange rates from the IMF, *International Financial Statistics* (end of period). Euro/dollar exchange rates are from the ECB. Data on the Taipei,China currency (NT$) is from the Bank of China.

Financial stress indices are from the IMF (personal communication).

9. Mapping global value chains and measuring trade in tasks

Hubert Escaith*

1. INTRODUCTION

Adequately measuring international trade taking place in global value chains (GVCs) and its impact on national economies is still a work in progress. Mapping GVCs, identifying where value-added is created, how much and by whom, are the challenges that trade statisticians face. Within supply chains, many production steps are carried out across different countries, with semi-finished products travelling along the production chain between these countries. Each time these products criss-cross national borders, international transactions are recorded at the full or gross value of the product, which leads to multiple counts. At the end of the supply chain, the parts are assembled for final use and then either consumed domestically or exported. Ordinary concepts of country of origin or country of destination do not fully apply anymore: if we look at the national origin of the value-added incorporated in the final product, we realize that significant shares of the value may come from other countries than from the country of origin as ascribed by customs records.

Rising to this statistical challenge and producing the right numbers is important for decision making in today's world: not only business models and strategies are changing, but also the way public policy makers should understand their "home" country and their defensive and offensive interests in trade policy. The old division of labor between industrialized and developing nations is losing its relevance, even if we are still far from living in the same village. Meeting at the Los Cabos Summit in June 2012, G20 Leaders noted ". . . the relevance of regional and global value chains to world trade, recognizing their role in fostering economic growth, employment and development and emphasizing the need to enhance the participation of developing countries in such value chains."

GVCs may also change the way we understand trade theory. Some researchers suggest they changed the old Ricardian law of comparative advantages, as we shall see later. Even if this remains an open question, the fact is that GVCs alter many of the stylized facts on which trade or economic development models are based. Even if for many dimensions, the changes are of degree and of speed, on balance this is not old wine in a new bottle: because of GVCs, something original and new is happening in the international economy, with profound economic and social implications at home. Theory and statistics go hand in hand; it is important to develop the right empirical tools to back academic research and, in turn, highlight new dimensions and identify gaps that require further attention.

The purpose of this chapter is to build on this compact between theory and statistics in order to provide a road map for empirical work. It analyzes the challenge posed to trade statisticians by looking in the first place for guidance from some relevant theoretical frameworks suggested by trade and development models or business practices. The subsequent sections enter into more detail on what kind of information needs to be collected, and how. The review covers basically three lines of work, starting from traditional trade statistics, then input–output accounting, then finally reviewing recent developments in collecting micro-data on trade by enterprise characteristics. At each step, examples involving the Asia-Pacific region will be introduced; those examples are provided for didactic purpose and do not pretend to offer an analysis, nor exhaust all the possibilities that a fully-fledged statistical exploration of trade in value-added data would provide. The conclusion summarizes the main results and looks for an integrating framework.

2.   WHY AND WHAT? (THOU SHOULDST NOT MEASURE WITHOUT A THEORETICAL FRAMEWORK)

While slicing up the production process through international outsourcing is not new, it is only recently that it became the dominant model in industrial organization. Technical advances in transportation and communications technology, as well as a series of institutional reforms, have "flattened the world" and enabled the fragmentation of the production process in different production stages, located in different countries. This phenomenon has variously been called fragmentation, unbundling, offshoring, vertical specialization, slicing-up of the value-added chain or trade in tasks (WTO, 2008). Grossman and Rossi-Hansberg (2006) advocate that the theory of trade in tasks is a new paradigm that differs from the Ricardian law of comparative advantages.[1]

Examples of processing trade existed since the 1970s; isolated cases can even be traced in the early years of the 20th century. More recently, fostering regional value chains was one of the driving factors behind the signature of the North American Free Trade Agreement in the early 1990s. Yet the accession of the People's Republic of China (PRC) to the WTO in 2001 led to a quantum leap. In less than 10 years, trade in intermediate products supplanted the old "Ricardian" trade in finished goods in explaining emerging trade patterns, creating *en passant* a series of accounting issues as goods in process of finalization criss-crossed several international borders and inflated traditional statistics based on customs values. While anecdotic data were available through case studies, aggregate level analyses were more limited. An off-shoring index for the United States (US) was calculated by Feenstra and Hanson in 1996, but it was not before the 2000s that more systemic efforts were put in place. The first worldwide estimates of trade in value-added were produced by scholars (e.g., Daudin et al., 2006, building on Hummels et al., 2001); professional statisticians joined efforts more recently and released in 2012 (WIOD) and 2013 (TiVA), the first "official" databases.[2]

Before revising the different approaches that the statistical community has adopted, the present chapter starts by taking the time to look at the underlying models that have guided the work of the statisticians. Data compiled by statisticians are the observed occurrences of a data-generating process (DGP), and have only a meaning when put in relation to relevant theoretical frameworks. Understanding the theoretical properties of this DGP guides the work of the statisticians when looking at relevant indicators, and provides the organizing principles that determine on which aspects of the observed variables their attention should be concentrated. Understanding that DGPs lie beyond the data is also important for the user of statistics. As Koopmans (1947) once commented, without a model, no practical inference for decision making is possible: "the rejection of the help that economic theorizing might give leaves a void. . . . Without resort to theory, in the sense indicated, conclusions relevant to the guidance of economic policies cannot be drawn." Oxley et al. (2008) go as far as describing most attempts to measure complex socio-economic developments without some proper understanding or a theoretical definition, as movies where "Mr Bean (counter) Measures the Economy".

2.1 Looking for Relevant Models

The nature of trade along global production networks is multifaceted and crosses several academic topics. The new trends in trade theory put much emphasis on the micro-economic dimension of firm heterogeneity. The management of international supply chains is now a profession and is taught as a subject matter in engineering and business schools. Park et al.

(2013) offer a commented review of the literature covering most, if not all, its relevant strands. We propose here to look selectively for theoretical guidelines in different places and then try to develop an integrating framework. Pursuing a general to specific approach, our first model of reference is network economics.

2.1.1 Network economics

The neoclassical approach to trade economics tends to focus on the bilateral commerce between two parties and ignores much of the interactions with other partners (for many years, the workhorse of the profession was the two countries-two goods model). Global production networks (or social networks, as the two share many points in common) are interested in describing what kind of other third party connections two participants have in common. A production network is, at its core, the nexus of interconnected functions, operations and transactions through which a specific product or service is produced, distributed and consumed (Coe et al., 2008).

In this framework, trade between two parties consists not only of the characteristics proper of each partner (what they produce at what cost), but also of their business environment (who they are in business with). A neoclassical market could be seen as a collection of independent buy and sell decisions, characterized by high entropy from a probabilistic perspective. In a trade and production network, what happens is the result of a series of business decisions, some of them of long-term nature, such as investment decisions. They will also involve a series of other partners downstream, or can take place only after another upstream partner has done its part of the contract and delivered the parts. The entropy of such a system is much lower: trade takes place among pre-determined partners glued together by arm's length contracts or intra-firm relationship and trade patterns that tend to reproduce themselves identically through time.

GVCs result from lead firms arbitraging between "make or buy" decisions. The chemically pure example of the new model of globalized manufactures is perhaps the so-called "factoryless" firm, which creates networks of workshops and manages its production lines in the cyberspace. Who you are connected with is important: those networks determine and organize the production, distribution and use of knowledge and information.

The first tool associated with network economics is graph theory, as this is the most intuitive way of representing the intricate relationships between various firms and how they interact in order to conceive, produce and deliver a product to its final market (Box 9.1). The graph model introduces three crucial concepts: nodes or vertices (firms, consumers), edges (connections) and orientation (upstream to downstream, loops).

BOX 9.1   WORLD TRADE NETWORK AS A GRAPH

Graph theory is particularly useful for analyzing international trade, if only for its (apparent) simplicity. Graphs, understood as mathematical constructs (Figure 9.1) are simplified maps composed exclusively of vertices (nodes) and edges (connections). Actual trade networks are best described as directed graphs, or digraphs, because they are made of directed edges (imports from, exports to). A digraph $G_{n,k}$ consists of a set of vertices and a set of directed edges (arcs), each linking a source vertex v_j to a target vertex v_i.

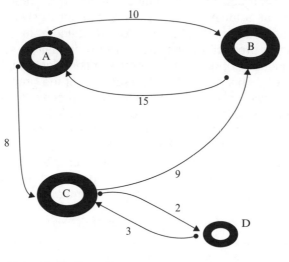

Source: Elaborated by the author.

Figure 9.1   Simple representation of trade as a graph

Despite their simplicity, graphs can be developed as relatively complex mathematical models, providing important insights on the way the actors (nodes) interact. From an historical perspective, the best-known example of graph analytics is the Königsberg Bridge Problem solved by the Swiss mathematician Euler (1707– 1783). Its modern version is the Traveling Salesman Problem, one of the cornerstones of operation research. The increasing importance of social networks and improved computer software has recently revived the interest in this subject, fostering the development of new indicators.

Graph theory, the mathematical approach to networks, may rapidly become cumbersome when graphs are densely populated (many nodes) and complex (many links between nodes). The World Trade Web (WTW), where countries are referred to as nodes and the flows between them as arcs, is an example of such a complex network (Tang and Wagner, 2010). Graphs that contain too many nodes and arcs to be effectively illustrated using standard graphs have to be analyzed in terms of their statistical properties.

The most common statistical approach to trade and production networks is through an input–output matrix. The graph can be reproduced as a table where the line shows for a given industry *i* the probability of intermediate product transiting from *i* to *j* while in process of production (the probability of industry *i* selling its output to industry *j*), or being absorbed in final demand as a finished product. This provides a forward view of the graph, where the product will go industry by industry to receive a series of transformations before reaching the stage of final product where it is consumed or invested domestically, or exported to a third country where it will be absorbed.[a] But the graph can also be read backward as a process where industry *j* purchases intermediate inputs from node *i*. Those inputs can be goods or services, and the suppliers may be located in different countries.

Table 9.1   Matrix representation of Figure 9.1

IO(G)	A	B	C	D
A	–	10	8	–
B	15	–	–	–
C	–	9	–	2
D	–	–	3	–

Source: Author's illustration.

Our previous example can be represented in a tabular form, as in Table 9.1. The backward and forward process is represented by the matrix form **IO(G)**, describing in a line the sales of outputs to the different nodes of the network, and in columns the purchase of inputs to these nodes. If we consider only the transactions in intermediate inputs (excluding sales for final demand, or absorbing state in the Markov chain terminology), then we obtain a square matrix listing all industries in all countries participating to the network. The diagonal (sales of an industrial sector to itself) does not need to be zero; as in our example, a sector/country is made of several firms, which may specialize in different varieties of the same product; obviously, the more aggregated the sector, the higher the frequency of inter-industry transactions.

Note: [a] Exports of intermediate products to an industry located abroad were already considered as part of the inter-industry network.

Those building blocks are the essential constituting elements identifying a network, thus are primary candidates on "what to measure". Using these simple building blocks, graph theory develops sophisticated indicators of connectedness.

The graph approach tends to emphasize connectivity, and the related field of network economics has developed several tools to qualify and measure connectedness. As mentioned in Box 9.1, production networks can also be analyzed using well-known input–output matrix algebra. The representation of the network graph through an input–output matrix extended to cover international transactions in intermediate goods captures directly or indirectly all the features of the graph, including the notion of connectedness strength and the average distance between connected nodes.

Value-added, finance and corporate ownership In a GVC network, the connections between the nodes (industries) go beyond the trade dimension. The difference between the total value of the sales of industry j (the sum of the weight of outgoing arcs) and the total value of inputs entering into node j (the total value of incoming arcs) gives the value that the industry created during the transformation of inputs into output. This value, called value-added by the national accountants, plays a significant role in the economic analysis of production networks: it serves to remunerate the primary inputs (labor and capital) as well as paying indirect taxes on production.

This value-added belongs also to another circuit – income flows – that runs parallel to the product circuit. Income flows are made, for example, of dividends, royalties and interest payments. Monetary income is created in one industry but can be transferred to households or firms that are resident in other countries. This secondary circuit makes possible the financial viability of the product circuit (its reproduction) when the final products are eventually purchased, consumed or invested thanks to the income generated. It is possible (Escaith and Gonguet, 2011) to superpose a monetary circuit to the product space defined by intra-industry international trade. Eventually, the trade and production network also relates to the corporate networks, as in a globalized world international trade is dominated by a subset of large multinational enterprises (MNEs) and many transactions take place within related firms and establishments. According to the UN Conference on Trade and Development (UNCTAD, 2013), MNE-coordinated GVCs account for some 80 percent of global trade.

For the same network, physical flows may differ from financial ones for a series of reasons, ranging from supply-chain governance (intra-firm trade may not entail change of ownership and actual payments for inputs purchased, or the banks issuing and receiving payments may be located in countries that differ from those involved in the physical flows) to tax planning.[3] Moreover, as we shall see later, physical flows between two partners may not provide anymore an adequate picture of the trade relationship between those countries. It is, in particular, the case when trade flows are intermediated by a third country that plays the role of a "hub". As Maurer and Degain (2010) highlight, what you see (through traditional trade statistics) is not what you get.

Besides their theoretical and statistical implications, the coexistence of three interconnected spaces – product, income and finance circuits – has important consequences for understanding the dynamics of globalized economies, the micro-macro interaction of national economies and the accumulation of imbalances. All those aspects, obviously, shall call the attention of the statistician when defining the new measures and indicators required for representing the economic implications of global production networks. Production is only one side of the GVC coin, as the rationales behind those chains are also closely related to international economics, which responds to its proper set of theoretical models.

2.1.2 Trade theory and development policy implications

The natural theoretical framework of reference for identifying the relevant dimensions to be measured when analyzing global value chains is trade theory, in particular its most recent avatars: new and "new" new trade theories. The new trade theory is strongly associated with, *inter alia*, Wilfred Ethier (1979) and Paul Krugman (1979) who, in the late 1970s, incorporated increasing returns to scale into previous models. Increasing returns are a deviation from the neo-classical hypothesis and tend to generate specialized and localized patterns. In particular, external benefits such as agglomeration effects facilitate the creation of localized industrial networks, as those discussed in the previous section. Those clusters are self-reinforcing, thanks to the benefits provided by the size of the cluster and the scope of specialization of participating firms. Thus, connectedness within networks is, once again, an important dimension to measure.

Reductions in trade costs are also even more important in the new trade theories. Not only do transaction costs explain the agglomeration of production in a specific location, but their reduction was a necessary factor in facilitating the international fragmentation of the production process (WTO, 2008). More generally, gravity models that use some measure of distance between trade partners as explanatory variables are standard features of the trade-economist's tool-box; a current topic of research is measuring the effect of distance on trade in intermediate products (typical of GVCs) and trade in final goods. Therefore, measuring those trade costs should be an important item on the trade statistician's agenda. Transaction costs include border aspects (tariff and non-tariff measures), as well as logistics and freight costs by mode of transport. Those transport modes are also relevant for the environmental implication of international trade.

The "new" new trade theory, by putting the emphasis on firm heterogeneity (Melitz, 2003) is another source of guidance on the relevant dimensions to take into account in our attempt at measuring global value chains. This new school, which has a clear empirical foundation, thrived on the increasing availability of firm-level data-tracking trade operations by firm characteristics.[4] Firms typically differ in terms of their productivity; some of them find it profitable to sell only on the domestic market, while the most productive export. Further empirical investigation shows that firm heterogeneity is closely related to ownership and governance structures, including global supply chain linkages. What the statistician should retain here are two things. First, that the "representative firm" approach adopted in input–output models is not sufficient for providing an adequate representation of modern trade. Second, foreign direct investment flows have to be part of the picture because foreign ownership is often a key factor explaining GVC trade patterns.

As part of the larger trend of "new" new trade theory, a growing strand is dedicated to analyzing trade within global value chains as "trade in tasks". Through GVCs, technology proper to lead firms (typically installed in developed countries) can be used effectively by first-tier providers and affiliates located in developing countries. This is analytically similar to a virtual migration of workers from cheap labor location to high productivity locations, without actually paying the full increase in labor cost. In more technical terms, trade in tasks is assimilated to a technological shock that changes a country's labor endowments measured in productivity-equivalent units. This shock may allow firms in high labor cost countries to remain competitive *vis-à-vis* the increasing competition from emerging countries; on the other hand, it may also help firms in developing countries to close their technological gap. Trade in tasks is also trade in skills, as differences in wages across countries is determined not only by the average wage level, but also by the relative abundance of skilled labor. In practical terms, this has important effects on wages and income distribution in both developed and developing countries. This theoretical branch of trade policy signals, therefore, that any attempt to "map" international trade in its new dimensions should include a measure of labor by skills and industries.

GVCs offer new options to developing countries. Gereffi and Sturgeon (2013) review the situation and policy options of emerging countries, but the potential is also high for small developing countries that did not find a niche in the older international division of labor. What Grossman and Rossi-Hansberg (2006) and Baldwin (2006) tell us is that globalization today differs from the old approach in that the opportunities for jobs and value creation is occurring at a much finer level of disaggregation. GVCs enable a finer degree of specialization, allowing the production process to be fragmented into narrowly defined segments or "tasks". Recently, development theory has borrowed from network sciences to define the concept of "product space". This is a network approach to trade by product grouping, similar to the idea of revealed comparative advantages (Hidalgo et al., 2007). Countries export products for which they have comparative advantages, but not all products have the same potential for export diversification at the extensive margin. Being able to diversify into new products depends not only on the relative situation of the developing country from the production frontier, but also the easiness of moving to other products (connectedness). Some areas of the product space may be denser than others and transition easier. Environmental impacts of natural resources based GVCs and international modes of transport are relevant issues for sustainable development analysis. Finally, the macro-economics of open economies – be they developing or developed – is also interested in the outcome of the statistical research agenda on trade in value-added, as signalled in Box 9.2.

2.1.3   International supply chain management

The last strand of literature to be called in the service of defining a theoretical framework for "measuring trade in global value chains" is the business school approach to international supply chain management. Actually, the term GVC originated in the management literature and is closely associated with international supply chains. Geoffrion and Powers

BOX 9.2   WHY IS TRADE IN VALUE-ADDED
            IMPORTANT? A MACRO-POLICY
            PERSPECTIVE

Rifflart and Schweisguth (2013) mention several areas where measuring trade in value-added brings a new perspective and is likely to impact policy choices:

1. Using accurate value-added trade data would improve exchange rate assessments. Real effective exchange rates based on value-added trade weights would reveal more accurate measures of competitiveness of a country than those based on gross trade weights.
2. Real effective exchange rates based on value-added trade would improve estimates of the impact of changes in relative prices, including that on global rebalancing. This reflects the higher foreign content in the downstream country's exports, which mitigates the impact of exchange rate changes.
3. Decomposing foreign value-added in exports by source country would help understand how disruptions to supply chains can have spillover effects. Disruptions of trade flows could be either policy induced, such as preferential/regional trade agreements, or naturally caused, such as the 2011 earthquake in Japan.
4. Bilateral balances, if discussed for political economy considerations, are better measured with value-added, rather than gross, trade data. Accounting for trade in intermediate parts and components, and taking into account "trade in tasks", does not change the overall trade balance of a country with the rest of the world, but it redistributes the surpluses and deficits across partner countries.
5. Measuring trade in value-added sheds new light on today's trade reality, where competition is not between nations, but between firms. Competitiveness in a world of global value chains means access to competitive inputs and technology. Optimum tariff structure in such a situation is flat (little or no escalation) and reliable (contractual arrangements within supply chains, especially between affiliated establishments, tend to be long term). As a consequence,

> tariffs, non-tariff barriers and trade measures such as
> anti-dumping rights are likely to impact domestic producers
> in addition to foreign producers.
> 6. The impact of macro-economic shocks would be better
>   assessed. The 2008–2009 financial crisis was character-
>   ized by a synchronized trade collapse in all economies.
>   What role did global supply chains play in the transmis-
>   sion of a demand shock in markets affected by a credit
>   shortage? A better understanding of value-added trade
>   flows would provide tools for policymakers to anticipate
>   the impact of macro-economic shocks and adopt the right
>   policy responses.

(1995) provide a comprehensive review of the early literature and how
the corporate status of logistics has changed dramatically since the late
1970s. The main object of the business approach is value creation, and
most of the present-day literature refers formally or informally to earlier
work by Michael Porter on cluster and competitive advantages (Porter,
1985). Another important contribution, if only to be able to understand
the variations in the value-added per unit of output, is attributed to Stan
Shih, the founder of IT Acer Company, in the early 1990s. Shih realized
that value-added ratios define a "smiley curve" through the product cycle.
Manufacturing lies at the bottom of the value-added curve, while higher
value-added content is found in services, either at the upstream part of
the chain (R&D) or closer to the customer, at the down-stream segment
(branding, distribution, after-sale services).

This analysis has important implications on the trade and development
perspective, as most developing countries enter GVCs through cheap
labor at assembly level. More directly relevant for our present purpose, the
smiley curve tends to indicate that what is important when analyzing trade
in tasks are the business functions, rather than the tasks themselves. Lanz
et al. (2011) highlight the importance of "working with others" and look
at the "task intensity" by clusters of tasks.

Analyzing trade through business practices may also help in identifying
potential issues in data collection. Trade practices show that not all exporting firms trade directly, but many go through trade agents, or wholesal-
ers. Some estimates put at about 20 percent the value of international
trade done by agents. In practice, this means that customs registers will
not reflect the true industrial origin of the exported goods. The business
perspective shows the limits of the value-added dimension when looking

at profitability and investment decisions from a micro-economic perspective. Value-added includes many elements that are actually costs for the firms (wages, taxes, even part of the capital income, which corresponds to the cost of capital). Similarly, high value-added per unit of output may not correspond to high technology or to high quality jobs: the rate of value-added in traditional agriculture is close to 100 percent, because the monetary cost of inputs is nil. Conversely, high technology means high volumes with good quality standards, but higher input consumption (i.e., lower value-added per unit of output).

2.2   What Should Be Counted?

The review of underlying theories and their main topics of interest should help us advance more rapidly with the next question: what? We saw that global production networks operate in many dimensions: trade in intermediate goods, trade in factors of production, trade in tasks, financial and income transfers, etc. Some of these dimensions may be more difficult to measure as they are hidden below several layers of superficial information. Moreover, trade in tasks itself (or the value-added content of trade) can only be measured indirectly: strictly speaking, therefore, we cannot measure it, but only provide an estimate.

A proper mapping of global value chains requires collecting information on operational, financial and corporate governance aspects. Those are fruits that hang at different heights of the tree, operational aspects being low-hanging, while governance ones stay unseen at the top. It is also important to compile the information, keeping the systemic dimension that relates all those bounties within a comprehensive and analytically relevant statistical model.

Our review of the relevant analytical approaches identified the following points of interest, which are either flows (visible or invisible; physical or financial) or actors (firms, households, markets):

- Trade in intermediate inputs, including goods and services. This is the glue connecting the firms participating in international supply chains and, at the same time, the belt that keeps them moving together. Trade flows are classified (according to the relevant classification for goods and services) and divided as incoming (inputs) or outgoing (output) for each relevant actor (firm or sector).
- Transaction costs: freight and insurance by modes of transport, border and "behind the border" costs (tariff duties and cost of complying with non-tariff measures).

- Balance between incoming and outgoing trade flows. This provides the measure of the value-added created by each firm in the value chain. Value-added should be disaggregated into its main components (wages, profit and taxes, to use common language).[5]
- Jobs and skills, if possible related within broader business functions.
- Capital and its ownership (tangible, intangible, technological content and intellectual property, as it relates to trade in income through royalties and fees).
- Non-reproducible capital or inputs (natural resources, land, water) used and consumed, as well as other environmental variables (trade and production related carbon dioxide (CO_2) emissions, etc.).

3.   HOW TO MAP AND MEASURE?

This section will review some of the approaches that have been used by trade statisticians to map the various dimensions of trade taking place within global value chains and estimate its value.

3.1   Mapping the Flow of Goods and Services

The obvious starting point for mapping value chains is to look at the intermediate inputs, which are used for the production of final (finished) products.[6] Unlike final products, intermediate goods or services produced by a given firm will be further processed by other downstream productive establishments before being sold, either to another firm further down the value chain, or as final products. Trade in intermediate inputs, including goods and services, is the glue connecting the firms participating in international supply chains and, at the same time, the belt that keeps them moving together. Mapping those flows, using available trade statistics, is therefore an intuitive way of describing the network. As mentioned by Sturgeon and Memedovic (2010), revisiting existing trade data sets with a new angle leads to considerable benefits, rapidly available and at relatively little cost. One early example in the specialized literature is Yeats (2001). Moreover, recent advances in the analysis of social networks provide a series of quantitative indicators (and dedicated software) that go beyond the simple mapping of trade patterns to compute synthetic indicators.[7]

Trade flows are classified according to the relevant classification for goods and services and divided as incoming (inputs) or outgoing (output) for each relevant actor (firm or sector). Trade in goods is relatively well mapped, and detailed information by products and partners is available at dedicated databases like COMTRADE, maintained by the United

Nations Statistical Division. Differentiating between intermediate and final goods can be solved relatively easily by doing a secondary classification on the UN Broad Economic Categories (BEC) classification that splits the Standard International Trade Classification (SITC) or, alternatively, the Harmonized System (HS) of merchandise, into their final use (intermediate, capital or consumer goods). Crossing BEC and SITC has the advantage of classifying each good by stage of production and by industry (OECD, 2005).

The case of services is much more complex. Most existing statistics are compiled for balance of payments purposes (the IMF BOP or the UN Extended Balance of Payments Services Classification or EBOPS classifications) rather than analytical purpose (as in the UN Central Product Classification or CPC). Moreover, only the most advanced countries publish bilateral flows of services. When only the most aggregate values are available (total imports and total exports of transport, travel and "other services"), imputing bilateral flows remains a matter of guesswork (Miroudot et al., 2009; and Timmer, 2012). The good news is that the task may become easier in the future, as work is under way to develop a correspondence table between EBOPS 2010 and CPC Version 2.0, which may help in the future.

Trade in intermediate goods and services within GVCs is sometimes seen as a statistical nuisance because it creates double counting. The value of parts and components that compose goods in process of elaboration are counted each time they (or the product in which they are embedded) cross a border. This double counting tends to artificially inflate the importance of trade and was probably one of the factors that led to a gradual increase in the world trade to GDP ratio up to 1995 (WTO, 2013a and b). Yet, far from being a double counting nuisance, trade in intermediate products can, to the contrary, provide invaluable information on the topology of value chains. Because the information on trade in intermediate inputs, at least in the domain of merchandise, is very detailed (the HS classification at its 6 digit level distinguishes some 5000 different categories of goods), the mapping can be very precise and provides information on the pattern of specialization of each country within regional or international productive clusters (Goyal, 2007; Flores and Vaillant, 2011). As we shall see later, this is a clear advantage over more holistic accounting approaches such as input–output models, because the mapping of trade in intermediate goods allows one to understand very detailed inter-industrial interactions.

According to Ferrarini (2011), Ng and Yeats (1999) were the first to compile detailed lists of the parts and components trade to assess the magnitude of processing trade in East Asia.[8] IDE-JETRO in the late 1970s was already compiling inter-industry trade flows of intermediate products in order to build its Asian input–output matrices, one of the first of such attempts. Indeed, compiling and allocating trade flows of intermediate products by country and sector of origin and destination is a critical step in building international input–output matrices. Ferrarini (2011) provides a very good example of the practical steps that statisticians must undertake in order to have a good database on intermediate flows.

The first practical issue a researcher has to solve is that trade partners usually have different perceptions of their mutual trade flows – something called asymmetry in data. One important source of discrepancy is that an export from A to B will usually be recorded 'free on board' (FOB), while imports of B from A will be recorded on their higher 'cost, insurance and freight' (CIF) basis.[9] Other sources of discrepancies are due to different ways of recording merchandise in the export and import countries, or the difficulty in tracing the actual country of origin or destination when goods are transiting through international hubs such as Rotterdam, Singapore or Hong Kong, China. As done by many other researchers, Ferrarini (2011) uses BACI, a data set compiled by the Centre d'Etudes Prospectives et d'Information Internationales (CEPII), which reconciles trade partners' import and export data to obtain a symmetric matrix of trade flows. Instead of using only one year, he averages two observation points (say 2006 and 2007), in order to reduce the incidence of outliers.

The next step is to differentiate between final and intermediate goods, based on the correspondence between the HS at 6 digits and the BEC. In practice, this can be quite a tricky issue because some items have mixed use. The Ferrarini paper gives the example of "Internal combustion engine spark plugs" (HS 851110), which can be mounted on an engine in a factory (intermediate consumption of manufacture), purchased by a garage (intermediate consumption of a service sector) or sold to car owners (administration and household final consumption). Besides the conceptual issues mentioned in Note 7, one of the biggest classification issues, at least in terms of value, is the treatment of fuels. When a taxi driver fills up the tank of her car, it is an intermediate consumption by the service sector; the same purchase done to fill a private or a government car will be final consumption. As it is very difficult to impute the imports of fuel according to their use (unless one uses supply-utilization tables, but this technique is proper to the IO approach and does not belong to the simpler trade flow approach), fuels are therefore usually excluded from the computation (it is at least the practice at WTO).

Once the dissociation between intermediate and final use is done, the next step is to assign the goods to their sector of production in order to have an economic perspective (this step is not compulsory if one needs only to map trade without looking into the sectoral implications). Here, it is often easier to use SITC rather than HS, as SITC has a clearer sectoral relationship. Fortunately, correspondence tables are maintained by the UN Statistical Division, even if some fine tuning may be required in specific cases.

To provide an example, Figure 9.2 shows the purchase of inputs by selected Asia-Pacific sectors using trade in intermediate goods data estimated for 2008 by IDE-JETRO for the Asia-Pacific region (Inomata, 2011). Note that a sector in one country can also be a provider for the same sector in another country. After filtering out the intermediate trade flows that represent less than 20 percent of the purchases of each importer, a visual analysis of the graph provides a few interesting indications. The main provider of inputs is the manufacturing sector (coded 3 in the graph). The People's Republic of China (C) and Japan (J) appear as the main source of manufacturing inputs. Note also the role of Singapore (S), especially as provider of manufacturing inputs to Malaysia (M).

Besides the actual mapping of trade in intermediate products, some quantitative indicators can be derived from this approach.[10] In-degree in such a directed graph (digraph) is the number of international suppliers (upstream connections) from which the sector sources its inputs (domestic inputs are excluded from the graph). "Betweenness centrality" can be best defined intuitively by the damage the removal of a vertex would do to the network if it was removed: some nodes work as "hubs" and have a systemic importance. Weighting this centrality criteria by the degree of connections each of the connected vertices have will lead to the "Eigenvector Centrality" indicator.

The list of indicators that can be constructed from a graph is long (and increasing thanks to the new interest graph theory has been receiving in the past decade).[11] Table 9.2 presents, for illustration purpose only, some of the network statistics calculated on the graph in Figure 9.2. Individual data show the first 15 vertices (country/sector) and the average for all other 55 vertices.

A diachronic approach of graphs is also a source of interesting results. Using the same set of countries that is used in Figure 9.2, Escaith and Inomata (2013) describe the evolution of industrial networks in Asia-Pacific through time, and the rise of the PRC as a hub. As shown in Figure 9.3, in 1985 there were only four key players in the region: Japan (J) as hub, Indonesia (I), Malaysia (M) and Singapore (S). With time, Japan also extended supply chain relationships to other East Asian economies, especially to the group known as the newly industrialized economies (NIEs). This is the phase when the relocation of Japanese production bases to neighboring countries was accelerating, triggered by the Plaza Accord in 1985. It saw the building of strong linkages between core parts

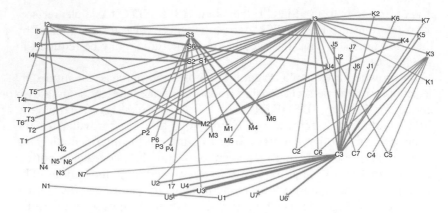

Notes:
Letters denote the reporting economy (C: People's Republic of China; I: Indonesia; J: Japan; K: Korea; M: Malaysia; N: Taipei,China; P: Philippines; S: Singapore; T: Thailand; U: USA) and numbers the sectors (1: Agriculture; 2: Mining; 3: Manufacturing; 4: Electricity, gas and water; 5: Construction; 6: Trade and transport; 7: Other services). To simplify the graph, flows lower than 20% of sectoral imported inputs were excluded.

Source: Digraph generated by NodeXL based on IDE-JETRO Asia Input–Output data.

Figure 9.2   Graph of intermediate inputs trade by industries in selected Asia-Pacific reporters, 2008

suppliers in Japan and their foreign subsidiaries. The United States (U) came into the picture in the late 1990s while the PRC began to emerge as the third regional giant. By 2005, the center of the network had completely shifted to the PRC, pushing the United States and Japan to the periphery. The PRC became the supply chain hub, where final consumption goods were produced for export to the US and European markets.

GVCs are primarily about making money (value-added, using the national accounts jargon). The graph approach is the first step toward analyzing the value-added that is generated at each step of the value chain. The difference between the value of out-going flows (sales) and incoming ones (purchases) provides a measure of the value-added generated in the process. Considering only imported inputs and exported output flows, Figure 9.4 shows, for example, that the countries which registered highest growth in their manufactured exports between 1995 and 2008 were those countries that had increased more rapidly their use of imported inputs.

Using traditional trade statistics for analyzing global value chains is particularly effective when the researcher is interested in a certain type of product. Different from the value-added approach – which will be

Table 9.2   Selected network indicators for the Asian input–output 2008 graph

Vertices[a]	In-degree	Betweenness centrality	Eigenvector centrality
S3	19	93.7	0.021
N3	25	95.6	0.021
K3	30	95.0	0.021
J3	31	94.1	0.021
J6	20	94.1	0.021
M3	25	97.0	0.021
U3	25	96.9	0.021
U6	18	96.9	0.021
I3	31	97.8	0.021
I6	18	97.8	0.021
T3	29	98.7	0.021
K6	20	87.7	0.021
C3	26	99.6	0.021
C6	22	99.6	0.021
S6	18	80.6	0.021
Other sectors[b] (simple average)	24	13.3	0.013

Notes:
a. First character denotes the trade partners, the number refers to the industrial sector (see Figure 9.2).
b. Simple average of all non-negative trade flows, including those inferior to 20% of total inputs.

Source: See Figure 9.2.

reviewed in the next section and provides information at aggregated sectoral level –merchandise trade statistics can be disaggregated into more than 5000 product categories in the Harmonized System. For example, many researchers interested in the trade-development nexus and the issue of value-chain upgrading want to analyze trade patterns according to the technological sophistication of the products. Lall et al. (2005) provide a detailed example of the calculation of sophistication scores for 237 exports at the 3-digit SITC level and 766 exports at the 4-digit level. This classification, while not pretending to be a world standard, has inspired analytical work in UN agencies such as Economic Committee for Latin America and the Caribbean (ECLAC) and UNCTAD. OECD and EUROSTAT also have defined a classification of high-technology sectors and products (Hatzichronoglou, 1997). The classification is based both on direct R&D intensity and R&D embodied in intermediate and investment goods.

1985

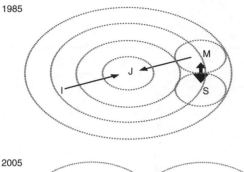

2005

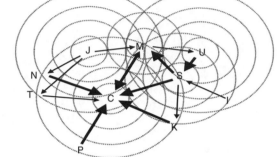

Note: See Figure 9.2.

Source: Escaith and Inomata (2013).

Figure 9.3   Evolution of Asia-Pacific intra-industry network, 1985–2005

Interestingly, the latest revision of the classification includes services (OECD, 2011).

Nevertheless, it remains important to keep in mind that such classifications – based on imported and exported goods – can be greatly misleading when trade takes place in GVCs where what is actually traded are the tasks and not the products. Relatively simple tasks (e.g., assembly) can be incorporated into very sophisticated electronic equipment. This does not imply that the sector/country's production frontier has moved toward high-technology. Therefore, popular indicators such as revealed comparative advantages have to be treated carefully when trade in tasks is prevalent.

Another aspect of interest for the researchers following the new "new" trade theory is product differentiation. Applying statistical filters to the raw data (e.g., splitting HS categories by quality, using unit values) should help to provide a better understanding of the industrial clusters participating in GVCs.

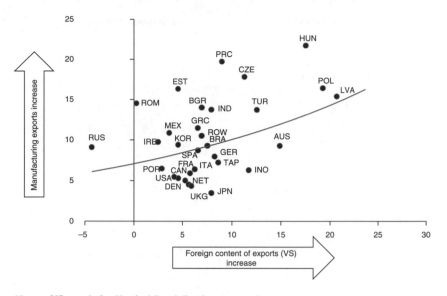

Note: VS stands for Vertical Specialization (see text).

Source: Adapted from WTR (2013) on the basis of OECD-WTO TiVA database.

Figure 9.4   *Export performance and reliance on imported inputs (1995–2007, % annual growth)*

Using OECD data, Figure 9.5 gives an example of trade indicators crossing technological content and quality differentiation for a selection. Industries are classified by technological content and, for each HS6 product they export, high, medium and low quality ranks are determined by looking at the relative position of their unit value compared to world trade in similar products (OECD, 2013). Within each of the industries, the graph nicely illustrates the specialization of high-income countries (Japan, the US) in high quality/high price products, while developing countries export low or medium quality varieties. The graph shows also that the US is still an exporter of medium and low priced products in the low technology sectors.

This specialization on different quality segments allows countries with different comparative advantage to trade in the same type of products, in apparent breach of the traditional trade theory that predicted a clear specialization by type of activity. This type of information is also relevant for development economists, as it shows that lesser developed economies are not condemned to compete head-to-head with emerging and developed countries, but may find an entry niche in low quality segments, before upgrading by climbing up the quality ladder.

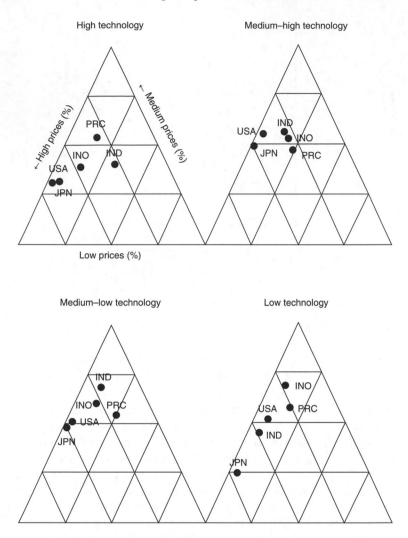

Note: The position of a point in the triangular graph represents the relative share of low-, medium- and high-priced products for each technological category.

Source: Based on an interpretation of data displayed in Figure 5.12 of OECD (2013).

Figure 9.5   *Exports by technology content and price level, selected Asia-Pacific countries (2010)*

Rauch (1999) looks into the issue from a different angle and offers a classification of merchandise into three categories (homogeneous, reference priced, and differentiated). Products traded on an organized exchange (Chicago Board of Trade, New York Mercantile Exchange, etc.) are considered homogeneous goods. When manufactured goods are not sold on mercantile exchanges but are sufficiently standardized to be benchmarked for price and quality (chemicals, special types of steel), they are classified as reference priced; all other products were deemed differentiated. The latter category includes the inputs specifically tailored to the end-user's needs (e.g., automobile parts).

3.2   Measuring Trade in Value-Added[12]

While mapping trade in intermediate inputs is important to understand the topology of the production process, a value-added approach enables one to assess the net economic contribution of each contributing sector/country and further disaggregate it into its main components (wages, profits and taxes).[13] Estimates of the value-added content of trade rely typically on Leontief inverse matrices based on international input output (IIO) tables, which integrate national accounts and bilateral trade statistics. IIO tables present the advantage of capturing in a cost-effective manner not only direct linkages and exchanges between countries and sectors, but also after applying the standard Leontief transformation, the indirect sectoral linkages. The IDE-JETRO's Asian Input–Output Tables are the earliest examples of systematic compilation of IIO with a clear statistical objective (most academic researchers have instead used non-official or ad-hoc data, such as GTAP or Eora databases).[14]

The most recent advances in compiling IIO rely principally on the increasing availability of country supply-use tables, which – for each sector – provide a detailed picture of the supply of goods and services inputs by origin (domestic production and imports) and the use of output for intermediate, consumption and final use (consumption, gross capital formation, exports). The supply-use table also provides information on the value-added components (compensation of employees, other net taxes on production, consumption of fixed capital, net operating surplus). From 2010 to 2012, best practices in compiling such data were greatly enhanced by the experience gained through an EU-funded project, the World Input–Output Data Base (WIOD). The WIOD project also developed socio-economic satellite accounts that allow deriving employment or environmental impact from the models (Box 9.3).

Once the IIO table is available, a series of trade indicators can be

---

BOX 9.3   DERIVING SOCIO-ECONOMIC IMPACT
FROM TRADE IN VALUE-ADDED

Since the 2008–2009 crisis, the trade-and-labor issue is particularly high on the research agenda. In a GVC framework, the demand for labor is affected by those industries that have to compete against imports of final goods and in industries that provide intermediate inputs. Foreign competition may induce a change in the absolute number of workers or in the skills required. For example, firms in developed countries may specialize in higher quality – high technology and high skills – processes. Conversely, off-shoring and international outsourcing are additional sources of jobs for firms that are able to qualify as GVC suppliers.

WTO and IDE-JETRO (2011) show that in the Asia-Pacific region, each country tends to specialize in exporting value-added that is generated by job skills that represent their comparative advantage (for example, Japan and the US are specializing in high-skill and high cost type of labor) while importing goods and services where they do not have such advantages from other developing Asian countries, especially the PRC. Foster et al. (2012), using WIOD data and a more formal methodology, examine the GVC-linked evolution of the skill-structure of labor demand for a sample of 18 countries.

The trade and environment nexus is another high-priority item in the research agenda. The Eora MRIO Database project has been developed with the objective of tracking the environmental "footprint" of consumption across countries. As we shall see, the "demand-side" approach to measuring trade in value-added builds largely on methodologies developed to track back to developing countries the source of CO_2 emissions of products consumed in developed countries.

---

produced, each one capturing a specific aspect of trade in value-added. Most, if not all, start from a simple accounting framework. The basic relationship, from a single country perspective, can be described as follows:[15]

$$g = A^*g + y$$

where:

g: is an n*1 vector of the output of n industries within an economy.

A: is an n*n technical coefficients matrix; where a_{ij} is the ratio of inputs from domestic industry i used in the output of industry j.

y: is an n*1 vector of final demand for domestically produced goods and services (final demand includes consumption, investment and exports).

A country's total value-added can be split in two parts: one is the VA embodied in goods and services absorbed domestically (consumption and investment), the other is the VA embodied in its exports. Assuming the homogeneity of products made for the domestic market and products made for exports, total imports embodied directly and indirectly within exports are given by:

Import content of exports $= m*(1 - A)^{-1}*e$, where:
m: is a 1*n vector with components m_j (the ratio of imports to output in industry j)
e: is a n*1 vector of exports by industry to the rest of the world.

In the same way, one can estimate the total indirect and direct contribution of exports to value-added by replacing the import vector m above with an equivalent vector that shows the ratio of value-added to output (v). So, the contribution of exports to total economy value-added is equal to:

$$VAE : v*(1 - A)^{-1}*e; \; (1 - A)^{-1} \text{ being the Leontief inverse matrix } (L)$$

Before revising in the following sections some of the main indicators that are derived from this basic relationship, it is important to highlight some of the limitations that are related to the definition of the technical coefficients matrix A. Those technical coefficients are derived by normalizing the intermediate coefficients Z_{ij} by the value of total production ($a_{ij} = Z_{ij}/Q_j$); where Z_{ij} is the intermediate consumption of products from sector i by j (i and j being possibly in different countries) and Q_j is the total production of sector j.

These I–O coefficients present the direct requirements of inputs from "i" for producing one unit of output of industry "j". For example, to produce one unit of output, sector *2* will require a_{12} units from sector *1*. The technical coefficients tell only part of the story of the productive chain. In order to be able to produce the a_{12} units demanded by sector *2*, the productive sector *1* will need inputs from other sectors. To satisfy this endogenous demand created by one additional unit of output in sector *2*, individual firms in each other connected sector will also require inputs produced by suppliers operating from other sectors. And so on and so forth, as the indirect demands generated at each step create in turn additional requirements.

The feedback sequence resulting from the initial demand injection can be obtained by the series

$$I + A + A^2 + A^3 + \ldots + A^n$$

where I is an identity matrix representing the initial demand injection and A^n is the progressive impact of initial demands at the nth stage of the production chain. When n tends to infinity, the series has a limit equal to L. The coefficients of the Leontief Inverse measure the depth (intensity) of the backward linkages between sectors. They describe entirely the direct and indirect flows of intermediate products involved by the productive chains.

But the elegance of the algebraic formulation hides some messy statistical issues. Q_i results from aggregating the production of all establishments surveyed when establishing the supply and use tables, mixing large and small firms. These firms may use different technologies and may therefore require different types and/or quantity of inputs. The higher the productive heterogeneity (as happens in developing countries), the less representative the average $a_{ij} = Z_{ij}/Q_j$ will be. Additionally, Q_i aggregates sales to the domestic sectors (firms, households and administration) and exports. It is well documented by the new "new" trade literature that, within each industrial sector, exporting firms are usually the largest and the most technically advanced ones. Therefore, one unit of additional export is unlikely to foster the same type of endogenous demand for intermediate inputs as one unit of additional domestic consumption. Typically, in least advanced countries, the multiplier effect through endogenous demand is low because traditional producers use little intermediate inputs (labor intensive production technologies) while most of the intermediate inputs required for non-traditional exports will be satisfied by imports. This aggregation bias has important implications when measuring trade in value-added and will be discussed more in detail.

3.2.1 Vertical specialization

Hummels et al. (2001) define vertical-specialization trade as "the value of imported intermediates embodied in a country's exports", or import content of exports. *VS* measures the value of imports that is required to produce one unit of exports. Intuitively (as we shall see, the issue is a bit more complex), the domestic value-added embodied in exports (VAE) is the difference between gross exports and *VS*. An additional definition is *VS*1, the value of exports that are embodied in a second country's export goods: "This occurs when the country exports goods that are used as inputs into another country's production of export goods." The first attempt at measuring vertical specialization was based on national input– output matrices and was not subject to the above-mentioned endogeneity issue. Daudin et al. (2006, 2011) and Johnson and Noguera (2012) develop further those concepts to an international IO framework. A subset of VS1 can actually return to the country in which the intermediate has been originally produced, that is, this country re-imports domestic value-added in final goods (VS1*). Johnson and Noguera (2012) follow similar lines and describe shipments from country *i* to *j* of final and intermediate goods (embodied in country *j* in consumption) as "absorbed" (the absorption state of the Markov chain described earlier in this chapter). Shipments of country A to B which return back to country A are called "reflected". Shipments from A to B that are processed in country B and afterwards sent to a third country C are called "re-directed".

At this stage, and discounting the reflected part of exports, we can define two types of domestic VA exports: for final demand (*fd*) and for intermediate (*imd*):

$$VAE(fd):v*(I - A)^{-1}*e^{fd} \text{ and}$$

$$VAE(imd):v*(I - A)^{-1}*e^{imd}$$

$$\text{with } e^{fd} + e^{imd} = e$$

As we shall see, $VAE(imd)$ should be further refined in order to avoid double counting and have a complete mapping of trade in value-added.

3.2.2 Full decomposition of gross exports

Koopman et al. (2012) develop a full decomposition of exports along these concepts, and build a consistent accounting framework that allows them to measure a country's gross exports according to its various value-added components. The net domestic value added content of exports is composed of the following four elements (Figure 9.6):

(i) and (ii)   The domestic value-added embodied either in *final* or *intermediate* goods/services and directly absorbed and consumed by the importing country. Those represent a strict bilateral trade pattern, as in the traditional Ricardian model.

(iii)   The domestic value-added contained in intermediates exported to a country and re-exported to a third country as part of a sale of goods or services. This represents a one-to-many

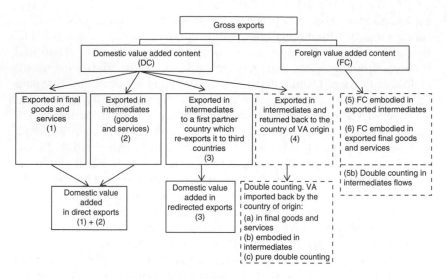

Source: Adapted from Koopman et al. (2012).

Figure 9.6   *Decomposition of gross exports into their value added components*

country transfer of value-added, when the embodied content of exported goods/services crosses borders more than once. This component would not have existed in the absence of global manufacturing, and is the source of trade creation from a trade in tasks perspective (Baldwin and Robert-Nicoud, 2010).

(iv)   The domestic value-added of exported goods/services which is sent back to the country of value-added origin. Such a value-added round-trip corresponds to the *reflected* case in Johnson and Noguera (2012).

The foreign value-added content of exports is similar to the *VS* index and corresponds to the value-added of inputs that was imported in order to produce intermediate or final goods/services to be exported. To avoid double counting and maintain the identity in trade balance measured in gross or in VA term, the domestic value-added sent back to its country of origin, or reflected, should not be included in the estimate of value-added exports.

The identification of "double counting" is a complex "accounting cum modelling" issue. From an accounting perspective, it has to do with trade in intermediates that are embodied in other intermediate or final goods/services, but not absorbed abroad. The issue is also conceptual. When moving from a national to an international IO matrix, the part of exports corresponding to intermediate inputs sent to industries in other countries for further processing are not included in final demand anymore. They are now endogenous to the global production process. The proper treatment of the endogenous portion of exports has been the source of some intense discussion in the expert community, as the limitations mentioned in Oosterhaven and Stelder (2002) apply in some cases (forecasting and simulation based on IIO models). Koopman et al. (2012) solve the accounting issue by distinguishing two occurrences: imported inputs used by a country to produce goods/services for export but already counted as domestic value-added amount by another country; domestic value-added content that returns home as imports but already included in the value-added of the country itself. The duplicated elements must be excluded from value-added exports to exclude double counting. Double counting may, nevertheless, provide useful information on vertical specialization (Box 9.4).

Table 9.3 presents a selection of results showing the decomposition of gross exports for Asia-Pacific countries based on the OECD-WTO Trade in Value Added Database (TiVA).[16] The average of the sampled countries indicates the foreign content of gross exports (similar to the *VS* criteria) increased from 24 percent to 32 percent between 1995 and 2008, showing a greater integration of the countries in GVC trade. Ranked on the *VS* criteria, Singapore is the most reliant on imported inputs for producing her exports, Australia – with a rich natural resources endowment – being at the other extreme of the sample. Interestingly, the PRC, far from being the downstream final assembly point for consumer goods, is exporting a high proportion of intermediate goods (see the column VA exported to third country). VA returning home is quantitatively marginal, but it is a good qualitative indicator of the back-and-forth trade typical of GVCs. The PRC ranked first on this indicator for 2008, showing a huge increase from 1995. The US is second (those indicators are computed on the basis of all reporters, and the US value is clearly influenced by the close trade relationship with Canada and Mexico).

3.2.3   The demand-side absorption approach

The previous approach entails complex calculation in order to avoid double counting. The WIOD project turned the tables and looked at trade flows from the final demand perspective. Reflecting a methodology previously used in environment economics to measure the CO_2 content imbedded in consumption and track its domestic and foreign origin, Stehrer (2012) measures the value-added of one country directly and indirectly contained in final demand of another country. The final demand approach has the advantage of looking at the issue from the exogenous side of the

BOX 9.4   DOUBLE COUNTING: ISSUE OR BLESSING?

One of the first motivations for measuring trade in value-added was to eliminate double counting. Because the value of intermediate inputs is double-counted each time the product into which the parts are embodied crosses a border, the sum of all customs registers will over-estimate the actual economic content of physical trade flows. This bias is eliminated by accounting only the net value aggregated at each step of the international value chain, exactly in the same way national accountants discard the value of intermediate transactions in the computation of the gross domestic product. The new IMF Balance of Payments Manual (BPM6) and the last revision of the UN System of National Accounts (SNA, 2008) goes further and recommends that one ignore trade in intermediates when no change of ownership takes place, as it is often the case in GVCs, and record only the manufacturing fees.

Yet, information on intermediate trade remains crucial for understanding how supply chains actually work. With the exception of the last step of the production network, all GVC trade is in intermediates. WTO (2013a) estimates that intermediates represent about 54 percent of global merchandise trade, excluding oil; in the OECD countries, they represent 56 percent and 73 percent of trade flows in goods and services, respectively (Miroudot et al., 2009). Knowing the composition, origin and destination of the flows of intermediate goods and services is key for understanding the architecture and topological properties of regional and international value chains.

Koopman et al. (2012) provide a detailed structural analysis of the trade in intermediate flows, identifying six categories of transactions, two of them being "pure" double-counting. Their estimates of double counting are particularly high for countries closely involved in value chains. The PRC normal exports (products exported by national firms) have a 3 percent incidence of such double counting while processing trade exports (firms operating in export processing zones) have a 10 percent incidence. The largest double counting in their paper is found for Singapore with 22 percent. Malaysia trade records 14 percent double counting while Indonesia, a natural resources-based economy, has only 7 percent.

Thus, double counting is well correlated with the "vertical specialization" index (*VS*). We see in Figure 9.8 that the incidence of double counting may also help in identifying linear GVCs ("snakes") from hub-and-spoke ones ("spiders"). In other words, far from being a nuisance because of double counting, trade in intermediates provides very valuable information on the industrial logic behind global production networks.

trade in value-added equation, avoiding endogeneity issues. The author goes further and proposes that this should be the proper measure of trade in value-added;[17] in an earlier paper of WIOD (Los et al., 2012), the two concepts were called the "direct trade flow (DTF)" perspective (corresponding to the decomposition of exports and value-added in trade) and the "global value chain (GVC)" perspective (for the foreign content in a unit of consumption). This battle of denominations was closed by Koopman et al. (2012) and Meng et al. (2012) who show that, properly measured, the two approaches (gross exports decomposition and final demand) lead to similar aggregated results.

Contrary to the previous approaches, which are supply-based and focus on exports (irrespective of their use by the importing country), the absorption approach relates to the demand side and estimates a country's value-added induced by its partners' final demand. When analyzing trade in value-added from the final demand side, the main building block is the measure of value-added used by an economy to satisfy its final demand but created in foreign countries. Foreign value-added can either come directly from one partner country or may have been indirectly transferred through several partner countries belonging to a same production chain. Symmetrically (a trade statistician would say, using mirror statistics), the exports of a country are defined as the domestic value-added exported to satisfy the final demand from other countries (this corresponds to the VAX definition of Johnson and Noguera, 2012).

3.2.4 Complementarity of the two approaches

At global level, the total trade measured from the supply side (exports) and the (final) demand side give the same results. Meng et al. (2012) show in a two country accounting framework that the demand-side approach can be expressed through two types of exports of value-added: the first component represents country value-added embodied in exports of final goods and the second one is composed from VA embodied in trade in

Table 9.3 Decomposition of gross exports of goods and services into their value-added components, 1995 and 2008 (% of total gross exports)

	Foreign value added content (vertical specialization)		Domestic value added (VA) content of gross exports						Total	
			VA directly absorbed by importer[a]		VA exported to third countries[b]		VA sent back to country of origin[b]			
	1995	2008	1995	2008	1995	2008	1995	2008	1995	2008
Singapore	46.7	53.1	39.2	25.5	13.8	21.1	0.3	0.3	53.3	46.9
Taipei,China	35.8	47.8	50.4	23.1	13.6	28.6	0.2	0.5	64.2	52.2
Republic of Korea	23.7	43.4	62.0	31.1	14.2	25.0	0.1	0.5	76.3	56.6
Philippines	30.9	41.7	52.4	27.0	16.6	31.1	0.0	0.2	69.1	58.3
Viet Nam	24.4	39.8	62.9	43.6	12.6	16.5	0.0	0.1	75.6	60.2
Malaysia	40.3	38.1	44.3	31.9	15.2	29.6	0.3	0.4	59.7	61.9
Thailand	29.8	37.8	58.1	43.4	12.0	18.7	0.1	0.2	70.2	62.2
Cambodia	26.0	36.1	56.3	59.1	17.8	4.8	0.0	0.0	74.0	63.9
People's Republic of China	11.9	33.3	74.1	51.2	13.9	14.4	0.1	1.1	88.1	66.7
Hong Kong, China	40.6	29.1	48.0	41.8	11.3	29.1	0.1	0.1	59.4	70.9
India	9.6	23.7	76.1	53.8	14.2	22.3	0.0	0.1	90.4	76.3
New Zealand	17.4	21.4	69.3	59.0	13.3	19.5	0.0	0.0	82.6	78.6
Japan	6.8	19.4	70.5	49.5	22.4	30.7	0.2	0.4	93.2	80.6
Indonesia	14.7	17.4	66.4	50.7	18.8	31.8	0.1	0.1	85.3	82.6
United States	8.4	14.6	66.6	55.0	24.5	29.7	0.5	0.7	91.6	85.4
Australia	11.8	13.9	66.3	50.8	21.8	35.1	0.1	0.2	88.2	86.1

Notes:
PRC = People's Republic of China.
a. One border crossing only.
b. Multiple border crossings.

Source: Based on OECD-WTO TiVA database.

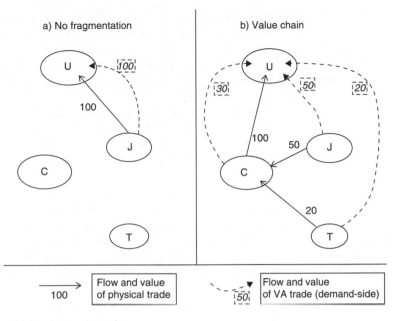

a) No fragmentation

b) Value chain

	Flow and value of physical trade
→ 100	

	Flow and value of VA trade (demand-side)
⇠ ⌐50¬	

Source: Elaborated by the author.

Figure 9.7   Imputed versus observed trade flows in value-added

intermediate goods and services. Degain et al. (2012) verify the result applying both methods to the WIOD table 2007.

From a practitioner's perspective, the actual "GVC", or "trade in tasks" perspective is perhaps better captured by the supply-side approach of export decomposition. This opinion stems from the network approach presented earlier in this chapter. Consider a simple example of a system of four countries (Figure 9.7). In the situation without fragmentation of production, all value-added is produced in the same country of origin. Here, for example (panel a), Japan (*J*) exports $100 of computers to US (*U*). In a distributed production network (panel b), *J* retains the production of key components (value of $50), outsources to Thailand (*T*) the production of hard disks ($20) and creates an affiliate in the PRC (C) that manufactures non-key components and does the assembly (value-added of $30). The final product is then shipped to *U* where it is consumed. The demand-side approach will decompose *U*'s final demand according to *C*, *J* and *T* respective contributions, even when no trade took place between *U* and *J* or between *U* and *T*.

This has the advantage of showing how *J* and *T*'s productive activities are influenced by *U*'s demand; something a traditional macroeconomic model based on gross trade would have difficulties to track. From a trade perspective, nevertheless, this creates two issues. One is that trade flows between *J* and *C* and between *T* and *C* disappear from the measure though they actually took place, while virtual ones are created (*U* and *J*, *U* and *T*) that did not occur in reality. In other words, the demand approach creates virtual bilateral flows that may not possibly exist in reality (due to physical or political impediments, for example).

The other argument is analytical. Focusing on demand-side only may blur our understanding of comparative advantages in trade in tasks and bias the results of some classical indicators such as gravity models. Losing the role of *C* as an intermediate step between *T* and *U* has implications when it comes to understanding comparative advantages in a trade in tasks environment. In a GVC *T*'s specialization is complementary with *C* and both *T* and *C* are competitive with respect to *J* and *U* (from a comparative advantage point of view) in their respective specializations. But there is no certainty that *T* individually would have a comparative advantage in the absence of *C*. For example, if Japan decides that computers sold to the US will be assembled in Mexico instead of the PRC, the hard disks used may come from Mexico or other places closer than Thailand. In other words, it is possible that for *T*, international competitiveness is conditional to supplying assembly lines in *C*.

From the topological perspective presented previously, this means that not all connections in the network are possible or have independent probabilities. Instead, the path trees of connections in GVC networks are usually Bayesian: connection probabilities at each node are path dependent and influenced by origin or ultimate destination. Translating probabilities into "distances" or "trade resistances", as in a gravity model where the probability of observing a high value of trade between two countries is inversely proportional to the distance separating them, we can say that the resistance to trade between *T* and *U* is higher for direct flows than triangular ones through *C*.

$$d(T,U) \; > \; d(T,C) \; + \; d(C,U)$$

Thus, "distances" in trade in tasks do not define a metric from a topological point of view.[18]

From a gravity model perspective, it means that some direct connections from suppliers to customers are "longer" (costlier) than indirect ones. Taking the US perspective in Figure 9.7, it may be cheaper to import a hard-disk drive made in Thailand and imbedded in a computer assembled in the PRC than importing it directly from nearby Mexico. But as soon as the assembly point is not the PRC, Mexico's hard disks may become competitive. The choice of sourcing components is not determined by the location of the final consumer, but depends on the cost of doing business with each of the intermediate nodes.

As trade analysts are interested in understanding these costs and their determinants (comparative advantage, competitiveness, trade policy, etc.), they are more attentive to tracking the exports side, and its successive steps, rather than simply identifying the foreign origin of domestic final demand. It is therefore important to be able to keep track of all intermediate steps and assign correctly the gross and net flows in the global production network, even if it results in additional data compilation and processing costs. Obviously, this is particularly relevant when supply chains are of the "linear" or "snake" type (various successive intermediate suppliers aggregating value-added to a good) rather than the "star" or "spider" type (a GVC organized as a hub and spikes, with various suppliers sending separately their inputs for final assembly).[19]

Comparing the bilateral flows of trade in value-added obtained from the export side and the demand side, as well as physical flows, may provide additional information on the topological structure of the GVC. The amount of double counting is higher in a snake configuration, as shown in Figure 9.8. In panel (a), C plays the role of a hub, a "spider" type, and the amount of double counting (the difference between the sum of physical flows and their VA content) is \$70 (\$170 of physical exports minus \$100 of value-added). In panel (b), J exports first to T and the resulting good in process is re-exported to C for further processing before its sale to U (in a "snake" configuration, all operations are successive), then the amount of double counting is \$120 (\$220 minus \$100).

A series of other indicators can be calculated from the IIO trade in value-added methodology. To cite a few:

- Bilateral balance of trade: comparison of value-added versus gross terms-based bilateral trade balances.
- Sectoral contributions to value-added exports, showing the direct and indirect contribution of each sector of the economy to the exports of one given sector. This is particularly important in the case of services, as they contribute to some 50 percent of "manufacture exports" in industrialized countries.
- Global value chain participation index; length of GVCs as measured by APL (see Box 9.5).
- Global value chain position index (relative length of upstream versus the downstream part of the chain), as in De Backer and Miroudot (2012).
- Relative comparative advantage (RCA) based on gross and value-added exports (incorporated in the OECD-WTO TiVA database).

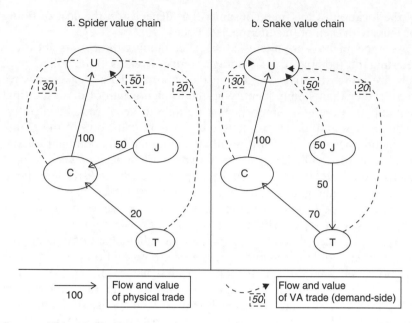

Source: Elaborated by the author.

Figure 9.8   Global value chains: snake and spider configurations

The list of possible indicators is much larger: on the basis of the international input–output matrices such as WIOD or OECD-WTO's TiVA that form today's backbone of trade in value-added indicators, it is possible to adapt most traditional input–output connectedness indicators. The 2013 version of the OECD-WTO TiVA database displays up to 39 indicators provided for 34 OECD countries and 23 non-OECD economies. Carlos-Lopes et al. (2008) offer a list of 12 of such indicators, some of them dating from the earliest years of input–output analysis. Miller and Blair (2009) is an example of a classic textbook on input–output analysis that can be revisited with a "trade in value-added mind".

To provide an example of how TiVA revisits traditional indicators and provides new insights, Figure 9.9 shows revealed comparative advantage (RCA), comparing on a 45° diagram gross and value-added indicators for machinery and transport equipment, one of the sectors most influenced by GVCs. Countries very active in the downstream part of the value chain (closest to final demand) have much higher RCA in gross values than in value-added, and fall below the 45° line. This is the case of the PRC and India in Asia, or Mexico in the Americas. On the contrary, countries will

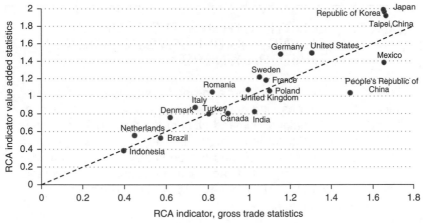

Source: Based on OECD-WTO TiVA database.

Figure 9.9   Revealed comparative advantage in machinery and transport equipment (gross versus value added, 2007)

rank higher on the value-added indicator when firms are more upstream (R&D, production of components). This is the case of Japan, Republic of Korea and Taipei,China in Asia, or the US in the Americas. Indonesia's relative situation in gross or value-added terms does not change much, which may be explained, either by a relatively low degree of GVC participation and/or a balanced mix of upstream and downstream exporting firms.

3.2.5   Limitations of the trade in value-added approach

The statistical limitations can be defined in two broad categories: data gaps and aggregation bias. The value-added approach suffers from all the shortcomings that afflict compiling intermediate trade flow statistics. Those flows are critical in "gluing" together the various industries and countries that are modelled in the IIO, but their estimation remains too often a guesswork exercise where statisticians have to ponder the relative merits of diverging sources and impute missing data. This is particularly true for trade in intermediate services. An additional challenge is the attribution of flows by sector of origin and sectors of destination (a "one to many" relationship). Identifying the sector of origin is a relatively easy task for good producing sectors, using the International Standard Industrial Classification (ISIC) and the SITC correspondence tables, but more of an issue for trade in services.[20] Sectors of destinations are allocated

BOX 9.5　LENGTH, STRENGTH OF SUPPLY CHAINS AND RELATIVE POSITIONS OF TRADE PARTNERS

The conventional input–output approach to supply chains focuses principally on measuring the strength of interconnectedness, based on the traditional demand-pull impact derived from technical coefficients. For trade analysts, the "length" of linkages also becomes important for mapping the geometry of supply chains. Length is most often estimated using the concept of average propagation length (APL) developed in Dietzenbacher et al. (2005).[a] It is defined as:

$$APL_{j-i} = 1 * \frac{a_{ij}}{(l_{ij} - \delta_{ij})} + 2 * \frac{[A^2]_{ij}}{(l_{ij} - \delta_{ij})} + 3 * \frac{[A^3]_{ij}}{(l_{ij} - \delta_{ij})} + \cdots$$

where l_{ij} is Leontief inverse coefficients, $[I-A]^{-1}$, δ_{ij} is a Kronecker delta product which is $\delta_{ij}=1$ if $i=j$ and $\delta_{ij}=0$ otherwise.

APL is the weighted average of the number of production stages, where an impact from industry j goes through until it ultimately reaches industry i, using the strength of an impact at each stage as a weight. APL was applied at the international level in Dietzenbacher and Romero (2007) for major European countries and by Inomata (2008) for Asia. Building on the APL methodology, Escaith and Inomata (2013) develop a graph showing the evolution of the length and upstreamness of regional supply chains in Asia-Pacific between 1985 and 2005.

Most economies have moved towards the northeast corner of the graph, indicating that the length of their supply chains linkages increased between 1985 and 2005. The PRC, in particular, shows a large increase in the length of the supply chains in which it participates (considering both its domestic supply chains and the overseas production networks). The exceptions to the trend are the US and Taipei,China, while Japan did not change much. The northwest-southeast diagonal distinguishes the relative position of each economy within the regional supply chains, as determined by the ratio of forward and backward APL. The US and Japan, the most advanced economies in the Asia-Pacific region,

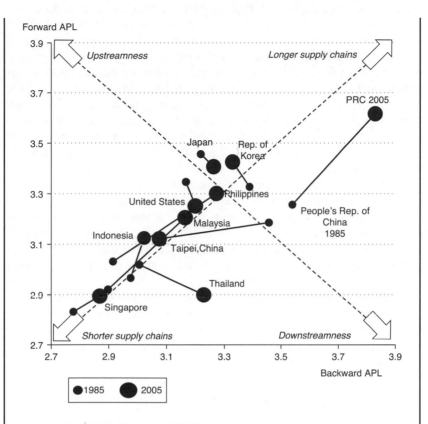

Forward APL

Source: Escaith and Inomata (2013).

Figure 9.10   Change of relative positions in the regional supply chains, 1985–2005

are located in the upstream position. The USA moved down-ward during the period and swapped its position with Republic of Korea. The PRC stays in the downstream segment of the regional supply chains, which reflects the country's position as a "final assembler" of the regional products.

Note: a Using a different method developed by Fally (2011), De Backer and Miroudot (2012) develop an index of "distance to final demand" for OECD.

on the basis of the import coefficients of SUT tables and some proportionality assumption with respect to the countries of origin. In other words, if the agricultural sector's consumption of imported chemicals represents 10 percent of the country's imports for this particular input, then 10 percent of all bilateral import flows of chemical inputs will be allocated to the agricultural sector. This "proportionality" assumption may not reflect the actual origin when the quality of intermediate products required is very different across the importing sectors, and that countries of origin specialize in particular qualities. Moreover, additional proportional imputations may be required when the SUT are not detailed enough by products, or simply not available.

Once flows of intermediates are allocated by sectors, the resulting IIO needs to be balanced, which raises complex issues of compatibilities. Some data conflicts can be solved using a priori inferences. For example, the multi-regional Eora tables, based on a mix of hard data and algorithmic imputations, are built by giving prominence to national input-output tables, followed by the UN Statistical Division series of national accounts and COMTRADE data.[21] Giving priority to national accounts (as is usually the case in order to satisfy balancing conditions) means that there are many occurrences where trade data are misrepresented. Even if precedence rules are established, many imputations rely ultimately on some value judgment. Timmer (2012) provides a detailed review of the numerous steps that eventually lead to the construction of the IIO table produced by the WIOD project. OECD (2013) discusses how the national input–output tables behind the TiVA database have been harmonized and linked together TiVA; Degain et al. (2013) compare three of the main databases used so far in the literature (GTAP, OECD-WTO's TiVA and WIOD).

Diachronic comparison of time series of IIO indicators also confronts the issue of price variations, in particular the impact of exchange rate. This complicates the chronological analysis of trade in VA indicators. WIOD provides chained time-series of its IIO tables that allow computing indicators in last-year's prices. For long term comparison Diakantoni and Escaith (2012) delineate a heuristic method to identify where exchange rate adjustments are taking place.[22]

Most analytical issues are related to aggregation. I mentioned two of them: firm heterogeneity and product differentiation. An aggregation bias is created when very different firms (and very different underlying GVCs) are aggregated together into a single sector. In developing countries' production technologies the use of imported inputs may differ widely between firms producing for exports and firms producing only for the domestic market. This is well documented in the case of the PRC and Mexico, as we shall see in the next section.

BOX 9.6   TOPOLOGICAL LIMITATIONS OF
           INTERNATIONAL INPUT–OUTPUT
           MATRICES

Despite their analytical advantages, international input–output matrices have topological limitations from a GVC perspective, most – if not all – of them due to aggregation biases and short-comings in the underlying formal statistical properties (i.e., from a probabilistic point of view). For example, APL computes the average length using $[a_{ij}]$ as probabilities for transiting from i to j Input–output matrices define a Markovian process where the transaction probabilities depend only on the current position of the node $[i]$ (a sector in a given country), but not on the manner a node gathered its inputs from other markets. We saw that in a GVC, suppliers are not undifferentiated as assumed, and the choice of suppliers may itself be conditioned by the market of final destination. High quality suppliers will be preferred if the market of final destination is of high income. From a statistical perspective, transition probabilities along the supply chain are not independent (Markovian), but conditioned by the market of final destination (Bayesian). A Markovian representation of the global network is only the expected value of the realization of a large number of mutually independent Bayesian trees. This is perfectly acceptable when APL is used for descriptive (ex post) reasons, but may be subject to serious aggregation bias if it is used to forecast or simulate the strength and length of a country/sector specific (supply or demand) shock. The "cascading" effect of a Markovian process will spread and dilute the shock, while a Bayesian approach would have called for a more concentrated effect.

The issue is better described through a simple example. A textile factory in Morocco imports cotton to produce fabric that is then cut and sown according to the specification of a Spanish fashion designer and exported. The shirts exported to the Italian market use long fiber cotton imported from Egypt, and T-shirts for the Portuguese tourism market use cotton imported from Mali. Due to the Spanish designer's price and quality constraints, the two types of cotton are not substitutable. If a supply shock affects agriculture in Egypt, only the shirt production will be affected; similarly, if demand for T-shirts increases only Malian producers will benefit from the surge in fabric production. Yet an input–output matrix will not be able to differentiate between those two differentiated value-chains and will aggregate them into a single set of coefficients. If the sales of the Moroccan factory split equally between Italy and Portugal, a 100 percent increase in demand for T-shirts exported to Portugal will translate, equivocally, to a 50 percent increase in Egyptian cotton (upward bias in measuring the strength of the demand shock) and a 50 percent increase in Malian cotton (downward bias, respectively).

Similarly, in an input–output perspective, the strength of backwards dependence at different stages (nodes) tends to decline as the "distance", as measured by the number of production steps (nodes), increases. Yet, this property is not consistent with the micro-economic and supply chain management views of the trade. In our previous example, the trade path is strictly determined by the market destination: if the final node of the graph is Italy (*alt. Portugal*), then the initial node is Egypt (*alt. Mali*). The path between nodes is not independent of initial or final states. From a topological perspective, the GVC network is closer to a Bayesian process than the Markovian setting that is implied by a usual input–output matrix. The local probability distribution associated with a given node is not independent of the final node (if the GVC is demand-driven), or of some particular intermediate node in the network (if the GVC is producer driven).

Product differentiation (quality, specifications) is a more complex issue and may actually reduce the possibility of sourcing inputs from all possible trade partners. This is particularly true when intermediate products are GVC specific. To take an example, sand is processed into silicon chips, which are assembled according to specific references. While sand and chips are both intermediate inputs, they respond to different market logics. Sand is a commodity: as long as it satisfies some physical specifications, its origin is not really important. Computer chips are much more specific and a chip made by a company according to very precise specifications required by the customer (e.g., a computer firm) may not be substitutable by other apparently similar products. The market powers associated with those two intermediate goods are very different.[23]

Implications, either in terms of the topological properties of the underlying network (Bayesian versus Markovian approaches) or in terms of economic analysis and market power, are very different when inputs are commodities or process-specific (see Box 9.6). While international input–output matrices can be differentiated to capture firm heterogeneity within a same industry (using a business register, as in the next section), they are not well equipped to deal with the heterogeneity in intermediate goods in a same product classification. As we saw previously in the chapter on mapping intermediate trade, these aspects have to be analyzed using the graph and network analysis tools on traditional trade statistics, after applying ad-hoc filters to discriminate products according to their specificity.

3.3   Linking Trade and Business Statistics

Input–output data, despite their great systemic value, are too aggregated to capture the business reality behind trade in global value chains. Sturgeon (2013) presents a state-of-the-art discussion on firm-level data requirements and data compilation strategies based on EUROSTAT experience. Some developing countries involved in GVCs have also developed appropriate statistical tools, be they large emerging economies such as the PRC or Mexico, or smaller countries such as Costa Rica. Obtaining firm-level data on global value chains requires dedicated surveys, something official statisticians look at with caution, considering the implementation cost, as well as the statistical fatigue of responding firms. Fortunately, there are cost-effective approaches at gathering relevant information without increasing the statistical burden on responding firms.

   Data already collected by national administrations are able to provide a detailed view of the trade activity generated by each firm. Administrative registers gather a lot of information on firms' activities, their corporate structure, their labor force and productive characteristics. By linking those administrative data with customs statistics, it is therefore possible to cross-check several existing databases and build very detailed maps of trade activity by firm characteristics. EUROSTAT has spearheaded a project called "Trade by Enterprise Characteristics" to understand the specific profiles of firms that actively engage into trade. This institutional initiative mirrors other initiatives from academia that burgeoned in response to the new "new" trade theory, which had a clear focus on empirical issues and micro-data. For example, Bernard et al. (2005) look at US data to provide an ID card of firms according to their trading activity. More recently, the Chinese Academy of Sciences (2013) has released detailed information on export activity by type of firms.

   These "trade by enterprise characteristics" (TEC) are so far restricted to national or custom union areas, because one needs to use a single identification for the firm across all administrative registers. In addition, confidentiality aspects constrain their dissemination. A second best solution is provided by disaggregating sectorial IIO by firm characteristics. De la Cruz et al. (2011) undertake such an exercise on Mexico; Tang et al. (2013) combine IO tables and firm census data to disaggregate Chinese GVC trade by firm size and type of ownership.

4. CONCLUSION: SEARCHING FOR AN INTEGRATING FRAMEWORK

Up to very recently, trade statistics were considered as a mature field by the profession; this sleeping beauty has recently awakened to transform herself into a vibrant teenager, curious to explore new areas, but yet unsure of the best avenues. While global production networks have been prevalent since the mid-1980s, the interest in this new form of globalization had remained largely circumscribed to the academic circle. The financial crisis of 2008–2009 and the resulting great trade collapse determined a new demand from policy makers for adequate statistical information regarding this phenomenon. The interest comes from various corners of policy making; from trade policy with the "Made in the World Initiative" launched by the WTO to the global governance and development objectives expressed by the G-20, the United Nations and regional institutions such as the ADB.

The objective of the present chapter was to tentatively map what we needed to know, while recognizing that there remain plenty of known unknowns and unknown unknowns. The starting point was to address the measurement issues by looking at the analytical and policy questions. Transactions between firms operating from different countries create new interdependencies between the national economies, with economic, financial, social and environmental dimensions. Statisticians have risen to the measurement challenge by making the best use of existing data. Using traditional trade statistics in innovative ways allows mapping more finely the World Trade Network, highlighting the specificities of trade in intermediate goods and the inter-industry linkages connecting production networks. Linking intermediary trade flows with national accounts data to construct international input–output tables and measuring the value-added content of trade were part of this effort.

We have so far only scraped the surface of the issue. The available statistics that the global trade in value-added databases provide today are estimates at macro-sectoral level. Having this information is already a great step in the right direction and helped in demonstrating that understanding the economic relevance of trade in today's globalized economy required new instruments and new methodologies. The results so far help in understanding the big picture, resizing the relative weight of services and manufactures and the real size of bilateral trade imbalances. Trade in value-added also helps understanding the complex relationships between trade in tasks and job creation.

The existing databases on trade in value-added still suffer from serious shortcomings. While they bring very valuable information on the relationship between international trade and economic development, existing databases developed on official data (AIO, OECD-WTO, WIOD) still need to cover many more developing and least developed countries, an effort hampered by data restrictions. So far, the incorporation of most developing countries in international IO tables results from the use of non-official estimates (GTAP) or algorithmic imputations (Eora) that may ignore the actual specificities of these countries. Extending the coverage of developing and least developed countries using official data should therefore be a priority.

From an analytical perspective, the indicators obtained so far suffer from sizable aggregation biases. These impair their use if one wishes to go beyond descriptive and exploratory statistics and look into causality factors and confirmatory analysis, using the sophisticated econometric models favored by the modern (new "new") trade theory. The new statistical frontier lies in the development of micro-databases to fully capture the heterogeneity of firms that are active in these global value chains and complements the trade data with information on firm characteristics, including the financial and corporate dimensions. The compilation of business data for international trade analysis calls for a revision of the existing classifications, in particular a better understanding of what are the "tasks" or "business functions" that are subject to outsourcing and eventually determine "trade in value-added".

The momentum created by this renewed interest was strong enough for calling the attention of the highest supra-national governing body, the United Nations Statistical Conference, which is in charge of setting international standards that are then applied by official statisticians.[24] Without prejudging of the future developments in this field of statistics, trends point toward integrating micro-economic data, including business registers, labor and financial information, using the national accounts as the organizing and integrating framework. The relevant data would be interrelated into a "satellite account" of the external sector, linked to the national accounts as far as residents are concerned, but also interlinked with other trading partners. A good example of such a statistical framework is provided by the satellite accounts for tourism, a branch of trade in services with complex interactions between many different economic and social actors.

Installing such accounts in the routine of national statistical institutes will be challenging for most developing countries, as it is very demanding in terms of the quality of administrative data and dedicated business surveys. It is nevertheless in these countries that the need for developing such an information system is the greatest, considering the relevance between global value chains, trade and development. On the other hand, the difficulty of the task should not be overstated, because most trade activity in developing countries is concentrated in a few firms, greatly simplifying the data compilation.

NOTES

*   I thank G. Daudin, B. Ferrarini, D. Hummels and anonymous editors for their comments on preliminary drafts. I also recognize the contribution of my colleagues at WTO, IDE-JETRO, OECD, UN, USITC, WIOD and the other researchers with whom I worked on "trade in value-added" in the past few years. I learned a lot from them, but most probably not enough to avoid errors and omissions in this chapter. Those, as well as any opinions expressed here, remain mine and do not reflect any position of the WTO or its members.

1.   Other economists contest the claim for paradigm shift and show that comparative advantages in trade in tasks can be analyzed through available mainstream models (Baldwin and Robert-Nicoud, 2010).

2.   TiVA, launched by OECD and WTO in January 2013, builds on a series of works by IDE-JETRO, US-ITC and the WIOD project.

3.   Vitali et al. (2011) present an analysis of intra-firm transaction within a large corporation, illustrating how graph and network theories can help in mapping a hierarchy across these relationships.

4.   As pointed out by Feenstra (2004), recent work in trade economics has been more empirical than theoretical, and about accounting for global trade flows rather than about testing hypotheses related to trade.

5.   National accounts would prefer to say compensation of employees and operating surplus (or labor and capital compensations) and net indirect taxes, after subsidies.

6.   Final goods are purchased for consumption or investment purposes. In practice, the boundaries are not clear. Gross investment includes changes in inventories, while final demand in national accounts covers total exports (of final and intermediate goods). International IO accountants separate exports of intermediate products from final demand, but the treatment of inventories remains an empirical issue.

7.   See, for a relatively nontechnical example, Hansen et al. (2011); Goyal (2007) develops a more formal approach of the economic theory of networks.

8.   V. Leontief, as early as 1950s, had already identified the potential of IO models for trade analysis. In 1953, Leontief published 'Domestic production and foreign trade; the American capital position re-examined,' resulting in the famed Leontief paradox. Later, he promoted the construction of international IO matrices to model economic interdependencies.

9.   Some countries, such as the US, record imports free alongside board (FAB) or free on board (FOB), but this remains exceptional and most countries favor a cost, insurance and freight (cif) recording for customs purposes, as it increases the statistical basis on which tax duties are levied.

10.   It is usual, in the social network literature, to call these indicators "metrics" albeit, from a strict mathematical perspective, they seldom define a true metrical space.

11. See, for example, Hansen et al. (2011) for a non-technical presentation of the main indicators used in this section.
12. The present section draws heavily on work done at OECD and WTO in co-operation with IDE-JETRO and USITC; see OECD-WTO (2012) and Degain et al. (2012) for the main technical conclusions of this research program.
13. Compensation of employees and operating surplus are primary factor income, and net indirect taxes after subsidies affect market pricing.
14. An introduction on international input–output can be found in the 'Explanatory Notes' of Inomata and Uchida (2009).
15. OECD-WTO (2012).
16. For more detailed review of TiVA indicators, see Ahmad (2013) and OECD (2013).
17. At more or less the same time, and independently of this debate, Sancho (2012) also criticized the use of input–output multipliers on gross output. Yet this criticism is not relevant when looking at ex-post data, as is usually done when measuring trade in value-added, because all endogenous effects have taken place.
18. Many researchers refer to trade in VA as a "new metric". Actually, trade in VA does not fulfill any of the necessary conditions for defining a metric space. Not even $d(U, U) = 0$ is verified, as we may have reflexive trade (exported VA returning home, as in Table 9.3).
19. See Goyal (2007) for a review of the network economics implications, and Baldwin and Venables (2010) for a trade perspective.
20. OECD has been developing a Bilateral Trade Database by industry and end-use category, where values and quantities of imports and exports are compiled according to product classifications and by partner countries. A similar Bilateral Trade in Services database, using detailed EBOPS data and the total services bilateral trade data is in prospect.
21. Eora is a project to estimate international input–output tables in order to assist environmental research, in particular footprint assessments of international trade; differing from WIOD or OECD-WTO TiVA, which use only official data, the aim of Eora is to cover as many countries as possible, relying on a mix of hard data and algorithmic procedures (Kanemoto et al., 2011).
22. Based on economic assumptions (the law of one-price and long-term adjustment of exchange rates to their purchasing parity), the heuristic is only indicative. Applied on Asian IIOs, the authors show that exchange rate corrections induced by the Asian crisis of 1997 had strong medium-term impact for the calculation of the indicators.
23. The aggregation bias relates not only to heterogeneity of quality within alternative sources, but may also reflect the monopolistic nature of GVCs: the sourcing inputs may be predetermined in an actual GVC, privileging intra-firm transactions (see Milberg and Winkler, 2013).
24. A report of the Statistical Commission (UNSC, 2013) provides a comprehensive review of the work undertaken so far at international level, and it proposes the development of an overreaching framework for ensuring consistency in methodology, data compilation and data dissemination.

REFERENCES

Ahmad, N. (2013),'Estimating trade in value-added: why and how?', in D. Elms and P. Low (eds), *Global Value Chains in a Changing World*, Fung Global Institute, Nanyang Technological University, and World Trade Organization.
Baldwin, R. (2006), 'Globalisation: the great unbundling (s)', paper contribution to the project Globalisation Challenges for Europe and Finland, Economic Council of Finland.
Baldwin, R. and F. Robert-Nicoud (2010), 'Trade-in-goods and trade-in-tasks: an

integrating framework', NBER Working Paper No. 15882, Cambridge, MA: National Bureau of Economic Research.

Baldwin, R. and A. Venables (2010), 'Relocating the value chain: offshoring and agglomeration in the global economy', NBER Working Paper No. 16611, Cambridge, MA: National Bureau of Economic Research.

Bernard, A.B., J.B. Jensen and P.K. Schott (2005),'Importers, exporters, and multinationals: a portrait of firms in the US that trade goods', NBER Working Paper No. 11404, Cambridge, MA: National Bureau of Economic Research.

Carlos-Lopes, J., J. Dias and J. Ferreira do Amaral (2008), 'Assessing economic complexity in some OECD countries with input–output based measures', International Conference on Policy Modelling, Berlin.

Chinese Academy of Sciences (2013), 'Interim report on global value chains and the value-added estimates in China's trade', June.

Coe, N., P. Dicken and M. Hess (2008), 'Global production networks: realizing the potential', *Journal of Economic Geography*, **8**, 271–295.

Daudin, G., P. Monperrus-Veroni, Ch. Rifflart and D. Schweisguth (2006), 'Le commerce extérieur en valeur ajoutée', Revue de l'OFCE 98, 129–165.

Daudin, G., Ch. Rifflart and D. Schweisguth (2011), 'Who produces for whom in the world economy?', *Canadian Journal of Economics*, **44**, 1403–1437.

De Backer, K. and S. Miroudot (2012), 'Mapping global value chains', WIOD Conference "Causes and Consequences of Globalization", Groningen, The Netherlands, 24–26 April.

De La Cruz, J., R. Koopman, Z. Wang and S.-J. Wei (2011), 'Estimating foreign value-added in Mexico's manufacturing exports', U.S. International Trade Commission, Office of Economics Working Paper No. 2011–04A.

Degain, Ch., H. Escaith and A. Maurer (2012), 'Comparison of methodologies to estimate trade in value-added terms', WTO-MIWI, draft note, mimeo, September.

Degain, Ch., L. Jones, Z. Wang and L. Xin (2013), 'The similarities and differences among the three major global inter-country input–output databases and their implications for trade in value-added estimates', 16th GTAP Conference on Global Economic Analysis, June.

Diakantoni, A. and H. Escaith (2012), 'Reassessing effective protection rates in a trade in tasks perspective: evolution of trade policy in factory Asia', WTO Working Paper ERSD 2012–11.

Dietzenbacher, E. and I. Romero (2007), 'Production chains in an interregional framework: identification by means of average propagation lengths', *International Regional Science Review*, **30**, 362.

Dietzenbacher, E., I. Romero and N.S. Bosma (2005), 'Using average propagation lengths to identify production chains in the Andalusian economy', *Estudios de Economia Aplicada*, **23**, 405–422.

Elms, D. and P. Low (eds) (2013), *Global Value Chains in a Changing World*, Fung Global Institute, Nanyang Technological University, and World Trade Organization.

Escaith, H. and F. Gonguet (2011), 'International supply chains as real transmission channels of financial shocks', *Journal of Financial Transformation*, **31**, 83–97.

Escaith, H. and S. Inomata (2013),'Geometry of global value chains in East Asia: the role of industrial networks and trade policies', in D. Elms and P. Low (eds),

Global Value Chains in a Changing World, Fung Global Institute, Nanyang Technological University, and World Trade Organization.

Ethier, W.J (1979), 'Internationally decreasing costs and world trade', *Journal of International Economics*, **9**, 1–24.

Fally, T. (2011), 'On the fragmentation of production in the US', presentation, University of Colorado-Boulder, July.

Feenstra, R. (2004), *Advanced International Trade: Theory and Evidence*, Princeton: Princeton University Press.

Feenstra R.C. and G.H. Hanson (1996), 'Globalisation, outsourcing and wage inequality', *American Economic Review*, **86**, 240–245.

Ferrarini, B. (2011), 'Mapping vertical trade', ADB Working Paper Series 263, Manila: Asian Development Bank.

Flores, M. and M. Vaillant (2011), 'Global value chains and export sophistication in Latin America', *Inter-American Development Bank-Integration and Trade Journal*, **32**, 15–35.

Foster, N., R. Stehrer, M. Timmer and G. de Vries (2012), 'Offshoring and the skill structure of labour demand', World Input–Output Database Working Paper Nr. 6.

Geoffrion A. and R. Powers (1995), '20 Years of strategic distribution system design: an evolutionary perspective', *Interfaces*, **25**, 105–127.

Gereffi, G. and T. Sturgeon (2013),'Global value chain-oriented industrial policy: the role of emerging economies', in D. Elms and P. Low (eds), *Global Value Chains in a Changing World*, Fung Global Institute, Nanyang Technological University, and World Trade Organization.

Goyal, S. (2007), *Connections: An Introduction to the Economics of Networks*, Princeton University Press.

Grossman, G.M. and E. Rossi-Hansberg (2006), 'Trading tasks: A simple theory of offshoring', NBER Working Paper No. 12721, Cambridge, MA: National Bureau of Economic Research.

Hansen, D., B. Shneiderman and M. Smith (2011), *Analyzing Social Media Networks with NodeXL: Insights from a Connected World*, Elsevier.

Hatzichronoglou, T. (1997), 'Revision of the high-technology sector and product classification', OECD Science, Technology and Industry Working Papers, No. 1997/02.

Hidalgo, C., B. Klinger, R. Hausmann and A. László Barabási (2007), 'The product space conditions the development of nations', *Science*, **317**, 482–487.

Hummels, D., Jun Ishii and Kei-Mu Yi (2001), 'The nature and growth of vertical specialization in world trade', *Journal of International Economics*, **54**, 75–96.

Inomata, S. (2008), 'Average propagation lengths: a new concept of the "distance" between industries, with an application to the Asia-Pacific region', *Sangyo-Renkan*, **16**–1 (in Japanese), Japan: Pan-Pacific Association of Input–Output Studies.

Inomata, S. (2011), 'Explanatory notes', in S. Inomata (ed.), *Asia Beyond the Global Economic Crisis: The Transmission Mechanism of Financial Shocks*, Cheltenham, UK and Northampton, MA, USA: Edward Elgar, in association with IDE-JETRO.

Inomata, S. and Y. Uchida (2009), 'Asia beyond the crisis: visions from international input–output analyses', IDE Spot Survey No. 31.

Johnson, R.C. and G. Noguera (2012), 'Accounting for intermediates: production sharing and trade in value added', *Journal of International Economics*, **86**, 224–236.

Kanemoto, K., M. Lenzen, A. Geschke and D. Moran (2011), 'Building Eora: a global multi-region input output model at high country and sector', 19th International Input-Output Conference.

Koopman, R., W. Powers, Z. Wang and S.-J. Wei (2012), 'Tracing value-added and double counting in gross exports', NBER Working Paper No. 18579, Cambridge, MA: National Bureau of Economic Research.

Koopmans, T.C. (1947), 'Measurement without theory', *Review of Economics and Statistics*, **29**, 161–172.

Krugman, P.R. (1979), 'Increasing returns, monopolistic competition, and international trade', *Journal of International Economics*, **9**, 469–479.

Lall, S., J. Weiss and J. Zhang (2005), 'The "sophistication" of exports: a new measure of product characteristics', Queen Elizabeth House Working Paper Series 123, Oxford University.

Lanz, R., S. Miroudot and H.K. Nordås (2011), 'Trade in tasks', OECD Trade Policy Working Papers, No. 117.Leontief, W. (1953), 'Domestic production and foreign trade; the American capital position re-examined', *Proceedings of the American Philosophical Society*, **97** (4), 28 September, 332–349.

Los, B., E. Dietzenbacher, R. Stehrer, M.P. Timmer and G. de Vries (2012), 'Trade performance in internationally fragmented production networks: concepts and measures", World Input–Output Database Working Paper Nr. 11.

Maurer, A. and Ch. Degain (2010), 'Globalization and trade flows: what you see is not what you get!', WTO Staff Working Paper No. 2010–12.

Melitz, M. (2003), 'The impact of trade on intra-industry reallocations and aggregate industry productivity', *Econometrica*, **71**, 1695–1725.

Meng, B., Y. Fang and N. Yamano (2012), 'Measuring global value chains and regional economic integration: an international input–output approach', IDE Discussion Paper 362.

Milberg, W. and D. Winkler (2013), *Outsourcing Economics: Global Value Chains in Capitalist Development*, Cambridge University Press.

Miller, R. and P. Blair (2009), *Input–Output Analysis: Foundations and Extensions* (second edition), Cambridge University Press.

Miroudot, S., R. Lanz and A. Ragoussis (2009), 'Trade in intermediate goods and services', OECD Trade Policy Papers 93.

Ng, F., and A. Yeats (1999), 'Production sharing in East Asia: who does what for whom, and why?', Policy Research Working Paper Series 2197, Washington, DC: The World Bank.

OECD (Organisation for Economic Co-operation and Development) (2005), *Handbook on Economic Globalization Indicators*, Paris.

OECD (2011), *ISIC REV. 3 Technology Intensity Definition: Classification of Manufacturing Industries into Categories Based on R&D Intensities*, Paris.

OECD (2013), *Interconnected Economies: Benefitting from Global Value Chains*, Paris.

OECD-World Trade Organization (WTO) (2012), 'Note on measuring trade in value added', e-document (WTO-MIWI website).

Oosterhaven, J. and D. Stelder (2002), 'Net multipliers avoid exaggerating impacts: with a biregional illustration for the Dutch transportation sector', *Journal of Regional Science*, **42**, 533–543.

Oxley, L., P. Walker, D. Thorns and H. Wang (2008). 'The knowledge economy/

society: the latest example of "measurement without theory"?', *The Journal of Philosophical Economics*, **2**, 20–54.

Park, A., G. Nayyar and P. Low (2013), 'Supply chains perspective and issues: a literature review', Fung Global Institute and World Trade Organization.

Porter, M.E. (1985), *Competitive Advantage: Creating and Sustaining Superior Performance*, The Free Press: New York.

Rauch, J.E. (1999), 'Networks versus markets in international trade', *Journal of International Economics*, **48**, 7–35.

Rifflart, Ch. and D. Schweisguth (2013), 'Draft report on new measures of international trade', in *European Framework for Measuring Progress*, e-Frame.

Sancho, F. (2012), 'Some conceptual difficulties regarding net multipliers', Department of Economics Universitat Autònoma de Barcelona, mimeo.

Stehrer, R. (2012), 'Trade in value added and the value added of trade', World Input–Output Working Paper No 8.

Sturgeon, T. (2013), 'Global value chains and economic globalization: towards a new measurement framework', EUROSTAT.

Sturgeon, T. and O. Memedovic (2010), 'Mapping global value chains: intermediate goods trade and structural change in the world economy', UNIDO Working Paper 05, Vienna: UNIDO.

Tang, K.K. and A. Wagner (2010), 'Measuring globalization using weighted network indexes', paper presented at the 31st General Conference of the International Association for Research in Income and Wealth, St. Gallen, Switzerland, August.

Tang, H., F. Wang and Z. Wang (2013), 'The domestic segment of global supply chain in China under state capitalism', paper presented at the International Conference on Global Value Chains and Structural Adjustments, Tsinghua University, Beijing, June.

Timmer, M. (2012), 'The World Input–Output Database: contents, sources and methods', World Input–Output Database Working Paper Number 10.

UNCTAD (2013), *World Investment Report 2013: Global Value Chains: Investment and Trade for Development*, Geneva.

UNSC (2013), *International Trade Statistics: Report to the Secretary General*, United Nations Statistical Commission, 44th session.

Vitali, S., J.B. Glattfelder and S. Battiston (2011), 'The network of global corporate control', PLoS ONE 6(10).

World Trade Organization (WTO) (2013a), *World Trade Report 2013: Factors Shaping the Future of World Trade*, Geneva.

WTO (2013b), *International Trade Statistics*, annual statistical yearbook, Geneva.

WTO (2008), *World Trade Report 2008: Trade in a Globalizing World*, Geneva.

WTO and IDE-JETRO (2011), *Trade Patterns and Global Value Chains in East Asia: From Trade in Goods to Trade in Tasks*, Geneva and Tokyo.

WTR (World Trade Report) (2013), *Factors Shaping The World Trade*, Geneva: World Trade Organization.

Yeats, A. (2001), 'Just how big is global production sharing?', in S. Arndt and H. Kierzkowski (eds), *Fragmentation: New Production Patterns in the World Economy*, New York: Oxford University Press.

10. The development and future of Factory Asia*

Richard Baldwin and Rikard Forslid

1. INTRODUCTION

Like a gigantic, impossibly complex but wonderfully efficient factory, East Asia churns out a vast array of manufactured goods with world-beating price-quality ratios. But this is not a series of national efforts. Manufacturing processes that used to be performed in single factories (mostly in Japan and Republic of Korea) have been fractionalized and dispersed across the region – creating what Baldwin (2006) called 'Factory Asia'.

This chapter looks at the underlying interconnected processes that have led to the development of Factory Asia – namely the fractionalization of the manufacturing process into stages and the dispersion of these stages around Asia. It does so by developing the TOSP (tasks, occupations, stages, products) framework that was informally introduced in Baldwin (2012). The TOSP framework views the production of goods as the performance of a range of tasks that are organized into occupations (collection of tasks) and stages (collections of occupations). Typically offshoring occurs at the level of stages rather than tasks or occupation.

This framework is then used to examine the likely effects of improving information and communication technology (ICT) on the future of Factory Asia. Two dimensions are distinguished: fractionalization of the production process (slicing up the value chain), and their spatial dispersion (offshoring stages).

A key premise of this chapter is that it is a trap to think of Factory Asia from the perspective of traditional trade theory. It is tempting to think of the fractionalization as simply a further step in the century's long march from autarky to free trade. After all, the fast lane of Factory Asia involves the offshoring of low-skill intensive stage to nations that are abundant in low-skill labor while knowledge-intensive stages remain in nations that are well endowed with knowledge workers. A natural, but incorrect, way to think of this is as nations' shifting resources to their comparative advantage sectors.

As this misthinking is pervasive, the rest of the introduction is devoted to contrast the old globalization paradigm – which views the process as driven by the steady lowering of trade costs – with an alternative narrative that views globalization as two processes rather than one.

1.1 Globalization as Two Unbundlings

Globalization is often viewed as linear – a progressive integration of national economies driven by lower technical and manmade trade costs. In trade economists' jargon, globalization is basically the move from autarky to free trade done slowly. The sharp trends in Figure 10.1 suggest that this is a mistake.

Globalization was associated with an agglomeration of economic activity in what used to be called the industrialized nations. From 1820 to 1988, the G7's share of global output rose from 22 percent to 67 percent. Since then, the share has plummeted and is now back to the level it first attained in 1900. About the same time, the world saw a massive shift in manufacturing activity from G7 nations to a handful of developing nations that

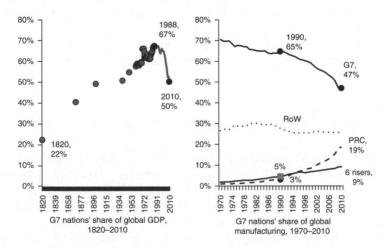

Note: 6 risers = Republic of Korea, India, Indonesia, Thailand, Turkey, and Poland; G7 = Canada, France, Germany, Italy, Japan, United Kingdom and United States of America; PRC = People's Republic of China; RoW = rest of the world.

Source: Authors' elaboration of data from unstats.un.org and Maddison's database.

Figure 10.1   Globalization: one process or two?

have come to be called Emerging Economies. In the two decades from 1970 to 1990, the G7's manufacturing share dropped from 71 percent to 65 percent. The subsequent two decades saw it plummet to 50 percent. The share shifts, however, were not generalized. Only seven nations saw their share of manufacturing rise by more than one-half of one percentage point (the People's Republic of China (PRC), the Republic of Korea, India, Indonesia, Thailand, Turkey and Poland). Plainly we are in a new phase of globalization – a phase that is distinct from earlier phases. There are many names for this new globalization paradigm – the global value chain (GVC) revolution, fragmentation, trade in tasks, etc.

On the back of this prima facie evidence, it would seem we need two processes to explain globalization's main outlines, not one. Falling trade cost will not cover it. In a 2006 paper for the Finnish Prime Minister's office, Baldwin (2006) characterizes this as globalization's two great unbundlings. The first unbundling – up to the mid or late 1980s is the traditional, linear process driven by lower trade costs. The second unbundling was driven by better information and communication technology. The first unbundling allowed consumption and production to be separated by great distances but production stages remained bundled in factories and industrial districts. The ICT revolution sparked the second unbundling by unbundling the factories. Improved ICT made it economical for stages of production formerly performed in a rich-nation factory to be unbundled and dispersed to low-wage nations.

The development of Factory Asia was one of the first manifestations of the second unbundling, although a similar development occurred in North America and Europe.

2.   FACTS: THE DEVELOPMENT OF FACTORY ASIA

We use here the Trade in Value-Added (TiVA) database, which contains the value-added in goods and services of a county's export (and import). The joint OECD–WTO Trade in Value-Added (TiVA) project traces the value-added by each industry and country in the production chain, and allocates the value-added to these source industries and countries.

One of the most striking features of Factory Asia is the very rapid growth of exports from emerging East Asian economies – measured in either gross or value-added (VA) terms. By 'gross exports' we mean the standard, customs-based numbers. By value-added exports, we mean the domestic value-added contained in a nation's gross exports. The difference is that the value-added figures net out the foreign value-added embedded in gross exports. For example, if Mexico exports a car that contains a US

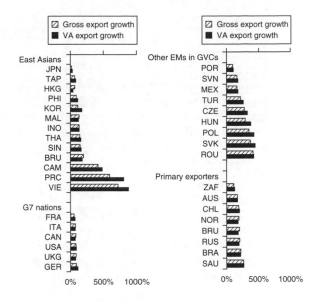

Notes:
EM = emerging market; G7 = Canada, France, Germany, Italy, Japan, United Kingdom
and United States of America; GVC = global value chain.
Country codes are listed in Appendix Table 10A.1.

Source: TiVA database with authors' calculations.

*Figure 10.2 Total export growth, 1995–2009, various nations, gross and
value-added*

engine, the gross export is the value of the whole car; the value-added
export is just the value that was added in Mexico.

As Figure 10.2 shows, the growth has been quite uneven. In general,
emerging markets have seen higher growth with the PRC, Cambodia, and
Viet Nam showing spectacular growth (although from very low bases in
the latter two cases).

For comparison, we include the export growth figures for the G7 and a
handful of emerging markets that are known to be active in outsourcing and
GVCs. A point we will explore more below is that there seems to be a connection between the magnitude of the growth and the size of the gap between
gross and value-added exports (a rough measure of supply-chain trade).

The commonality of emerging markets' rapid export growth hides an
important distinction. Some of these nations – like Brazil and the Russian
Federation – achieve high export growth on the back of the booming
demand for commodities. Others are doing it via manufactured goods.

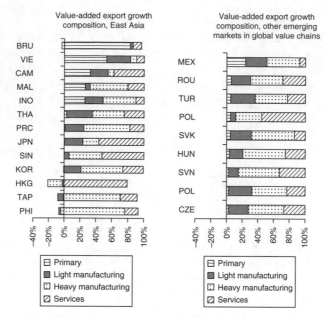

Note: Country codes are listed in Appendix Table 10A.1.

Source: TiVA database with authors' calculations.

Figure 10.3   Decomposition of value-added export growth by broad sector, 1995–2009

To provide hints as to the sources of the growth, Figure 10.3 shows the growth decomposition by broad sector – focusing on primary exports, light manufactured exports, heavy manufactured exports, and service exports. The left panel shows a wide diversity among East Southeast Asian (EA) nations. Some nations – such as Brunei Darussalam, Viet Nam, and Cambodia have seen their natural resource based exports account for substantial fractions of their total export growth. For most, however, the key driver was manufactured exports. Only in three economies (Hong Kong, China; Singapore and Japan) have service exports played a large role in VA export growth.

The role of commodity exports has been smaller in the emerging markets involved in Factory North America (Mexico), and Factory Europe (Poland, Turkey, etc.). The commonality is that manufacturing exports account for the lion's share of the growth – often two-thirds or more.

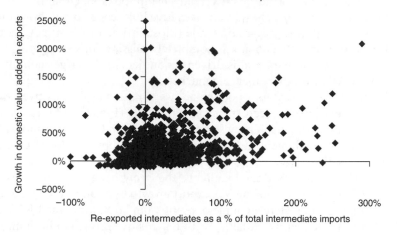

Re-exported intermediates as a % of total intermediate imports versus growth in domestic value-added in exports

Source: TiVA database with authors' calculations.

Figure 10.4   *Growth in supply-chain participation and domestic value-added in exports*

2.1   Connection to Supply-chain Trade

A property of fast growers that rely on manufacturers is that they seem to be linking-up to global supply chains to a much larger extent. This section presents prima facie evidence that this link is indeed important for many of the East Asian nations.

The measure of supply-chain trade involvement we use is the share of re-exported intermediates (REI), that is, imported intermediates that are re-exported either as parts and components, or embedded in final goods. Our aim is to explore the connection between increases in this measure of supply chain trade (SCT) and increases in the domestic value-added contained in exports. In both cases, we look at the percentage increase from 1995 to 2009 (which is the full span of the TiVA database). The first look at the raw data is not encouraging. Figure 10.4 shows the scatter plot of the change in 57 nations' SCT measure in 18 different sectors against the same nations' growth of domestic value-added in exports in the same sectors. The overall correlation is unclear.

The second unbundling logic, however, suggests that the correlation should differ greatly for 'headquarters (HQ) economies' and 'factories economies' – as well as across sectors (since production unbundling has not happened equally in all sectors). Once we separate the East Asia nations from the others, a positive relationship looks much more plausible. Indeed, Figure 10.5 shows that a positive link seems to hold for other nations involved in supply-chain trade (those in Factory North America and Factory Europe). The link is completely missing for G5 nations, the headquarters economies, and is driven by outliers in the large economies outside of Asia for other emerging markets.

When we look at sectors – pooling across of nations – the positive association is clear in some sectors but not in others (Figure 10.6). It is particularly clear in the machinery sectors, electrical and optical equipment, transportation equipment, and machinery and equipment not elsewhere classified (nec).

The last cut of the data highlights the growth correlation between supply-chain participation and VA export growth by country group and by sector (Figure 10.7). Here a couple of points stand out. First, the PRC and Viet Nam are frequently outliers – with big positive growth in both measures. Second, East Asian nations seem to systematically have more positive links between the two measures than the other nations. This, however, is less true in the classic outsourcing sectors such as textiles and machinery of various sorts. Indeed in transportation, the correlation of the East Asian nations and other factory economies (Other SCTers) is not at all clear.

2.2 Evolution of Factory Asia

Data for the early days of Factory Asia are difficult to come by. One rough indicator that does reach back to the 1960s is a simple intra-industry trade index (IIT) (Brülhart 2009). The idea here is that two-way trade in similar products that is either North-South, or South-South is likely to be largely supply-chain trade, i.e. two-way trade in parts and components. Plainly this is a crude measure, but it is transparent, widely understood and available for most nations going back to the early 1960s.

Figure 10.8 shows the paths of Japan's and the Republic of Korea's IIT with each of seven Association of Southeast Asian Nation (ASEAN) economies. The first salient point is that Japan's exchange with the other Asian nations has been growing since the 1960s. In the early days, much of this was in microelectronics (Grunwald and Flamm, 1985). Japan's IIT with three of the big ASEAN economies – Malaysia, Thailand and the Philippines – took off at about the same time, i.e. mid- to late-1980s. The sharp rise in IIT with Indonesia and Viet Nam came a decade later. For Indonesia (which is still a big commodity exporter), the rise was much less marked than for the others. Lao People's Democratic Republic and Cambodia have not really joined the Japanese supply chains according

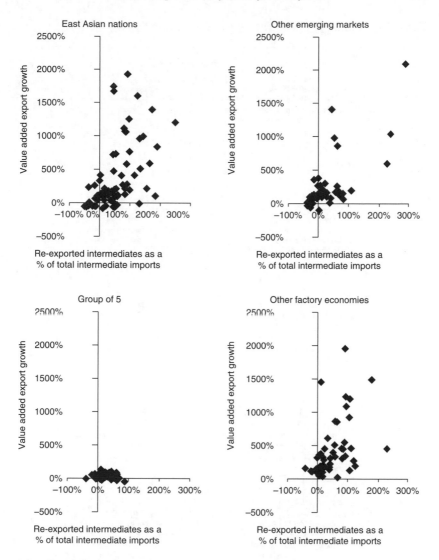

Note: East Asian nations = China, People's Rep. of, Indonesia, Korea, Rep. of, Malaysia, Philippines, Taipei,China, Thailand and Viet Nam; Group of 5 = France, Germany, Japan, United Kingdom and United States of America; other factory economies = Hungary, Mexico, Poland, Slovakia and Turkey; other emerging markets = Brazil, Canada, India, South Africa and Russian Federation.

Source: TiVA database with authors'calculations.

Figure 10.5 Supply chain participation and value-added exports, by nation groups

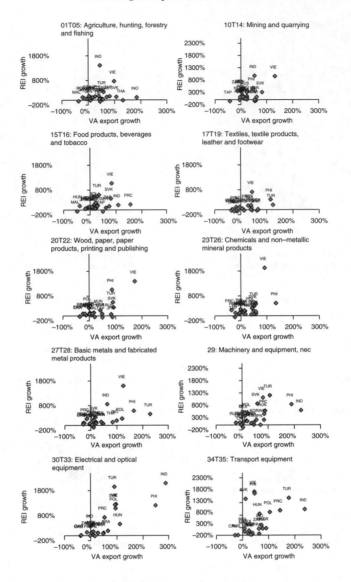

Notes:
Country codes are listed in Appendix Table 10A.1.
nec = not elsewhere classified; REI = re-exported intermediates; VA = value-added.

Source: TiVA database with authors' calculations.

Figure 10.6 *Supply chain participation and value-added exports, by all nation groups by sectors*

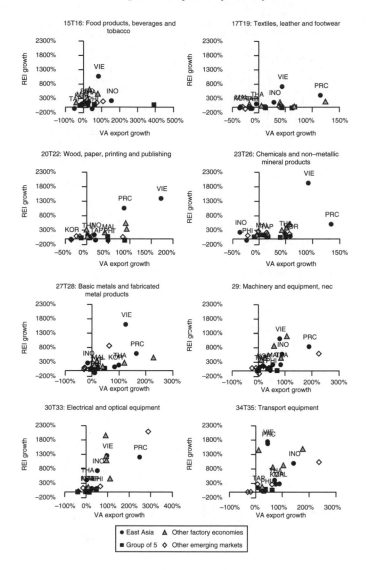

Notes:
nec = not elsewhere classified; REI = re-exported intermediates; VA = value-added.
Follows country codes list in Appendix Table 10A.1.

Source: TiVA database with authors' calculations.

Figure 10.7 Supply chain participation and value-added export growth, by sector and country group

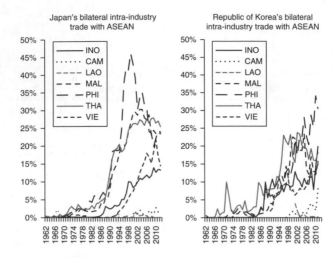

Note: Country codes are listed in Appendix Table 10A.1.

Source: Author's calculations on COMTRADE data.

Figure 10.8   *Japan's and the Republic of Korea's bilateral intra-industry trade with ASEAN, 1962–2012*

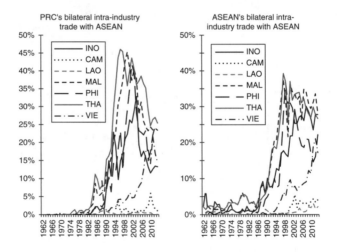

Note: Country codes are listed in Appendix Table 10A.1.

Source: Author's calculations on COMTRADE data.

Figure 10.9   *PRC's and each ASEAN's bilateral intra-industry trade with ASEAN, 1962–2012*

to this indicator. For the Republic of Korea, the timing is similar but the engagement with ASEAN economies is muted compared to Japan.

Figure 10.9 shows the IIT proxy for Factory Asia participation for the PRC with each of seven ASEAN economies and for each ASEAN with the others. What we see is that PRC's bilateral IIT with Thailand and Malaysia jumped in the mid-1980s, but it did not start until the early 1990s with Indonesia and the Philippines. The IIT measure slopes up from the later 1990s for Viet Nam but does not really take off until the early 2000s. Cambodia's IIT with PRC has taken off only in the 2010s. As for the ASEANs among themselves, we see a similar timing. The 'big four' ASEANs, Thailand, Malaysia, Indonesia and the Philippines, see their IIT scores jump in the mid-1980s. Viet Nam's jump is delayed till the late 1990s with a significant acceleration in the 2000s.

More direct evidence comes from the IDE-JETRO international input–output table. This shows the country of origin of imported manufactured goods purchased by the manufacturing sector of each East Asian economy. Table 10.1 has three panels corresponding to the shape of Factory Asia in 1985, 1990 and 2000.

The top panel shows the situation in 1985 when Factory Asia was very simple. With the exception of Singapore, East Asian nations sourced their imported manufactured inputs from Japan and the rest of the world – all the rows are dominated by zeros except those of Japan and the rest of the world (mainly the US and Europe). By 1990 (second panel), it was more complex: 'Triangle trade' still dominated the picture with the low-wage nations (first five columns) buying inputs from Japan and the rest of the world but providing no inputs in return. Now, however, Japan is not the only headquarters economy. Taipei,China, the Republic of Korea, and Hong Kong, China experienced their own hollowing-out phases and new triangle trade appears. This new triangle trade involves the shipment of parts from the new HQ economies to the 'factory economies' (the PRC and the advanced ASEANs, Indonesia, Malaysia, the Philippines and Thailand). This can be seen from the emergence of new non-zero entries in the rows for Taipei,China, the Republic of Korea and Singapore.

By 2000, Factory Asia was really complex. Firms based in the 'factory economies' began to source parts from other factory economies rather than from the HQ economy alone. In particular, Thailand, Malaysia and the PRC became important suppliers of parts to other 'factory economies' including each other. In short, the input–output matrix went from simple triangle trade to a much more complex situation where the 'factory economies' were both makers and buyers of parts and components.

This rise of the PRC position in the Matrix between 1990 and 2000 is especially noteworthy. At the beginning of the decade, it neither bought

Table 10.1 Widening and deepening of the Asian manufacturing matrix, 1985, 1990, 2000 (%)

	PRC	Indonesia	Malaysia	Philippines	Thailand	Singapore	Taipei,China	Republic of Korea	Japan
1985									
Indonesia						8			
Malaysia						16			
Philippines						0			
Thailand						0			
PRC				2		14			
Taipei,China						3			
Republic of Korea									
Singapore	3	3	7						
Japan		12	14	4	9	12	7	8	
Rest of the world		15	19	19	14	11	10	16	8
1990									
Indonesia									
Malaysia						5			
Philippines									
Thailand									
PRC						3			
Taipei,China			3	4	3	3			
Republic of Korea				2		2			
Singapore			7	2	3				
Japan		8	10	8	14	18	10	8	
Rest of the world	8	23	20	21	22	44	17	13	5

2000

	Indonesia	Malaysia	Philippines	Thailand	PRC	Taipei,China	Rep. of Korea	Singapore	Japan	Rest of world
Indonesia									2	4
Malaysia				3	4			12	2	
Philippines										
Thailand					3	3			3	
PRC	2			4		4	3	5	5	2
Taipei,China	3			3	5	3	3	3	3	
Republic of Korea	2	3		4	8	3	4	4	4	
Singapore				13	6	4				
Japan	2	7		15	20	16	19	20	14	7
Rest of the world	4	16		20	20	17	38	20	15	11

Notes:

PRC = People's Republic of China.

Percentage share of manufactured inputs bought by column nation's manufacturing sector from the row nation; numbers less than 2% are zeroed out; own-nation purchases are also zeroed out.

The columns would sum to 100% if we had included each nation's supply of inputs to its own manufactured sector (a number that is often greater than 50%) and if we had not zeroed out the low numbers (less than 2%).

Source: IDE-JETRO, Asian input–output matrix (7 sectors) for 1985, 1990 and 2000; see, for example, www.ide.go.jp/English/Publish/Books/Sds/082.html.

nor sold much manufactured inputs in East Asia. By the end of the decade, we see many entries for the Chinese column (which shows its purchase pattern) and the Chinese row (which shows which nations depend a lot on inputs from the PRC). The flourishing of intra-ASEAN trade is also clear from the comparison of 1990 and 2000.

The message of Table 10.1 is clear. By 2000, the competitiveness of manufacturing firms in East Asia depended in a serious way on the smooth functioning of regional trade. A disruption of trade between, say, Malaysia and the PRC, could cause serious problems for Japanese and Korean firms trying to sell in the US.

3. ECONOMICS OF SUPPLY-CHAIN UNBUNDLING

Globalization's second unbundling shifted the locus of globalization from sectors to stages of production. This requires an analytic focus on supply chains. The economics of this change is best looked at by decomposing it into two phenomena: fractionalization and dispersion.

- Fractionalization concerns the unbundling of supply chains into finer stages of production.
- Dispersion concerns the geographic unbundling of stages.

The two are linked in so far as the organization of stages may be crafted with dispersion, i.e. offshoring, in mind. This section considers them in turn and their interlinks.

3.1 Supply Chain Unbundling: The Functional Dimension

A prime assumption behind our conceptualization of Factory Asia is that the ICT revolution triggered the second unbundling and this resulted in Factory Asia. The main avenue of investigation is thus to understand how ICT improvements fostered production unbundling. Here we start with fractionalization, putting off issues of dispersion (offshoring) temporarily.

To this end, it is useful to view a firm's supply chain at four levels of aggregation (Figure 10.10):

1. Tasks: This is the list of everything that must get done to produce value for the corporation; the list includes all pre-fabrication and post-fabrication services.
2. Occupations: One natural intermediate aggregation of tasks is an 'occupation' – the group of tasks performed by an individual worker.

The TOSP Framework

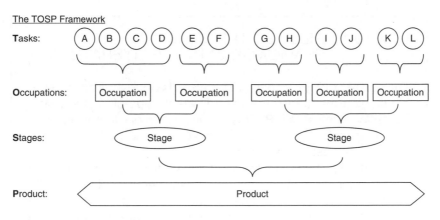

Source: Authors' illustration.

Figure 10.10   Tasks, occupations, stages and products – the TOSP framework

3. Stages: Stages are defined as a collection of occupations that are performed in close proximity due to the need for face-to-face interaction, fragility of the partially processed goods, etc. This is a critical level of aggregation since supply chain internationalization typically involves the offshoring of stages rather than individual occupations or individual tasks.
4. Products: The product is the supply chain's output broadly viewed.

3.1.1   Optimal tasks per occupation and occupations per stage

With this aggregation scheme in mind, consider the economics of the optimal:

1. Tasks per occupation; and
2. Occupations per stage.

Adam Smith illustrated the first issue with an example – an 18th-century pin factory where making a pin involved twelve distinct 'tasks', or what Smith called 'operations'. The full list of tasks/operations was: drawing out the wire, straightening the wire, cutting the wire, sharpening the pointy end, grinding the top end, making the pinhead (which itself involves three distinct tasks/operations), attaching the pinhead, whitening the completed pin, and putting the pins into the packaging.

Smith reported that pin factory managers had workers specialize in particular tasks. Workers did not make pins; they performed particular

---

BOX 10.1 RELATED THEORETICAL FRAMEWORKS IN THE LITERATURE

The Costinot (2009) model looks at optimal 'team size' (akin to our stages) that turns on a very different trade-off, namely specialization versus risk. Big teams allow workers to specialize in particular tasks and this lowers average time cost. Big teams, however, are assumed to be riskier.

Specifically, the model assumes an exogenous probability that each worker will fail to complete the assigned task. To avoid risk pooling – which would obviate all the analysis and results – the paper adopts a series of strong assumptions. First no worker can help any other; a failure in any task is a failure in all tasks, so more workers mean more failure. Second, there can be no inventory that would smooth over task-level failures. Third, the firm cannot reduce the probability of failure with managers a la Garicano (2000).

While specialization-versus-risk is the fundamental trade-off in the model, the paper discusses this trade-off as if it were a specialization-versus-transaction-costs trade-off.[a] That is, the discussion simply asserts that the failure-risk is due to contracting problems, and then it simply asserts that contracting problems are transaction costs.

Bloom et al. (2009) also model the team size choice based on a trade-off that is quite different to ours. Drawing on the seminal work by Garicano (2000), they focus on firm hierarchy, where production requires problems to be solved and hierarchy is a way of economizing on workers' problem-solving-training. Their core trade-off is between spending more to train workers to solve problems by themselves, and spending more on managers who are not directly productive but who have the knowledge to solve all problems.

Note: [a] The independent and identically distributed nature of the risk is adopted for technical reasons, namely to convexify outcomes in a way that allows the authors to work in a general setting.

---

sets of tasks. This allowed each worker to get really good at his or her assigned task. The downside of splitting up tasks is the difficulty of coordinating the whole process. This is the fundamental trade-off we focus on – the benefit of specialization versus the cost of coordination. Our key trade-off differs fundamentally from Costinot (2009) and Bloom et al. (2009); see Box 10.1.

Fractionalization and improved communication technology versus informa-tion technology   Since we are addressing the history and future of Factory Asia, we focus on how ICT developments alter fractionalization. Here the important point is that ICT affects the optimal division of labor via two channels, as Bloom et al. (2009) have stressed.

- First, communication and organizational technologies – call them coordination technologies (CT) for short – lower the marginal cost of coordination. Intuitively, better CT will make it easier to slice up production processes into more stages, and will make it easier to disperse stages internationally. Thus CT will tend to foster the current trends in Asia toward more vertical specialization, more offshoring, more foreign direct investment and more intra-industry trade.
- Second, information technology (IT) lowers the marginal benefit to specialization; think of how robots make it easier for individual workers to master more tasks without loss of efficiency.
- 3D printing is the extreme where IT allows a single worker to perform all tasks simply by operating one machine. For example Japanese industry is a leading user of industrial robots. Without these machines far more stages of production would have been offshored to low-skill abundant neighbors.

Plainly, CT and IT cut in opposite directions. Better CT favors greater fractionalization by making it cheaper; better IT discourages it by making it less necessary.[1] To explain and explore these effects in greater detail and with greater precision of thought, we present a one-line sketch model of optimal fractionalization.

3.1.2   Functional unbundling: a basic model
To crystalize thinking about our specialization-versus-coordination trade- off, this subsection provides a simple model that allows us to be more precise about the basic trade-off between specialization gains versus coordination costs, as well as the very different effects that better CT and IT have on supply chain fractionalization. We work in a partial equilibrium setting since when firms make these choices, they are likely to ignore the impact of their decisions on labor and product markets. Likewise, we initially work in a closed economy to separate the organization issues from the offshoring issues. Even though they are ultimately linked, intuition is served by first dealing with them separately.

One factor, one-tier organization   Consider a firm with a constant-returns-to-scale process whereby producing a good requires performance of a given list of tasks. To be concrete, view this as a continuum of tasks that we arbitrarily list along the range from zero to unity. The tasks are performed using homogenous labor and there is, in the simplest model, only one organizational choice – the number of occupations into which the tasks are organized. Stages are left out of the analysis for the time being.

The problem is to assign tasks to occupations optimally. In principle this assignment would involve a matching of task-types to worker-types. Even with homogenous workers the assignment problem could be complex if the degree of task-level efficiency depended upon the group of tasks assigned per worker. For example, it would be reasonable to assume that a worker would gain more efficiency by specializing in related tasks – say, painting tasks or welding tasks. In such a case, it would be natural to define the occupation by the nature of tasks assigned to it (e.g. painters, welders, etc.). While this degree of resolution is desirable, making progress would require seemingly arbitrary specificity concerning the efficiency effects of task specialization.

To keep the analysis streamlined and transparent, we assume that the tasks, as well as the workers, are homogenous. With this simplification, all occupations are symmetric and the only choice is the range of tasks assigned to a typical worker. That is, each worker's 'occupation' is defined by his/her range of assigned tasks and all occupations will be identical.

The gains from specialization are modeled as a link between the amount of labor per task and the range of tasks per occupation. Specifically, the labor input coefficient increases with the range of tasks performed by a single worker. There are many ways of micro-founding such an outcome but to keep things focused on essentials we simply assume the hours per tasks rises with the range of tasks per worker. What we have in mind is some sort of learning curve.

From the production-cost perspective, the least efficient arrangement is to have each worker doing every task. The most efficient is to have each worker specialized in only one task. The least cost for an organization with a given number of occupations will be to assign an equal range of tasks to each occupation; occupations are symmetric in equilibrium. Specifically, if there are n_o occupations, a range of $1/n_o$ tasks is assigned to each occupation.

Greater specialization, however, engenders greater coordination costs among occupations. A worker specializing in a range of tasks that is one-n_o^{th} of all tasks must coordinate with $(n_o - 1)$ other occupations. For simplicity, the between-occupation coordination costs are all identical and given by the parameter as χ_o (chi is a mnemonic for coordination). Ignoring within-occupation coordination, the number of coordination-pairs is $n_o(n_o - 1)/2$.

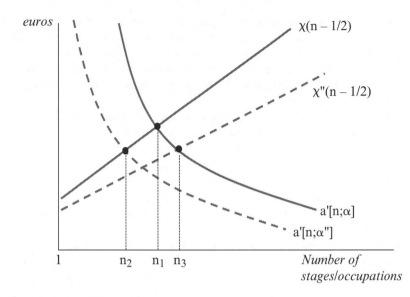

euros

χ(n − 1/2)

χ"(n − 1/2)

a'[n;α]

a'[n;α"]

1   n_2 n_1 n_3 *Number of*
stages/occupations

Source: Authors' illustration.

Figure 10.11   *Functional unbundling: stages and occupations in symmetric*
case

More formally, the organizational cost-minimization problem is:

$$min_{\{n_o\}} w_l\, a\, [n_o;\alpha]\, 1 w_l \chi_o n_o \left(\frac{n_o - 1}{2}\right); a'[\,\cdot\,] < 0 \qquad (10.1)$$

Here w is the wage; the function $a\,[\,\cdot\,;\alpha]$ captures the efficiency-inducing effect of specialization. That is, the per-task labor input coefficient 'a' falls as the number of occupations goes up (the range of tasks per work is $1/n_o$ with no symmetric occupations, so a higher n_o is associated with greater specialization of workers). Here 'α' – a mnemonic for automation – parameterizes the impact of IT on the efficiency-specialization effect; $a'n_o$; α] indicates the first derivative with respect to n_o as usual.

The first-order condition is:

$$0 = a'\,[n_o;\alpha]\, n_o + \chi_o\left(n_o - \frac{1}{2}\right) \qquad (10.2)$$

The second order condition holds if $a'\,[\,\cdot\,;\alpha]$ is decreasing (i.e. the second derivative is positive) which is true if there are diminishing returns to specialization – an assumption we maintain throughout.

The solution is illustrated in Figure 10.11. The marginal benefit of increased specialization (i.e. more occupations) is shown $a'[n_o;\alpha]$ while the marginal coordination cost is rising with the number of occupations as shown. The optimal specialization is n_1 as shown. This illustrates the specialization-coordination trade-off that is central to our thinking on functional fragmentation.

With this framework, it is straightforward to illustrate the distinct impact of IT and CT. Improved IT makes it easier for one worker to master many tasks without loss of efficiency – this is why $a'[n_o;\alpha]$ is downward sloped. Improved IT, which is parameterized as a rise in α (automation) to α'', shifts down the marginal benefit of specialization. In other words, the marginal benefit of additional specialization is lower, when a is higher. With the higher a'', the optimal number of occupations is n_2 rather than n_1.

Improved CT (communications), by contrast, makes it easier to coordinate occupations; this shows up as a reduction χ to χ''. The result is a lower marginal cost of increasing the number of occupations; graphically this shows up as a shift down in $\chi(n - 1/2)$. The resulting optimal number of occupations is therefore n_3 rather than n_1.

One factor, two-tier organization   It is straightforward to introduce additional levels of organizational hierarchy. We do this by assuming that occupations can be organized into 'stages' as a means of economizing on coordination costs. The occupation-level coordination costs remain as before, but we assume that workers only face this for an occupation inside their own stage. The new element is the cost of coordinating among stages. For simplicity, we assume that all stages are symmetric from this perspective. Specifically, if all occupations are broken up into n_s stages, each stage will have to coordinate with $n_s(n_s - 1)/2$ other stages. The modified cost minimization problem then becomes:

$$\min_{\{n_o,n_s\}} w_l a\,[n_o n_s;\alpha] + w_l\left(\chi_o n_o\left(\frac{n_o - 1}{2}\right)\right) + \chi_s n_s \frac{n_s - 1}{2} \quad (10.3)$$

Note that the range of tasks per symmetric occupation is now $1/n_o n_s$, so the argument of $a[\,\cdot\,;\alpha]$ is $n_o n_s$, and the coordination cost parameter for stage-coordination is denoted as χ_s. The first-order conditions are:

$$0 = a'\,[n_o n_s;\alpha]\,n_s + \chi_o\left(n_o - \frac{1}{2}\right),\ 0 = a'\,[n_o n_s;\alpha]\,n_o + \chi_s\left(n_s - \frac{1}{2}\right) \quad (10.4)$$

The simplest solution occurs when the χ's are equal so the solution involves an equal number of stages and occupations. In this case, Figure 10.11 continues to characterize the basic trade-off between coordination and specialization – as well as the role of CT and IT. More complex combinations of parameters would yield a different number of occupations and stages.

With a basic framework in place for the fractionalization of production processes, we turn to the issue of spatial dispersion.

3.2 Geographical Unbundling: Balancing Dispersion and Agglomeration Forces

If it were not for offshoring, fractionalization would be purely a matter of industrial organization. To put it in an international dimension we now turn to location decisions. The touchstone principle is that firms seek to put each stage in the lowest cost location.

In reality, places differ along many dimensions that matter for the location. The World Economic Forum's competitiveness index, for example, has 110 different measures. Our goal here, however, is to illustrate the first order trade-off that has influenced the development of Factory Asia. What we focus on is factor costs – for example, low versus high wage – as the gain from offshoring. The cost of offshoring is the downside.

The cost calculation involves a trade-off between direct factor costs and 'separation' costs.

- The direct costs include wages, capital costs and implicit or explicit subsidies.
- The separation costs should be broadly interpreted to include both transmission and transportation costs, increased risk and increased face-to-face managerial time.

The location decision may also be influenced by local spillovers of various types. In some sectors and stages, say fashion clothing, proximity between designers and consumers may be critical. In others, product development stages may be made cheaper, faster and more effective by co-location with certain fabrication stages. Yet other stages and sectors are marked by strong technological spillovers that make clustering of producers the natural outcome.

3.2.1 Production efficiency versus coordination costs

The first aspect of spatial unbundling turns on a trade-off that is closely aligned with the functional unbundling discussed above. Offshoring a particular stage can save on production costs but raise coordination costs.

To crystalize the fundamental economic logic, we adopt a simple setting with two nations – high-tech North and low-wage South – and stages that vary continuously in their technology intensity. We work with a 'spider-like' production process (Baldwin and Venables 2013) whereby the engineering of the production process implies no particular sequencing of stages. Each stage produces a 'part' and the parts get assembled into the good in the final stage called 'assembly'. This permits us to order the stages in analytically convenient ways.

Specifically, the stages – exogenously defined in this section – are arranged in order of increasing tech-intensity, i.e. in order of increasing North comparative advantage. This means that the high-tech North tends to have a comparative advantage in 'high' stages (those with indices near unity) while low-wage South has a comparative advantage in 'low' stages.

More specifically, the per-stage production cost is $w_n a_{ni}$ in North and is $w_s a_{si}$ in South, where a_{ni} and a_{si} are the North and South unit labor input coefficient for stage i and the w's are the national wages. Since there are only two locations, relative cost is all that matters, so we normalize North's $w_n a_{ni}$ to unity for all stages.[2] Recalling that we have arranged stages such that North's comparative advantage is greatest in stages with high indices, South's cost per stage starts below North's (i.e. below unity) and rises steadily to a number above unity.

A particularly simple case is illustrated in Figure 10.12 where $w_s a_{si}$ rises linearly with the sophistication of the stage; β is the slope of this relationship, i.e. $w_s a_{si} = \beta' i$ where 'i' indexes the stages and i ranges from 0 to 1. Plainly South is the low cost producer in stages from zero to $1/\beta'$ and North is the low cost producer in the rest. It is convenient to think of as β the strength of North's comparative advantage in stages, since as β rises more stages are most cheaply produced in the North.

To study the offshoring solution, the first anchor point is the cost-minimizing outcome when coordination costs are zero. As mentioned, the answer is that the lower tech stages are placed in South – namely, stages from 0 to $1/\beta$ – with the rest in North. Separating stages, however, has implications for coordination costs. The nature of these costs matters greatly.

Products with complex coordination demands   We begin with a case where coordination demands are complex, in the sense that every stage needs to coordinate with every other stage. An illustration of this is given in Table 10.2, which is drawn for the six-stage case where stages 1 to 2 are

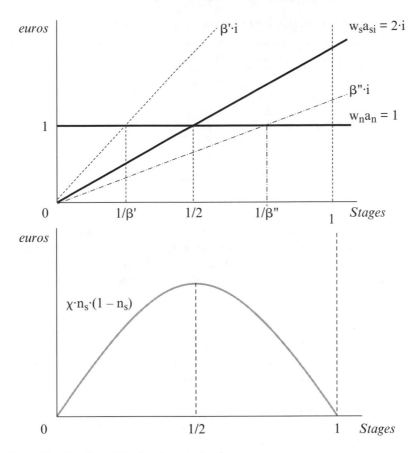

Note: Here North is offshoring stages to South.

Source: Authors' illustration.

*Figure 10.12 Comparative advantage, coordinate cost and optimal
unbundling*

undertaken in South and the rest in North. The table allows for different
coordination costs for coordination of stages within North, χ_n, within
South, χ_s, and 'international', χ_I.

To keep the expressions simple and to sharpen the intuition, we start
with the simple example where within-nation coordination costs are zero,
i.e. $\chi_n = \chi_s = 0$ but $\chi_I > 0$, so total coordination costs are:

$$w_n \chi_I n_s (1 - n_s)$$

Table 10.2   Coordination-cost matrix: complex good case

	Stage 1	Stage 2	Stage 3	Stage 4	Stage 5	Stage 6
Stage 1	χ_s					
Stage 2	χ_s	χ_s				
Stage 3	χ_I	χ_I	χ_n			
Stage 4	χ_I	χ_I	χ_n	χ_n		
Stage 5	χ_I	χ_I	χ_n	χ_n	χ_n	
Stage 6	χ_I	χ_I	χ_n	χ_n	χ_n	χ_n

Note: This table discretizes the continuum of parts for the sake of illustration.

where w_n, n_s, and n_n are the North wage and number of stages in South and North respectively. We assume that international coordination costs involve North labor, and have assumed that the mass of stages equals unity. Here coordination cost varies with the range of stages offshored to South according to a parabola.

It is important to note that this convexity means that coordination costs act as an agglomeration force. That is to say, the coordinate-cost-minimizing solution is to keep all stages bundled together. Coordination costs are maximized when stages are split evenly between North and South. Production cost considerations, by contrast, act as a dispersion force. The optimal unbundling and offshoring of stages from North to South involves the usual balancing of dispersion and agglomeration forces.

More formally, taking coordination and production costs together (assuming the linear example, i.e. $w_s a_{si} = \beta_i$ where $0 < \beta < 1$), total costs as a function of the range of stages in South, $(0, n_s)$, are:

$$\{\beta n_s^2/2 + 1 - n_s\} + \{\chi_I n_s(1 - n_s)\}$$

This is a quadratic function whose second derivative is negative if and only if coordination costs are not too high relative to the strength of North's comparative advantage, specifically $\chi < \beta/2$. We assume this regularity condition so that the first order conditions indicate cost minimizing rather than cost maximizing solutions.

The first order condition with respect to the range of stages placed in South, n_s, is:

$$\{\beta n_s - 1\} + \{\chi_I(1 - 2n_s)\} = 0$$

Solving the first order condition with respect to the range of stages placed in South, we have:

$$n = \frac{1 - \chi_I}{\beta - 2\chi_I}$$

This spatial unbundling setting presents some unusual features.

First, it is subject to threshold behavior, with the threshold at $\chi_I > \beta/2$. The reason for this is simple. The solution is the cost-maximizing solution for $\chi_I > \beta/2$ but the cost-minimizing solution for $\chi_I < \beta/2$. Thus:

If coordination costs are high relative to North's comparative advantage (as measured by β), then we have a corner solution, i.e. all stages are clustered in one nation.[3]

Which nation it is depends upon North's comparative advantage.[4] Production is cheaper in the North if and only if $\beta > 2$; otherwise the cluster is in South.

For coordination costs lower than the clustering threshold (i.e. $\chi_I < \beta/2$), stages will be dispersed internationally according to 0.

Thus a continuous reduction in coordination costs starting from a very high level would have a discontinuous effect on offshoring at the threshold.

A second unusual feature is that cheaper coordination may lead to more or less production in South. The sign of the impact of χ_I on n_s switches at $\beta = 2$. If South has a strong comparative advantage, in the sense that more than half the stages would be produced there based solely on production cost considerations (e.g. β'' as in Figure 10.12), then considerations of communication costs will lead to 'too much' production in the South. The point is that even though Southern production costs are higher, the fact that more than half the stages are there already means that sending more stages lowers coordination costs. In this case, lower communication costs will lead to less offshoring to South. By contrast, if β is high, say β' in Figure 10.12, then lower χ_I will increase the offshoring to South.

One particularly intuitive case is when North has a strong comparative advantage in parts, e.g. β' in the diagram, so more than half the parts are produced in North. In this case, coordination cost considerations tend to reduce the amount of offshoring from the North to the South. As coordination costs fall, the range of stages placed in the South rises.

To summarize, even in the simplest framework that allows a trade-off between efficiency and coordination costs, the relationship between easier communication and offshoring is far from monotonic. The convex nature of coordination costs tends to create tipping points and comparative static results that can flip signs according to parameters that may be hard for the econometrician to observe.

4.   CONCLUDING REMARKS

This chapter looks at the underlying interconnected processes that drove Factory Asia's development from the mid-1980s. We focused on two complementary trends: fractionalization of the manufacturing process into stages, and the dispersion of these stages around Asia. The chapter organized the thinking by providing a formal model for the TOSP (tasks, occupations, stages, products) framework that was informally introduced in Baldwin (2012). The TOSP framework views the production of goods as the performance of a range of tasks that are organized into occupations (collection of tasks) and stages (collections of occupations). Typically offshoring occurs at the level of stages rather than tasks or occupation.

4.1   Policy Issues

While no formal evidence-based policy recommendations can be made based on our chapter's contribution, a number of important themes emerge.

First, geography is an important determinant of the ease of participating in Factory Asia. Just as it is easier to set up a supply plant in or near an industrial district, joining Factory Asia is much easier for nations that are proximate to the headquarters economies in East Asia – Japan, the Republic of Korea, Taipei,China, Singapore, and Hong Kong, China. As Factory Asia is not so developed, proximity to other factory economies is also important – especially proximity to the PRC, which is a massive and highly competitive producer of industry inputs (parts and components).[5] This is nothing more than an assertion that forward and backward linkages matter at the regional level as well as at the national or industrial district level.

The intuition is similarly straightforward. In the main production unbundling sectors – electrical and mechanical machinery – fractionalized production processes involve time-sensitive and shipping-cost sensitive elements. Being near other supply-chain traders – both headquarters and factory economies – makes it easier to join Factory Asia. Another way to put this is that 'regional comparative advantage' matters as well as 'national comparative advantage' when it comes to joining an international production network.

Second, size matters. Nations that have over a billion consumers (the PRC and India) can pursue policies that smaller nations cannot. In essence the two giants can leverage their local market as a powerful attraction force for supply chain segments.

Third, providing assurances to tangible and intangible property rights is likely to be an important element in attracting supply chain production.

As such production is necessarily networked, some firms or networks of firms must be coordinating the process. Such firms are naturally reluctant to expose their managerial, technical and marketing knowhow to tacit or explicit expropriation, which would facilitate the emergence of new competitors.

4.2 Future Research

The charts in the chapter suggest many correlations and relationships that can and should be tested more formally using the newly developed TiVA database. Such empirical work will be critical in developing evidence-based policy recommendations. How important are intellectual property rights protection versus quick port clearance? How damaging is distance to participation in international supply chains (controlling for other factors)? How important are formal free trade agreements overall, and particular provisions specifically (e.g. investment provisions, versus capital mobility provisions).

A wide range of institutional measures exist in databases such as the World Bank's Doing Business and the World Economic Forum's Global Competitiveness Report, and the detailed work from the trade facilitation literature. These are essentially right-hand side variables that have been used to explain macro growth trends. It would be important to sort out how these various 'institutional or policy' measures interact with more fundamental determinants such as distance from headquarters economies, distance from final goods markets, wages, etc. The key contribution of the new value-added databases is that we now have left-hand side measures of supply-chain participation. Moreover, the network nature of the new data should allow us to go beyond simple nation-by-nation approaches where a nation's own right-hand side features are all that is allowed to affect outcomes. This would allow us to look at regional as well as national comparative advantage and perhaps better identify which sectors are more likely to be successful in which nations.

Factory Asia has been deepening and widening at a historically unprecedented rate since the 1980s. Despite the Global Crisis, the Great Trade Collapse and the rise of anti-globalization elements in rich nations, Factory Asia does not seem to be leveling off. New nations like Viet Nam seem to be joining with success. In short, the future of Factory Asia seems bright. The key questions are: How can developing nations join, and how can they make sure that joining leads to an ever-denser participation in value networks? Those are questions that economists would be well advised to tackle.

NOTES

* This chapter was written for the ADB's project 'The Future of Factory Asia'. Our contribution draws heavily on the authors' earlier works; it is intended to inform policy and help direct future research.
1. This insight – which is due to Bloom et al. (2009) – has recently received some empirical support from Lanz et al. (2011). They find that offshoring of business services complements manufacturing activities, in the sense that increased import penetration in business services is associated with a shift in local task content from information and communication related tasks toward tasks related to handling machinery and equipment. Offshoring of other services complements local information-intensive tasks in that it shifts local task composition towards ICT-related tasks.
2. As wages are exogenous here, we could do this by choosing North labor as numeraire and choosing units for all stages since that $a_{ni} = 1$ for all i.
3. Note that β measures North's comparative advantage in the sense that the range of stages where North is the low cost producer ranges from $1/\beta$ to unity, so this expands as β rises.
4. Total cost with all stages in the South and North, respectively, will be $\beta/2$ and 1.
5. It is a quirk of language, but remarkable that one can get from 'supply chain' to 'supply China' by moving just one letter!

REFERENCES

Baldwin, R. (2006),'Globalisation: the great unbundling (s)', paper contribution to the project Globalisation Challenges for Europe and Finland, Economic Council of Finland.

Baldwin, R. –(2012),'Global supply chains: why they emerged, why they matter, and where they are going', Centre for Economic Policy Research Discussion Papers No. 9103.

Baldwin, R., and A.J. Venables (2013), 'Spiders and snakes: offshoring and agglomeration in the global economy', *Journal of International Economics*, **90**, 245–254.

Bloom, N., L. Garicano, R. Sadun, and J. Van Reenen (2009),'The distinct effects of information technology and communication technology on firm organization', NBER Working Papers No. 14975, Cambridge, MA: National Bureau of Economic Research.

Brülhart, M. (2009), 'An account of global intra-industry trade, 1962–2006', *The World Economy*, **32**, 401–459.

Costinot, A. (2009),'On the origins of comparative advantage', *Journal of International Economics*, **77**, 255–264.

Costinot, A., L. Oldenski, and J. Rauch (2011),'Adaptation and the boundary of multinational firms', *The Review of Economics and Statistics*, **93**, 298–308.

Garicano, L. (2000),'Hierarchies and the organization of knowledge in production', *Journal of Political Economy*, **108**, 874–904.

Grunwald, J., and K. Flamm (1985), *The Global Factory: Foreign Assembly in International Trade*, Brookings Institution Press.

Lanz, R., S. Miroudot, and H.K. Nordås (2011), 'Trade in tasks', OECD Trade Policy Papers No 117, OECD Publishing, available at: http://dx.doi.org/10.1787/5kg6v2hkvmmw-en.

APPENDIX 10A.1

Table 10A.1   Country codes

Country name	Country code
Australia	AUS
Brazil	BRA
Brunei Darussalam	BRU
Cambodia	CAM
Canada	CAN
Chile	CHL
Czech Republic	CZE
France	FRA
Germany	GER
Hong Kong, China	HKG
Hungary	HUN
Indonesia	INO
Italy	ITA
Japan	JPN
Korea, Republic of	KOR
Malaysia	MAL
Mexico	MEX
Norway	NOR
People's Republic of China	PRC
Philippines	PHI
Poland	POL
Portugal	POR
Romania	ROU
Russia	RUS
Saudi Arabia	SAU
Singapore	SIN
Slovakia	SVK
Slovenia	SVN
South Africa	ZAF
Taipei,China	TAP
Thailand	THA
Turkey	TUR
United Kingdom	UKG
United States	USA
Viet Nam	VIE

Source: Authors' listing.

Index